MATH*FOCUS* 8

MATH*FOCUS* 8

**Senior Author and
Senior Consultant**
Marian Small

Authors
Jack Hope
David Kennedy
Carolyn Martin
Carol Shaw
Marian Small
Michèle Wills
David Zimmer

Assessment Consultants
Sandra Carl Townsend
Gerry Varty

NELSON EDUCATION

NELSON / EDUCATION

Nelson Math Focus 8

Authors
Jack Hope, David Kennedy,
Carolyn Martin, Carol Shaw,
Marian Small, Michèle Wills,
David Zimmer

Director of Publishing
Kevin Martindale

General Manager, Mathematics, Science, and Technology
Lenore Brooks

Publisher, Mathematics
Colin Garnham

Associate Publisher, Mathematics
Sandra McTavish

Managing Editor, Development
David Spiegel

Product Manager
Linda Krepinsky

Program Manager
Colin Bisset

Senior Project Editor
Robert Templeton, First Folio
Resource Group, Inc.

Developmental Editors
Margaret McClintock
Tony Rodrigues
Carmen Yu
First Folio Resource Group, Inc.:
Susan Lishman
Wendi Morrison
Bradley T. Smith

Assistant Editors
Linda Watson, First Folio Resource
Group, Inc.
Carmen Yu

Editorial Assistant
Caroline Winter

Executive Director, Content and Media Production
Renate McCloy

Director, Content and Media Production
Sujata Singh

Content Production Editor
Montgomery Kersell

Copy Editor
Margaret Holmes

Proofreader
Arthur Lee

Indexer
Noeline Bridge

Production Manager
Helen Jager-Locsin

Senior Production Coordinator
Sharon Latta Paterson

Assessment Consultants
Sandra Carl Townsend
Gerry Varty

Design Director
Ken Phipps

Interior Design
Kyle Gell
Allan Moon

Cover Design
Eugene Lo

Cover Image
Courtesy of Shelley Yearley

Compositor
Allan Moon

Photo Shoot Coordinator
Lynn McLeod

Studio Photographer
Dave Starrett

Photo/Permissions Researcher
Lynn McLeod

Printer
RR Donnelley/Willard

Advisory Panel

The authors and publisher gratefully acknowledge the contributions of the following educators:

Nicole Bell
Assistant Professor
School of Education and
Professional Learning
Trent University
Peterborough, Ontario

Gerry-Lynn Borys
Teacher
St. Francis of Assisi Middle School
Red Deer Catholic
Regional Division 39
Red Deer, Alberta

Cathy Canavan-McGrath
Program Coordinator
South Slave Divisional
Education Council
Fort Smith, Northwest Territories

Anett Chicomny
Math Specialist
Siksika Nation High School
Siksika Board of Education
Siksika, Alberta

Sheila Crane
Grade 5 Teacher
Mother Teresa Catholic School
Edmonton Catholic Schools
Edmonton, Alberta

Shona Dobrowolski
Mathematics Consultant
Okotoks, Alberta

Lenée Fyfe
Teacher
G.S. Lakie Middle School
Lethbridge School Division No. 51
Lethbridge, Alberta

Kathy Gu
Teacher
McNally Composite High School
Edmonton Public Schools
Edmonton, Alberta

Sharon Laflamme
Principal
Muskoday First Nation
Community School
Saskatoon Tribal Council
Muskoday, Saskatchewan

Allan Macdonald
Department Head/Teacher
Lakeland Ridge School
Elk Islands Public Schools
Sherwood Park, Alberta

Moyra Martin
Principal
Cardinal Newman Elementary/Junior
High School
Calgary Catholic School District
Calgary, Alberta

Dave McCann
Principal
Big Valley School
Clearview School Division
Big Valley, Alberta

Jacinthe Moquin
Teacher
J.H. Picard School
Edmonton Catholic Schools
Edmonton, Alberta

D.S. Moss
Teacher
Father Michael Troy
Catholic School
Edmonton Catholic Schools
Edmonton, Alberta

Roswitha Nowak
Middle Years Learning Support
West St. Paul School
7 Oaks School Division
Winnipeg, Manitoba

Rita Paquette
Math Coordinator/Teacher
Sherwood Heights
Junior High School
Elk Island Public Schools
Sherwood Park, Alberta

Susie Robinson
Cree Language Consultant
Edmonton Catholic School District
Edmonton, Alberta

Shelina Samji-Kassam
Mathematics Teacher
Lester B. Pearson High School
Calgary Board of Education
Calgary, Alberta

Rupi Samra-Gynane
Vice Principal
Princess Margaret Secondary School
School District #36
Surrey, British Columbia

Doug Super
Teacher
Mulgrave Independent School
West Vancouver, British Columbia

Rosita Tam
Vice Principal
Kenneth Gordon School
Burnaby School Board
Burnaby, British Columbia

Tracy Welke
Mathematics Teacher
Vegreville, Alberta

Chris Yang
Teacher
South Delta Secondary School
School District #37
Delta, British Columbia

Literacy Consultants

Vicki McCarthy
Vancouver School District
Vancouver, British Columbia

Melanie Quintana
Mathematics Educator
St. Julia School
Dufferin-Peel Catholic
District School Board
Mississauga, Ontario

Equity Consultant

Mary Schoones
Educational Consultant
Ottawa-Carleton District
School Board
Ottawa, Ontario

Contents

Chapter 2: Fraction Operations 42

Chapter 3: Ratios and Rates 102

Chapter 4: Percents   140

Chapter 5: Measurement 190

Chapter 6: Integers 240

Chapter 7: Tessellations

Chapter 8: Data Analysis 328

Chapter 9: Linear Relations and Linear Equations 362

Chapter 10: Probability 416

Chapter 11: 3-D Geometry

Number Relationships

GOAL

You will be able to

- model perfect squares and square roots
- use a variety of strategies to recognize perfect squares
- use a variety of strategies to estimate and calculate square roots
- explain and apply the Pythagorean theorem
- solve problems by using a diagram

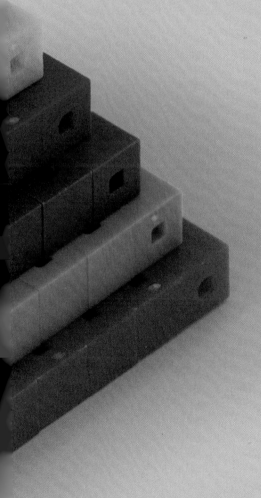

◀ This is a model of the pyramid at Chichen Itza, in Mexico. Each of the layers of the model is a square built from centimetre cubes. How many cubes are needed to make the model pyramid?

Getting **Started**

Tatami Mats

Vanessa presented a report on Japanese tea rooms to her class. The floors are usually covered with square and rectangular tatami mats. She drew one way to cover a square floor with a square half mat and four rectangular full mats. The area of the half mat is 8100 cm² and is half the size of a full mat.

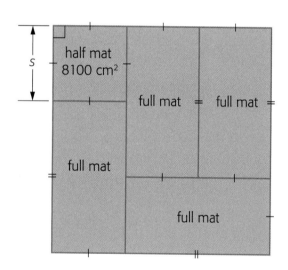

❓ What are the dimensions of the mats and the room?

A. The variable s represents the side length of the square mat. Why can you use the equation $s \times s = 8100$ to determine the side length of the square mat?

B. How do you know that the side length of the square mat must be between 50 cm and 100 cm?

C. Is the side length of the square mat closer to 50 cm or 100 cm? Explain.

D. What is the side length of the square mat? Show your work.

E. What are the dimensions of the rectangular mats and the room? Explain what you did.

What Do You Think?

Decide whether you agree or disagree with each statement.
Be ready to explain your decision.

1. When you multiply a number by itself, the product is always greater than the number you multiplied.

2. You can use the area to estimate the dimensions of the square.

10 cm²

3. This equation has no solution.
$a \times a = 12.25$

4. A right triangle has sides of 6 cm and 8 cm. The length of the third side must be about 10 cm.

1.1

Representing Square Numbers

GOAL

Use materials to represent triangular and square numbers.

EXPLORE *the Math*

Mark read that the ancient Greeks used to arrange pebbles to represent numbers. He used squares on a grid instead of pebbles to model both triangular and square numbers.

6

Six is called a triangular number because you can arrange 6 pebbles in a triangle in which each row is 1 greater than the row above it.

9

Nine is called a square number because you can arrange 9 pebbles into a 3-by-3 square.

❓ How can you divide a square number into two triangular numbers?

Recognizing Perfect Squares

GOAL

Use a variety of strategies to identify perfect squares.

LEARN ABOUT *the Math*

There are 441 students and teachers in my school. I can display photos of them all in a square because 441 is a perfect square.

perfect square

the product of a whole number multiplied by itself; e.g., 49 is a perfect square because $49 = 7 \times 7$.

❓ Is Elena correct?

Communication | Tip

- Perfect squares can also be called square numbers.
- A 2 written above and to the right of a number shows it has been "squared."
  7^2 represents 7×7 and can be read as "7 squared."

Example 1 | Identifying a perfect square using diagrams

I determined whether 441 is a perfect square by drawing a square.

Elena's Solution

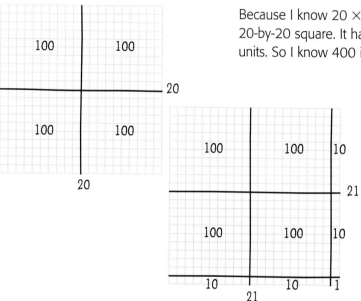

Because I know $20 \times 20 = 400$, I sketched a 20-by-20 square. It has an area of 400 square units. So I know 400 is a perfect square.

I modified my sketch to show a 21-by-21 square. $21 \times 21 = 441$, so it has an area of 441 square units.

I can draw a square with 441 square units, so 441 is a perfect square.

Example 2 | Identifying a perfect square using factors

I determined whether 441 is a perfect square using prime factors.

Mark's Solution

If 441 is a perfect square, then there are two equal factors that have 441 as a product. I decided to factor 441 to look for them.

I represented the factors in a tree diagram.
I know 441 is divisible by 9, because the sum of its digits is divisible by 9. One factor is 9. Another factor is $441 \div 9 = 49$.
9 and 49 are not equal.

I continued until all the factors were prime.

$441 = 3 \times 3 \times 7 \times 7$

I wrote 441 as the product of prime factors.

$441 = 3 \times 7 \times 3 \times 7$
$441 = (3 \times 7) \times (3 \times 7)$
$441 = 21 \times 21$

I rearranged them to create a pair of equal factors.

441 can be renamed as two equal factors, so 441 is a perfect square, and Elena is correct.

Reflecting

A. Is there a perfect square between 400 and 441? Explain.

B. Would you use prime factors to determine whether 400 is a perfect square? Why or why not?

WORK WITH *the Math*

| **Example 3** | Identifying a square number using factors |

Determine whether 256 is a perfect square using prime factors.

Solution

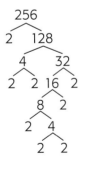

$256 = 2 \times 2 \times 2 \times 2 \times 2 \times 2 \times 2 \times 2$

$256 = (2 \times 2 \times 2 \times 2) \times (2 \times 2 \times 2 \times 2)$
$= 16 \times 16$
$256 = 16 \times 16$ or 16^2, so it is a square number.

Determine the prime factors of 256 using a tree diagram. Each time you divide by a factor, you continue to get another even number. So the only prime factor is 2.

Write 256 as the product of the prime factors.

Group the factors to rename 256 as the product of two equal factors.

A Checking

1. Which numbers are perfect squares? Show your work.
   a) 64
   b) 100
   c) 120
   d) 900
   e) 1000
   f) 10 000

2. How do you know that each number is a perfect square?
   a) $1225 = 35 \times 35$
   b) $484 = 2 \times 2 \times 11 \times 11$
   c) $2025 = 45^2$

B Practising

17 units

17 units

3. The area of this square is 289 square units. How do you know that 289 is a perfect square?

4. Show that each number is a perfect square.
   a) 16
   b) 144
   c) 1764

5. Barrett is making a display of 225 square photos of the students in his school. Each photo is the same size. Can he arrange the photos in a square? Explain.

6. Calculate.
   a) 6^2
   b) 9^2
   c) 11^2
   d) 12^2
   e) 25^2
   f) 40^2
   g) 100^2
   h) 1000^2

2025
5   405
   5   81
      9   9

7. Maddy started to draw a tree diagram to determine whether 2025 is a square number.
   How can Maddy use what she has done so far to determine that 2025 is a square number?

8. Guy says: "My street address is a square number when you read the digits forward or backward."
   Is Guy correct? Explain.

9. Star's grandmother makes square patchwork quilts. They usually contain two different squares and two congruent rectangles. What other squares and rectangles could Star's grandmother have shown in her 10-by-10 quilt?

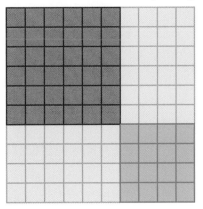

10. a) How many perfect squares are between 900 and 1000? Show your work.

   b) How can you use your answers in part a) to determine the greatest perfect square less than 900 and the least perfect square greater than 1000?

11. Are 0 and 1 both square numbers? Explain.

12. When you square a number, how do you know whether the result will be odd or even?

13. How do you know that the product of two different square numbers will also be a square number? Use an example to explain.

14. Square each whole number from 11 to 20. What are the ones digits?

15. Use your answers in question 14 to predict the ones digit in each calculation. Explain what you did.
   a) 21^2 b) 32^2 c) 45^2 d) 58^2

16. Suppose you know the ones digit of a square number. Can you always figure out the ones digit of the number that was squared? Explain, using your answers from questions 14 and 15.

17. Because 289 has only three factors: 1, 17, and 289, explain how you can use this information to show that 289 is a square number.

1.3

Square Roots of Perfect Squares

GOAL

Use a variety of strategies to determine the square root of a perfect square.

LEARN ABOUT the Math

Vanessa needs to place square mats in the middle of the gym floor. The floor is 15 m by 20 m, and the mats have an area of 144 m². Vanessa wants to know the distances between the sides of the floor mats and the walls of the gym. She drew a diagram to help her understand the problem.

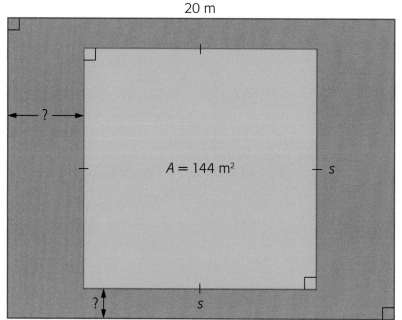

❓ How can Vanessa determine the distances between the sides of the floor mats and the walls of the gym?

A. How does Vanessa's diagram help her to understand the problem?

B. What does the variable s represent in Vanessa's diagram?

C. How does the equation $s \times s = 144$ help you determine the side length of the square mats?

D. Why can you solve the equation in part C by calculating the **square root** of 144? Use the diagram of the square mats to help you explain.

E. How would you solve $s \times s = 144$?

F. What is the side length of the mats?

G. What are the distances between the sides of the floor mats and the walls of the gym? Show your work.

Reflecting

H. Can you use the ones digit of 144 to predict the ones digit of the square root of 144? Explain.

I. How can you check your answer when you calculate the square root of a number? Use $\sqrt{144}$ to explain.

---

square root

one of two equal factors of a number; for example, the square root of 81 is 9 because 9×9, or 9^2, $= 81$.

Communication | *Tip*

The square root symbol is $\sqrt{}$. You can write "the square root of 100" as $\sqrt{100}$.

WORK WITH *the Math*

| **Example 1** | Determining a square root by guess and test |

The floor mat in rhythmic gymnastics is a square with an area of 169 m². What is its side length?

Vanessa's Solution

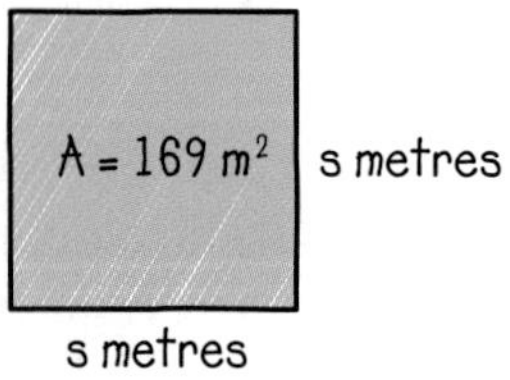

$A = 169\ m^2$ s metres

s metres

I drew a diagram to help understand the problem.

$s \times s = 169$
$s = \sqrt{169}$

I have to determine a number that equals 169 when multiplied by itself, or squared. Each equation represents this situation.

$10^2 = 100$ too low
$20^2 = 400$ too high

The side length of the mat must be between 10 m and 20 m, but closer to 10 m than 20 m.

$3 \times 3 = 9$
$7 \times 7 = 49$

I know the ones digit of the side length must be 3 or 7, because both 3^2 and 7^2 have ones digits of 9. No other digit squared will end in 9.

Try 13.
$13^2 = 169$
So $\sqrt{169} = 13$

I tried 13 because it is between 10 and 20, but closer to 10 than 17.

The side length of the mat is 13 m.

| Example 2 | Determining a square root by factoring |

Determine the square root of 225.

Sanjev's Solution

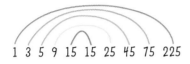

I made a factor rainbow to show the factors of 225.

I know 3 and 9 are factors because the sum of the digits in 225 is 9.

I know 5 is a factor because the ones digit of 225 is 5.

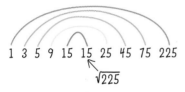

Because 3 and 5 are factors, 3×5, or 15, must also be a factor of 225.

The square root of 225 is 15.

The factor with an equal partner is the square root. So I can express 225 as 15×15 or 15^2.

A Checking

1. Judo mats are squares with a minimum area of 36 m² and a maximum area of 64 m². The side length of each mat is a whole number in metres.
   a) Sketch each possible mat on grid paper.
   b) What are the possible side lengths of the mats?

2. Calculate.
   a) $\sqrt{4}$ **b)** $\sqrt{16}$ **c)** $\sqrt{81}$ **d)** $\sqrt{400}$

1 3   9   49   147 441

B Practising

3. a) Complete the factor rainbow. Show how to use the factors to determine the square root of 441.

   b) How can you check your answer in part a)?

4. Determine the square root of 729 by factoring. Show how to check your answer.

5. Maddy listed rectangles with whole number sides and an area of 64 m^2 to determine $\sqrt{64}$.

               64 m   32 m
                               1 m   2 m

   a) What other rectangles can Maddy list?

   b) How can she use her complete list to determine $\sqrt{64}$?

   c) Use Maddy's strategy to determine $\sqrt{144}$.

   d) How is Maddy's strategy for determining a square root like Sanjev's?

6. Determine the square root of each number using mental math.

   a) 1   **c)** 25   **e)** 400

   b) 0   **d)** 100   **f)** 900

7. Explain how to determine each square root.

   a) $\sqrt{31 \times 31}$ **b)** $\sqrt{43^2}$ **c)** $\sqrt{2 \times 2 \times 3 \times 3}$

8. a) The square of 32 is 1024. What is the square root of 1024?

   b) The square root of a perfect square is 11. What is the perfect square?

9. At the 2006 Winter Olympics in Turin, Italy, 196 Canadian athletes were at the opening ceremonies. Would they have been able to arrange themselves in a square? Explain.

10. The area of a square weightlifting platform is 16 m^2. What is the perimeter of the platform?

11. a) Explain how you know the square root of 225 is between 10 and 20.

   b) How can you predict the ones digit of the square root of 225?

   c) How can you use your answers to parts a) and b) to predict the square root of 225?

676
2 338
2 169
13 13

12. This tree diagram shows the prime factors of 676.

    a) Is 676 a perfect square? Explain.

    b) What is the square root of 676?

13. Iris said, "If the ones digit of a perfect square is 0, then the ones digit of the square root will be 0. If the ones digit of a perfect square is 1, then the ones digit of the square root will be 1 or 9."

    a) Complete Iris's table.

Ones digit of perfect square	0	1	2	3	4	5	6	7	8	9
Ones digit of square root	0	1 or 9								

    b) Can you always use the ones digit of a perfect square to predict its square root? Explain.

14. Determine each square root using estimation and your chart from question 13. Show your work for one answer.

    a) 289   **b)** 441   **c)** 2209   **d)** 3025

15. Describe two strategies to calculate $\sqrt{324}$.

16. Determine

    a) $\sqrt{100}$ **b)** $\sqrt{10\ 000}$ **c)** $\sqrt{1\ 000\ 000}$

17. Predict $\sqrt{100\ 000\ 000}$ using your answers in question 16. Explain your prediction.

18. **a)** Jason listed all factors of 5929.

        1, 7, 11, 49, 77, 121, 539, 847, 5929

        How can you determine the square root of 5929 using Jason's list of factors?

    b) Show how to use squaring to check your answer.

19. A whole number has an odd number of factors. How do you know that one of the factors must be the square root?

20. Why might squaring a number and calculating the square root of a number be thought of as opposite operations? Use an example to explain.

Reading Strategy

Evaluating

Write your answer to question 20. Share it with partners. Do they agree or disagree?

Number Relationships   **15**

1.4

Estimating Square Roots

YOU WILL NEED
- grid paper
- a calculator

GOAL

Estimate the square root of numbers that are not perfect squares.

LEARN ABOUT *the Math*

Kaitlyn and her father drilled a hole in the ice in the lake to measure its thickness. The ice was 30 cm thick. Their total mass is 125 kg. Can the ice support them safely? They used this formula to check.

Required thickness (cm) $\doteq 0.38\sqrt{\text{load in kilograms}}$

Communication | ***Tip***

- The multiplication symbol is often omitted from formulas when the meaning is clear. For example, $0.38\sqrt{}$ means the same as $0.38 \times \sqrt{}$.
- The symbol "$\doteq$" means "approximately equal to." For example, $\sqrt{2} \doteq 1.414$.

❓ Is the ice thick enough to support Kaitlyn and her father?

A. Draw a 10-by-10 square, an 11-by-11 square, and a 12-by-12 square on grid paper. Calculate the area of each square.

B. How can you calculate the side length of a square if you know only the area of the square?

C. Does a square with an area of 125 square units have a whole-number side length? Use your diagrams in part A to help you explain.

D. How can you use the side lengths of the squares you drew in part A to estimate $\sqrt{125}$?

E. Determine $\sqrt{125}$ to two decimal places using a calculator.

F. Will the ice support Kaitlyn and her father? Show your work.

Reflecting

G. Explain how to use the square key $\boxed{x^2}$ or the power key $\boxed{\wedge}$ on your calculator to check your answer in part E.

H. When you square your answer in part E, why do you not get exactly 125?

WORK WITH *the Math*

Example 1	Estimating a square root using squaring

A square floor has an area of 85 m². About how long are its sides?

Kaitlyn's Solution

A = 85m²   n metres

n metres

$n \times n = 85$
$n^2 = 85$

$9^2 = 81$
$9.1^2 = 82.81$
$9.2^2 = 84.64$
$\sqrt{85} \doteq 9.2$

The sides of the floor are about 9.2 m long.

I can determine the side length of a square with an area of 85 square units by calculating $\sqrt{85}$.

The square root of 81 is 9, so the square root of 85 must be a bit more than 9.

I squared 9.1 and 9.2.
The square of 9.2 is very close to 85.

So the square root of 85 is about 9.2.

Example 2 | Determining a square root using a calculator

A truck has a mass of 5000 kg. What thickness of ice is needed to support the truck? Use the formula:
Required thickness (cm) $\doteq 0.38\sqrt{5000}$.

Guy's Solution

5000 must be close to 70 because $70^2 = 4900$.

First, I estimated $\sqrt{5000}$.

Multiplying 70 by 0.38 is less than half of 70, or about 30 cm.

Then I estimated 0.38×70.

0.38 ⊠√‾ 5000 ⎵ ⊟  **26.87005769**

Then I used these keystrokes and entered these numbers into my TI-15 calculator.

The ice needs to be about 27 cm thick to support the truck; 27 cm is close to my estimate of 30 cm, so the answer is reasonable.

Calculator | Tip

Your calculator might use this key sequence:
5000 √‾⊟ 70.710678
⊠ .38 ⊟ 26.870057

A Checking

1. Estimate each square root to one decimal place using squaring. Show what you did.
   a) $\sqrt{15}$　　　　　　　　b) $\sqrt{30}$

2. Determine each square root to one decimal place using the square root key on your calculator.
   a) $\sqrt{8}$　　b) $\sqrt{42}$　　c) $\sqrt{163}$　　d) $\sqrt{979}$

3. Choose one of your answers from question 2 and explain how you know your answer is reasonable.

B Practising

4. Estimate to determine whether each answer is reasonable. Correct any unreasonable answers using the square root key on your calculator.
   a) $\sqrt{10} \doteq 3.2$　　c) $\sqrt{30} \doteq 5.5$　　e) $\sqrt{342} \doteq 28.5$
   b) $\sqrt{15} \doteq 4.8$　　d) $\sqrt{289} \doteq 27$　　f) $\sqrt{1482} \doteq 38.5$

5. Calculate each square root to one decimal place. Choose one of your answers and explain why it is reasonable.
   a) $\sqrt{18}$ **c)** $\sqrt{38}$ **e)** $\sqrt{800}$
   b) $\sqrt{75}$ **d)** $\sqrt{150}$ **f)** $\sqrt{3900}$

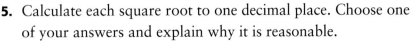

$A = 3000 \text{ m}^2$

6. A square field has an area of 3000 m^2.
   a) Explain how you can use $\sqrt{3000}$ to estimate the side length of the square.
   b) How do you know the side length is between 50 m and 60 m?
   c) Calculate the side length of the square field. Round your answer to one decimal place.

7. What can you add to each number to make a perfect square?
   a) 42   **b)** 101   **c)** 399   **d)** 875

8. Tiananmen Square in Beijing, China, is the largest open "square" in any city in the world. It is actually a rectangle of 880 m by 500 m.
   a) What would be the approximate side length of a square with the same area as Tiananmen Square?
   b) Explain how you know your answer is reasonable.

9. a) How do you know the square root of 29 is between 5 and 6?

b) List three other whole numbers whose square roots are between 5 and 6.

10. Estimate the time an object takes to fall from each height using this formula: time (s) $\doteq 0.45\sqrt{\text{height (m)}}$. Record each answer to one decimal place.

a) 100 m   **c)** 400 m   **e)** 2000 m
b) 200 m   **d)** 900 m   **f)** 10 000 m

11. Kim estimated that the square root of a certain whole number would be close to 5.9. What might the whole number be? Explain your reasoning.

12. a) Try Mark's number trick.
- Choose any whole number greater than 0.
- Square it.
- Add twice the original number.
- Add one.
- Calculate the square root of the sum.
- Subtract your original number.
- Record your answer.

b) Try Mark's number trick with four other numbers. What do you notice about all your answers?

13. The year 1936 was the last year whose square root was a whole number. What is the next year whose square root will be a whole number? Explain your reasoning.

14. Calculate each square root with a calculator to three decimal places.

a) $\sqrt{5}$ **b)** $\sqrt{500}$ **c)** $\sqrt{50\ 000}$ **d)** $\sqrt{5\ 000\ 000}$

15. a) Describe any patterns you saw in question 14.
b) Determine $\sqrt{500\ 000\ 000}$ without a calculator.

16. Explain how to use the diagram to estimate $\sqrt{5}$.

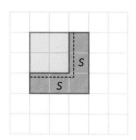

Subtracting to Calculate Square Roots

You can calculate the square root of a perfect square by subtracting consecutive odd numbers, starting with 1. The square root is the number of odd numbers subtracted to get to 0.

$$\begin{array}{r} 16 \\ -1 \\ \hline 15 \end{array}$$ one subtraction

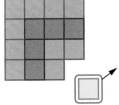

$$\begin{array}{r} 15 \\ -3 \\ \hline 12 \end{array}$$ two subtractions

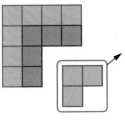

$$\begin{array}{r} 12 \\ -5 \\ \hline 7 \end{array}$$ three subtractions

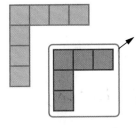

$$\begin{array}{r} 7 \\ -7 \\ \hline 0 \end{array}$$ four subtractions

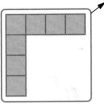

The first four odd numbers were subtracted from 16 to get 0, so $\sqrt{16} = 4$.

1. Calculate each square root by subtracting consecutive odd numbers, starting at 1.

    a) $\sqrt{9}$ **b)** $\sqrt{25}$ **c)** $\sqrt{64}$ **d)** $\sqrt{81}$

Mid-Chapter **Review**

Frequently Asked Questions

Q: How do you determine whether a number is a perfect square?

A1: You can try to draw a square, with whole number side lengths, that has the area of the number. For example, to determine if 225 is a perfect square, try to figure out a whole number side length, s, for a square with that area.

$15^2 = 225$, so $s = 15$, a whole number, and 225 is a perfect square.

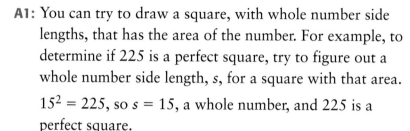

A2: You can use prime factors. For example, to determine if 1225 is a perfect square, draw a tree diagram to identify the prime factors. Then group the prime factors to rename 1225 as 35×35 or 35^2. So 1225 is a perfect square.

$$1225 = (5 \times 7) \times (5 \times 7)$$
$$= 35 \times 35$$

Q: How do you calculate or estimate a square root?

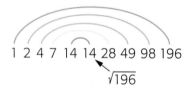

A1: If a number is a perfect square, you can factor to determine its square root. For example, to calculate $\sqrt{196}$, list all its factors. The partner of 14 is itself, so $14 \times 14 = 14^2$ or 196. $\sqrt{196} = 14$.

A2: If a number is not a perfect square, you have to estimate its square root. For example, to determine $\sqrt{10}$:

Estimate that $\sqrt{10}$ is between 3 and 4 and closer to 3 than 4.	$\sqrt{9} = 3$ $\sqrt{10} = \blacksquare$ $\sqrt{16} = 4$

Square 3.1. $3.1^2 = 9.61$ (too low)
Square 3.2. $3.2^2 = 10.24$ (too high)
So $\sqrt{10}$ is between 3.1 and 3.2.

A3: You can use the square root key on a calculator. You can use the square key $\boxed{x^2}$ to check your answer.

Practice

1. Show that each number is a perfect square by drawing a square. Label each side length.

   a) 49   **b)** 64   **c)** 144   **d)** 196

2. List the square numbers between 49 and 100. Show your work.

3. Which number is not a perfect square? Show your work.

   A. 100   **B.** 121   **C.** 135   **D.** 400

4. Show that 11 025 is a perfect square using its prime factors.
   11 025 = 3 × 3 × 5 × 5 × 7 × 7

5. What square number and its square root can be represented by this square? Explain.

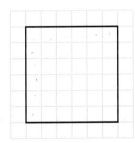

6. A square park has an area of 900 m². How can you use a square root to determine the side length of the park?

7. How can you use the factors of 81 to determine the square root of 81?

8. Estimate each square root to one decimal place using squaring. Show your work for one answer.

   a) $\sqrt{12}$ **b)** $\sqrt{17}$ **c)** $\sqrt{925}$ **d)** $\sqrt{1587}$

9. What is the perimeter of a square with an area of 625 cm²? Show your work.

1.5 Exploring Problems Involving Squares and Square Roots

YOU WILL NEED
- grid paper
- square tiles
- playing cards (optional)

GOAL

Create and solve problems involving a perfect square.

EXPLORE the Math

Joseph read about a game played with two decks of square playing cards (104 cards). You deal the cards in equal rows and equal columns to form a square. Four cards are left over and not used.

He wanted to know how many rows and columns are in the square.

He drew a diagram and wrote an equation to solve the problem.

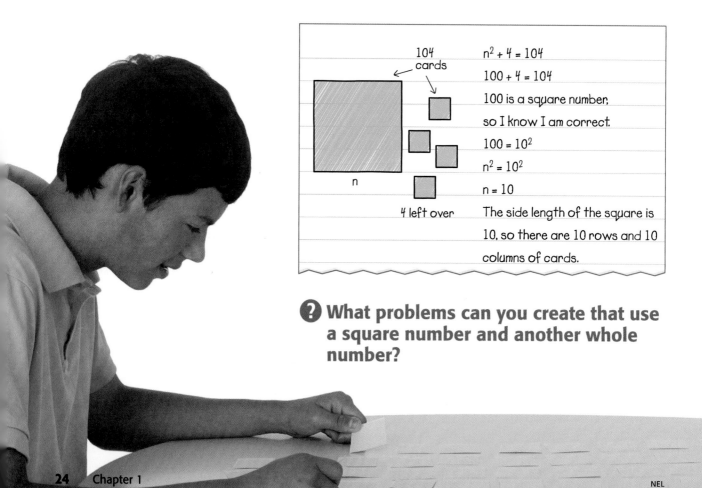

104 cards

n

4 left over

$n^2 + 4 = 104$

$100 + 4 = 104$

100 is a square number, so I know I am correct.

$100 = 10^2$

$n^2 = 10^2$

$n = 10$

The side length of the square is 10, so there are 10 rows and 10 columns of cards.

❓ What problems can you create that use a square number and another whole number?

Tossing Square Roots

YOU WILL NEED
- a die
- a calculator

Number of players: 2 to 4

How to Play

1. For each turn, toss a die three times to form a three-digit number.

2. Each player estimates the square root of the tossed number without using a calculator. Each player then records his or her estimate.

3. Each player calculates the square root.

4. Each player scores points for the estimate:
   - Estimate within 2:   1 point
   - Estimate within 1:   2 points
   - Estimate within 0.5: 3 points

5. Continue for five turns. The player who has the most points wins.

Mark's Turn

We rolled 654.

I estimated that the square root of 654 is between 20 and 30 and probably close to 25.

My estimate of 25 is within 1 of the answer. I score 2 points.

1.6

The Pythagorean Theorem

GOAL

Model, explain, and apply the Pythagorean theorem.

LEARN ABOUT the Math

Guy was doing research on Pythagoras, a mathematician who lived 2500 years ago. Guy discovered that Pythagoras is known for the **Pythagorean theorem,** which is used to solve problems involving the side lengths of **right triangles.** He wondered if this theorem applied to other types of triangles as well.

Pythagorean theorem

a relationship that says the sum of the squares of the lengths of the legs of a right triangle is equal to the square of the length of the hypotenuse. This is written algebraically as $a^2 + b^2 = c^2$.

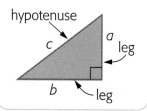

Communication | **Tip**

In a right triangle, the two shortest sides are called the legs. The longest side, opposite the right angle, is called the hypotenuse.

❓ Is the Pythagorean theorem true for all types of triangles?

A. Construct two obtuse triangles, two acute triangles, and one right triangle. Each triangle should have one side 60 mm long and another side 80 mm long, such as the ones shown.

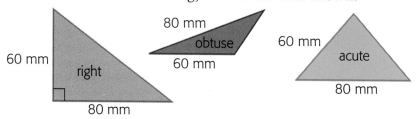

B. Measure the third side of each triangle to the nearest millimetre. Record the length of the longest side as $c = $ ▨ mm. Record the lengths of the two shorter sides as $a = $ ▨ mm and $b = $ ▨ mm.

C. For each triangle, calculate $a^2 + b^2$ and c^2. Compare the two values. Record each comparison.

D. Is the Pythagorean theorem true for all types of triangles drawn in your class? Explain.

Reflecting

E. Guy drew three triangles, with these results:
Triangle 1: $a^2 + b^2 < c^2$
Triangle 2: $a^2 + b^2 = c^2$
Triangle 3: $a^2 + b^2 > c^2$
What types of triangles did Guy draw? Explain your answer.

WORK WITH *the Math*

| Example 1 | Identifying a right triangle |

Determine whether $\triangle ABC$ is a right triangle.

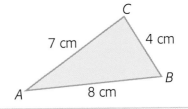

Elena's Solution

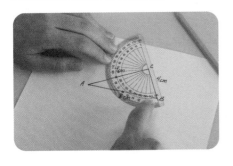

I measured $\angle C$. It is 89°. That is close to 90°, but not exactly 90°, so I am not sure.

$a^2 + b^2 = 4^2 + 7^2$
$ = 16 + 49$
$ = 65$
$c^2 = 8^2$
$ = 64$

I decided to use the Pythagorean theorem to be sure.

$a^2 + b^2 \neq c^2$
So $\triangle ABC$ is not a right triangle.

$a^2 + b^2$ does not equal c^2.

Example 2 | Using the Pythagorean theorem

A cowhand rode a horse along the diagonal path, instead of around the fence of the ranch. What distance did the cowhand save by riding the diagonal path?

Joseph's Solution

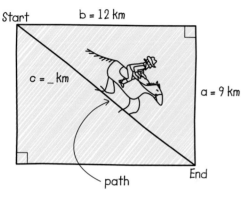

I drew a diagram to represent the problem.

$c^2 = a^2 + b^2$
$c^2 = 9^2 + 12^2$
$\quad = 81 + 144$
$\quad = 225$

$c = \sqrt{225}$
$\quad = 15$

I used the Pythagorean theorem to create an equation.
I solved the equation to determine c, the length of the hypotenuse.

I solved for c by calculating the square root.

Distance along fence
$= 9 \text{ km} + 12 \text{ km}$
$= 21 \text{ km}$
Distance saved
$= 21 \text{ km} - 15 \text{ km}$
$= 6 \text{ km}.$
The cowhand saved 6 km.

I calculated the distance around two sides and the distance the cowhand saved.

| Example 3 | Calculating a missing side length |

Determine the length of *a* in △*ABC*.

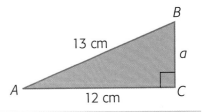

Vanessa's Solution

$$a^2 + b^2 = c^2$$
$$a^2 + 12^2 = 13^2$$
$$a^2 + 144 = 169$$
$$a^2 + 144 - 144 = 169 - 144$$
$$a^2 = 25$$
$$a = \sqrt{25}$$
$$= 5$$

The missing length, *a*, is 5 cm.

△*ABC* is a right triangle, so I can determine *a* using the Pythagorean theorem.
I know *b* = 12 and *c* = 13. So I can square these numbers and solve the equation for *a*.

A **Checking**

1. Which triangle is a right triangle? Show your work.

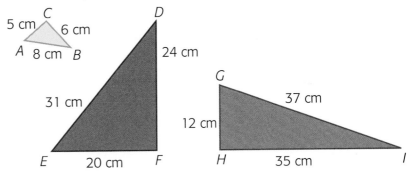

2. Calculate the unknown length in each right triangle. Show your work.

a)

b)

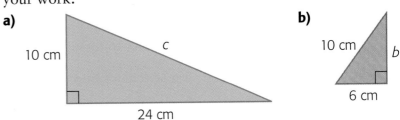

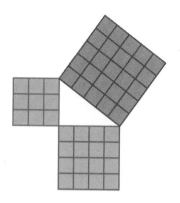

B Practising

3. Hernan formed a triangle with grid paper squares. How can you tell that he formed a right triangle?

4. a) Draw a triangle with side lengths 8 cm, 10 cm, and 13 cm.
   b) Does your diagram look like a right triangle? Explain.
   c) Show how to use the Pythagorean theorem to determine whether it really is a right triangle.

5. A Pythagorean triple is any set of three whole numbers, a, b, and c, for which $a^2 + b^2 = c^2$. Show that each set of numbers is a Pythagorean triple.
   a) 3, 4, 5   c) 7, 24, 25   e) 9, 40, 41
   b) 5, 12, 13   d) 8, 15, 17   f) 11, 60, 61

6. a) Choose a Pythagorean triple in question 5. Double each number. Is the new triple also a Pythagorean triple? Explain.
   b) Choose another Pythagorean triple from question 5. Multiply each number by the same whole number greater than 2. Is the new triple also a Pythagorean triple? Explain.

7. In 2003, the old-time players of the Edmonton Oilers and Montreal Canadiens played an outdoor hockey game before more than 57 000 fans in Commonwealth stadium.

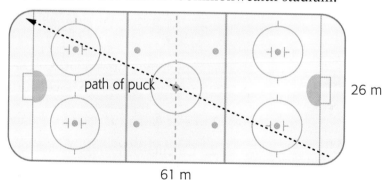

About how far would a hockey puck travel when shot from one corner to the opposite corner?

8. A wheelchair ramp must be 12 m long for every metre of height.
   a) What is the length of a ramp that rises 2.0 m?
   b) About how long is side b to one decimal place?

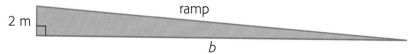

9. Calculate each unknown side to one decimal place.

a)

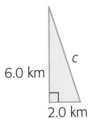

6.0 cm

c

5.0 cm

c)

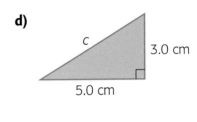

9.0 cm

a

8.0 cm

b)

c

6.0 km

2.0 km

d)

c

3.0 cm

5.0 cm

10. What is the distance between points *A* and *B*? Show your work.

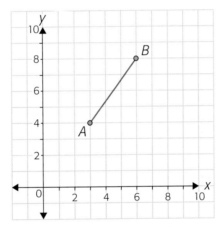

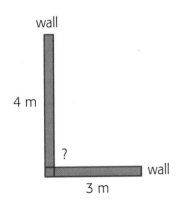

wall

4 m

?

3 m

wall

11. The hypotenuse of an isosceles right triangle is 10 cm. How long are the legs? Show your work.

12. How can a carpenter use a measuring tape to ensure that the bases of these two walls form a right angle?

13. One side of a right triangle is 9 cm and another side is 12 cm. Draw sketches to show that there are two possible triangles.

14. Why is there only one square but many rectangles with a given diagonal length? Use a diagonal length of 8 cm to help you explain.

Solve Problems Using Diagrams

YOU WILL NEED
- grid paper
- a calculator
- a ruler

> **GOAL**
>
> Use diagrams to solve problems about squares and square roots.

LEARN ABOUT *the Math*

Joseph is building a model of the front of a famous Haida longhouse. He wants the model to have these measurements.

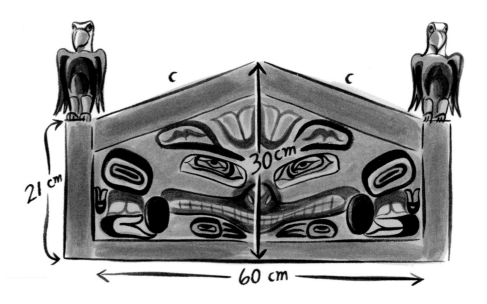

❓ How can Joseph calculate the two lengths at the top of the model?

Example 1 | Solve a problem by identifying a right triangle

I used a diagram to identify right triangles.

Joseph's Solution

1. Understand the Problem

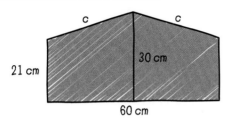

I drew a diagram that included all I knew about the model. I used c to represent the two lengths I want to know.

2. Make a Plan

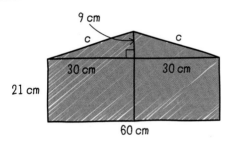

I drew a line to connect the top of the opposite sides of the model. I noticed two right triangles in my diagram.

Each triangle has a base of half of 60 cm or 30 cm.
The height of each triangle is
$30 - 21 = 9$ cm.
I can use the Pythagorean theorem to calculate the hypotenuse of each right triangle.

3. Carry Out the Plan

$$c^2 = 9^2 + 30^2$$
$$= 81 + 900$$
$$= 981$$
$$c = \sqrt{981}$$
$$\doteq 31.32 \text{ cm}$$

Each length at the top of the model is about 31.32 cm.

I know that, in a right triangle, $a^2 + b^2 = c^2$. I used 9 cm for the length a, and 30 cm for the length b.
I solved for c.

Reflecting

A. How did Joseph's diagrams help him solve the problem?

WORK WITH *the Math*

Example 2 | Visualizing a problem using diagrams

A green square mat in a martial arts competition has an area of 64 m². Around the mat is a red danger zone 1 m wide. Around the red zone is a safety area 3 m wide. What is the side length of the overall contest area?

Kaitlyn's Solution

1. Understand the Problem

I have to figure out the overall dimensions of a square mat surrounded by two zones of different widths.

2. Make a Plan

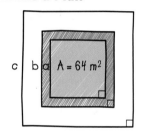

I decided to draw a diagram to help me visualize the mat and two zones. I used letters to show the dimensions that I need to know to figure out the size of the contest area.

3. Carry Out the Plan

$$\text{Area} = a^2$$
$$64 = a^2$$
$$\sqrt{64} = a$$
$$8\text{ m} = a$$

The square mat is 8 m by 8 m.

First, I calculated the side length of the square mat using the formula for the area of a square.

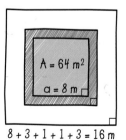

$$8 + 3 + 1 + 1 + 3 = 16\text{ m}$$

The overall contest area is a square measuring 16 m by 16 m.

I added the new information from the calculations to my diagram.

The red zone and the danger zone add 3 m + 1 m to each side of the mat.

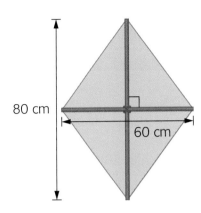

80 cm

60 cm

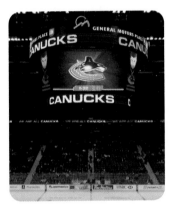

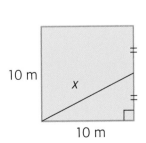

10 m

x

10 m

A Checking

1. The two cross-pieces of a kite measure 60 cm and 80 cm. The cross-pieces are tied at their middles. What is the perimeter of the kite? Show your work.

B Practising

2. The LED scoreboard at General Motors Place in Vancouver, BC, has four rectangular video displays. Each display measures about 412 cm by 732 cm. What is the side length of a square with the same area as the four video displays? Show your work.

3. How many squares are on an 8-by-8 chessboard?

4. When Maddy drew a 3-by-3 square, she counted a total of 5 squares along both diagonals.

   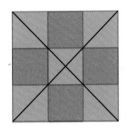

   a) What is the total number of squares along the two diagonals of a 5-by-5 square? Show your work.

   b) What is the side length of a square with a total of 21 squares along both diagonals? Show your work.

5. The diagonal of a rectangle is 25 cm. The shortest side is 15 cm. What is the length of the other side?

6. Fran cycles 6.0 km north along a straight path. She then rides 10.0 km east. Then she rides 3.0 km south. Then she turns and rides in a straight line back to her starting point. What is the total distance of her ride?

7. The floor of a square room is covered in square tiles. There are 16 tiles on the outside edges of the floor. How many tiles cover the floor?

8. Create and solve a problem about this diagram.

Chapter **Self-Test**

1. **a)** What is the least square number greater than 100? Show your work.
   b) What is the greatest square number less than 200? Show your work.

2. **a)** Explain how you know that 25 is a perfect square. Show two different strategies.
   b) Express 25 as the sum of two other perfect squares.

3. Each number is the square root of some number. Determine each square number.
   a) 1   **b)** 7   **c)** 15   **d)** 30

4. How many squares can you create by combining one or more of these puzzle pieces? Use linking cubes to help you. Draw each square to show how you arranged the pieces.

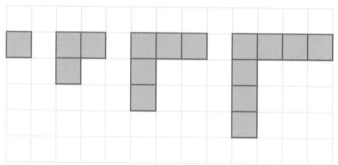

5. Calculate the side length of each square. Show your work.
   a)

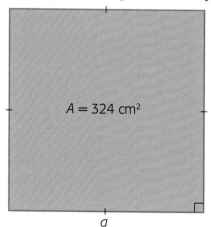

$A = 324$ cm²

a

   b) $A = 42$ cm²

6. Explain how you can estimate $\sqrt{90}$.

7. Saskatchewan is about 652 000 km² in area. What would the approximate side lengths be if the province were shaped like a square? Explain.

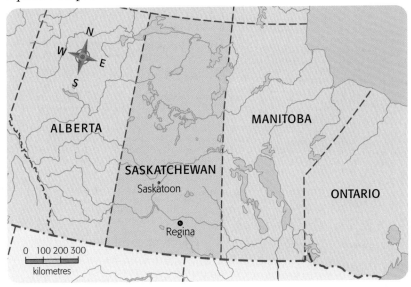

8. Which of these two triangles is a right triangle? Explain.

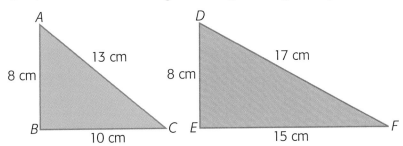

9. The length of line segment *A* on the geoboard is 1 unit. What is the length of line segment *B*? Show your work.

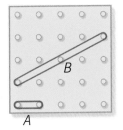

10. A square has an area of 100 cm². The midpoints of the square are connected to form another square. What are the side lengths of the outer and inner square? Draw a diagram to help you explain.

What Do You Think Now?

Revisit What Do You Think? on page 3. How have your answers and explanations changed?

Frequently Asked Questions

Q: How can you use the Pythagorean theorem?

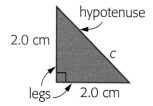

A1: You can calculate the length of the hypotenuse if you know the lengths of the legs. For example, the hypotenuse is about 2.8 cm.

$$c^2 = 2^2 + 2^2$$
$$= 8$$
$$c = \sqrt{8}$$
$$\doteq 2.8 \text{ cm}$$

A2: You can calculate the length of one leg if you know the lengths of the hypotenuse and the other leg. For example, side a is 5 cm.

$$a^2 + 12.0^2 = 13.0^2$$
$$a^2 + 144.0^2 = 169.0$$
$$a^2 = 25.0$$
$$a = \sqrt{25.0}$$
$$= 5.0 \text{ cm}$$

A3: You can determine whether a triangle is a right triangle by comparing $a^2 + b^2$ with c^2.

For example: $a^2 + b^2 = 14^2 + 18^2$
$$= 196 + 324$$
$$= 520$$
$$c^2 = 23^2$$
$$= 529$$

$520 \neq 529$, so $\triangle ABC$ is not a right triangle.

Practice

Lesson 1.2

1. Determine whether each number is a perfect square using its prime factors. Explain what you did.
   a) $3969 = 3 \times 3 \times 3 \times 3 \times 7 \times 7$
   b) $6615 = 3 \times 3 \times 3 \times 7 \times 5 \times 7$
   c) $1521 = 3 \times 13 \times 3 \times 13$
   d) $125 = 5 \times 5 \times 5$

Lesson 1.3

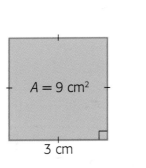

A = 529 cm²

2. Zack drew a square and its area. How can you use his diagram to determine the side length of the square?

3. What is the perimeter of a square parking lot with an area of 1600 m²? Show your work.

Lesson 1.4

4. How can you use the two squares to show that $\sqrt{11}$ is between 3 and 4?

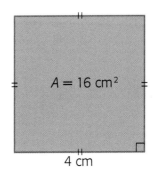

A = 9 cm²

3 cm

A = 16 cm²

4 cm

5. Estimate each square root to one decimal place using squaring. Show your work for one answer.
   a) $\sqrt{7}$ b) $\sqrt{33}$ c) $\sqrt{425}$ d) $\sqrt{922}$

6. The official size of a doubles tennis court is 23.9 m by 11.0 m. What is the side length of a square with the same area as a doubles tennis court? Show your work.

= 130 chairs

Lesson 1.5

7. Chairs in a gym were arranged in the shape of square. Nine chairs were placed in front of the square. A total of 130 chairs were used. How many rows and columns were in the square?
   a) Explain how the diagram represents this problem.
   b) What equation would you use to represent this problem?
   c) Show how to solve the equation.
   d) How many rows and columns were in the square?

Lesson 1.6

8. This map shows the route of a helicopter. About how far did the helicopter travel? Show your work.

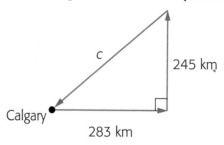

9. The area of the square is 25 cm². What are the side lengths of the red triangle?

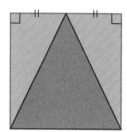

Lesson 1.7

10. Draw a diagram to solve this problem from a medieval military book. Explain what you did.

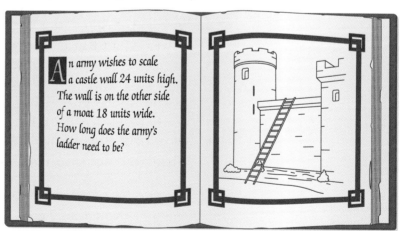

An army wishes to scale a castle wall 24 units high. The wall is on the other side of a moat 18 units wide. How long does the army's ladder need to be?

Chapter **Task**

Pythagorean Spiral

You can use the Pythagorean relationship to create a spiral design.

❓ How many right triangles do you need to draw to get a hypotenuse just longer than 6 cm?

A. Draw this right triangle in the centre of a large sheet of paper. Use the Pythagorean theorem to show that c is about 2.828 cm. How do you know that 2.828 cm is reasonable?

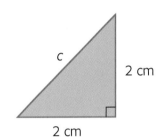

B. Draw a new right triangle on the hypotenuse of the first triangle. Make the outer leg 2 cm long. What is the length of c? Round your answer to three decimal places.

C. How do you know your answer in part B is an estimate?

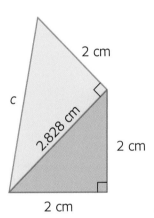

D. Draw another right triangle on the hypotenuse of the second triangle. What is the length of d? Round your answer to three decimal places.

E. Repeat drawing right triangles with an outer side of 2 cm long. How many right triangles in total do you need to draw to get a hypotenuse just longer than 6 cm?

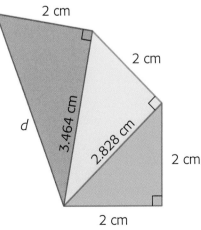

Chapter 2

Fraction Operations

GOAL

You will be able to

- multiply and divide fractions by whole numbers, other fractions, and mixed numbers using models, drawings, and symbols

- estimate products and quotients of whole numbers, fractions, and mixed numbers

- solve and create problems using fraction operations

- calculate the value of expressions involving fractions, using the proper order of operations

- communicate clearly about fraction operations

◀ **How could you use fractions to describe this "musical instrument"?**

Getting **Started**

Pattern Block Designs

Allison made a design using pattern blocks.

❓ What fractions can you use to describe the pattern block design?

A. If a yellow hexagon has an area of 1 unit, what is the area of each block?

    a) the red block   **b)** the blue block   **c)** a green block

B. The equation $3 + \frac{3}{6} = 3\frac{1}{2}$ tells the sum of the areas of two of the colours.

    • Which are the two colours?

    • How do you know?

C. The equation $3 - \frac{1}{2} = 2\frac{1}{2}$ describes how much more of the design is one colour than another.

    • Which are the two colours?

    • How do you know?

D. Write equations with fractions and/or **mixed numbers** to describe the areas defined below, using the units in part A. Solve the equations. Show your work.
- the red and blue parts
- how much more is green than blue
- how much more is yellow and red than green and blue
- how much more is red than green

E. Write three other fraction equations that describe areas in Allison's design.

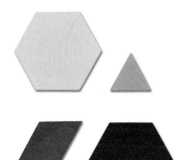

F. Make your own design using
- yellow, red, blue, and green pattern blocks
- a total of eight blocks
- at least two yellow blocks
- at least one block of each other colour

Repeat steps D and E for your design.

G. Is it possible to create a design using the rules in step F where each is true? Explain.
- The yellow area is $1\frac{1}{3}$ units greater than the blue area.
- The blue and red area, together, is $\frac{1}{6}$ unit greater than the green area.

What Do You Think?

Decide whether you agree or disagree with each statement. Be ready to explain your decision.

1. If you add two fractions, the result is always less than 1, but if you add three fractions, it is greater than 1.

2. If you subtract two fractions, the difference is usually somewhere between the two fractions you are subtracting.

3. The product of two numbers is always greater than the sum.

4. The quotient of two numbers is always less than the product.

5. One way to calculate $a \div b$ is to figure out how many bs make up a.

2.1

Multiplying a Whole Number by a Fraction

YOU WILL NEED
- grid paper
- counters
- Fraction Strips Tower
- Number Lines

GOAL

Use repeated addition to multiply fractions by whole numbers.

LEARN ABOUT *the Math*

Nikita is having a party. After a few hours, she notices that six pitchers of lemonade are each only $\frac{3}{8}$ full. She decides to combine the leftovers to use fewer pitchers.

❓ How many pitchers will the leftover lemonade fill?

A. Estimate how many whole pitchers the lemonade will fill completely. Explain your thinking.

B. Use a model to represent $\frac{8}{8}$ of a pitcher.

C. Use this model to represent all the lemonade from the six partially full pitchers. Write the number of pitchers, after the lemonade has been combined, as both an **improper fraction** and a **mixed number**.

D. Why could you write either $\frac{3}{8} + \frac{3}{8} + \frac{3}{8} + \frac{3}{8} + \frac{3}{8} + \frac{3}{8}$ or $6 \times \frac{3}{8}$ to describe the total amount of lemonade in the pitchers?

E. Now use another model to represent the pitchers and solve the problem.

Reflecting

F. How could you have predicted that the amount left in the last pitcher would be a fraction with a denominator of 8?

G. Describe a procedure for multiplying a whole number by a fraction. Explain why you think that procedure will work.

WORK WITH *the Math*

Example 1	Multiplying with grids and counters

Calculate $4 \times \frac{5}{6}$ using grids and counters.
Represent the answer as an improper fraction and as a mixed number.

Brian's Solution

$4 \times \frac{5}{6}$ is four sets of $\frac{5}{6}$.

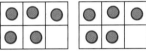

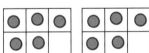

$4 \times \frac{5}{6} = \frac{4 \times 5}{6} = \frac{20}{6}$

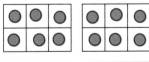

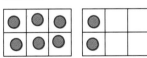

$4 \times \frac{5}{6} = \frac{20}{6}$, or $3\frac{2}{6}$, or $3\frac{1}{3}$

I used 3-by-2 rectangles, since I wanted to show sixths and $3 \times 2 = 6$. Each rectangle represents one whole.

I showed four sets of $\frac{5}{6}$ by putting counters on 5 out of 6 squares in each of the four rectangles.

$4 \times 5 = 20$, so 20 squares are covered.

Since each square represents $\frac{1}{6}$, the 20 squares represent $\frac{20}{6}$.

To write the improper fraction as a mixed number, I moved the counters to fill as many grids as I could.

I moved 3 counters from the last grid to fill up the other 3 grids.

That means 3 grids were full and there were 2 counters, each representing $\frac{1}{6}$, in the last grid.

You can write the fraction part $\frac{2}{6}$ as $\frac{1}{3}$ if you want to.

Example 2 | Multiplying with fraction strips

Calculate $3 \times \frac{2}{3}$ using fraction strips. Write the product as an improper fraction and as a whole or mixed number.

Misa's Solution

$3 \times \frac{2}{3}$ is 3 sets of $\frac{2}{3}$.

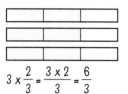

$$3 \times \frac{2}{3} = \frac{3 \times 2}{3} = \frac{6}{3}$$

I can look at the model and see that there are 6 thirds altogether.

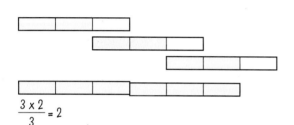

$$\frac{3 \times 2}{3} = 2$$

To rename the product as a whole or mixed number, I needed to know how many whole strips there were and how many thirds were left over. I lined up the strips to see.

The total length matched 2 full strips and there were no extra thirds

Example 3 | Multiplying with a number line

Calculate $5 \times \frac{3}{2}$ using a number line. Write the product as an improper fraction and as a whole or mixed number.

Preston's Solution

$5 \times \frac{3}{2} = 5 \times 3$ halves

$= 15$ halves

$= \frac{15}{2}$

I knew that there would be 15 halves since there are 5 sets of 3 halves.

```
 ├─┼─┼─┼─┼─┼─┼─┼─┼─┼─┼─┼─┼─┼─┼─┼─┼─┼─┼─┼─→
 0  1  2  3  4  5  6  7  8  9  10
```

I drew a number line marked in halves to see how much $\frac{15}{2}$ is.

I knew it would be less than 10 since $\frac{20}{2} = 10$.

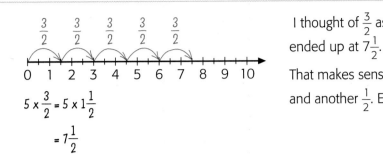

I thought of $\frac{3}{2}$ as $1\frac{1}{2}$. I made 5 jumps of $1\frac{1}{2}$ and ended up at $7\frac{1}{2}$.

That makes sense since $\frac{15}{2}$ is 7 sets of 2 halves and another $\frac{1}{2}$. Each set of 2 halves is one whole.

$5 \times \frac{3}{2} = 5 \times 1\frac{1}{2}$

$= 7\frac{1}{2}$

Reading Strategy

Questioning

Write three questions that can help you solve this problem.

A Checking

1. Jennifer pours $\frac{2}{3}$ of a cup of water into a pot and repeats this 7 times. How many cups of water, in total, does she pour into the pot? Write your answer as a mixed number.

2. **a)** Write $5 \times \frac{3}{4}$ as a repeated addition sentence.
   b) Use a model to calculate the answer.
   c) Write your answer as an improper fraction and as a mixed number.

B Practising

3. Multiply. Write your answer as a fraction and, if it is greater than 1, as a mixed number or whole number. Use a model and show your work for at least two parts.

   a) $2 \times \frac{1}{3}$ **c)** $6 \times \frac{3}{8}$ **e)** $3 \times \frac{7}{6}$

   b) $5 \times \frac{3}{5}$ **d)** $4 \times \frac{2}{5}$ **f)** $8 \times \frac{4}{2}$

4. Estimate to decide which products are between 5 and 10. Calculate to check.

   a) $2 \times \frac{5}{3}$ **c)** $8 \times \frac{4}{5}$ **e)** $6 \times \frac{5}{4}$

   b) $6 \times \frac{6}{7}$ **d)** $7 \times \frac{7}{10}$ **f)** $7 \times \frac{7}{6}$

5. Art class is $\frac{5}{6}$ of an hour each school day. How many hours of art does a student have in five days?

6. Jason needs $\frac{2}{3}$ of a cup of flour to make one batch of bannock. How many cups of flour will he need if he decides to make six batches, one for each of his aunts?

7. Katya says that multiplying $17 \times \frac{1}{4}$ will tell her how many dollars 17 quarters is worth. Do you agree? Explain.

8. a) How much farther are four jumps of $\frac{3}{5}$ on a number line than three jumps of $\frac{4}{5}$? Explain.

   b) Select two other pairs of jumps that would be the same distance apart as the jumps in part a).

9. a) Multiply $2 \times \frac{2}{5}$.

   b) Rewrite $\frac{2}{5}$ as a percent, and then multiply by 2.

   c) Explain how you can use the calculation in part b) to check your answer to part a).

10. Multiply 5×2.3. Show how to use fraction multiplication to check your result.

11. Ki multiplied a whole number by a fraction. The numerator of the fraction product was 30. List three possible whole number and fraction combinations he could have been using.

12. Carmen multiplied a whole number by a fraction. Her answer was between 6 and 8. List three possible multiplications Carmen might have performed.

13. Describe a situation where you might multiply $4 \times \frac{2}{3}$.

14. Lea modelled the product of $5 \times \frac{\blacksquare}{\blacksquare}$ using grids and counters and filled exactly four grids. What fraction did she multiply by?

15. At a party, Raj notices that 15 pitchers of lemonade are filled to the same level, but not to the top. He combines all the lemonade to fill six whole pitchers. What fraction of each of the 15 pitchers was full?

16. a) Why do the products for $5 \times \frac{2}{3}$, $5 \times \frac{2}{5}$, and $5 \times \frac{2}{7}$ all have the same numerator?

   b) Why are the denominators different?

2.2

Exploring Calculating a Fraction of a Fraction

YOU WILL NEED
- Fraction Strips Tower
- scissors
- pencil crayons

GOAL

Represent one fraction as part of another fraction.

EXPLORE the Math

Aaron is playing a fraction game with his friends.
The game board is a fraction strip tower.
Each player picks a card and covers sections of fraction strips.
For example, if the player picks [B. Cover $\frac{1}{4}$ of $\frac{1}{3}$], the player would cover $\frac{1}{12}$, since $\frac{1}{12}$ fits into $\frac{1}{3}$ four times.

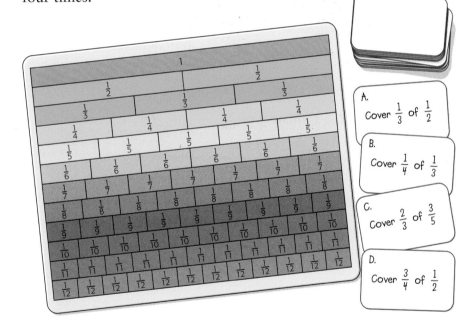

❓ Which cards might Aaron pick from the deck to cover each of $\frac{1}{6}$, $\frac{2}{5}$, and $\frac{3}{8}$?

2.3 Multiplying Fractions

YOU WILL NEED
- Fraction Strips Tower
- grid paper
- coloured pencils

GOAL

Multiply two fractions less than 1.

LEARN ABOUT *the Math*

About $\frac{1}{10}$ of Canadians who are 12 and older downhill ski. About $\frac{2}{5}$ of these skiers are between the ages of 12 and 24.

? What fraction of the Canadian population between the ages of 12 and 24 are downhill skiers?

Example 1 | Using a fraction strip model

I needed to determine $\frac{2}{5}$ of $\frac{1}{10}$.

Allison's Solution

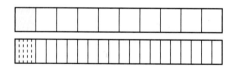

I used fraction strips.

I divided $\frac{1}{10}$ into 5 equal sections. I realized that, if I divided each $\frac{1}{10}$ up, that would make 50 equal sections. I coloured $\frac{2}{5}$ of the first tenth.

$\frac{2}{5}$ of $\frac{1}{10} = \frac{2}{50}$

About $\frac{2}{50}$ of Canadians between the ages of 12 and 24 downhill ski.

So 2 of 50 sections were coloured.

I could write that as $\frac{2}{50}$.

Example 2 | Using a grid

I calculated $\frac{2}{5} \times \frac{1}{10}$.

Nikita's Solution

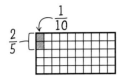

Since ■ groups of ■ is another way of saying ■ × ■, I figured that $\frac{2}{5}$ of $\frac{1}{10}$ would be $\frac{2}{5} \times \frac{1}{10}$.

One way to multiply whole numbers is to draw a rectangle with those dimensions and calculate its area.

To show fifths, I wanted the rectangle to have 5 sections in one direction. To show tenths, I wanted it to have 10 sections in the other direction. So I made a 5-by-10 rectangle. Inside of it, I drew a rectangle that was $\frac{2}{5} \times \frac{1}{10}$. Its area was 2 × 1 squares out of the total 5 × 10 squares.

$$\frac{2}{5} \times \frac{1}{10} = \frac{2 \times 1}{5 \times 10}$$
$$= \frac{2}{50}$$
$$= \frac{1}{25}$$

I noticed that 2 and 50 had a common factor, so I wrote the product in lower terms.

Reflecting

A. How did Nikita's model show both $\frac{2}{5} \times \frac{1}{10}$ and $\frac{1}{10} \times \frac{2}{5}$?

B. How can you use a model to determine the numerator and denominator of a product?

C. Suggest a possible procedure for multiplying two fractions less than 1. Explain why you chose that procedure.

WORK WITH *the Math*

Example 3 | Multiplying fractions less than 1

If $\frac{2}{3}$ of the students in Windham Ridge School are in Grades 7 and 8, and if $\frac{5}{8}$ of these students are girls, what fraction of the students in the school are girls in Grades 7 and 8?

Solution A: Using fraction strips

This model shows $\frac{5}{8}$ of $\frac{2}{3}$.

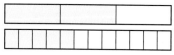

$$\frac{5}{8} \times \frac{2}{3} = \frac{5}{12}$$

So $\frac{5}{12}$ of the students are girls in Grades 7 and 8.

To take $\frac{5}{8}$ of $\frac{2}{3}$, you need a strip that divides the $\frac{2}{3}$ into 8 sections.

A strip to divide each third into 4 sections would work. Use twelfths since $3 \times 4 = 12$.

Divide $\frac{2}{3}$ into 8 equivalent sections, and colour 5 of the sections.

Solution B: Using an area model

$$\frac{5}{8} \times \frac{2}{3} = \frac{5 \times 2}{8 \times 3}$$

$$= \frac{10}{24}, \text{ or } \frac{5}{12}$$

So $\frac{5}{12}$ of the students are girls in Grades 7 and 8.

Colour a 3-by-8 rectangle to show $\frac{5}{8}$ by $\frac{2}{3}$.

Ⓐ Checking

1. What multiplication expression does each model represent?

a)

b)

2. Draw a model for $\frac{3}{4} \times \frac{2}{5}$. Use your model to determine the product.

3. About $\frac{2}{11}$ of Canadian downhill skiers are from British Columbia. About $\frac{1}{10}$ of Canadians downhill ski. What fraction of all Canadians are downhill skiers from British Columbia?

B Practising

4. What multiplication expressions does each model represent?

   a)

   b)

   c)

5. Draw a model for each multiplication expression. Determine the product. Write the result in lowest terms.

   a) $\frac{1}{2} \times \frac{3}{8}$ c) $\frac{1}{6} \times \frac{2}{5}$ e) $\frac{1}{4} \times \frac{4}{5}$

   b) $\frac{4}{5} \times \frac{1}{3}$ d) $\frac{3}{4} \times \frac{2}{6}$ f) $\frac{3}{5} \times \frac{2}{3}$

6. Match each expression with its product in the box.

   a) $\frac{5}{6} \times \frac{7}{10}$ c) $\frac{2}{6} \times \frac{9}{10}$

   b) $\frac{3}{8} \times \frac{4}{9}$ d) $\frac{4}{7} \times \frac{14}{15}$

$\frac{1}{6}$	$\frac{8}{15}$
$\frac{3}{10}$	$\frac{7}{12}$

7. a) Draw a picture to show why $\frac{2}{5} \times \frac{3}{8} = \frac{6}{40}$.

   b) List two other pairs of fractions with a product of $\frac{6}{40}$.

8. Matthew's bed takes up $\frac{1}{3}$ of the width of his bedroom and $\frac{3}{5}$ of the length. What fraction of the floor area does the bed use up?

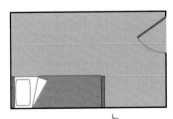

9. Jessica is awake for $\frac{2}{3}$ of the day. She spends $\frac{5}{8}$ of that time at home.

   a) What fraction of the day is Jessica awake at home?

   b) How many hours is Jessica awake at home?

10. The Grade 8 class raised $\frac{2}{5}$ of the money to support the school's winter production. The Grade 8 boys raised $\frac{2}{3}$ of the Grade 8 money. What fraction of the whole production fund did the Grade 8 boys raise?

11. **a)** In Manitoba, Francophones make up about $\frac{1}{20}$ of the population. Only about $\frac{1}{8}$ of Francophones in Manitoba are under 15. What fraction of Manitoba's total population is made up of Francophones under 15?

   b) Aboriginal peoples make up about $\frac{3}{20}$ of the population of Manitoba. Of those, only about $\frac{1}{3}$ are under 15. What fraction of Manitoba's total population is made up of Aboriginal peoples under 15?

12. Cheyenne gets home after 4 p.m. on school days about $\frac{1}{2}$ of the time. She gets home after 5 p.m. on about $\frac{2}{5}$ of those days. On what fraction of school days does she get home after 5 p.m.?

13. Describe a situation where you might multiply $\frac{3}{5} \times \frac{2}{3}$.

14. **a)** Complete this pattern and continue it for three more products.

   $$4 \times \frac{1}{2} = \blacksquare \qquad 2 \times \frac{1}{2} = \blacksquare \qquad 1 \times \frac{1}{2} = \blacksquare \qquad \frac{1}{2} \times \frac{1}{2} = \blacksquare$$

   b) How does this pattern explain the product of $\frac{1}{2} \times \frac{1}{2}$?

15. How much greater is the first product than the second?

   a) $\frac{2}{7} \times \frac{2}{5}$ than $\frac{1}{7} \times \frac{3}{5}$

   b) $\frac{3}{8} \times \frac{4}{9}$ than $\frac{1}{8} \times \frac{2}{3}$

   c) $\frac{3}{5} \times \frac{2}{3}$ than $\frac{1}{5} \times \frac{1}{4}$

16. **a)** Calculate 0.4×0.3.

   b) Rename each decimal as a fraction and multiply. What do you notice?

17. Use a pattern to help you determine the product of $\frac{1}{2} \times \frac{2}{3} \times \frac{3}{4} \times \frac{4}{5} \times \ldots \times \frac{99}{100}$.

18. How does the product of two fractions less than 1 compare to the two fractions? Is the product equal to, greater than, or less than each fraction? How do you know?

19. Daniel multiplied $\frac{3}{5}$ by another fraction less than 1.

   a) What do you know about the denominator of the product?

   b) What do you know about the numerator of the product?

2.4

Exploring Estimating Fraction Products

YOU WILL NEED
- fraction models
- Fraction Spinner

GOAL

Estimate to predict whether a fraction product is closer to 0, $\frac{1}{2}$, or 1.

EXPLORE the Math

Brian and Preston are playing a spinner game. Brian is getting ready to spin.

Game Rules

Spin twice and multiply.
Score 1 point if the fraction is closer to $\frac{1}{2}$ than 0.
Score 1 more point if the fraction is closer to $\frac{1}{2}$ than 1.

❓ **What combinations can Brian spin to win 2 points?**

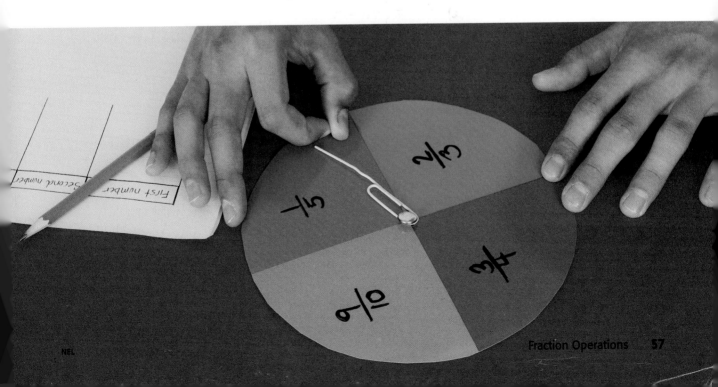

2.5 Multiplying Fractions Greater Than 1

YOU WILL NEED
• grid paper

GOAL

Multiply mixed numbers and improper fractions.

LEARN ABOUT the Math

A large bag of popcorn holds $2\frac{1}{2}$ times as much as a small bag.
Aaron has $1\frac{1}{2}$ large bags.
He is pouring the popcorn into smaller bags to give to friends.

❓ How many small bags will his popcorn fill?

Example 1 | Adding partial areas

I used an area model.

Aaron's Solution

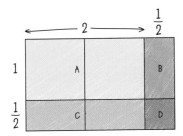

The area of A is $1 \times 2 = 2$ square units.

The area of B is $1 \times \frac{1}{2} = \frac{1}{2}$ square unit.

The area of C is $\frac{1}{2} \times 2 = 1$ square unit.

The area of D is $\frac{1}{2} \times \frac{1}{2} = \frac{1}{4}$ square unit.

The total area is $2 + \frac{1}{2} + 1 + \frac{1}{4}$ square units, or $3\frac{3}{4}$ square units.

He could fill $3\frac{3}{4}$ small bags of popcorn.

I knew this was a multiplication problem since I wanted $1\frac{1}{2}$ groups of $2\frac{1}{2}$.

One way to multiply is to get the area of a rectangle with side lengths the numbers you are multiplying. I drew a rectangle with side lengths $1\frac{1}{2}$ and $2\frac{1}{2}$.

I divided the rectangle into parts and calculated the area of each part.

I added up the partial areas.

Example 2 | Applying a procedure

I used a procedure.

Misa's Solution

$$1\frac{1}{2} \times 2\frac{1}{2} = \frac{3}{2} \times \frac{5}{2}$$

$$= \frac{3 \times 5}{2 \times 2}$$

$$= \frac{15}{4}$$

Area is $\frac{15}{4} = 3\frac{3}{4}$

He could fill $3\frac{3}{4}$ small bags of popcorn.

I knew this was a multiplication problem. When you multiply fractions less than 1, you can multiply the numerators and multiply the denominators.

I renamed $1\frac{1}{2}$ as $\frac{3}{2}$ and $2\frac{1}{2}$ as $\frac{5}{2}$ and multiplied the way I would multiply fractions less than 1.

Reflecting

A. Would you use Aaron's or Misa's method to multiply $1\frac{2}{3} \times 1\frac{4}{5}$? Explain your reasons.

B. How would you use each model to multiply $2\frac{1}{3} \times 3\frac{1}{2}$?

WORK WITH the Math

| Example 3 | Multiplying two mixed numbers |

Multiply $2\frac{1}{2} \times 3\frac{1}{3}$.

Solution A: Adding partial areas

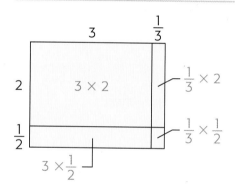

Calculate the area of the rectangle by calculating the four partial areas and then adding.

$$2\frac{1}{2} \times 3\frac{1}{3} = \left(2 \times 3\frac{1}{3}\right) + \left(\frac{1}{2} \times 3\frac{1}{3}\right)$$

$$= (2 \times 3) + \left(2 \times \frac{1}{3}\right) + \left(\frac{1}{2} \times 3\right) + \left(\frac{1}{2} \times \frac{1}{3}\right)$$

$$= 6 + \frac{2}{3} + \frac{3}{2} + \frac{1}{6}$$

$$= 6 + \frac{4}{6} + 1 + \frac{3}{6} + \frac{1}{6}$$

$$= 7 + \frac{8}{6}$$

$$= 8\frac{2}{6} \text{ or } 8\frac{1}{3}$$

Solution B: Using grids

$2\frac{1}{2} = \frac{5}{2}$ and $3\frac{1}{3} = \frac{10}{3}$

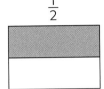

If you were multiplying $\frac{1}{2} \times \frac{1}{3}$, you would draw 2-by-3 grids.

$\frac{1}{2}$ $\frac{1}{3}$ of $\frac{1}{2} = \frac{1}{6}$

Start with 2-by-3 grids to represent 1 whole.

Then extend the grid in both directions so there is space to draw a rectangle that is 5 halves wide and 10 thirds long.

The dimensions are $\frac{5}{2} \times \frac{10}{3}$.

There are 5 x 10 = 50 squares.

Each square is $\frac{1}{6}$ of 1 whole.

The area is $\frac{50}{6}$.

$$2\frac{1}{2} \times 3\frac{1}{3} = \frac{5}{2} \times \frac{10}{3}$$
$$= \frac{5 \times 10}{2 \times 3}$$
$$= \frac{50}{6}, \text{ or } 8\frac{2}{6}, \text{ or } 8\frac{1}{3}$$

A Checking

1. Estimate each product.

   a) $\frac{5}{8} \times 6\frac{1}{2}$ b) $7\frac{2}{9} \times 6\frac{3}{4}$

2. Show each multiplication using a different model. Determine the product.

   a) $2\frac{2}{3} \times 1\frac{4}{5}$ b) $\frac{1}{2} \times 4\frac{4}{7}$

3. Miriam is making $3\frac{1}{2}$ dozen cookies. If $\frac{2}{7}$ of the cookies have icing, how many dozen cookies have icing?

B Practising

4. Calculate each product.

a) $\dfrac{2}{3} \times 2\dfrac{1}{4}$ c) $\dfrac{1}{5} \times 2\dfrac{2}{3}$ e) $\dfrac{5}{6} \times 1\dfrac{5}{7}$

b) $\dfrac{5}{8} \times 1\dfrac{1}{2}$ d) $\dfrac{3}{4} \times 2\dfrac{5}{6}$ f) $\dfrac{2}{9} \times 1\dfrac{1}{6}$

5. Use a model to show $2\dfrac{3}{4} \times 4\dfrac{1}{3}$. Then calculate the product.

6. Draw a sketch to show a model for each multiplication.

a) $\dfrac{4}{3} \times \dfrac{3}{2}$ b) $\dfrac{1}{4} \times 4\dfrac{4}{7}$ c) $2\dfrac{1}{5} \times 3\dfrac{1}{6}$

7. Calculate each product. Write the fraction parts in lowest terms.

a) $2\dfrac{1}{4} \times 3\dfrac{1}{3}$ c) $1\dfrac{4}{5} \times 2\dfrac{2}{3}$ e) $3\dfrac{1}{6} \times 2\dfrac{2}{3}$

b) $1\dfrac{1}{2} \times 2\dfrac{1}{2}$ d) $3\dfrac{1}{5} \times 2\dfrac{1}{4}$ f) $1\dfrac{1}{6} \times 1\dfrac{1}{4}$

8. A muesli recipe requires $1\dfrac{1}{4}$ cups of oatmeal. How many cups of oatmeal do you need for each number of batches?

a) $2\dfrac{1}{2}$ batches   b) $3\dfrac{1}{3}$ batches

9. Zoë had $3\dfrac{1}{3}$ times as much money as her brother. She spent $\dfrac{2}{5}$ of her money on a new CD player. Now how many times as much money as her brother does Zoë have?

10. Tai calculated $3\dfrac{1}{3} \times 4\dfrac{3}{8}$. He multiplied the whole number parts together and then the fraction parts together to get an incorrect product of $12\dfrac{3}{24}$.

a) Why would estimation not help Tai realize he made a mistake?

b) How could you show Tai that his answer is incorrect?

11. Andrea's bedroom is $1\dfrac{1}{3}$ times as long as Kit's bedroom and $1\dfrac{2}{3}$ times as wide. What fraction of the area of Kit's bedroom is the area of Andrea's bedroom?

12. The highest point in Alberta is Mount Columbia. Mount Columbia is about $4\frac{3}{5}$ times as high as the highest point in New Brunswick, Mount Carleton. Mount Carleton is about $5\frac{3}{4}$ times as high as the highest point in Prince Edward Island. Compare the height of Mount Columbia to the highest point in Prince Edward Island.

13. a) Multiply $3\frac{4}{10}$ by $2\frac{3}{10}$.

    b) Rename these two fractions as decimals, and multiply the decimals.

    c) How was the decimal multiplication similar to the fraction multiplication?

14. The product of three improper fractions is $\frac{14}{3}$. What could the fractions be?

15. Describe a situation at home in which you might multiply $3\frac{1}{2}$ by $2\frac{1}{3}$.

16. Do you agree or disagree with the following statement? Explain. When you multiply a mixed number using thirds by a mixed number using fourths, the answer has to be a mixed number using twelfths.

Frequently Asked Questions

Q: How can you multiply a fraction by a whole number?

A: You can represent repeated addition using a variety of models.
For example, $3 \times \frac{4}{5}$ means 3 sets of $\frac{4}{5}$.

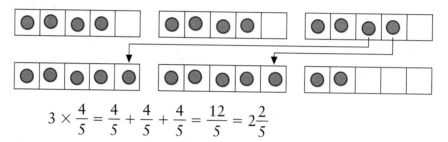

$$3 \times \frac{4}{5} = \frac{4}{5} + \frac{4}{5} + \frac{4}{5} = \frac{12}{5} = 2\frac{2}{5}$$

Q: How can you multiply two fractions less than 1?

A1: You can model one fraction and then divide it into the appropriate number of pieces. For example, to show $\frac{2}{3} \times \frac{6}{7}$, you can model $\frac{6}{7}$ and divide each of the 6 sevenths into thirds.
Then, to show $\frac{2}{3}$ of each section, colour 2 of the thirds.

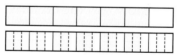

$$\frac{2}{3} \times \frac{6}{7} = \frac{12}{21}, \text{ or } \frac{4}{7}$$

A2: You can determine the area of a rectangle. For example, to model $\frac{2}{3} \times \frac{2}{5}$, create a rectangle that is $\frac{2}{5}$ of a unit wide and $\frac{2}{3}$ of a unit long and calculate its area. There are 2×2 squares, each with an area of $\frac{1}{15}$. So the total area is $\frac{4}{15}$ square units.

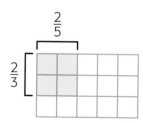

$$\frac{2}{3} \times \frac{2}{5} = \frac{4}{15}$$

A3: You can multiply the numerators together and the denominators together: $\frac{a}{b} \times \frac{c}{d} = \frac{a \times c}{b \times d}$.
For example, $\frac{3}{5} \times \frac{6}{7} = \frac{3 \times 6}{5 \times 7} = \frac{18}{35}$.

Q: How can you estimate the product of two fractions?

A: The product of two fractions close to 1 is close to 1.

The product of two fractions close to $\frac{1}{2}$ is close to $\frac{1}{4}$. The product of two fractions close to 0 is close to 0.

For example, $\frac{5}{6} \times \frac{7}{8}$ is close to 1 because $\frac{5}{6}$ is close to 1 and $\frac{7}{8}$ is close to one.

Q: How can you multiply two mixed numbers?

A1: You can use an area model to multiply two mixed numbers.

For example, suppose that you wanted to calculate the area of a rectangle that is $1\frac{1}{3}$ units long and $2\frac{1}{2}$ units wide.

There are $4 \times 5 = 20$ squares. Each has an area of $\frac{1}{6}$ of 1 whole.

$$\frac{4}{3} \times \frac{5}{2} = \frac{20}{6}, \text{ or } 3\frac{2}{6}, \text{ or } 3\frac{1}{3}$$

A2: You can write each mixed number as an improper fraction. You can multiply the improper fractions like proper fractions.

$$1\frac{1}{3} \times 2\frac{1}{2} = \frac{4}{3} \times \frac{5}{2}$$
$$= \frac{20}{6}$$

Practice

1. Write as a repeated addition. Use fraction strips or a number line to add.
   Write each answer as an improper fraction and as a mixed number. Write the fractions in lowest terms.

   a) $6 \times \dfrac{1}{5}$

   c) $8 \times \dfrac{3}{5}$

   b) $4 \times \dfrac{5}{12}$

   d) $5 \times \dfrac{4}{9}$

2. Use grid paper and counters to multiply.

   a) $3 \times \dfrac{3}{8}$

   c) $5 \times \dfrac{5}{6}$

   b) $2 \times \dfrac{5}{9}$

   d) $4 \times \dfrac{2}{5}$

3. The product of a fraction and a whole number is $\dfrac{24}{5}$. What could the fraction and the whole number be?

Lesson 2.2

4. Draw a picture to show $\dfrac{2}{3}$ of $\dfrac{3}{8}$.

5. What is the missing fraction?

   a) $\dfrac{1}{4}$ of $\dfrac{2}{7}$ is ▇.

   b) $\dfrac{3}{5}$ is ▇ of $\dfrac{4}{5}$

   c) ▇ of $\dfrac{3}{4}$ is $\dfrac{3}{12}$.

Lesson 2.3

6. Draw a model for each multiplication. Use your model to determine the product.

   a) $\dfrac{1}{3} \times \dfrac{1}{6}$

   b) $\dfrac{3}{7} \times \dfrac{4}{5}$

7. What fraction multiplication does each model represent?

   a)

   b)

   c)

8. If you multiply $\frac{2}{8}$ by another fraction, can the denominator be 20? Explain.

9. About $\frac{3}{4}$ of the traditional dancers of a First Nations school are girls. About $\frac{1}{4}$ of these students are in Grade 8. What fraction of the students who dance are Grade 8 girls?

Lesson 2.4

10. Which products are greater than $\frac{1}{2}$?

   a) $\frac{3}{4} \times \frac{5}{6}$

   b) $\frac{1}{6} \times \frac{7}{8}$

   c) $\frac{3}{9} \times \frac{8}{9}$

   d) $\frac{3}{5} \times \frac{2}{3}$

Lesson 2.5

11. Calculate.

   a) $\frac{3}{7} \times 3\frac{1}{2}$

   b) $\frac{2}{5} \times 1\frac{3}{5}$

   c) $1\frac{1}{3} \times 1\frac{2}{3}$

   d) $\frac{5}{6} \times 6\frac{12}{25}$

   e) $2\frac{3}{4} \times 3\frac{3}{4}$

   f) $3\frac{1}{5} \times 6\frac{3}{8}$

12. Eileen used to be on the phone $3\frac{1}{2}$ times as much as her sister every day. As a New Year's resolution, she decided to cut down to about $\frac{2}{5}$ of the time she used to be on the phone. About how many times as much as her sister is Eileen now on the phone?

2.6

Dividing Fractions by Whole Numbers

YOU WILL NEED
- counters
- grids
- Fraction Strips Tower

GOAL

Use a sharing model to represent the quotient of a fraction divided by a whole number.

LEARN ABOUT the Math

Three-tenths of the possible donors still have to be called. Two of the students are going to share the job.

❓ What fraction of all the possible donors will each student be calling?

A. Suppose $\frac{4}{10}$ of the list of donors still need to be called. Use counters on a grid to represent $\frac{4}{10}$.

B. Arrange the counters into two equal groups.

C. What fraction of the grid is covered by each group?

D. What fraction of the donors will each student phone?

E. How can you change what you did in step B to solve the problem if only $\frac{3}{10}$ of the donors need to be called?

Reflecting

F. What whole number division did you need to do to solve the problem in step D?

G. Why did you need to change your strategy to solve step E?

H. Why is dividing a fraction by 2 the same as multiplying it by $\frac{1}{2}$?

WORK WITH *the Math*

Example 1	Relating dividing and multiplying

Allison had art class on 9 out of the 20 school days last month. She worked with a partner about $\frac{1}{3}$ of the time. For what fraction of the school days last month did she work with a partner in art?

Allison's Solution

9 out of 20 is $\frac{9}{20}$.

$\frac{9}{20} \div 3$

I wrote 9 out of 20 as a fraction.
Then I needed to divide it into 3 equal parts.

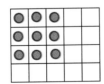

$\frac{3}{20}$ are in each group.

$\frac{9}{20} \div 3 = \frac{9 \div 3}{20}$

$= \frac{3}{20}$

I used a grid. I chose a grid with 20 squares to represent 20ths. I made sure my grid had at least 3 rows so I could put the 9 counters into 3 separate rows.

I figured out the fraction in each row.

Example 2 | Relating dividing and multiplying

Allison had art class on 9 out of the 20 school days last month.
She worked with a partner about $\frac{1}{3}$ of the time. For what fraction
of the school days last month did she work with a partner in art?

Nikita's Solution

$$\frac{9}{20} \div 3 = \frac{1}{3} \times \frac{9}{20}$$

$$= \frac{1 \times 9}{3 \times 20}$$

$$= \frac{9}{60}$$

$$= \frac{9 \div 3}{60 \div 3}$$

$$= \frac{3}{20}$$

I wanted $\frac{1}{3}$ of 9 out of 20.

I wrote 9 out of 20 as $\frac{9}{20}$.

I multiplied by $\frac{1}{3}$ since $\frac{1}{3}$ of something is the same as $\frac{1}{3}$ times that thing.

After I wrote the fraction in lowest terms, to $\frac{3}{20}$, I realized I could have just divided the numerator 9 by 3 and left the denominator as twentieths.

Example 3 | Using a fraction strip model

Divide $\frac{2}{3}$ by 4.

Preston's Solution

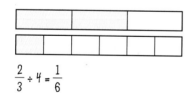

$$\frac{2}{3} \div 4 = \frac{1}{6}$$

I used fraction strips to represent $\frac{2}{3}$.

I needed to find strips that were the right length so that four sections made up the $\frac{2}{3}$.

I realized each strip had to be half of $\frac{1}{3}$, which is $\frac{1}{6}$.

A Checking

1. Two-thirds of a room still has to be tiled. Three workers are going to share the job. What fraction of the room will each worker tile if they all work at the same rate?

2. a) Divide $\frac{6}{7}$ by 3 using a grid and counters. Sketch your work.

b) Divide $\frac{5}{7}$ by 3 using a model. Sketch your work.

c) Why might your denominators for parts a) and b) be different?

3. a) How can you solve $\frac{5}{6} \div 4$ using multiplication of fractions?

b) Explain why this works.

B Practising

4. Divide. Use a model for at least two of your solutions and show your work.

a) $\frac{8}{9} \div 4$

c) $\frac{6}{9} \div 4$

e) $\frac{2}{3} \div 5$

b) $\frac{2}{9} \div 4$

d) $\frac{3}{5} \div 6$

f) $\frac{7}{8} \div 3$

5. Which quotients are less than $\frac{1}{4}$? How do you know?

a) $\frac{2}{3} \div 3$

b) $\frac{7}{8} \div 2$

c) $\frac{8}{9} \div 3$

6. Kevin used $\frac{5}{6}$ of a can of paint to cover four walls. How much of a can did he use for each wall?

7. Sheldon used $\frac{1}{6}$ of his blue seed beads to make a Native regalia breastplate. He wanted to use the same colour of beads to make two pairs of moccasins. What fraction of the beads that he originally had could he use for one moccasin?

8. a) Divide $\frac{4}{5}$ by 5.

b) Rewrite $\frac{4}{5}$ as a percent, and divide by 5.

c) Explain how you can use the calculation in part b) to check your answer to part a).

9. a) Create a problem you might solve by dividing $\frac{2}{3}$ by 4.

b) Solve your problem.

10. a) Why do the quotients for $\frac{8}{9} \div 2$, $\frac{8}{12} \div 2$, and $\frac{8}{15} \div 2$ all have the same numerator?

b) Why are the denominators different?

11. Aaron noticed that $\frac{2}{3} \div 5 = \frac{2}{3 \times 5}$, $\frac{4}{5} \div 6 = \frac{4}{5 \times 6}$, and $\frac{3}{5} \div 7 = \frac{3}{5 \times 7}$. What is the pattern he noticed? Is it always true?

2.7 Estimating Fraction Quotients

YOU WILL NEED

• Fraction Strips Tower

GOAL

Interpret and estimate the quotient of fractions less than 1.

LEARN ABOUT *the Math*

Participants last year

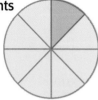

Participants this year

The fraction of students in a school who participate in school sports has increased from $\frac{1}{8}$ to $\frac{2}{5}$.

? **Is the fraction of participating students closer to double or closer to triple what it was?**

Example 1 | Comparing fractions by multiplying

I used fraction strips to compare $\frac{3}{8}$ and $\frac{2}{5}$.

Brian's Solution

$2 \times \frac{1}{8} = \frac{2}{8}$

$\frac{2}{8} < \frac{2}{5}$ since 8 > 5.

$3 \times \frac{1}{8} = \frac{3}{8}$

Double $\frac{1}{8}$ means $2 \times \frac{1}{8}$.

I wanted to compare $\frac{2}{5}$ to $\frac{2}{8}$. When you compare two fractions with the same numerator, the one with the lower denominator is greater since the whole is divided into fewer parts.

Triple $\frac{1}{8}$ means $3 \times \frac{1}{8}$.

I compared $\frac{3}{8}$ and $\frac{2}{5}$ using fraction strips. They are pretty close in size.

The new fraction is closer to triple $\frac{1}{8}$.

Example 2 | Fitting one fraction into the other fraction

I used fraction strips to visualize the quotient.

Preston's Solution

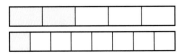

$\frac{2}{5}$ is about triple $\frac{1}{8}$.

To find out how $\frac{2}{5}$ relates to $\frac{1}{8}$, I need to see how many times $\frac{1}{8}$ fits into $\frac{2}{5}$. That is dividing.

I can see that $\frac{1}{8}$ fits into $\frac{2}{5}$ almost 3 times.

Example 3 | Comparing using equivalents

I used compatible numbers.

Nikita's Solution

$\frac{2}{5} = \frac{2 \times 8}{5 \times 8}$

$= \frac{16}{40}$

$\frac{1}{8} = \frac{1 \times 5}{8 \times 5}$

$= \frac{5}{40}$

$\frac{16}{40}$ is close to $\frac{15}{40}$.

Since $3 \times \frac{5}{40} = \frac{15}{40}$,

$\frac{2}{5}$ is about triple $\frac{1}{8}$.

I want to know, is $\frac{2}{5}$ closer to twice $\frac{1}{8}$ or to three times $\frac{1}{8}$?

I wrote equivalent fractions with the same denominator. Then I used a fraction that was close to one of these and where the numerators divided easily.

Reflecting

A. Brian and Preston both used fraction strips. Why could Brian solve by multiplying, but Preston solve by dividing?

B. Why did Nikita use equivalent fractions with the same denominator?

WORK WITH *the Math*

Example 4 | Estimating a fraction quotient

To win a recycling contest, the student council knew that at least $\frac{8}{9}$ of the students in the school had to participate. At one point, only $\frac{1}{4}$ of the students had signed up. How many more groups of that size had to sign up to have a chance to win?

Solution A

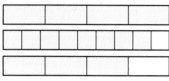

$\frac{8}{9}$ is closer to 1 than $\frac{3}{4}$.

Almost 4 groups of $\frac{1}{4}$ of the students are needed for the school to have a chance to win.

To determine about how many groups of $\frac{1}{4}$ are in $\frac{8}{9}$, estimate using a whole number of groups.

4 groups is $\frac{4}{4}$.

3 groups is $\frac{3}{4}$.

To decide if $\frac{8}{9}$ is closer to 1 or $\frac{3}{4}$, use a model.

Solution B

$\frac{8}{9} \div \frac{1}{4}$

is close to

$1 \div \frac{1}{4} = 4$

$\frac{8}{9}$ is close to 1.

There are 4 fourths in 1.

A Checking

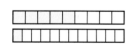

1. How does the picture show that $\frac{5}{9} \div \frac{1}{12}$ is about 7?

2. Estimate the quotient as a whole number.

   a) $\frac{3}{5} \div \frac{1}{4}$ b) $\frac{7}{8} \div \frac{2}{5}$ c) $\frac{3}{7} \div \frac{1}{10}$

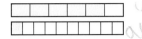

B Practising

3. How does the picture show that $\frac{5}{6} \div \frac{1}{10}$ is about 8?

4. Draw a picture to estimate about how many times $\frac{2}{5}$ fits into $\frac{8}{9}$.

5. Estimate each quotient as a whole number.

   a) $\frac{11}{12} \div \frac{3}{12}$ c) $\frac{11}{12} \div \frac{1}{7}$ e) $\frac{5}{6} \div \frac{1}{10}$

   b) $\frac{11}{12} \div \frac{1}{6}$ d) $\frac{3}{4} \div \frac{1}{10}$ f) $\frac{10}{11} \div \frac{2}{3}$

6. Amber needs $\frac{3}{4}$ of a cupful of berries to make a Saskatoon berry soup. She can find only a $\frac{1}{3}$-cup measure. About how many times will she have to fill the cup to have the right amount of berries?

7. Why might you estimate $\frac{7}{8} \div \frac{2}{7}$ by dividing 1 by $\frac{1}{4}$?

8. List two fractions you can divide to get the quotient specified.

   a) about 2 b) a bit more than 3

9. You divide a fraction less than $\frac{1}{2}$ by a fraction less than $\frac{1}{8}$. How could the result be each of the following?

   a) close to 4 b) close to 8 c) close to 20

10. Tom used 25 tiles to tile $\frac{3}{8}$ of the floor. About how many tiles does he need to finish the job? How do you know?

11. Describe a situation that can be answered by estimating $\frac{7}{8} \div \frac{1}{3}$.

12. How do you know that $\frac{3}{4} \div \frac{5}{6}$ is less than 1?

13. a) Describe two different ways to estimate $\frac{7}{8} \div \frac{2}{11}$.
    b) Which way would you choose? Why?

Fraction Operations **75**

2.8

Dividing Fractions by Measuring

YOU WILL NEED

- Fraction Strips Tower

GOAL

Divide fractions using models and using equivalent fractions with a common denominator.

LEARN ABOUT *the Math*

Misa exercises for $\frac{3}{4}$ of an hour several times a week.

? **How many times does Misa have to exercise if she wants to exercise for a total of 4 h every week?**

A. Line up 4 whole fraction strips to show a total of 4 ones.

B. Line up enough $\frac{3}{4}$ strips to fit along the four whole strips from step A.

C. Divide each whole strip into 4 fourths.

D. How many times does the $\frac{3}{4}$ strip fit along the 4 whole strips?

E. How many times does Misa have to exercise to achieve her goal of 4 h?

Reflecting

F. Why does finding out how many $\frac{3}{4}$ strips fit along the length of 4 whole strips help you solve the problem?

G. How could you solve the problem using equivalent fractions for 4 and $\frac{3}{4}$, and then dividing the numerators?

WORK WITH the Math

Example 1 | Using a model

Calculate $\frac{4}{5} \div \frac{1}{3}$.

Aaron's Solution

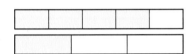

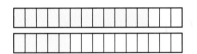

$$\frac{4}{5} \div \frac{1}{3} = \frac{12}{15} \div \frac{5}{15}$$

$$= \frac{12}{5}$$

$$= 2\frac{2}{5}$$

To divide $\frac{4}{5}$ by $\frac{1}{3}$, I asked myself how many thirds are in $\frac{4}{5}$.

Since $\frac{1}{3} < \frac{4}{5}$, the answer is more than 1. I lined up fraction strips to estimate.

It looked as if a bit more than 2 thirds fit into $\frac{4}{5}$.

I decided to use equivalent fractions. I chose fifteenths since I was using thirds and fifths.

I counted how many times $\frac{5}{15}$ fits into $\frac{12}{15}$.

I realized that the quotient was just $12 \div 5$. Once the denominators are equal, you only have to divide the numerators.

Example 2 | Using common denominators

Calculate $\frac{1}{3} \div \frac{2}{5}$.

Allison's Solution

$$\frac{1}{3} \div \frac{2}{5} = \frac{1 \times 5}{3 \times 5} \div \frac{2 \times 3}{5 \times 3}$$

$$= \frac{5}{15} \div \frac{6}{15}$$

$$= \frac{5}{6}$$

To calculate $\frac{1}{3} \div \frac{2}{5}$, I wanted to find out how many times $\frac{2}{5}$ fits into $\frac{1}{3}$.

I cannot fit an entire $\frac{2}{5}$ into $\frac{1}{3}$, so the answer must be less than 1. But I can fit most of $\frac{2}{5}$ into $\frac{1}{3}$, so the answer should be close to 1. I solved the problem using a common denominator.

A common denominator for $\frac{1}{3}$ and $\frac{2}{5}$ is $3 \times 5 = 15$.

I divided the numerators to determine how many $\frac{6}{15}$ are in $\frac{5}{15}$. The answer makes sense. It is less than 1, but close to 1.

Example 3 | Dividing a mixed number by a fraction

There were $2\frac{1}{2}$ containers of orange juice in Jeff's fridge. How many glasses of juice can he pour if each glass uses about $\frac{1}{5}$ of a container?

Misa's Solution

$$2\frac{1}{2} = \frac{(2 \times 2) + 1}{2}$$

$$= \frac{5}{2}$$

$$\frac{5}{2} \div \frac{1}{5} = \frac{25}{10} \div \frac{2}{10}$$

$$= 25 \div 2$$

$$= 12\frac{1}{2}$$

I needed to divide $2\frac{1}{2}$ by $\frac{1}{5}$ to figure out how many glasses Jeff can pour.

I renamed $2\frac{1}{2}$ as an improper fraction.

Then I divided by $\frac{1}{5}$ using a common denominator of 2×5.

I just had to divide the numerators.

A Checking

1. What division expression does this picture represent?

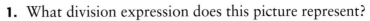

2. Draw a fraction strip model to show the number of times $\frac{1}{4}$ fits into $\frac{7}{8}$.

3. Calculate.

   a) $\dfrac{5}{8} \div \dfrac{3}{4}$ b) $2\dfrac{1}{2} \div \dfrac{2}{3}$

4. Craig needs to measure $3\dfrac{1}{3}$ cups. How many times must he fill a $\dfrac{1}{2}$-cup measure?

B Practising

5. What division expression does each picture represent?

   a)
   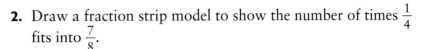

   b)
   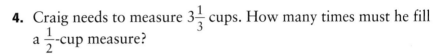

6. Calculate each quotient using equivalent fractions. Explain your thinking for part d).

   a) $5 \div \dfrac{1}{3}$ c) $2\dfrac{1}{2} \div \dfrac{3}{8}$

   b) $1\dfrac{3}{4} \div \dfrac{5}{6}$ d) $\dfrac{3}{5} \div \dfrac{5}{6}$

7. Frederika has written $\dfrac{2}{5}$ of a page for her report in 1 h. About how much time will she need to complete the entire report at this rate?

8. Create and solve a problem that can be solved by dividing $\dfrac{1}{3}$ by $\dfrac{1}{10}$.

9. Alana is cooking a turkey. It takes $4\dfrac{1}{2}$ h to cook. She checks it every 20 min, or $\dfrac{1}{3}$ of an hour.

   a) How many times will she check the turkey before it is cooked?

   b) Why can you keep subtracting $\dfrac{1}{3}$ from $4\dfrac{1}{2}$ to answer the question?

10. How can you calculate $\frac{3}{5} \div \frac{1}{2}$ using equivalent fractions with a common denominator?

11. Calculate. Write fractions in lowest terms.

a) $\frac{1}{4} \div \frac{4}{6}$ **c)** $\frac{4}{9} \div \frac{3}{4}$ **e)** $2\frac{1}{4} \div 1\frac{5}{6}$

b) $\frac{3}{5} \div \frac{2}{3}$ **d)** $2\frac{1}{3} \div 1\frac{7}{8}$ **f)** $1\frac{7}{9} \div 2\frac{1}{3}$

12. Craig has only a $\frac{1}{3}$-cup measuring cup. What operation would you perform to answer each question?

a) How much flour could Craig measure by filling the cup 5 times?

b) How many times would Craig have to fill his measuring cup to measure $2\frac{3}{8}$ cups of flour?

13. Does order matter when you divide fractions? For example, is $\frac{2}{3} \div \frac{1}{5}$ the same as $\frac{1}{5} \div \frac{2}{3}$? Explain.

14. How do you know that dividing by $\frac{1}{6}$ is the same as multiplying by 6?

15. Teo made a video that was $2\frac{1}{2}$ h long. He made it by clipping together sections that were each about $\frac{1}{3}$ of an hour long.

a) What operation could you perform to decide about how many sections Teo clipped together?

b) How do you know that the sections were not all exactly $\frac{1}{3}$ of an hour long?

16. How would you explain to someone why $\frac{5}{a} \div \frac{2}{a} = 2\frac{1}{2}$, no matter what the denominator is?

It Is Just Like Multiplying!

Did you know that you can divide fractions by dividing numerators and dividing denominators?

I bet dividing is *just* like multiplying.

For example,

$$\frac{15}{16} \div \frac{3}{4} = \frac{15 \div 3}{16 \div 4}$$

$$= \frac{5}{4}$$

It is just like multiplying numerators and denominators to multiply fractions.

1. How do you know that $\frac{15}{16} \div \frac{3}{4}$ really is $\frac{5}{4}$?

2. How does using the equivalent fraction $\frac{9}{15}$ help you use this "dividing numerators/dividing denominators" method to calculate $\frac{3}{5} \div \frac{1}{3}$?

3. How could you use equivalent fractions to calculate $\frac{2}{3} \div \frac{3}{4}$ using this method?

4. Why do you think this method works?

5. When would you be most likely to use this method?

2.9 Dividing Fractions Using a Related Multiplication

YOU WILL NEED

• Fraction Strips Tower

GOAL

Divide fractions using a related multiplication.

LEARN ABOUT *the Math*

Allison has 2 large cans of paint. Nikita has $\frac{7}{8}$ of a large can of paint. Each student is pouring paint into small cans that hold $\frac{1}{3}$ as much as the large ones.

? **How many small cans of paint will each student fill?**

Example 1	Dividing a whole number by a fraction

To find out how many small cans I can fill, I divided 2 by $\frac{1}{3}$.

Allison's Solution

$2 \div \frac{1}{3} = 2 \times 3$

$\qquad = 6$

My 2 large cans of paint will fill 6 small cans.

I needed to divide 2 by $\frac{1}{3}$ to see how many $\frac{1}{3}$-size cans would be filled by 2 large cans.

The small can is $\frac{1}{3}$ the size, so each large can fills 3 small ones. I double that for 2 large cans.

Example 2 | Dividing a fraction by a fraction

Calculate $\frac{7}{8} \div \frac{1}{3}$.

Nikita's Solution

$1 \div \frac{1}{3} = 3$

$\frac{7}{8} \div \frac{1}{3} = \frac{7}{8} \times 3$

$\qquad = \frac{21}{8}$

$\qquad = 2\frac{5}{8}$

My $\frac{7}{8}$-full large can will fill $2\frac{5}{8}$ small cans.

I used a related multiplication to divide $\frac{7}{8}$ by $\frac{1}{3}$.

I needed to divide $\frac{7}{8}$ by $\frac{1}{3}$ to see how many $\frac{1}{3}$-size cans fit into $\frac{7}{8}$ of a large can.

I realized it would have to be $\frac{7}{8}$ as much as the amount that 1 whole large can of paint fills. Since 1 large can fills 3 small ones, I multiplied $\frac{7}{8}$ by 3.

It makes sense that the answer is less than 3, but close to it.

---

reciprocal

the fraction that results from switching the numerator and denominator; for example, $\frac{4}{5}$ is the reciprocal of $\frac{5}{4}$

Reflecting

A. Why did Allison and Nikita divide by $\frac{1}{3}$ to solve the problem?

B. The result when Allison divided by $\frac{1}{3}$ was twice as much as the **reciprocal** of $\frac{1}{3}$. Why does that make sense?

C. Suppose the small can had held $\frac{2}{3}$ as much as the large can instead of only $\frac{1}{3}$ as much. Why could Allison and Nikita have multiplied both 2 and $\frac{7}{8}$ by the reciprocal of $\frac{2}{3}$?

WORK WITH the Math

Example 3 | Dividing a mixed number by a fraction

Misa wants to pour $1\frac{7}{8}$ large cans of paint into small cans. Each small can holds $\frac{3}{5}$ as much paint as a large can. How many small cans will Misa fill?

Solution A: Using fraction strips to divide

Estimate:

$\frac{3}{5}$ is about $\frac{1}{2}$

$1\frac{7}{8}$ is about 2

There are 4 halves in 2.

Number of small cans in 1 large can.
$1 \div \frac{3}{5} = \frac{5}{3}$, or $1\frac{2}{3}$ small cans

large can

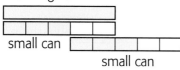

small can

small can

$1\frac{2}{3} \times 1\frac{7}{8}$

$= \frac{5}{3} \times \frac{15}{8}$

$= \frac{75}{24}$, or $\frac{25}{8}$, or $3\frac{1}{8}$

Misa will fill $3\frac{1}{8}$ small cans with paint.

Estimate first.

It takes about 2 small cans to fill one large one.

Since there are almost 2 large cans, Misa will need about 4 cans.

Calculate next.

You can use fraction strips to see how many times $\frac{3}{5}$ fits into 1.

The fraction part is $\frac{2}{3}$ since, even though it is $\frac{2}{5}$ of a can, it is $\frac{2}{3}$ of a small can.

Then figure out how many times $\frac{3}{5}$ fits in $1\frac{7}{8}$ cans by multiplying the number for 1 large can by $1\frac{7}{8}$.

Solution B: Using a common denominator

$1\frac{7}{8} \div \frac{3}{5} = \frac{15}{8} \div \frac{3}{5}$

$= \frac{15 \times 5}{8 \times 5} \div \frac{3 \times 8}{5 \times 8}$

$= \frac{75}{40} \div \frac{24}{40}$

$= \frac{75}{24}$, or $3\frac{3}{24}$, or $3\frac{1}{8}$

Misa will fill $3\frac{1}{8}$ small cans with paint.

Solution C: Multiplying by the reciprocal

$$1\frac{7}{8} \div \frac{3}{5} = \frac{15}{8} \div \frac{3}{5}$$

$$= \frac{15}{8} \times \frac{5}{3}$$

$$= \frac{75}{24}, \text{ or } 3\frac{3}{24}, \text{ or } 3\frac{1}{8}$$

Misa will fill $3\frac{1}{8}$ small cans with paint.

A Checking

1. Calculate.

a) $\dfrac{3}{8} \div \dfrac{1}{2}$ b) $\dfrac{7}{8} \div \dfrac{1}{3}$

2. Lynnsie has $1\frac{1}{2}$ large cans of paint. Each small can holds $\frac{3}{5}$ as much paint as a large can. How many small cans can Lynnsie fill?

B Practising

3. Calculate.

a) $\dfrac{3}{9} \div \dfrac{2}{9}$ c) $\dfrac{4}{8} \div \dfrac{7}{8}$ e) $\dfrac{1}{5} \div \dfrac{2}{5}$

b) $\dfrac{1}{2} \div \dfrac{1}{3}$ d) $\dfrac{4}{5} \div \dfrac{2}{3}$ f) $\dfrac{9}{20} \div \dfrac{3}{5}$

4. Rahul has $\frac{2}{3}$ of a container of trail mix. He is filling snack packs that each use about $\frac{1}{5}$ of a container. How many snack packs can Rahul make?

5. Why does it make sense that $\frac{7}{8} \div \frac{3}{4}$ is greater than $\frac{7}{8}$?

6. Which quotients are $1\frac{1}{4}$? How do you know?

a) $\dfrac{5}{2} \div \dfrac{1}{2}$ c) $\dfrac{3}{5} \div \dfrac{3}{4}$

b) $\dfrac{3}{4} \div \dfrac{3}{5}$ d) $5 \div 4$

7. Estimate each quotient. Then express the mixed numbers as improper fractions and calculate the exact quotient.

a) $6\dfrac{2}{5} \div 3\dfrac{1}{2}$ b) $5\dfrac{2}{3} \div 1\dfrac{1}{4}$ c) $8\dfrac{3}{4} \div 2\dfrac{1}{3}$

8. Calculate.

a) $\dfrac{9}{8} \div \dfrac{3}{8}$ **c)** $\dfrac{11}{4} \div \dfrac{3}{2}$ **e)** $5\dfrac{1}{3} \div 2\dfrac{3}{4}$

b) $\dfrac{7}{3} \div \dfrac{5}{6}$ **d)** $1\dfrac{2}{3} \div \dfrac{3}{7}$ **f)** $6\dfrac{3}{5} \div 2\dfrac{1}{3}$

9. a) Which quotients are greater than 1?

i) $\dfrac{3}{5} \div \dfrac{2}{3}$ **ii)** $\dfrac{9}{2} \div \dfrac{5}{6}$ **iii)** $\dfrac{3}{7} \div \dfrac{1}{8}$

b) How could you have predicted the answers to part a) without calculating the quotients?

10. Which quotients are greater than 2? Calculate these quotients only.

a) $\dfrac{5}{9} \div \dfrac{1}{4}$ **b)** $3\dfrac{1}{3} \div \dfrac{4}{5}$ **c)** $\dfrac{8}{9} \div \dfrac{3}{4}$ **d)** $\dfrac{7}{8} \div \dfrac{1}{3}$

11. Choose two fractions where the quotient is less than the product.

12. Printers print at different rates. How many pages does each printer print each minute?

a) 20 pages in $1\dfrac{1}{2}$ min

b) 20 pages in $1\dfrac{1}{3}$ min

13. Miri filled $2\dfrac{1}{2}$ pitchers with $\dfrac{2}{3}$ of the punch she made. How many pitchers would she fill if she used all the punch she made?

14. Trevor takes $4\dfrac{1}{2}$ min to run once around his favourite route. How many laps can he do in each time period?

a) 30 min   **b)** 20 min   **c)** 15 min

15. a) Calculate $0.45 \div 0.3$ using decimal division.

b) Calculate $\dfrac{45}{100} \div \dfrac{3}{10}$ using fraction division.

c) What do you notice?

16. A pattern block design is made up of the equivalent of $3\dfrac{1}{3}$ red blocks. How many blue blocks could cover that design?

17. Describe a situation in which you might use each calculation.

a) $\dfrac{9}{8} \div \dfrac{2}{3}$ **b)** $1\dfrac{2}{5} \div 2\dfrac{2}{3}$

Target $\frac{2}{3}$

In this game, you will roll a pair of dice twice to create two fractions. Then you will add, subtract, multiply, or divide your fractions to get an answer as close as possible to $\frac{2}{3}$.

Number of players: 2, 3, or 4

How to Play

1. Each player rolls the pair of dice twice, then uses the four numbers as the numerators and denominators of two fractions.

2. Each player can add, subtract, multiply, or divide the two fractions to get an answer as close as possible to $\frac{2}{3}$.

3. The player with the answer closest to $\frac{2}{3}$ gets a point. Both players get a point if there is a tie.

4. Keep playing until one player has 10 points.

Preston's Turn

I rolled a 2 and a 6, then I rolled a 1 and a 4.

+	−	×	÷
$\frac{2}{4} + \frac{1}{6}$	$\frac{4}{6} - \frac{1}{2}$	$\frac{1}{2} \times \frac{4}{6}$	$\frac{1}{6} \div \frac{2}{4}$
$= \frac{6}{12} + \frac{2}{12}$	$= \frac{4}{6} - \frac{3}{6}$	$= \frac{4}{12}$	$= \frac{1}{6} \times \frac{4}{2}$
$= \frac{8}{12}$	$= \frac{1}{6}$	$= \frac{1}{3}$	$= \frac{4}{12}$
$= \frac{2}{3}$			$= \frac{1}{3}$

I could use $\frac{2}{4} + \frac{1}{6}$ to get exactly $\frac{2}{3}$.

2.10

Order of Operations

GOAL

Use the order of operations in calculations involving fractions.

LEARN ABOUT the Math

Allison and Preston are playing a math game called Target 1.

If I do the operations from left to right, the value is $\frac{65}{120}$.

If you use the rules for order of operations, you will get a different answer.

$$\frac{2}{3} + \frac{1}{5} \times \frac{5}{8}$$

Rules for Target 1

1. Pick three fraction (F) cards.

2. Pick two operation (O) cards.

3. Put them in this order:
   F O F O F

4. Rearrange the cards to get a value as close as possible to 1.

5. The closest value gets 1 point.

6. The first player to get 5 points wins.

? **How close to 1 can Allison get with her cards?**

A. Show how Preston got $\frac{65}{120}$.

B. What would Allison's answer be if she were to use the rules for the order of operations? Can she get any closer to 1 by rearranging her cards?

Reflecting

C. How could you use brackets to get the same answer as Preston in step A?

D. What is the correct order of operations for Allison's original calculation?

WORK WITH *the Math*

Example 1	Using the order of operations with fractions

Calculate $\frac{7}{3} - \frac{4}{5} \times \left(\frac{5}{6} \div \frac{1}{2}\right) + \frac{1}{4}$

Preston's Solution

$\frac{7}{3} - \frac{4}{5} \times \left(\frac{5}{6} \div \frac{1}{2}\right) + \frac{1}{4}$

$= \frac{7}{3} - \frac{4}{5} \times \frac{10}{6} + \frac{1}{4}$

First I had to do $\frac{5}{6} \div \frac{1}{2}$ since it was in brackets.

I used the reciprocal to calculate $\frac{5}{6} \div \frac{1}{2} = \frac{5}{6} \times \frac{2}{1}$ using mental math.

$= \frac{7}{3} - \left(\frac{4}{5} \times \frac{10}{6}\right) + \frac{1}{4}$

$= \frac{7}{3} - \frac{40}{30} + \frac{1}{4}$

You are supposed to do multiplications before additions.

I added brackets to show the multiplication I would do next.

$= \left(\frac{7}{3} - \frac{4}{3}\right) + \frac{1}{4}$

$= \frac{3}{3} + \frac{1}{4}$

I rewrote the product $\frac{40}{30}$ in lower terms. Then, I subtracted and added from left to right.

I added brackets to show my thinking.

$= 1\frac{1}{4}$

A Checking

1. Calculate using the rules for order of operations.

   a) $3 + \dfrac{1}{2} \div \dfrac{2}{3} \times 8$

   b) $\dfrac{2}{3} + \left(\dfrac{1}{6}\right)\left(\dfrac{1}{6}\right)$

2. Suppose that Nikita picked these cards in the game Target 1:

   | $\dfrac{1}{4}$ | $\dfrac{2}{5}$ | $\dfrac{3}{8}$ | $\div$ | $+$ |

   List three different ways that she could arrange the cards. Then calculate the value for each arrangement.

B Practising

3. Calculate using the rules for order of operations.

   a) $\dfrac{3}{4} + \dfrac{1}{2} \times \dfrac{2}{3}$

   b) $\dfrac{5}{6} \div 5 + 3 \times \dfrac{1}{2}$

   c) $\dfrac{1}{2} - \dfrac{1}{3} \times \dfrac{1}{4} + \dfrac{1}{5} \div \dfrac{1}{6}$

   d) $\left(\dfrac{1}{2} - \dfrac{1}{3}\right) \times \left(\dfrac{1}{4} + \dfrac{1}{5} \div \dfrac{1}{6}\right)$

   e) $\left(\dfrac{1}{2} - \dfrac{1}{3} \times \dfrac{1}{4} + \dfrac{1}{5}\right) \div \dfrac{1}{6}$

   f) $\dfrac{5}{4} \times \dfrac{1}{2} - \dfrac{2}{3} \div 2 + \dfrac{1}{2}$

4. Suppose that Nikita picked these cards in Target 1:

   | $\dfrac{1}{2}$ | $\dfrac{4}{5}$ | $\dfrac{2}{9}$ | $\div$ | $-$ |

   a) List three values greater than 0 that she could calculate, without using brackets, by placing the cards in different positions.

   b) Show another value she could calculate if she were allowed to use brackets.

5. Which expressions have the same value?

   a) $\dfrac{2}{3} \div \dfrac{5}{7} \times \dfrac{3}{6} + \dfrac{1}{2}$

   b) $\dfrac{2}{3} \div \left(\dfrac{5}{7} \div \dfrac{3}{6}\right) + \dfrac{1}{2}$

   c) $\dfrac{2}{3} \div \dfrac{5}{7} \times \left(\dfrac{3}{6} + \dfrac{1}{2}\right)$

   d) $\dfrac{2}{3} \div \left(\dfrac{5}{7} \times \dfrac{3}{6} + \dfrac{1}{2}\right)$

6. Calculate.

a) $\dfrac{6}{7} - \dfrac{3}{4} \times \left(\dfrac{3}{5} + \dfrac{2}{10} \right)$

b) $\dfrac{5}{8} \div \dfrac{1}{10} + \dfrac{1}{3}$

c) $\dfrac{5}{4} + 2\dfrac{1}{2} \times 3 \div \dfrac{2}{3}$

d) $\dfrac{3}{7} \div \dfrac{4}{5} + \dfrac{1}{4}$

e) $\dfrac{4}{9} + \dfrac{2}{3} \times \dfrac{4}{5} \div \dfrac{1}{10}$

f) $\dfrac{8}{9} \times \left(\dfrac{2}{5} + \dfrac{3}{7} \times \dfrac{1}{3} + \dfrac{3}{5} \right) \times 4$

7. a) Calculate each.

i) $\dfrac{2}{3} + \left(\dfrac{1}{4} \times \dfrac{4}{5} \right) - \dfrac{1}{10}$

ii) $\dfrac{2}{3} + \dfrac{1}{4} \times \left(\dfrac{4}{5} - \dfrac{1}{10} \right)$

iii) $\left(\dfrac{2}{3} + \dfrac{1}{4} \right) \times \dfrac{4}{5} - \dfrac{1}{10}$

b) How do your results in part a) show the importance of using brackets in mathematical expressions?

8. What is the missing digit in the following equation?

$$\dfrac{5}{\blacksquare} + \left(\dfrac{3}{4} - \dfrac{2}{3} \right) \times \left(\dfrac{3}{4} - \dfrac{2}{3} \right) = \dfrac{1}{24}$$

9. Use two pairs of brackets to make the following equation true.

$$2 + \dfrac{1}{4} + \dfrac{1}{3} \times \dfrac{3}{7} - \dfrac{2}{5} \times \dfrac{3}{8} \div \dfrac{1}{10} + \dfrac{1}{5} = 1\dfrac{3}{4}$$

10. What values of a, b, and c will make the value of the expression below greater than $1\dfrac{1}{2}$? Determine two sets of possibilities using only proper fractions.

$$a - b + c \times c$$

11. Which expressions have values less than 1?

a) $\dfrac{1}{2} + \left(1 - \dfrac{3}{4} \right) \times \dfrac{1}{2}$

b) $2 \div \dfrac{7}{10} \times \dfrac{1}{3}$

c) $\dfrac{7}{8} \times 1\dfrac{1}{4} \div \left(\dfrac{3}{16} - \dfrac{1}{8} \right)$

d) $2\dfrac{2}{3} \times \dfrac{1}{5} + \dfrac{1}{5}$

12. Create an expression involving fractions and operation signs that results in a whole number only if the correct order of operations is used.

13. How does knowing the order of operations help make sure that you get the same answer to $\dfrac{2}{3} + \dfrac{1}{3} \times \dfrac{1}{12}$ as other students in the class?

2.11 Communicate about Multiplication and Division

Describe situations involving multiplying and dividing fractions and mixed numbers.

LEARN ABOUT the Math

Preston created a problem that could be solved using this calculation: $3 + \frac{2}{3} \times 3\frac{1}{2}$

A cookie recipe used $3\frac{1}{2}$ cups of sugar and $4\frac{1}{2}$ cups of flour. Preston had only 3 cups of flour so he used $\frac{2}{3}$ of $3\frac{1}{2}$ cups of sugar. Altogether, how much flour and sugar did he use?

He was trying to explain why the problem was a correct one to use.

Preston's Explanation

Aaron's Questions

The problem has an adding part and a multiplying part.

The adding part has to be about combining things, and the multiplying part has to be about taking part of something.

Why does the multiplying have to be about taking part of something?

Since I needed $3\frac{1}{2}$ of something, I decided to use cups in a recipe.

Why did you take $\frac{2}{3}$ of $3\frac{1}{2}$ instead of $3\frac{1}{2}$ of $\frac{2}{3}$?

I decided the problem would involve taking $\frac{2}{3}$ of the $3\frac{1}{2}$ and adding it to the 3 that was already there.

Why did 3 already have to be there?

The 3 also had to be cups. I made the recipe start with $4\frac{1}{2}$ cups of flour, because I know 3 is $\frac{2}{3}$ of $4\frac{1}{2}$.

❓ How can you improve Preston's explanation?

A. How can you respond to Aaron's questions to improve Preston's explanation?

B. What other questions could Aaron have asked?

Reflecting

C. Which parts of the Communication Checklist did Preston cover well? Which parts did Aaron cover in his questions?

D. How would you modify Preston's explanation to explain why his problem is appropriate?

WORK WITH *the Math*

Example 1	Describing a situation for dividing fractions

Create a problem that requires division of $1\frac{1}{2}$ by $\frac{4}{5}$.
a) Explain why the problem requires that division.
b) Explain how and why the problem could also be solved using multiplication.

Misa's Solution

a) Jeff's mom was installing new baseboards in a room. She had a lot of strips of wood. Most were one length, and there were a few shorter ones that were $\frac{4}{5}$ of that length.

> I know that one meaning of division is how many of one thing fit into another. I decided to use that meaning. I picked a problem about strips of wood.

She had to fill a space that required $1\frac{1}{2}$ of the longer strips. If she decided to use the shorter strips, how many of them would she need?

> I made sure one strip was $\frac{4}{5}$ as long as a certain distance and the other strip was $1\frac{1}{2}$ times as long as that same distance.

b) $1\dfrac{1}{2} \div \dfrac{4}{5} = \dfrac{3}{2} \div \dfrac{4}{5}$

$\qquad = \dfrac{3}{2} \times \dfrac{5}{4}$

$\qquad = \dfrac{15}{8}$

> I know that one way to solve a division question involving fractions is to multiply by the reciprocal. So to solve the problem I created, I could use multiplication of fractions.

A Checking

1. **a)** Create a problem that requires multiplying $\frac{2}{3} \times \frac{8}{9}$ and solve it.

   b) Explain why multiplying these numbers is appropriate for the problem.

   c) How do you know your answer is reasonable?

B Practising

2. Use words and these grids to explain why $\frac{3}{5}$ of $\frac{2}{3}$ is the same as $\frac{2}{3}$ of $\frac{3}{5}$.

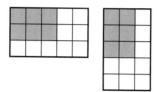

3. **a)** Create a problem that requires calculating $\frac{3}{5} \div 4$ as well as a multiplication by 3.

   b) Explain why a different computation could solve that problem.

4. Explain why you can calculate $2 \div \frac{2}{3}$ using each method below. Use the Communication Checklist and the picture.

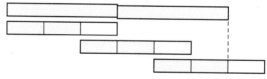

   a) Divide equivalent fractions with the same denominator.

   b) Multiply 2 by 3 and then divide by 2.

5. Complete Diane's explanation for calculating 1.2×3.55.

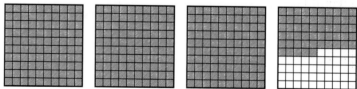

   1.2 is $1\frac{2}{10}$. This is the same as $1\frac{1}{5}$. So I need 3.55 and another $\frac{1}{5}$ of 3.55.

6. How can you use fraction multiplication to explain why $4.2 \times 0.2 = 0.84$?

7. a) Why can you calculate 60% of 1.5 by multiplying $\frac{3}{5} \times \frac{3}{2}$?

   b) Do you think this is the easiest way to calculate the percent? Explain.

8. Fabienne said that she now understands why she needs to multiply the numerator and denominator of a fraction by the same amount to get an equivalent fraction. Explain her reasoning, shown below.

$$\frac{3}{5} \times 1 = \frac{3}{5}$$

$$1 = \frac{2}{2}$$

$$\frac{3}{5} \times \frac{2}{2} = \frac{3}{5}$$

$$\frac{3 \times 2}{5 \times 2} = \frac{3}{5}$$

9. Robin said that, when he multiplies or divides mixed numbers, he usually uses decimal equivalents instead because it is easier. Do you agree or disagree? Explain using examples.

10. Explain how multiplying fractions is like multiplying whole numbers and how it is different.

11. Explain how you know that $3\frac{1}{2} \times 6\frac{1}{3}$ must be greater than 21 before you do the calculation.

12. Explain why $\frac{15}{16} \div \frac{5}{8}$ is half of $\frac{15}{16} \div \frac{5}{16}$.

1. Draw a model to show that $4 \times \frac{2}{3} = \frac{8}{3}$.

2. Use fraction strips to model each.

   a) $\frac{2}{3}$ of $\frac{1}{4}$ is ▪.   **b)** $\frac{1}{2}$ of $\frac{6}{9}$ is ▪.   **c)** $1\frac{1}{5}$ of $\frac{4}{7}$ is ▪.

3. Explain why multiplying a fraction by $\frac{5}{6}$ results in a value that is less than the original fraction.

4. Calculate.

   a) $\frac{3}{5} \times \frac{5}{8}$ **b)** $\frac{2}{6} \times \frac{5}{6}$ **c)** $\frac{3}{7} \times \frac{1}{6}$ **d)** $\frac{5}{8} \times \frac{3}{7}$

5. Show two ways to calculate $1\frac{2}{3} \times 2\frac{1}{4}$.

6. Calculate.

   a) $\frac{3}{5} \times 5\frac{1}{2}$ **c)** $1\frac{2}{5} \times 1\frac{3}{4}$

   b) $\frac{7}{10} \times 6\frac{3}{4}$ **d)** $\frac{2}{9} \times 5\frac{1}{3}$

7. **a)** Draw a picture to show that $\frac{3}{4} \div \frac{5}{8}$ is $1\frac{1}{5}$.

   b) Use a multiplication equation to show that $\frac{3}{4} \div \frac{5}{8} = 1\frac{1}{5}$.

8. Calculate.

   a) $\frac{4}{5} \div \frac{2}{5}$ **b)** $\frac{5}{8} \div \frac{1}{5}$ **c)** $\frac{1}{5} \div \frac{5}{8}$ **d)** $3\frac{1}{2} \div 1\frac{1}{4}$

9. Calculate.

   a) $\frac{2}{3} - \frac{1}{4} \times \frac{5}{6} \div 2$

   b) $\left(\frac{2}{3} - \frac{1}{4}\right) \times \left(\frac{5}{6} \div 2\right)$

   c) $\frac{2}{3} - \left(\frac{1}{4} + \frac{9}{12}\right) \times \frac{5}{2} \times \frac{5}{6} \div 5$

What Do You Think Now?

Revisit What Do You Think? on page 45. How have your answers and explanations changed?

Chapter **Review**

Frequently Asked Questions

Q: How can you divide a fraction by a whole number?

A1: You can think of it as sharing. For example, $\frac{4}{5} \div 3$ tells you the share size if 3 people share $\frac{4}{5}$ of something.

A2: You can use a model.

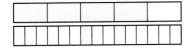

$$\frac{4}{5} \div 3 = \frac{4}{15}$$

A3: You can multiply by a fraction.

$$\frac{4}{5} \div 3 = \frac{4}{5} \times \frac{1}{3}$$
$$= \frac{4}{15}$$

A4: You can divide using an equivalent fraction where the numerator is a multiple of the whole number.

$$\frac{4}{5} \div 3 = \frac{12}{15} \div 3$$
$$= \frac{4}{15}$$

Q: How can you divide two fractions?

A1: You can determine the number of times the divisor fits into the dividend using fraction strips and a common denominator.

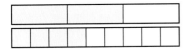

$$\frac{2}{3} \div \frac{4}{9} = \frac{6}{9} \div \frac{4}{9}$$
$$= 6 \div 4$$
$$= 1\frac{2}{4} \text{ or } 1\frac{1}{2}$$

A2: You can multiply by the reciprocal. For example,

$$\frac{2}{3} \div \frac{4}{9} = \frac{2}{3} \times \frac{9}{4}$$

$$= \frac{18}{12}$$

$$= 1\frac{6}{12} \text{ or } 1\frac{1}{2}$$

Q: In what order do you perform a series of fraction calculations?

A: Use the rules for the order of operations:

Perform the operations in brackets first.

Next, divide and multiply from left to right.

Then, add and subtract from left to right.

Then, convert the final answer to a mixed number.

For example,

$$\frac{3}{2} - \frac{2}{5} \div \frac{1}{5} \times \frac{3}{10} + \frac{2}{3}$$

$$= \frac{3}{2} - \left(\frac{2}{5} \div \frac{1}{5}\right) \times \frac{3}{10} + \frac{2}{3}$$

$$= \frac{3}{2} - 2 \times \frac{3}{10} + \frac{2}{3}$$

$$= \frac{3}{2} - \left(2 \times \frac{3}{10}\right) + \frac{2}{3}$$

$$= \frac{3}{2} - \frac{6}{10} + \frac{2}{3}$$

$$= \left(\frac{3}{2} - \frac{6}{10}\right) + \frac{2}{3}$$

$$= \left(\frac{15}{10} - \frac{6}{10}\right) + \frac{2}{3}$$

$$= \frac{9}{10} + \frac{2}{3}$$

$$= \frac{27}{30} + \frac{20}{30}$$

$$= \frac{47}{30}, \text{ or } 1\frac{17}{30}$$

Practice

Lesson 2.1

1. Draw a model to represent $3 \times \frac{5}{6}$.

2. Calculate each. Express the answer as a whole or mixed number.

   a) $8 \times \frac{4}{5}$ b) $6 \times \frac{3}{5}$ c) $9 \times \frac{2}{7}$ d) $12 \times \frac{2}{3}$

Lesson 2.2

3. What is the value of each expression?

   a) $\frac{1}{5}$ of $\frac{1}{2}$ b) $\frac{3}{8}$ of $\frac{8}{9}$ c) $\frac{2}{3}$ of $\frac{6}{8}$ d) $\frac{4}{6}$ of $\frac{1}{2}$

4. What is the missing fraction in each sentence?

   a) $\frac{2}{5}$ is $\frac{2}{3}$ of ▮   b) ▮ of $\frac{4}{9}$ is $\frac{1}{3}$

Lesson 2.3

5. Sketch a model for this calculation.

   $$\frac{3}{4} \times \frac{2}{5} = \frac{6}{20}$$

6. Calculate.

   a) $\frac{2}{9} \times \frac{2}{7}$ b) $\frac{3}{7} \times \frac{2}{5}$ c) $\frac{5}{8} \times \frac{2}{3}$ d) $\frac{1}{5} \times \frac{5}{7}$

7. About $\frac{2}{3}$ of the students in Andee's school come by bus. About $\frac{1}{3}$ of these students are on the bus for more than an hour and a half each day. What fraction of the students in Andee's school are on the bus for more than an hour and a half each day?

   $2/3 \times 1/3 = 2/9$

Lesson 2.4

8. Which products are closer to $\frac{1}{2}$ than either 0 or 1?

   a) $\frac{3}{4} \times \frac{5}{6}$ b) $\frac{1}{6} \times \frac{7}{8}$ c) $\frac{3}{9} \times \frac{8}{9}$ d) $\frac{3}{5} \times \frac{2}{3}$

Lesson 2.5

9. Draw two models to represent $1\frac{3}{4} \times 2\frac{1}{5}$.

10. Calculate. Express the answer as an improper fraction.

    a) $2\frac{1}{3} \times \frac{3}{5}$ b) $3\frac{1}{4} \times 2\frac{2}{5}$

11. The supermarket has $2\frac{1}{2}$ times as many employees just before dinnertime as in the late morning. There are 18 employees in the late morning. How many employees are there just before dinnertime?

    $2\frac{1}{2} \div 18 = 5/2 \times 1/18 = 5/36$

$5/2 \times 18/1$

$5/1 \times 9/1 = 45$

x

12. Draw a diagram to show that $\frac{6}{8} \div 3 = \frac{2}{8}$.

13. Calculate.

   a) $\frac{9}{10} \div 3$ **b)** $\frac{9}{10} \div 2$ **c)** $\frac{4}{5} \div 6$

14. Explain why $\frac{\blacksquare}{2} \div 3$ is a fraction that can be written with a denominator of 6.

15. Which quotients are between 4 and 6?

   a) $\frac{9}{10} \div \frac{1}{5}$ **b)** $\frac{9}{10} \div \frac{1}{8}$ **c)** $3\frac{1}{2} \div \frac{3}{4}$

16. What fractions might you use to estimate $\frac{7}{16} \div \frac{6}{20}$?

17. Sketch a model to show $\frac{5}{6} \div \frac{1}{3} = 2\frac{1}{2}$.

18. Explain how you know that $\frac{4}{6} \div \frac{3}{6}$ has the same quotient as $\frac{4}{5} \div \frac{3}{5}$.

19. Calculate.

   a) $\frac{5}{6} \div \frac{1}{6}$ **b)** $\frac{5}{8} \div \frac{1}{4}$ **c)** $\frac{5}{6} \div \frac{1}{4}$ **d)** $\frac{3}{8} \div \frac{2}{9}$

20. What fraction calculation can you use to determine the number of quarters in $4.50?

21. Pia used $\frac{2}{3}$ of her sugar to make $\frac{3}{4}$ of a batch of cookies. How much of her sugar would she have needed to make a whole batch?

22. Which expression has the greater value? How do you know?

   A. $\frac{4}{5} \times \frac{2}{3} - \frac{1}{5} \times \frac{5}{8}$ **B.** $\frac{4}{5} \times \left(\frac{2}{3} - \frac{1}{5}\right) \times \frac{5}{8}$

23. Where can you place brackets to make this equation true?

$$3 \times \frac{2}{3} + \frac{1}{3} \div \frac{1}{4} = 12$$

24. Use fractions to explain why 4.5×0.5 equals 2.25.

Chapter **Task**

Computer Gizmos

Brian likes to write mini-applications for his computer. One application automatically displays a bar to show what fraction of a megabyte of memory a file is using at any point in time.

Megabyte Minder		
File name	**Memory (in MB)**	
Science project		$\frac{1}{3}$
Journal		$\frac{7}{8}$
Short story		$\frac{2}{5}$
Book report		$\frac{5}{6}$

❓ How can you describe how the sizes of Brian's files compare?

A. Which of Brian's files have room to be doubled before they reach the 1 MB mark? How do you know?

B. Compare the science project file to all the others by indicating what fraction of the larger file it is.

C. Compare the journal file to all the others by indicating what fraction of the smaller file it is.

D. How much memory is still available for the book report file compared to the science project file? Why is there more than one way to answer this question?

E. What other fraction comparisons related to these files can you make? Calculate the comparisons.

NEL

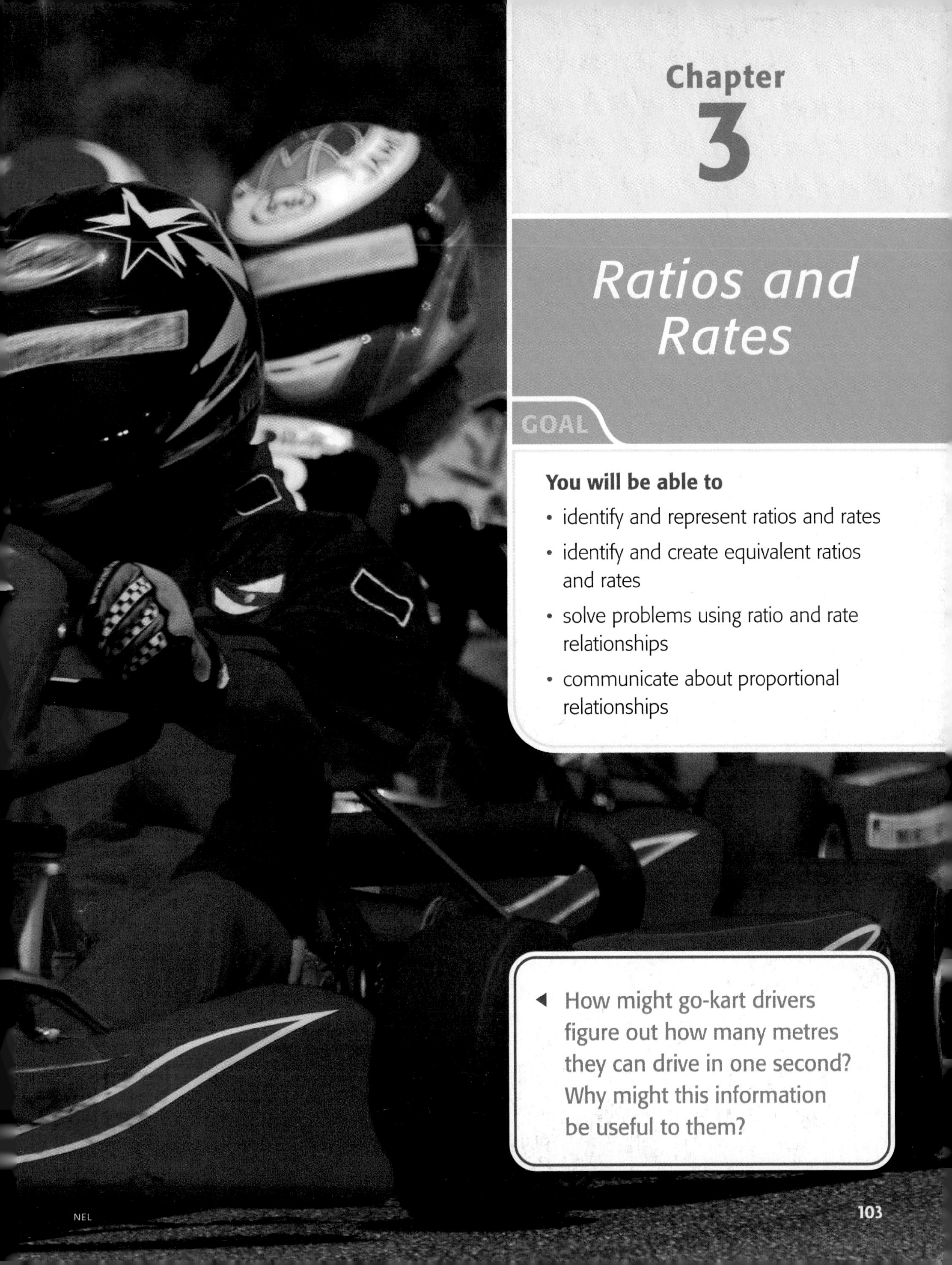

Ratios and Rates

GOAL

You will be able to

- identify and represent ratios and rates
- identify and create equivalent ratios and rates
- solve problems using ratio and rate relationships
- communicate about proportional relationships

◄ How might go-kart drivers figure out how many metres they can drive in one second? Why might this information be useful to them?

Getting **Started**

Seating Arrangements

Ten girls and eight boys are sitting in the cafeteria as shown.

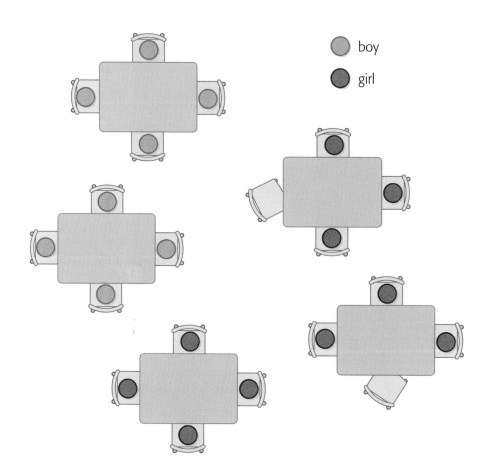

boy

girl

ratio

a comparison of two numbers (e.g., 5 : 26 is the ratio of vowels to letters in the alphabet) or of two measurements with the same units (e.g., 164 : 175 is the ratio of two students' heights in centimetres). Each number in the ratio is called a term.

❓ What ratios could describe their seating arrangement?

A. Explain how the **ratio** 10 : 8 describes the students.

B. Write another **part-to-part ratio** to describe the students.

C. Write a part-to-part ratio to compare the number of tables with boys to the number of tables with girls.

D. Write a **part-to-whole ratio** to compare the number of tables with boys to all the tables. Write the ratio as a fraction.

E. Write a part-to-whole ratio to describe the number of tables with girls to all the tables. Write the ratio in the form "▢ to ▢".

F. Suppose three boys and one girl sat at one table. What would each of these ratios describe?
- 3:1
- 1 to 4
- $\frac{3}{4}$

G. Suppose the ratio 2:2 represents the students at a table. Who might be sitting at the table?

H. Draw five squares to represent the five tables.
- Arrange 10 red and 8 blue counters to represent the girls and boys at the tables.
- Sketch your model.
- List all the different ratios your diagram shows.
- Explain how each ratio represents your seating arrangement.

What Do You Think?

Decide whether you agree or disagree with each statement.
Be ready to explain your decision.

1. The first term of a ratio should always be less than the second term.

2. The ratios 2:2 and 3:3 describe the same comparison.

3. If you know a part-to-part ratio, you can always calculate the related part-to-whole ratio.

4. Prices are like ratios since they compare two numbers.

Using Two-Term Ratios

GOAL

Compare two quantities using ratios.

LEARN ABOUT the Math

Nikita used a Ukrainian recipe for cold fruit soup, but to make more, she used 6 cups of cranberry juice.

Cold Fruit Soup

Liquids

4 cups cranberry juice

3 cups white grape juice

8 cups water

Solids

2 cups sugar

1 cup raspberry jam

equivalent ratio

a ratio that represents the same relationship as another ratio; e.g., 2:4 is an equivalent ratio to 1:2 because both ratios describe the relationship of the blue counters to the red counters. There are 2 red counters for each blue counter, but also 4 red counters for every 2 blue counters.

❓ How much water and grape juice should she use?

A. Write the part-to-part ratio of cranberry juice to water.

B. Draw a picture to show why 2:4 is an **equivalent ratio** to the ratio in part A.

C. Write a **proportion** to determine the amount of water needed for 6 cups of cranberry juice.

D. Write the part-to-part ratio of cranberry juice to grape juice.

E. Write equivalent ratios you can use to determine how much grape juice is needed in each case.

- You use 2 cups of cranberry juice.
- You use 6 cups of cranberry juice.

F. How much water and grape juice should Nikita use?

Reflecting

G. How are the three ratios in parts A, B, and C related?

H. How is creating an equivalent ratio like creating an equivalent fraction?

WORK WITH the Math

Example 1	Representing situations with ratios

Compare the lengths of the blister beetle and the hydraena beetle to the length of the giant stag beetle using ratios.

blister beetle	hydraena beetle	giant stag beetle

2 cm	2 mm	3 cm

Brian's Solution

blister beetle and giant stag beetle:

2 cm : 3 cm

The ratio is 2 : 3.

hydraena and giant stag :

3 cm = 30 mm

2 mm : 30 mm

The ratio is 2 : 30.

I think the ratios should be different since the beetles are such different sizes.

The ratio 2 : 3 makes sense since the stag beetle is $1\frac{1}{2}$ times as long as the blister beetle, just like 3 is $1\frac{1}{2}$ times 2.

I renamed 3 cm as 30 mm. That way, I was comparing 2 mm to 30 mm.

That seems right, since $30 = 15 \times 2$ and the stag beetle looks like it is 15 times as long as the hydraena beetle.

Example 2 | Creating equivalent ratios using fractions

Misa has chat room buddies from Canada and the U.S.A. in a ratio of 30 : 20.
She has 135 Canadian buddies. How many U.S. buddies does she have?

Allison's Solution

$30 : 20 = \dfrac{30}{20}$

I wrote the ratio as a fraction.

$\dfrac{30}{20} \overset{\div 10}{\underset{\div 10}{=}} \dfrac{3}{2}$

I renamed $\dfrac{30}{20}$ in lower terms by dividing the numerator and denominator by the common factor of 10.

$\dfrac{\text{Canadian buddies}}{\text{U.S. buddies}} = \dfrac{3}{2}$

$= \dfrac{135}{\blacksquare}$

I wrote a proportion comparing Canadian buddies to U.S. buddies.

$135 \div 3 = 45$

$\dfrac{3}{2} \overset{\times 45}{\underset{\times 45}{=}} \dfrac{135}{90}$

I divided 135 by 3 to figure out what to multiply 2 by.

Misa has 90 U.S. buddies.

Example 3 | Solving a ratio problem using a proportion

The ratio of the mass of oats to barley in some horse feed is 4 : 11.
How many kilograms of each grain are in 150 kg of feed?

Aaron's Solution

O O O O B B B B B B B B B B B
⎣___⎦ ⎣_____⎦
  4 parts   11 parts

I represented the ratio with a diagram. I represented oats with O and barley with B.

The whole is 15.

4 : 11 is a part-to-part ratio. I added the parts to determine the whole.

Oats = $\frac{4}{15}$ of total mass

Barley = $\frac{11}{15}$ of total mass

I wrote fractions to describe what part of 15 kg of feed is oats and what part is barley.

Oats: $\frac{4}{15} = \frac{\blacksquare}{150}$
      ×10

To find out the amount of oats in 150 kg of feed, I needed an equivalent fraction for $\frac{4}{15}$ with a denominator of 150.

    ×10
$\frac{4}{15} = \frac{40}{150}$
    ×10

I multiplied the denominator by 10, so I had to multiply the numerator by 10.

Mass of oats = 40 kg

Mass of barley = 150 − 40
            = 110

In 150 kg of feed, there are 40 kg of oats and 110 kg of barley.

I subtracted to figure out how much of the mass is barley.

Misa's Solution

4 + 11 = 15

I figured that if there were 4 kg of oats and 11 kg of barley, there would be 15 kg of feed.

150 ÷ 15 = 10
  4 × 10 = 40 kg oats
11 × 10 = 110 kg barley

I realized that 150 is 10 times as much as 15, so the parts would also have to be 10 times as much.

A Checking

1. **a)** Write a part-to-part ratio to compare the items in the top row in each diagram.
   b) The bottom row represents an equivalent ratio. Write a proportion you could solve to calculate the missing term.
   c) Calculate the missing term.

A.

2 oranges	5 apples
4 oranges	▦ apples

B.

3 women	5 men
▦ women	15 men

C.

2 stars	5 bells
8 stars	▦ bells

D.

3 triangles	9 squares
4 triangles	▦ squares

2. Calculate each missing term.
   a) $3:8 = $ ▦ $:16$ **b)** $20:$ ▦ $= 32:24$

B Practising

3. Copy the grid on the right. Shade it so the ratio of coloured squares to the total number of squares is the same as for the grid on the left.

   a)   **b)**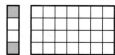

4. Write three equivalent ratios for each ratio.
   a) 21 to 56 **c)** $48:36$ **e)** 7 to 42
   b) $6:54$ **d)** $\dfrac{22}{55}$ **f)** $\dfrac{3}{8}$

5. Show that the ratio of the number of blue sections to the total number of sections is the same for all three diagrams.

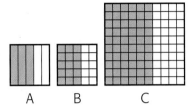

A   B   C

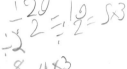

6 ÷ 3 = 2

6. Determine the missing term in each proportion.

a) $27:45 = \blacksquare : 5$

c) $\blacksquare : 9 = 2:3$

b) $\dfrac{2}{6} = \dfrac{3}{\blacksquare}$

d) $\dfrac{16}{\blacksquare} = \dfrac{12}{15}$

7. Write each comparison as a ratio. Remember, the units should be the same so the comparison is meaningful.

a) 400 g to 1 kg   b) 6 cm to 7 mm   c) 200 s to 3 min

8. a) Draw one picture to show the ratios $3:1$ and $\dfrac{3}{4}$ at the same time.

b) Explain how each ratio is in the picture.

c) Change your picture to show two equivalent ratios to the ones in part a).

9. Katherine spends 7 h each day in school, including 30 min for lunch.

a) Write a ratio to compare the time for lunch with the total time in school each day.

b) Write a ratio to compare the total time for lunch for a school week with the total school time for a school week.

c) Calculate the number of hours of lunch time in 30 school days.

10. Suppose you add the same amount to both terms of a ratio. Which of the following is true? Explain.

A. You never get an equivalent ratio.

B. You usually do not get an equivalent ratio.

C. You usually get an equivalent ratio.

Reading Strategy

Activating Prior Knowledge

What do you know about fractions? How can what you know about fractions help you with ratios?

11. Park rangers captured, tagged and released 82 grizzly bears. A month later, the rangers captured 20 bears, two of which had tags. Estimate the park's grizzly bear population.

12. Lucas is 9 years old and 129 cm tall. Medical charts show that a boy's height at age 9 is $\frac{3}{4}$ of his predicted adult height. Predict Lucas's adult height.

13. Using a ratio, compare two related quantities or measurements you find in a newspaper article, on the Internet, or on TV. Describe the ratio and explain why it is actually a ratio.

14. George rolled a die 30 times, with these results.

Roll of						
How many times	4	5	6	5	8	2

   a) Explain how $\frac{8}{30}$ describes the experimental probability of rolling a 5. What sort of ratio is it?
   b) Write a part-to-part ratio to compare the rolls of 5 to the rolls of 1.
   c) Are any other part-to-part ratios equivalent to the ratio in part b)?
   d) Suppose George were to roll a die 10 times instead of 30. About how many rolls would you expect for each number? Explain.

15. Describe a situation you might represent with each ratio.
   a) $\frac{3}{60}$ b) 9:20

16. The sides of a rectangle with an area of 192 cm² are in the ratio 3:4. What are the side lengths?

17. A ratio can be called a multiplicative comparison of two amounts. Why is a ratio about multiplication?

3.2

Using Ratio Tables

GOAL

Use ratio tables to solve problems.

LEARN ABOUT *the Math*

The students in Preston's school signed up for a snowboard trip.
Two girls signed up for every three boys who signed up.
In all, 42 boys signed up.

? **How many girls signed up for the trip?**

Example 1 | Using a ratio table

I used a ratio table to help me solve the problem.

Preston's Solution

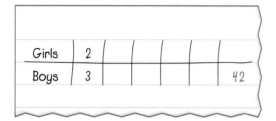

The ratio of girls to boys is 2 : 3.
I drew a two-row table and wrote the ratio of girls to boys in the first column. I decided to put girls on the top row, but I did not have to. I needed an equivalent ratio for 42 boys.

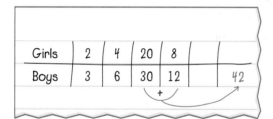

I created some equivalent ratios, hoping I would see a connection to a ratio with 42 boys. I got equivalent ratios by multiplying both numbers in a column by the same amount. I picked numbers that were easy to multiply by. I wrote the equivalent ratios in other columns.

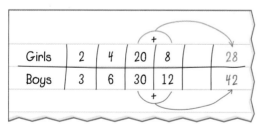

I saw that I had a column with 30 boys, and I knew I needed to have a column with 42 boys in it. I realized that, if I multiplied the second column by 2, I would get a column with 12 boys. Then I could add the columns with 30 boys and 12 boys to get a column with 42 boys.

So 28 girls signed up for the trip.

The ratio 28 : 42 is equivalent to the original ratio of 2 : 3.

Reflecting

A. Why do you get an equivalent ratio when you multiply the numbers in one column by the same amount?

B. Why did Preston get an equivalent ratio when he added the column with 20 and 30 and the column with 8 and 12?

C. What other ratio table could you have used to solve the same problem?

WORK WITH *the Math*

Example 2	Solving a proportion using a ratio table

Solve $\dfrac{6}{\blacksquare} = \dfrac{20}{90}$ using a ratio table.

Allison's Solution

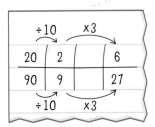

$\dfrac{6}{27} = \dfrac{20}{90}$

The missing term is 27.

I started the table with the ratio I knew, $\dfrac{20}{90}$.
I wanted a first term of 6.
I noticed that 20 and 90 had a common factor of 10, so I divided them by 10 to get an equivalent ratio in lower terms.
Then I multiplied 2 by 3 to get 6.
I multiplied 9 by 3, since both terms must be multiplied by the same number.

Brian's Solution

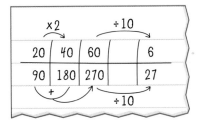

$\dfrac{6}{27} = \dfrac{20}{90}$

The missing term is 27.

I started the table with the ratio in which I knew both terms.
I wanted a first term of 6.
Doubling is easy to do, so I did that. I realized that the sums of the first two columns would give 60 as the first term and 270 as the second.
I divided by 10 to get 6 as the first term.

Example 3 | Determining part of a whole

A bag of trail mix has 70 g of raisins for every 30 g of sunflower seeds. There are no other ingredients. In 500 g of trail mix, how many grams are raisins?

Misa's Solution

raisins	70		
sunflower seeds	30		
package			500

I used the first two rows of a ratio table to represent the parts; I added a third row to represent the whole. I did that since I knew about the parts for a smaller mixture, but not the whole amount for the package.

raisins	70		
sunflower seeds	30		
package	100		500

x 5

The whole for the small mixture was 100 g (70 g + 30 g).

x 5

raisins	70		350
sunflower seeds	30		150
package	100		500

x 5

I multiplied all the numbers by 5 since I wanted a total of 500.

There are 350 g of raisins in the package.

A **Checking**

1. Complete each ratio table.

a)

Boys		2	20	40			
Girls		3	30			15	45

b)

Bottles of juice	60				54
Bottles of water	90	9	27	99	

B Practising

2. Solve using a ratio table. Show your steps.

   a) $2:3 = 36:\blacksquare$ **c)** $6:8 = \blacksquare:44$

   b) $12:18 = 30:\blacksquare$ **d)** $80:\blacksquare = 50:60$

3. Mary made 2 L of orange juice from concentrate.
   She used 3 parts of water for each 1 part of concentrate.
   How much concentrate did she use?

4. Create two different ratio tables that would let you solve each
   proportion. Explain your thinking in creating the tables.

   a) $\blacksquare:20 = 63:84$ **c)** $8:\blacksquare = 20:35$

   b) $8:84 = 90:\blacksquare$ **d)** $30:45 = \blacksquare:54$

5. It takes 27 kg of milk to make 4 kg of butter.

   a) How much milk is needed to make 3 kg of butter?

   b) How much butter can you make from 540 kg of milk?

6. A map is drawn with a ratio of $3:2\,000\,000$.

   a) Why does the ratio $3:2\,000\,000$ mean that 3 cm on the
   map represents 20 km? Use the fact that 1 km = 1000 m.

   b) How many centimetres on the map represent 68 km?

7. A survey showed that residents of a city were $2:1$ in favour of
   higher parking fines. In all, 4500 people were surveyed. How
   many were in favour of higher parking fines?

8. Two bags have the same ratio of red to blue marbles. The ratio
   is not 1:1. There are 9 red marbles in one bag and 16 blue
   marbles in the other.

   a) How many of each colour might be in each bag?

   b) Show that part a) has at least three other answers.

9. Barney says ratio tables are a good way to solve ratio
   problems since you can decide what to add, subtract, multiply,
   or divide to get the answer. What do you think Barney means?

Ratio Match

In this game, you make as many equivalent ratios as possible with six cards.

Number of players: 2–4

YOU WILL NEED
- a deck of playing cards with no face cards (aces represent 1s)

How to Play

1. Shuffle the cards and place them face down.

2. Each player takes six cards.

3. Make as many equivalent ratios as you can using your cards.

4. You get one point for each set of equivalent ratios that do not use the same four cards.

5. After six rounds, the player with the most points wins.

Nikita's Turn

I picked 4, 6, 7, 1, 1, and 2.
I created two pairs of equivalent ratios:
- 1:2 and 7:14
- 6:12 and 7:14
I got 2 points.

Preston's Turn

I drew 8, 10, 2, 1, 5, and 4.
I created four pairs of equivalent ratios:
- 1:4 and 2:8
- 4:5 and 8:10
- 5:10 and 1:2
- 2:5 and 4:10
I got 4 points.

3.3

Exploring Ratios with Three Terms

YOU WILL NEED
- Fraction Strips Tower, base ten blocks, counters, or play money
- chart paper
- coloured markers

EXPLORE *the Math*

three-term ratio

a ratio that compares three quantities; e.g., the ratio 2 : 3 : 5 (or, 2 to 3 to 5) describes the ratio of red to blue to yellow squares.

Allison, Nikita, and Misa pool their money to buy one lottery ticket. The **three-term ratio** 6 : 3 : 1 describes their shares of the ticket.

ENTER TO WIN
the
Hospital Lottery
to buy
new medical equipment

Tickets are only $10!

Grand prize	$10 000
2nd prize	$2500
3rd prize	$500

Brian, Preston, and Aaron also buy a ticket. The ratio 6 : 2.50 : 1.50 describes their shares of the ticket.

❓ **If either ticket wins one of the prizes, how much should each person get?**

Frequently Asked Questions

Q: **When do you use ratios?**

A: You use ratios when you want to compare quantities with the same units. For example

- the amount of water and concentrate needed to make orange juice
- the amount of time spent doing activities in a day
- the areas of two rectangles

Q: **How can you use equivalent ratios to solve problems?**

A1: You can use equivalent fractions or set up a proportion to figure out an appropriate equivalent ratio. For example:

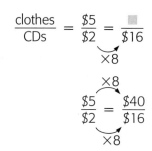

- You spent $5 on CDs for every $2 you spent on clothes. You spent $16 on clothes. How much did you spend on CDs?

You multiply $2 by 8 to get the amount spent on CDs, so multiply $5 by 8 to get the amount spent on clothes.

You spent $40 on clothes.

A2: You can use a ratio table and a given ratio to create an equivalent ratio. You can do this in several ways:

- Multiply or divide both terms in one column by the same amount.
- Add or subtract corresponding numbers in two or more columns to get one number in the equivalent ratio you need and read the table to get the other number.

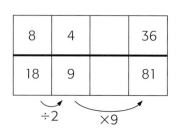

For example, to solve $8 : 18 = \blacksquare : 81$, you might notice that 81 is not a multiple of 18, but it is a multiple of 9, which is also a factor of 18, so you try to get a 9 as the second term.

Practice

Lesson 3.1

1. a) List three ratios equivalent to $4:9$.

b) Can one term of a ratio equivalent to $4:9$ be 360? Is there more than one way? Explain.

2. Calculate each missing term.

a) $\blacksquare:11 = 11:121$

b) $5:2 = \blacksquare:14$

c) $\blacksquare:5 = 17:2.5$

3. Green paint is mixed with white paint in the ratio $5:3$ to make the green paint lighter.

a) What fraction of the paint is white?

b) There are 2 L of mixed paint. How many litres of green paint were used to make it?

4. Determine each ratio for the numbers from 1 to 100, including 1 and 100.

a) the number of even numbers to the number of odd numbers

b) the number of multiples of 6 to the number of multiples of 8

Lesson 3.2

5. Complete each ratio table.

a)

Number of days	7			28	
Number of school days	5	35	100		40

b)

Number of dimes		9		6	
Value of dimes	10¢	90¢	80¢		800¢

6. The ratio of Grade 8 students to Grade 7 students on a field trip is $7:5$. In all, 84 students went on the trip. Determine the number of Grade 8 students on the trip using a ratio table.

Lesson 3.3

7. Jerry makes bead necklaces. Each necklace has red, blue, and purple beads in the ratio $5:3:1$. One necklace has 36 beads altogether. How many of each colour does it have?

3.4

Using Rates

YOU WILL NEED

• a calculator

GOAL

Use rates and equivalent rates to solve problems.

speed

the rate at which a moving object travels a certain distance in a certain time; for example, a sprinter who runs 100 m in 10 s has a speed of 100 m/10 s = 10 m/s.

rate

a comparison of two amounts measured in different units; for example, cost per item or distance compared to time. The word "per" means "to" or "for each" and is written using a slash (/); for example, a typing rate of 250 words/8 min.

unit rate

a rate in which the second term is 1; for example, in swimming, 12 laps/6 min can be rewritten as a unit rate of 2 laps/min

LEARN ABOUT the Math

Adam Sioui of Calgary won a gold medal in 2007 for swimming the 100 m backstroke in just under 56 s.

? **On average, how long did Adam take to swim 1 m?**

A. **Speed** is an example of a **rate**. It compares the distance travelled to the time in which the distance is travelled. How do you know that Adam's speed was less than two metres each second?

B. Describe how you would calculate Adam's speed as a **unit rate** of metres per second (m/s).

C. How do you know that Adam swam 1 m in less than 1 s?

D. What is Adam's unit rate in seconds per metre (s/m)?

Communication | Tip

The 1 in a unit rate is usually not written; e.g., 95.2 km/1 h is written as 95.2 km/h.

Reflecting

E. Why was your answer to part D an **equivalent rate** to 56 s/100 m?

F. How are rates like ratios? How are they different?

WORK WITH *the Math*

Example 1	Using a proportion to solve a rate problem

At last year's school picnic, the helpers served about 160 L of lemonade to 250 people. About how much lemonade did each person have?

Aaron's Solution

The rate is 160 L/250 people.

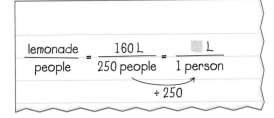

$$\frac{\text{lemonade}}{\text{people}} = \frac{160\ L}{250\ \text{people}} = \frac{\blacksquare\ L}{1\ \text{person}}$$

$\div 250$

$160 \div 250 = 0.64$

Each person could have had 0.64 L, or 640 mL, of lemonade.

I want to know the amount of lemonade each person had: that is a unit rate. I used the information to write a proportion.

I realized that I had to divide 250 by 250 to get 1, so I had to divide 160 by 250. I used my calculator.

Example 2 | Calculate equivalent rates using a ratio table

Allison's favourite cereal comes in two sizes. The small box is 750 g and costs $3.99. The giant box is 2.5 kg and costs $12.49. How much does Allison save by buying the giant box?

Allison's Solution

2.5 kg = 2500 g

I converted 2.5 kg to grams since the mass of the other box was in grams.

Grams	750			2500
Cost	$3.99			

I used a ratio table to figure out the cost of the giant box at the small-box rate.

I noticed that, if I divided 750 by 3 and then multiplied by 10, I would get the number of grams for the big box.

		÷3		×10	
Grams	750	250		2500
Cost	$3.99	$1.33		$13.30

So 2500 g would cost $13.30 at the small-box rate.

$13.30 – $12.49 = 81¢
I save 81¢ by buying the giant box.

I subtracted the cost for the giant box from what it would have cost at the small-box rate.

Ⓐ Checking

1. Write two equivalent rates for each case. One of your rates should be a unit rate.

    a) 5 goals in 10 games

    b) 10 km jogged in 60 min

    c) 10 penalties in 25 games

2. On a hike, Peter walked 28 km in 7 h.

    a) What was his speed in kilometres per hour?

    b) How far would he walk in 2 h at that speed?

3. Determine the missing term.
   a) Three trucks have 54 wheels. Six trucks have ▦ wheels.
   b) In 5 h, you drive 400 km. In 2 h, you drive ▦ km.
   c) In 2 h, you earn $20. In 9 h, you earn ▦.
   d) Six boxes contain 72 doughnuts. ▦ boxes contain 48 doughnuts.

4. Brad pays $56 for four CDs.
   a) At this rate, how many CDs can he buy with $42?
   b) Why might you use a different strategy to figure out how many CDs he could buy with $28?

5. Calculate the unit cost (the cost for 1 kg, 1 L, or 1 m²).
   a) $3.70 for 2 kg of peaches
   b) $2.99 for 1.89 L of juice
   c) $283.28 for 22.5 m² of floor tiles

6. Wayne Gretzky scored 2857 points in 1487 NHL hockey games.
   a) Calculate his average points per game to the nearest hundredth.
   b) At this rate, how many more points would he have scored in 79 more games?

7. Suppose 6 kg of oranges cost $14. How many kilograms of oranges can you buy for $21?

8. A grey whale's heart beats 24 times in 3 min. How many times does it beat in a day?

9. When might you use the concept of rate in a grocery store?

10. Jason's mom drove 160 km to a stampede at 100 km/h. Then she drove back home at 90 km/h. What was the difference in time between the trips?

11. Create a problem that involves calculating speed, in which you know the distance travelled and the time taken to travel that distance. Solve the problem in two ways.

3.5

Communicate about Ratios and Rates

GOAL

Explain your thinking when solving ratio and rate problems.

LEARN ABOUT the Math

Nikita asked Misa to check her explanation to this problem.

A computer downloads a 1577 KB file in 10.455 s. How long will it take to download a 657 KB file? Explain.

Nikita's Explanation

$1577 \div 10.455 = 150.8369201$

$657 \div 150.84 = 4.355608692$

It will take 4.36 s to download the file.

Misa's Questions

Why did you divide 1577 by 10.455?

Why did you divide again?
Where are the units for the numbers?
Why did you use 150.84 when you divided?

Why did you say 4.36 s and not 4.356 s?

❓ How can Nikita improve her explanation?

A. How can you answer Misa's questions to improve Nikita's explanation?

B. What other questions could Misa have asked?

Reflecting

C. Which parts of the Communication Checklist did Nikita cover well? Which parts did Misa cover in her questions?

D. How else could you change Nikita's explanation to make it better?

WORK WITH *the Math*

Example 1	Communicating about ratios

The Coyotes have won 8 of their first 20 soccer games. If this continues, how many games would you expect them to win out of 30 games? Explain your thinking.

Preston's Solution

$8:20 = \blacksquare:30$

Wins	8	4		12
Games	20	10		30

$\div 2 \qquad \times 3$

In 30 games, they would probably win 12.

I realized this was a ratio problem and I assumed that the team's winning ratio would stay the same.
I set up a proportion in which the first value was wins and the second was total games.

I like ratio tables, so I used one to solve the problem.
It was hard to figure out what to multiply 20 by to get 30, so I divided 8 and 20 by 2 to get 4 and 10 and then I multiplied both terms by 3.

This answer is reasonable, since if they played 40 games, they would win 16, and 12 is between 8 and 16.

A Checking

1. You are asked to solve this problem:
   Marlene can run 4 km in 30 min. Can she run 6 km in 45 min?
   Complete the calculation and explanation. Use the
   Communication Checklist to help you.

B Practising

2. Mahrie was given this problem to solve:
   Sam has a part-time job delivering flyers. He earns 25¢ for
   every 10 flyers he delivers. He needs $45 to buy his mom's
   birthday gift. How many flyers must he deliver?

   Mahrie wrote this. How would you improve her explanation?

   $45 \times 4 = 180 \rightarrow 1800$ flyers

3. The capacity of a glass is 270 mL, and the capacity of a
   Thermos flask is 1 L. Akeem said the ratio 270:1 compares
   the capacity of the glass with the capacity of the Thermos. Is
   he correct? Explain.

golden raisins
$0.66/100 g

dark raisins
$0.55/100 g

4. Raisins in a bulk-food store are priced as shown.
   a) A recipe calls for 500 g of raisins. How much money will
      you save if you buy the cheaper raisins? Explain.
   b) Raj bought $3.63 worth of one kind of raisins.
      What was the mass in grams?
   c) Is there more than one answer to part b)? Explain.

5. Jake downloaded three files, all at the same rate. The 1600 KB
   file downloaded in 14 s. The other two files downloaded in 21 s
   and in 10.5 s. About how large are the other two files? Explain.

6. A school district report says its student-to-teacher ratio is
   21:1. The district has 50 teachers and 1280 pupils. Is the
   report accurate? Explain.

7. Without solving, say which is greater, the solution to
   $8:10 = 20:\blacksquare$ or the solution to $8:10 = \blacksquare:20$. Explain.

8. In Ellen's school, four boys play sports for every three girls who
   play sports. Can there be exactly 80 girls who play sports?

Birth Rates

This map shows the birth rate per 1000 people for Alberta, British Columbia, and the Northwest Territories in 2005. But does it tell you where the most babies were born?

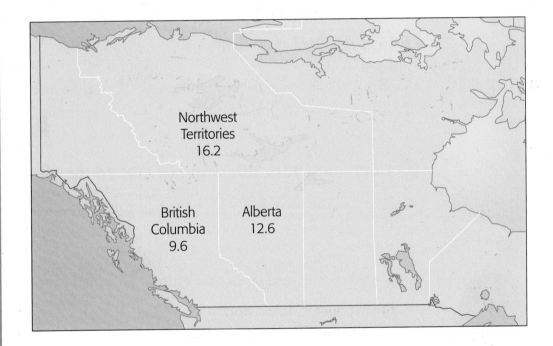

Northwest Territories
16.2

British Columbia
9.6

Alberta
12.6

1. Where do you predict the most and least babies were born? Why?

2. Why do you need to know the populations of those regions to be sure?

3. Using the table, calculate the approximate number of births in each region.

Region	Approximate population in 2005
Alberta	3.3 million
B.C.	4.3 million
N.W.T.	43 thousand

4. Does the highest birth rate mean the most births? Explain.

3.6 Using Equivalent Ratios to Solve Problems

YOU WILL NEED
• a calculator

GOAL

Solve rate and ratio problems using proportions and ratio tables.

LEARN ABOUT *the Math*

Allison and Nikita sorted their CD collections. The three-term ratio of rap CDs to pop CDs to rock CDs is $4:6:8$. They have 63 pop CDs.

❓ How many rock CDs and rap CDs do they have?

A. Why can you solve $8:6 = \blacksquare:63$ to figure out the number of rock CDs?

B. Why can you replace the ratio $8:6$ with the ratio $8 \times 63:6 \times 63$ and replace the ratio $\blacksquare:63$ with the ratio $6 \times \blacksquare:6 \times 63$?

C. Why can you write the proportion in part A as $8 \times 63:6 \times 63 = 6 \times \blacksquare:6 \times 63$?

D. The second terms of the ratios in part C are equal. What does that tell you about the first terms? Explain how you know.

E. Why can you use the equation $8 \times 63 = 6 \times$ ▨ to solve for the number of rock CDs?

F. What proportion can you use to solve for the number of rap CDs?

G. What equation can you use to solve for the number of rap CDs?

H. Use the equations in parts E and G to calculate the number of rock CDs and rap CDs they have.

Reflecting

I. Why should the number of rap CDs be half the number of rock CDs?

J. Why might you call the method you used to solve the proportions "cross-multiplying"? Why does it work?

WORK WITH *the Math*

Example 1	Solving part-to-part ratio problems

To make green paint, the paint store mixes yellow and blue paint in the ratio of $2:3$. If they used 15 L of yellow paint, how much blue paint did they use?

Aaron's Solution

$\dfrac{2}{3} = \dfrac{15}{▨}$

To determine the amount of blue paint, I set up a proportion.

$\dfrac{2 \times ▨}{3 \times ▨} = \dfrac{15 \times 3}{▨ \times 3}$

I can multiply each side of the equation by 1 without changing the equation. To get a common denominator, I multiplied the right side by $\dfrac{3}{3}$ and the left side by $\dfrac{▨}{▨}$. $\dfrac{1}{1} = \dfrac{3}{3} = \dfrac{▨}{▨}$

$2 \times ▨ = 15 \times 3$

I knew the numerators were equal since two fractions with the same denominator are only equal if their numerators are equal.

$▨ = \dfrac{15 \times 3}{2}$

I solved by dividing 3×15 by 2.

$= \dfrac{45}{2}$, or 22.5

They used 22.5 L of blue paint.

A Checking

1. A girl who measures 50 cm in length at birth will probably grow to an adult height of 165 cm. Based on this, what will be the likely adult height of a girl whose length at birth is 48 cm?

B Practising

2. For every 1.5 m of an iceberg that is above the water, 12.0 m of the iceberg is below the water. Suppose 9 m of an iceberg is above the water. Is the iceberg 72 m in length from top to bottom? Explain.

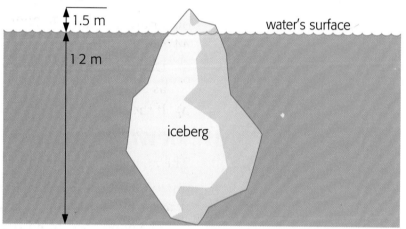

3. A water tank holds 80 L. It is leaking at a rate of 1.5 L/min. How long will it take before these amounts leak out?
   a) 5 L   b) 20 L   c) 35 L

4. About 22 out of 99 adult Canadians have difficulty reading. There are about 900 000 adults in Manitoba. How many adults in Manitoba might have difficulty reading?

5. A 13-year-old's heart might beat about 84 times per minute. About how long would it take her heart to beat 10 000 times?

6. The ratio of the running speed of cats to domestic pigs to chickens is 30:11:9. Approximately how many metres could a pig and a chicken run in the time a cat takes to run 1 km? 1 km = 1000 m.

7. On a 1035 km trip from Calgary, to Abbotsford, B.C., Dave's dad drove at 85 km/h. On the trip back, there were construction problems and his speed was 75 km/h. What was his average speed for the whole trip?

8. Digital televisions often have a width-to-height ratio of $16:9$. The width of a TV screen is 104.0 cm. What is its height?

9. In 2005, 4 in 10 Canadian teens aged 12 to 17 were exposed to second-hand smoke. About how many students in your school would have been exposed to second-hand smoke in 2005?

10. In 2007, the amount of ozone over Antarctica dropped 30.5 million tonnes. In 2006, the amount of ozone dropped 44.1 million tonnes.
  a) Describe the drop in the amount of ozone for the two years as a ratio.
  b) If the drop in 2008 could be described by an equivalent ratio, what would the drop in tonnes be?

11. The population density of an area tells how many people there are for each square kilometre. For example, the population density of Canada is $3.2/km^2$.
  a) The population of Edson, Alberta, is 8098. What would its area be, based on the Canadian population density?
  b) The actual area of Edson is $29.54 \ km^2$. Is Edson more crowded or less crowded than Canada in general? Explain.
  c) The population density of South Korea is $460/km^2$. There are about 34 million people in Canada. How many people would live in Canada if it were as crowded as South Korea?

12. On average, a certain baseball player has 212 hits in 1000 times at bat. Describe three different strategies you can use to determine how many hits he is likely to get in 400 times at bat.

13. Create and solve a problem that uses $\frac{2}{3}$ as a ratio and as a rate.

Reading Strategy

Finding Important Information

Use a KSO chart to help you solve the problem.
What do you **K**now?
What do you want to **S**olve?
What **O**ther information do you need?

Chapter **Self-Test**

blue	3	24	27	54	51
yellow	4				
red	8				

	A	B	C	D	E
1	25	Tom	3	Theo	14
2	16	Billie	12	Aaron	14
3	7	Evelyn	19	Charlotte	13
4					

1. **a)** Write two ratios equivalent to $5:9$, using only odd numbers.

   b) Write two ratios equivalent to $5:9$, each with one term of 90.

2. Complete the ratio table in the margin.

3. Calculate the missing term in each proportion.

   a) $2:11 = \blacksquare:55$

   b) $\dfrac{6}{\blacksquare} = \dfrac{10}{15}$

   c) $\dfrac{3}{4} = \dfrac{21}{\blacksquare}$

   d) $4.2:6.3 = \blacksquare:31.5$

4. A spreadsheet has cells that hold either numbers or words. There are three cells with numbers for every two cells with words. There are 250 cells in the spreadsheet. How many cells have numbers?

5. Nicole earned $78 in 9 h. How much would she earn in 12 h?

6. The ratio of cats to dogs at an animal shelter is $5:2$. Currently, 63 cats and dogs are up for adoption. How many cats are up for adoption?

7. In Canadian universities, 6 out of every 10 graduates from a first degree are women. If about 160 000 students graduated last year, about how many were women?

8. Jason's mom drove 70 km to the city at 80 km/h. Then she drove back home at 90 km/h. What was the difference in time between the trips?

9. Three granola bars cost $2.67. Use three strategies to figure out the cost of 10 bars.

What Do You Think Now?

Revisit What Do You Think? on page 105. Have your answers and explanations changed?

Chapter **Review**

Frequently Asked Questions

Q: How can you solve a rate problem using an equivalent rate?

A: You can set up a proportion to figure out an appropriate equivalent rate. For example: You travel 650 km in 8 h. How far would you travel in 3 h?

$$\frac{650}{8} = \frac{\blacksquare}{3}$$

$$\frac{650 \times 3}{8 \times 3} = \frac{\blacksquare \times 8}{3 \times 8} \qquad \text{write the two rates as equivalents with a common denominator}$$

$$650 \times 3 = \blacksquare \times 8 \qquad \text{the numerators are equal}$$

$$1950 = \blacksquare \times 8$$

$$1950 \div 8 = \blacksquare$$

$$243.75 = \blacksquare$$

You would travel 244 km in 3 h.

Q: How can you solve a ratio problem using a fraction?

A: You can set up an equation with two equivalent fractions. For example, to solve $5 : 6 = 12 : \blacksquare$

$$\frac{5}{6} = \frac{12}{\blacksquare} \qquad \text{write the ratios as fractions}$$

$$\frac{5 \times \blacksquare}{6 \times \blacksquare} = \frac{12 \times 6}{\blacksquare \times 6} \qquad \text{write the fractions as equivalents with the same denominator}$$

$$5 \times \blacksquare = 6 \times 12 \qquad \text{the numerators are equal}$$

$$5 \times \blacksquare = 72$$

$$\blacksquare = 72 \div 5$$

$$= 14.4$$

Practice

Lesson 3.1

1. Write two equivalent ratios for each of the following.

   a) $9:20$ **b)** $\dfrac{4}{5}$ **c)** 21 to 3   **d)** $18:1.5$

2. Solve each proportion.

   a) $5:9 = 40:\blacksquare$ **b)** $30:80 = 51:\blacksquare$ **c)** $\blacksquare:18 = 60:270$

3. Draw a rectangle. Draw another rectangle twice as long and twice as wide. Describe each ratio.

   a) ratio of the smaller diagonal to the larger one

   b) ratio of the smaller area to the larger one

Lesson 3.2

4. Complete the ratio table in the margin.

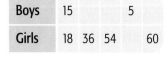

Boys	15			5	
Girls	18	36	54		60

5. Solve the proportion $6:15 = 33:\blacksquare$ in more than one way using ratio tables. Show what you did.

Lesson 3.3

6. A stick is cut into four pieces of different lengths. The ratio of the length of one piece to the next shorter one is always 2 to 1. What is each piece as a fraction of the whole stick?

Lesson 3.4

7. Rewrite each rate as a number of items for $1.

   a) 4 cookies for 50¢   **b)** 3 kg of sugar for $1.20

8. Which of the games on the left is the best deal? Explain.

3 tosses for 50¢

5 tosses for $1.00

9 tosses for $1.60

Lesson 3.5

9. Sally asks, "If $20 + 5 = 25$ and $30 + 5 = 35$, then why does $20:30$ not equal $25:35$?" How would you answer Sally's question?

Lesson 3.6

10. In a 750 g bag of salad mix, the ratio of lettuce to cabbage to carrots is $8:4:3$ by mass. What is the mass of each ingredient?

11. A car odometer reads 14 985 km at the start of a trip, and the car has a full tank of gas. At the end of the trip, the odometer reads 15 235 km, and 30 L of gas is needed to refill the tank. How much gas does the car use per 100 km?

Chapter **Task**

"If the world ..."

Suppose you were writing a book in which each two-page spread began, "If the whole school (or town or city) were just like our classroom, then ..."

? What would your pages say?

A. Select three items from the following list that apply to your classmates.
- the ratio of right-handed students to the total number of students
- the ratio of boys to the total number of students
- the ratio of students who climb stairs to get to their bedroom to those who do not
- the total number of minutes of TV that your classmates watched last night
- the approximate number of litres of water that your classmates drank yesterday

B. Find out how many students are in your school and how many people live in your community.

C. Use the information from parts A and B to create equivalent ratios for your three choices from part A for your whole school and your community.

D. Come up with two of your own ideas for ratios and rates that apply in your class and figure out how to use them to find out about your whole school or community.

E. Suppose your page said, "If the world were a village of 1000 people, there would be...." What would your page say for your five ratio choices?

If the World Were a Village

A Book about the World's People

Cumulative **Review**

1. Which of the following is a perfect square?
   A. 8 **B.** 9 **C.** 10 **D.** 11

2. Which digit is a possible last digit of a perfect square?
   A. 2 **B.** 3 **C.** 5 **D.** 7

3. Which factor of 324 is its square root?
   A. 4 **B.** 9 **C.** 18 **D.** 36

4. To one decimal place, the square root of a number shown on a calculator is 12.3. Which statement is true?
   A. The number is between 150 and 155.
   B. The number is between 155 and 160.
   C. The number is less than 150.
   D. The number is greater than 160.

5. Erik is flying a kite. Calvin is directly under the kite. The boys are 60 m apart, and the kite string is 100 m long. How high is the kite above Calvin?
   A. 40 m **B.** 80 m **C.** 160 m **D.** 6400 m

6. An airplane travels between two cities that are 1500 km apart. It climbs steadily from takeoff to cruise at 10 000 m during the first 200 km of the trip. It descends steadily from 10 000 m for 300 km to land. About what distance do climbing and descending add to the flight?
   A. 0.4 km **B.** 4 km **C.** 10 km **D.** 20 km

7. Ron's cookie recipe requires $2\frac{3}{4}$ cups of flour and makes 20 cookies. He wants to make 75 cookies. Which expression describes the amount of flour he should use?
   A. $\dfrac{75}{20}$ **B.** $\dfrac{75}{20} + 2\frac{3}{4}$ **C.** $2\frac{3}{4} + \dfrac{75}{20}$ **D.** $2\frac{3}{4} \times \dfrac{75}{20}$

8. Which expression is equivalent to $3\frac{3}{8}$?
   A. $\dfrac{17}{8}$ **B.** $\dfrac{24}{8}$ **C.** $\dfrac{27}{8}$ **D.** none of these

9. Which expression has the same value as $\frac{1}{2} \times \frac{2}{3}$?
   A. $\dfrac{5}{6} \times \dfrac{2}{5}$ **B.** $\dfrac{3}{4} \times \dfrac{8}{9}$ **C.** $\dfrac{3}{8} \times \dfrac{4}{9}$ **D.** $\dfrac{3}{5} \times \dfrac{5}{6}$

10. Which expression has the greatest value?

A. $\dfrac{5}{6} \div \dfrac{2}{5}$ **B.** $\dfrac{5}{6} \times \dfrac{2}{5}$ **C.** $\dfrac{2}{5} \div \dfrac{5}{6}$ **D.** $\dfrac{6}{5} \times \dfrac{2}{5}$

11. Calculate $6\dfrac{1}{4} \div 2\dfrac{1}{2}$.

A. $2\dfrac{1}{4}$ **B.** $2\dfrac{1}{2}$ **C.** $3\dfrac{1}{8}$ **D.** $3\dfrac{1}{2}$

12. Calculate $\dfrac{3}{4} - \dfrac{5}{8} \times \dfrac{4}{5} + \dfrac{3}{5}$.

A. $\dfrac{7}{10}$ **B.** $\dfrac{1}{8}$ **C.** $\dfrac{5}{7}$ **D.** $\dfrac{17}{20}$

13. Which represents a ratio that is NOT equivalent to the others?

A. 4 to 5 **B.** 3 to 4 **C.** 8:10 **D.** 2 to 2.5

14. A candy mixture contains 55 g of chocolate-coated raisins and 45 g of chocolate-coated peanuts. What fraction of the mixture is peanuts?

A. $\dfrac{9}{11}$ **B.** $\dfrac{11}{9}$ **C.** $\dfrac{9}{20}$ **D.** $\dfrac{11}{20}$

15. Determine the missing terms in the proportion.

$6 : \underline{\quad} : 15 = \underline{\quad} : 20 : 10$

A. 1 and 25 **C.** 10 and 12
B. 2.5 and 0.5 **D.** 30 and 4

16. Which vehicle in the Vehicle Comparison chart has the best fuel efficiency?

17. Concrete is made by mixing cement, sand, and gravel in the ratio $1:3:4$ by mass. Michael needs to make 160 kg of concrete. How many kg of gravel does he need?

A. 156 **B.** 80 **C.** 40 **D.** 20

18. Rena walked for $2\dfrac{3}{4}$ h and travelled $7\dfrac{1}{2}$ km. Which expression should you use to determine her speed?

A. $2\dfrac{3}{4} \times 7\dfrac{1}{2}$ **B.** $2\dfrac{3}{4} \div 7\dfrac{1}{2}$ **C.** $7\dfrac{1}{2} \times 2\dfrac{3}{4}$ **D.** $7\dfrac{1}{2} \div 2\dfrac{3}{4}$

19. Marie rides her bike at 10 km/h along the legs of the right-triangle path shown. Imelda walks along the hypotenuse at 2 km/h. How much of a head start should Imelda get so that the two girls arrive at the destination at the same time?

A. 72.5 min **B.** 24.0 min **C.** 21.6 min **D.** 12 min

Vehicle Comparison

Vehicle	Gas used (L)	Distance travelled (km)
A	65	650
B	60	700
C	55	600
D	50	550

1 km

0.6 km

Percents

You will be able to

- interpret, represent, and use percents greater than 100%

- interpret, represent, and use percents between 0% and 1%

- relate percents to fractions and decimals

- solve problems involving percents

◀ **What percent of Canadians do you think use the Internet regularly?**

YOU WILL NEED
- a coin
- grid paper

Hitchhiker's Thumb

About 25% of people have hitchhiker's thumb.

Hitchhiker's thumb   Not hitchhiker's thumb

❓ Do more students in your class have hitchhiker's thumb than would be expected?

A. What fraction does 25% represent? Draw a picture to show why.

B. In your class, how many people would you expect to have hitchhiker's thumb?

C. What multiplication could you do to answer part B?

D. What division could you do to answer part B?

E. About how many students in a school of 600 would you expect to have hitchhiker's thumb? Explain your thinking.

F. Find out how many students in your class have hitchhiker's thumb. Compare that number with your answer to part B. Do more students have hitchhiker's thumb than expected or not?

What Do You Think?

Decide whether you agree or disagree with each statement. Be ready to explain your decision.

1. A percent of a number is always less than that number.

2. Every number is some percent of every other number.

4 and 16
4 is 25% of 16

9 and 20
9 is 45% of 20

3. 0.5% means one half.

4. To get 15% of a number, you can take 30% of the number's double.

4.1

Percents Greater than 100%

YOU WILL NEED

- 10 × 10 Grids
- a calculator

> **GOAL**
>
> Represent and interpret percents greater than 100%.

LEARN ABOUT the Math

Ivan is 160 cm tall. Taira is 152 cm tall.
Both Ivan and Taira are 13 years old.

An adult's height is normally 107% of his or her height at age 13.

❓ How tall are Ivan and Taira likely to be as adults?

A. What percent of this grid is shaded?

100%

B. Shade the grids to show 107%. Circle the part that represents the 100%.

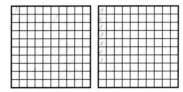

C. Suppose the grid in part A represents Ivan's present height. How many centimetres does each small square in the grid represent?

D. Use your answer to part C to figure out what 107% of Ivan's present height is, to the nearest tenth of a centimetre.

E. Repeat parts C and D for Taira.

F. How tall do you predict that Ivan and Taira will be?

Reflecting

G. Why did you use more than one 10-by-10 grid to represent 107%?

H. Why did you have to decide that the first grid represented 100% to interpret the percent you showed in part B?

WORK WITH *the Math*

| Example 1 | Using a grid to solve a percent problem |

Renée's CD collection is 125% the size of Angèle's collection.
Renée has 75 CDs. How many CDs does Angèle have?

Renée's Solution

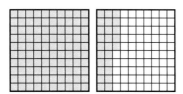

125% = 100% + 25%

I drew a 10-by-10 grid to represent Angèle's collection. I thought of that amount as 100%.

To show 125% for my collection, I needed to use part of a second grid.

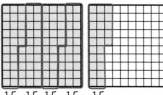

15 15 15 15   15

125% = 5 groups of 25%
75 ÷ 5 = 15
Each of the 5 groups represents 15 CDs.

4 x 15 = 60

If 125% is 75, then 100% is 60.
Angèle has 60 CDs.

There were 125 squares to represent the 75 CDs in my collection.

I divided the 125 into 5 equal sections. I did that because I wanted to create sections I could add to make up 100%.

Each section represented 125% ÷ 5 and also represented 75 ÷ 5 CDs.

Angèle's collection is the full first grid. It has 4 sections of 15.

Example 2 | Using reasoning to solve a percent problem

A bacon double cheeseburger, king-size fries, and a medium milkshake provide a Grade 8 student with 390% of the recommended daily grams of fat allowance for a person that age.

How many grams of fat are in the meal if the recommended daily allowance is 20 g?

Lam's Solution

100% of 20 g = 20 g

400% of 20 g = 4 x 20 g = 80 g

10% of 20 g = (20 ÷ 10) g = 2 g
390% of 20 g = (80 – 2) g = 78 g

The meal has 78 g of fat.

100% of something is the whole thing.

390% = 400% – 10%
400% is four times 100%.

To get 10%, I divided 100% by 10.
I calculated 390% by subtracting 10% from 400%.

A Checking

1. What percent does the diagram show? One full grid represents 100%.

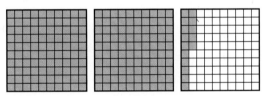

2. Represent 167% using 10-by-10 grids. Use one full grid to represent 100%.

3. A girl usually grows to be 125% of the height she was at age 9. If a girl is 132 cm tall at age 9, what will her adult height likely be?

B Practising

4. Represent each percent using 10-by-10 grids. Use one full grid to represent 100%.

   a) 135%   b) 250%   c) 310%

5. Paul says that the grids show 150%. Rebecca says that they show 75%. How could each be correct?

6. Solve.

   a) 120% of 40 = ▨   c) 110% of 48 = ▨
   b) 130% of 200 = ▨   d) 220% of ▨ = 99

7. A fast food meal contains 70 g of fat. What percent of the recommended daily allowance of 20 g is this?

70 g	Fast food meal

20 g	Recommended daily allowance

8. Yanir has $50 in pennies. Use grids to model and calculate each amount.

   a) 90% of $50   b) 310% of $50

9. A faucet is dripping at a rate of 1 L/h. Why would you not use a percent to describe the rate?

10. The population of a town is 600. Use grids to model and calculate each percent of that population.

a) 185%
185 × 600 = 1100

b) 225%
1350

11. Last year, 800 students were enrolled at Susan's school. This is 250% of the enrolment in the school 15 years ago.

a) Use a diagram to help you calculate the enrolment 15 years ago.

b) What percent of the current enrolment is your answer to part a)?

12. **a)** What percent of the side length of a square is its perimeter?

b) What percent of the shortest side length of this triangle is its perimeter?

c) Estimate. What percent of the side length of the square is its diagonal?

d) Create and solve your own question involving measurements where the answer is a percent greater than 100%.

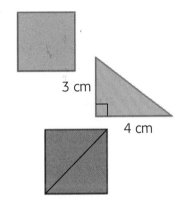

3 cm

4 cm

13. A download speed using high-speed Internet was 1316 KB/s. An upload speed on the same network was 327 KB/s.

a) Estimate the percent of the upload speed that represents the download speed.

b) Estimate the percent of the download speed that represents the upload speed.

14. One number is 500% of another.

a) What could the numbers be?

b) What percent is the lower number of the higher one? How do you know?

4.2

Fractional Percents

YOU WILL NEED
- 10 × 10 Grids
- Thousandths Grids
- a calculator

GOAL

Represent and interpret percents between 0% and 1%.

LEARN ABOUT the Math

You can taste sweetness if 0.5% of a sugar-and-water mixture is sugar.

? **What is the least amount of sugar that must be in a 250 g sugar-and-water mixture for it to taste sweet?**

A. Why should 0.5% be less than 1%?

B. How could you represent 0.5% on this grid?

C. Suppose the full grid represents 250 g of a sugar-and-water mixture. What does your answer to part B represent?

D. What is the least amount of sugar, in grams, that is in the mixture if it tastes sweet? Explain.

You can read fractional percents like 0.5%, for example, as five-tenths of a percent, or 0.23% as twenty-three hundredths of a percent.

Reflecting

E. How would you represent 2.5% using the grid you used in part B? How do you know?

F. Why is 0.5% not equal to $\frac{1}{2}$?

WORK WITH *the Math*

Example 1	Representing percents less than 1%

How could you use a thousandths grid to show 0.6% and 4.6%?

John's Solution

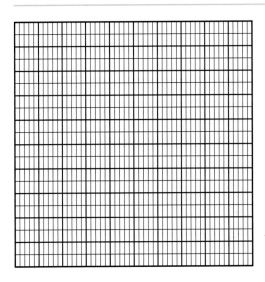

1% is one hundredth, so 0.1% is one tenth of one hundredth.

$$0.1\% = \frac{1}{10} \times \frac{1}{100} = \frac{1}{1000}$$

There are 1000 thousandths in the full grid. Each of the small rectangles is $\frac{1}{1000}$, or 0.1%.

0.6% = 6 x 0.1%

4.6% = 4% + 0.6%

Example 2 | Solving a problem involving percents

About 0.9% of the Canadian population is Sikh. If Canada's population is about 34 million, about how many people are Sikh?

Holly's Solution

1% of 34 000 000 = 340 000

0.1% of 34 000 000 = 340 000 ÷ 10
$\qquad$ = 34 000

0.9% of 34 000 000 = 340 000 − 34 000 = 306 000

There are about 306 000 Sikhs in Canada.

I know that 0.1% is $\frac{1}{10}$ of 1%.

To calculate 0.9%, I calculated 1% and then subtracted 0.1%.

Ivan's Solution

$0.9\% = \dfrac{0.9}{100}$

Multiply numerator and denominator by 10 to get an equivalent fraction.

$\dfrac{0.9}{100} = \dfrac{9}{1000}$
$\qquad = 0.009$

0.009 × 34 000 000 = 306 000

There are about 306 000 Sikhs in Canada.

I wrote 0.9% as a decimal and then wrote it as a fraction.

I knew that one way to calculate percents is to multiply by the equivalent decimal.

A Checking

1. Use a thousandths grid to represent each of these percents.
   a) 0.75% b) 1.4% c) 4.9%

2. How many grams of sugar would you need to make a 1 kg sugar-and-water mixture that is 0.5% sugar?

B Practising

3. What percent does each of these grids represent? The full grid is 100%.

a)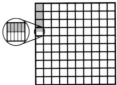

b)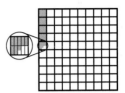

handwritten left margin:
1000
1mm = 1 m

3000
3 mm = 3 m

3.2 mm = ? m

4. How can knowing that 5% of a mass is 25 g help you to calculate each of these?

a) 1%   b) 0.1%   c) 2.5%

5. a) Explain how you might estimate the value of 0.3% of 630.
   b) Represent 0.3% on a 10-by-10 grid.
   c) Calculate 0.3% of 630. Explain your strategy.

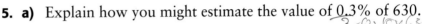

handwritten right margin:
2 0.15×630
= 94.5
÷ 2
18940

6. You can taste saltiness if 0.25% of a mixture is salt. At least how many grams of salt would there have to be in 1 kg of salt water to taste the salt?

handwritten: 0.0025 × 1000 = 2.5

7. Air contains 0.93% argon and 0.03% carbon dioxide. In 1 L of air, how much of each would there be?

a) argon   b) carbon dioxide

8. About 0.8% of Canada's exports go to Germany. For each million dollars in exports, how many dollars' worth goes to Germany?

9. a) How do you know that 1 mm is 0.1% of 1 m?
   b) What percent of 1 m is 3.2 mm?

handwritten: 3.2 / 1000 =

handwritten: —% of 1 m is 3.2

10. Which of these ways of calculating 2.5% of a number is correct? Explain.
    a) Calculate 5% and then divide by 2
    b) Calculate 25% and then divide by 10
    c) Divide by 4 and then divide by 10
    d) Divide by 4 and then divide by 100

11. When is 0.1% of a number a whole number?

12. Is 5.1% of a number always very close to 5% of the number? Explain using examples.

4.3

Relating Percents to Decimals and Fractions

YOU WILL NEED

- 10 × 10 Grids
- Thousandths Grids

GOAL

Express a percent as an equivalent decimal or fraction, or a decimal or fraction as an equivalent percent.

LEARN ABOUT the Math

One pair of skis costs 150% of the cost of another pair of skis.

❓ What fraction of the price of the cheaper skis is the price of the more expensive skis?

A. A full 10-by-10 grid represents 100%. Use a decimal and a mixed number or improper fraction to write the number of grids you would shade to represent 150%.

B. Why does the ratio 150:100 compare the costs of the two pairs of skis?

C. What fraction and decimal of the price of the cheaper skis is the price of the more expensive skis?

Reflecting

D. How could you have predicted that the fraction in part C would be a mixed number or improper fraction and that the decimal would be greater than 1?

E. How are the ratio in part B and the fraction and decimal in part C related?

WORK WITH the Math

| **Example 1** | Relating fractions, decimals, and percents |

Use a fraction, a decimal, and a percent to describe the shaded area.
Use one full 10-by-10 grid to represent 100%.

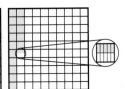

Ivan's Solution

Percent:
100% + 100% + 15% + 0.5% = 215.5%

Each full grid is 100%.

Decimal:
1 + 1 + 0.15 + 0.005 = 2.155

Each full grid is 1.

Fraction:
$$2 + \frac{15}{100} + \frac{5}{1000} = \frac{2000}{1000} + \frac{150}{1000} + \frac{5}{1000}$$
$$= \frac{2155}{1000}$$

There are 2 full grids and another $\frac{15}{100} + \frac{5}{1000}$ of a third grid.

Example 2 | Relating a circle graph to percents

This circle graph shows what fraction of the students in a school is in each grade. What percent of the students are in Grade 8?

Fraction of students in each grade

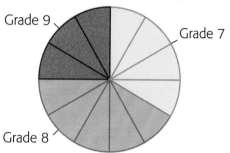

Taira's Solution

$\frac{5}{12}$ are in Grade 8.

Each section of the graph represents $\frac{1}{12}$.

$\frac{5}{12} = 5 \div 12$

$5 \div 12 \doteq 0.417$

$0.417 = 41.7\%$

The first two decimal places tell the whole-number percent. The third decimal place is tenths of a percent.

Example 3 | Writing a fraction as a percent

A group sponsoring a contest says that 1 out of 16 tickets wins a prize. What percent of the tickets win a prize?

Angèle's Solution

$1 \div 16 = \frac{1}{4}$ of $\frac{1}{4}$

$\frac{1}{4} = 0.25$

$0.25 \div 4 = 0.0625$

$0.0625 = 6.25\%$

I could divide 1 by 16 to write $\frac{1}{16}$ as a decimal.
I knew $\frac{1}{16}$ is $\frac{1}{4}$ of $\frac{1}{4}$.

First I thought of the decimal for $\frac{1}{4}$. Then I took $\frac{1}{4}$ of that by dividing by 4.

Then I wrote the percent by multiplying the decimal by 100.

A Checking

1. Shade in each fraction of a grid. Use one full grid to represent 1. Write the percent for the fraction.

   a) $\frac{3}{4}$

   b) $1\frac{1}{5}$

2. 1.1% of Canadians are Jewish.
   a) Write the percent as a decimal.
   b) Write it as a fraction.

B Practising

3. Use a fraction, a decimal, and a percent to describe each shaded area. A single full grid represents 100%.

   a)

   b)

   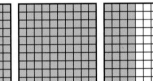

4. Complete the chart.

	Percent	Equivalent fraction	Equivalent decimal
a)	3.2%	3 1/5	0.032
b)	1, 25%	$\frac{5}{4}$	0.0125
c)	6.4 %	6.4(10) 64/1000 (100 10)	0.064

5. The population of Abbotsford, BC, is 136% of the population of Kamloops, BC. Write the percent as a fraction and as a decimal.   1.36 $\frac{136}{100}$

6. Joel's class did a traffic survey and drew a circle graph to show what kinds of vehicles passed the school on a particular morning.
   a) What percent of the traffic was trucks?
   b) What percent was foreign cars?
   c) What percent was North American cars?

Kinds of Vehicles That Passed the School

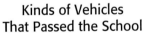

trucks

North American cars

foreign cars

7. You are downloading a file. The progress bar looks like this.
  a) Estimate the percent of the file that has been downloaded.
  b) Test your estimate by measuring.
  c) Use part b) to write the percent as a decimal and as a fraction.

8. The average Canadian spends about 0.09 of a 24 h day watching television.
  a) What fraction of a day is this?
  b) What percent of a day is this?
  c) About how many minutes is this?

9. The percent of people with blood type A is 410% of the fraction of people with blood type B. Write this percent as a fraction and a decimal.

10. The fraction of people with blood type O is $\frac{9}{2}$ the number of people with blood type B. Write this as a percent.

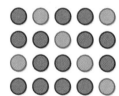

11. a) Write the number of red counters as a fraction and as a percent of the number of blue counters.
  b) Remove 5 counters so that there are 400% as many red counters as blue ones. How many of each colour of counter did you remove?

12. Franca knew that 20 was 2.5% of a number. Explain why you can use each of these methods to calculate the number.
  a) Divide 20 by 2.5 and then multiply by 100.
  b) Divide 20 by 0.025.

13. Use what you know about fractions to calculate 50% of 200%.

14. Why is it usually easier to express a decimal as a percent than a fraction as a percent? Why is it not always easier?

4.4

Solving Problems Using a Proportion

YOU WILL NEED
- a ruler (optional)
- a calculator

GOAL

Solve a percent problem using an equivalent ratio.

LEARN ABOUT the Math

Lam has a mass of 62.0 kg. After a season of lacrosse, his body fat was reduced from 18% of his total mass to 12.5% of his total mass, but his total mass did not change.

❓ How much body fat did Lam lose?

Example 1 | Using separate calculations

Calculate the mass of fat loss.

Lam's Solution

18% – 12.5% is about 5%   First I estimated.
  10% of 62 = 6.2
    5% of 62 = 6.2 ÷ 2   The answer is about 5% of 62.
         = 3.1   That is half of 10%.
I lost about 3.1 kg of fat.

18% – 12.5% = 5.5%   I calculated the percent change.

$$5.5\% = \frac{5.5}{100}$$

$$= \frac{55}{1000}$$

$$\frac{55}{1000} = \frac{\blacksquare}{62}$$ Then I set up a proportion to solve the problem.

$$\frac{55 \times 62}{1000 \times 62} = \frac{\blacksquare \times 1000}{62 \times 1000}$$

$$\frac{3410}{62\,000} = \frac{1000 \times \blacksquare}{62\,000}$$

$$3410 = 1000 \times \blacksquare$$

$$3410 \div 1000 = \blacksquare$$

$$3.410 = \blacksquare$$

I lost 3.4 kg of fat.   I know my answer is reasonable, because it is close to my estimate.

Reflecting

A. How did Lam choose the values for the proportion?

B. Why did solving the proportion solve Lam's problem?

WORK WITH *the Math*

Example 2 | Using a visual model to set up a proportion

7.5% of the boys in Joe's school play lacrosse. This is 30 boys.
How many boys are in the school?

Solution

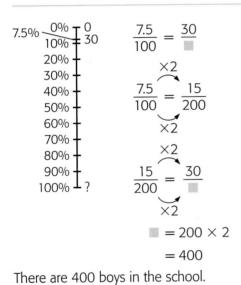

$$\frac{7.5}{100} = \frac{30}{\blacksquare}$$

$$\frac{7.5}{100} \overset{\times 2}{=} \frac{15}{200}$$
$$\times 2$$

$$\frac{15}{200} \overset{\times 2}{=} \frac{30}{\blacksquare}$$
$$\times 2$$

$$\blacksquare = 200 \times 2$$
$$= 400$$

There are 400 boys in the school.

Think of the problem as figuring out the answer to the question: "30 is 7.5% of what number?"

That means you know what 7.5% is, but you want to know what 100% is.

Draw a diagram to visualize the proportion. Place 7.5% close to, but above, 10%. You can see that 100% should be a lot more than 30. Use equivalent fractions to make it easier to solve the proportion.

Since the numerator was multiplied by 2, the same must be true for the denominator.

A Checking

1. How does this diagram show that 425% of 85 is more than 4 × 85?

2. The body mass for muscle should be about 310% of the mass for fat. Luc's fat mass is 10.4 kg. What should his muscle mass be?

B Practising

3. Solve.

a) ▦ = 225% of 48

b) ▦ = 37.5% of 480

c) 78 = 325% of ▦

d) 84.7 = 770% of ▦

4. Explain how to use the diagram to estimate the solution to 62.5% of ▦ = 20

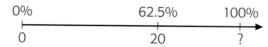

5. Draw a diagram to show each.
   a) 20% of 115 is 23.
   b) If 40 is 80% of ▦, then ▦ must be 50.

6. A popular music download site reported these statistics: In April 2007, there were 5.6 million downloads a day. This was 0.2% of all downloads from that site since it started. How many downloads were there from the site from when it started until April 2007?

7. a) The ratio 5:1000 describes the scale on a map. Write the ratio as a fraction.
   b) What percent describes the distance on the map compared to the actual distance?
   c) What percent describes the actual distance compared to the map distance?

8. The population of Alberta in 2006 was 110.6% of its population in 2001. The population in 2001 was 2 974 807. Estimate the population in 2006.

9. Use the information in the graph to estimate the attendance at the Calgary Stampede in 2006.

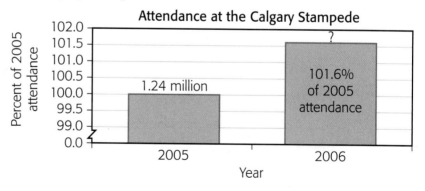

10. How does knowing how to create equivalent ratios help you to calculate the percent of a number?

4.5

Solving Percent Problems Using Decimals

YOU WILL NEED
- a calculator

GOAL

Use the decimal representation of a percent to solve a problem.

LEARN ABOUT the Math

In Canada, more and more people are living in towns and cities. In January 2007, about 13.5% of Saskatchewan's population of 987 939 was Aboriginal. About 46.7% of the Aboriginal people were living in towns and cities.

987 939 × 0.467 = 461367.5 5

❓ About how many Aboriginal people in Saskatchewan live in towns and cities?

Example 1 | Using simpler decimals to estimate

The question said "about," so I decided to estimate.

Angèle's Solution

Saskatchewan's population

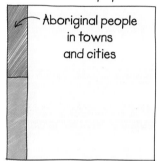

Aboriginal people in towns and cities

I drew a diagram to help me figure out what to do.

I realized I had to calculate 46.7% of 13.5% of 987 939.

13.5% is close to 10%
46.7% is close to 50%

I estimated 13.5% as 10%.
Since I rounded 13.5% down, I rounded 46.7% up to 50% to estimate.

10% of 50% = 0.1 x 0.5
         = 0.05
987 939 is close to 1 000 000
0.05 x 1 000 000 = 50 000
About 50 000 Aboriginal people in Saskatchewan live in towns and cities.

I needed 50% of 10%, so I multiplied equivalent decimals.
Then I multiplied by an estimate of the population. I used 1 million for that estimate.

Reflecting

A. Why could you not have just calculated 46.7% of 1 000 000 directly to solve the problem?

B. Angèle rewrote the percents as decimals to solve the problem. How else could you have solved the problem?

WORK WITH *the Math*

| Example 2 | Solving a problem using decimal division |

Online sales in Canada in 2006 were 139.8% of online sales in 2005. The value of the sales in 2006 was $49.98 billion. What was the value of the sales in 2005?

Solution

139.8% = 1.398

Write 139.8% as a decimal.

1.398 × 2005 sales = 2006 sales
1.398 × 2005 sales = $49.98 billion

Write the equation relating the sales for 2005 and 2006.

Divide both sides by 1.398.

2005 sales = $49.98 billion ÷ 1.398
          = $35.75 billion

Use a calculator to do the division.

Sales in 2005 were $35.75 billion.

A Checking

1. Rewrite these equations with decimals you could use to solve each, then solve them. *0.055*
   0.152
   a) 15.2% of 35 = ▨
   b) 124% of 18 = ▨ *1.24*
   c) 5.5% of ▨ = 40
   d) 160% of ▨ = 30 *1.6*

2. In November, the number of visitors to the school blog rose to 112% of the number in October. There were 500 visitors to the blog in October. How many visitors were there in November?

   | October: 500 visitors to the school blog |

   | November: 112% of the number of October visitors |

   1.12 × 500 = 560

B Practising

3. Solve each by using a decimal equivalent for the percent.
   a) 1.4% of 500 = ▨ *0.014*
   c) 560 = 350% of ▨
   b) 0.45% of 250 = ▨ *0.0045*
   d) 24 = 0.8% of ▨

4. What percent question is Ellen solving when she performs each computation? For example, a question for the calculation 40 ÷ 0.2 could be, "40 is 20% of a number. What is the number?"
   a) 0.45 × 36
   c) 0.004 × 180
   e) 36 ÷ 1.8
   b) 1.2 × 45 *1.2.0 × 45*
   d) 56 ÷ 0.07 *56 ÷ 7.00*
   f) 90 ÷ 0.005 *90 ÷ 0.5*

5. The cost of an item in Alberta is 105% of the listed price to include the GST. What is the cost of each of these items with tax included?

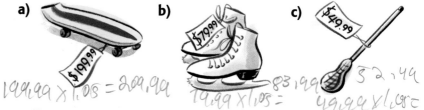

   a) $199.99 *199.99 × 1.05 = 209.99*
   b) $79.99 *79.99 × 1.05 = 83.99*
   c) $49.99 *52.44 49.99 × 1.05 =*

6. Jeff's parents bought new flooring for his room. There was a sale, so they only had to pay 80% of the regular cost. If they paid $400, what was the regular price? *400 ÷ 320 = 0.8 × 400 = 320*

7. The chart below shows the most popular computer screen resolutions in Canada in 2007.
   In a school where 400 students had computers, about how many would be using a screen resolution of 800 × 600?

Screen resolution	Percent of users
1024 × 768	54.31%
800 × 600	19.94% *93 7/2*
1280 × 1024	12.06%
1280 × 800	3.93%
1152 × 864	3.75%

8. Refer to the graph. In a school with 480 boys aged 11 to 15, how many boys drink the amount of milk they should?

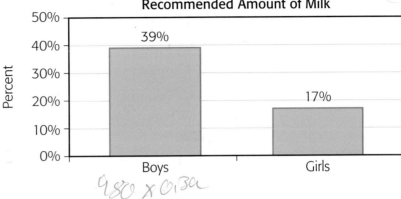

11- to 15-Year-Old Canadians Who Drink the Daily Recommended Amount of Milk

9. It is predicted that Aboriginal people will make up 32.5% of Saskatchewan's population in 2045. They made up 13.3% of the population in 1995. Why is the population increase not 32.5% − 13.3% = 19.2% of the 2045 population?

10. The population of China is divided into 56 different ethnic groups. The population of the Han group is 90.56% of the Chinese population. Among the 55 other groups, the Dai people has the least population, which is 1.12% of the population of those 55 other groups. If the Chinese population is 1.6 billion, what is the Dai population?

11. Manuel is saving for a new mountain bike that costs 212% of the amount currently in his savings bank. The bike costs $349. How much has he saved?

12. In a survey, 365 girls and 345 boys in Grade 8 were asked, "What is your favourite weekend activity?" If 7.4% of the girls and 10.1% of the boys chose watching TV and videos, how many more boys than girls chose this activity?

13. Describe a percent question you would solve using each of these calculations.
    a) 1.25×400 b) $400 \div 1.25$ c) 0.035×400

Frequently Asked Questions

Q: How can you represent percents greater than 100%?

A: You have to say what you mean by 100%. Then you can represent the percent greater than 100% based on that.

For example, you can represent 250% on grids.

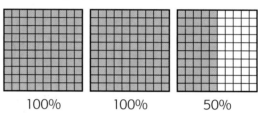

100%   100%   50%

You can also represent the percent as the decimal 2.5 (1 + 1 + 0.5) or the fraction $\frac{5}{2}$ or mixed number $2\frac{1}{2}$.

Q: How can you represent percents that involve parts of 1%?

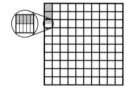

A: You can divide 1% into parts.
For example, you can represent 2.5% as 2% + 0.5%.
0.5% is half of 1%.
Then you can represent that on a grid.
You can also write 2.5% as a decimal or fraction.
2% = 0.02 and 0.5% = 0.005
2% + 0.5% = 0.02 + 0.005 = 0.025

$$2.5\% = \frac{2.5}{100} \overset{\times 2}{\underset{\times 2}{=}} \frac{5}{200} \overset{\div 5}{\underset{\div 5}{=}} \frac{1}{40}$$

Q: How can you solve a percent problem?

A: You can use a proportion or you can multiply or divide by a decimal.

For example, suppose you know that 30 is 150% of a number and you want to figure out that number.

You could set up the proportion $\dfrac{30}{\blacksquare} = \dfrac{150}{100}$. You notice
that $150 = 5 \times 30$, so $5 \times \blacksquare = 100$, and $\blacksquare = 20$.

Or, you can write 150% as 1.5. If $1.5 \times \blacksquare = 30$, then
multiply both sides by 2.

$$3 \times \blacksquare = 60$$
$$\blacksquare = 20$$

Practice

Lesson 4.1

1. Represent each percent. Use a 10-by-10 grid to represent 100%.
   a) 140%   b) 315%   c) 284%

Lesson 4.2

2. Represent each percent. Use a thousandths grid.
   a) 0.8%   b) 3.7%   c) 15.5%

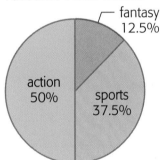

Favourite Video Games

fantasy 12.5%

action 50%

sports 37.5%

3. In a survey, 40 students were asked this question: What type
   of video game do you prefer? The circle graph shows their
   responses. Use a hundredths grid to calculate the number of
   students who preferred each type of game.

Lesson 4.3

4. Estimate the equivalent percent for each fraction. Explain your
   reasoning.
   a) $\dfrac{135}{95}$ b) $\dfrac{29}{26}$ c) $\dfrac{3}{640}$

Lesson 4.4

5. On a multiple-choice science test, Marcus answered 67.5% of
   the questions correctly. If there were 40 questions on the test,
   how many did he answer correctly?   27

Lesson 4.5

6. There are 15 girls in Daniel's school choir. 37.5% of the students
   in the choir are girls. How many students are in the choir?
   ⊆ girls

7. When water freezes, its volume increases by 10.1%.
   150 × 0.101 =
   a) If 150 L of water freezes, what is the increase in volume?
   b) Estimate the original volume of water if the increase in
       volume is 22 L.

4.6

Solve Problems by Changing Your Point of View

YOU WILL NEED
- a calculator

GOAL

Solve problems by looking at situations in different ways.

LEARN ABOUT the Math

Holly lives in British Columbia, where the PST is 7%. She wants to buy a new guitar. She finds the guitar she wants on sale for 25% off the regular price of $329.98.

❓ How can Holly calculate the cost of the guitar, including taxes?

Example 1	Solving a problem using related percents

What is the cost of the guitar, including taxes?

Holly's Solution

1. Understand the Problem

The cost has two parts.
Cost = discounted price + taxes

2. Make a Plan

First I will calculate the discounted price = original price − 25% discount.
Then I will add 7% for the PST.
Then I will add 5% for the GST.

3. Carry Out the Plan

Original price = $329.98

25% of original price = $329.98 ÷ 4

$$= \$82.50$$

Discounted price = $329.98 − $82.50

$$= \$247.48$$

PST = 7% of $247.48

$$= 0.07 \times \$247.48$$

$$= \$17.32$$

GST = 5% of $247.48

$$= \frac{1}{2} \text{ of } 10\% \text{ of } \$247.48$$

$$= \frac{1}{2} \text{ of } \$24.75$$

$$= \$12.38$$

Total cost = $247.48 + $17.32 + $12.38

$$= \$277.18$$

4. Look Back

I realized I could have thought about the problem differently and it would have been a lot easier.

The discounted price = 75% of the original price.

Adding 7% and then 5% to the discounted price is the same as taking 112% (100% + 12%) of the discounted price.

I could have calculated:

Total cost = 112% of 75% of $329.98

$$= 1.12 \times 0.75 \times \$329.98$$

$$= \boxed{277.1832}$$

Reflecting

A. How did Holly change her point of view when she looked back?

B. Why was changing her point of view useful?

WORK WITH *the Math*

Example 2 | Solving a percent problem using a ratio table

Ivan made a poster by enlarging a 10 cm by 5 cm picture to 380%
of its size. What is the area of the poster?

Ivan's Solution

1. Understand the Problem

I have to calculate the area of the poster.

2. Make a Plan

I can calculate the area of the picture and then figure out 380% of that area.

3. Carry Out the Plan

area of the picture = 10 cm x 5 cm

= 50 cm^2

I set up a ratio table. The top row is the area and the bottom row is the
enlargement percent.

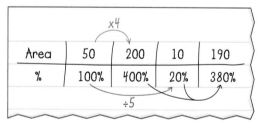

Area	50	200	10	190
%	100%	400%	20%	380%

To get 380%, I calculated 400% and subtracted 20%.
The area of the poster is 190 cm^2.

4. Look Back

I can estimate; 380% is about 400%. So 50 cm^2 × 4 = 200 cm^2,
which is close.
I could have written the percent as a decimal and then multiplied it by the
area of the picture.

A Checking

1. For each, write the single multiplication that will give you the necessary information.
   a) the price of an item on sale for 20% off if you know the regular price
   b) the total cost, with 5% tax, of an item if you know the price without tax

2. Describe two ways to calculate 50% of a number if you know the value of 20% of the number.

B Practising

3. Daniel buys a video game, which is on sale for 30% off the regular price of $69.98. In Alberta, he pays 5% GST. How much does Daniel pay? 48,99×1,00=8 1.44

4. A used kayak sells for $450. The combined taxes are 13%. What is the purchase price?
   508

5. A picture for a school yearbook has an area of 80 cm² and a perimeter of 42 cm. The picture was reduced by 20% to fit into the available space. What is the area of the reduced picture?

6. Alan missed 20% of the number of days of school that Richard did. Richard missed 150% as many days as Bella did. How many days could they each have missed? Give two possible answers.

7. Use two different ratio tables to solve this problem: After working at a part-time job, Rhea has 450% as much money saved as she had before. She had $120 before. How much does she have now?

8. Why is solving a percent problem using a ratio table a way of solving a problem by changing your point of view?

Reading Strategy

Predicting

Use the Activate, Predict, Read, and Connect Chart to predict the solution.

Solving Percent Problems Using Fractions

YOU WILL NEED

- a coin
- grid paper

GOAL

Create and solve a percent problem using fractions.

EXPLORE *the Math*

> **Problem**
> 12 boys were in a class. They made up 40% of the class. How big was the class?

To solve the problem on the card, Angèle divided 12 by $\frac{2}{5}$.

? **What problems involving percent can you create that could be solved by taking $\frac{5}{8}$ of a number?**

4.8 Combining Percents

YOU WILL NEED
• a calculator

GOAL

Use percents to solve problems involving two percentages.

LEARN ABOUT *the Math*

John wants to buy an MP3 player. In a newspaper, he sees a player that regularly sells for $119.95. It is advertised at 20% off, but, because he lives in British Columbia, he has to pay 5% GST and 7% PST. He has saved $115 from babysitting.

? Does John have enough money to buy the MP3 player?

| Example 1 | Working with discounts and sales tax |

I needed to calculate the total cost of the player.

John's Solution

$0.2 \times \$119.95 = \$23.99$
sale price = regular price - discount
$\qquad = \$119.95 - \$23.99$
$\qquad = \$95.96$

$5\% + 7\% = 12\%$

$0.12 \times \$95.96 = \$11.5152$
The tax would be $11.52.
The total price would be
$\$95.96 + \$11.52 = \$107.48.$
I have enough money.

The discount is 20% of $119.95. I wrote 20% as the decimal 0.2.

I had to calculate the sale price before I used the GST and PST. The two tax percents could be added since they are both percents for the same amount.

I wrote 12% as a decimal. I used a calculator to multiply. I rounded the decimal to the nearest hundredth.

I added the tax to the price to get the total cost.

I compared it to the $115 I had saved.

Reflecting

A. Why could you have calculated 80% of the regular price instead of subtracting 20% from the regular price?

B. Why could you have multiplied the sale price by 1.12 instead of adding the tax to the sale price?

C. Why might you have calculated the total cost this way: $0.8 \times 1.12 \times 119.95$?

WORK WITH *the Math*

Example 2	Calculating interest

Miranda took out a loan to buy a computer. The computer cost $1299. The interest rate on the loan is 8.25% of the original price each year. Calculate the amount of interest Miranda will pay over the two years.

Solution

Yearly interest = amount of loan × annual interest rate
        = $1299 × 8.25%
        = $1299 × 0.0825
        = $107.1675

Calculate the interest on the loan for one year

The interest for one year is $107.17.

Total interest = number of years × yearly interest
        = 2 × $107.17
        = $214.34

Calculate the interest for 2 years.

Miranda will pay $214.34 in interest.

Ⓐ Checking

1. A television is on sale for 25% off the regular price of $339.95. Calculate the discount and the final cost if the tax is 5% in Alberta, where there is no PST.

B Practising

2. Mikael's father bought a new car for $35 500. The car decreased in value by 20% after one year. What was the value of the car after the one year? ~~28 400~~

3. Calculate the total tax in Manitoba for each item (7% PST and 5% GST).

   a)
   $299.95
   35.99

   b)
   $1099.95
   131.99

   c)
   $14.98
   LIVE
   1.80

4. Jake purchased these items in Yukon, where there is no PST but there is 5% GST.

   a) Calculate the sale price for each item before taxes.

   i)
   $149.95
   10% OFF
   134.96

   ii)
   $99.99
   25% OFF
   74.99

   iii)
   $35.49
   30% OFF
   24.84

   b) Calculate the price for each item with taxes.
   i) 26.09   ii) 78.74   iii) 141.71

5. Lawrence added the taxes to the price of an item before taking off the discount. Tina took off the discount and then added the taxes. Will they get the same purchase price? Explain.
   Yes, because they just did it the same way. Different way.

6. Calculate the interest on a deposit of $500 that pays 3.5% per year over five years. 87.5

7. Miriam wants to buy a pair of inline skates. One store is selling the skates at 15% off the regular price of $149.95. Another store is selling the skates for $139.95, with 10% off. Which store has the better price?
   1) 127.46   2) 126.96

8. Complete.
   a) 6% of 100 + 8% of 100 = ▧% of 100   14%
   b) 6% of 100 + 8% of 120 = ▧% of 100
   15.6

9. The price of a $150 item is increased by 25%. After a couple of weeks, it is reduced by 25%. Why is the final price not $150?

150 × 0.25 = 187.5 × 0.75 = 140.6
Reduced by 25% does not cancel.

Greatest Number

YOU WILL NEED
- a standard deck of cards

The goal of the game is to end up with the greatest value possible.

Number of players: 2 to 5

How to Play

1. Shuffle the cards. Deal five cards to each player.

2. The aces count as 1, the face cards count as 0, and numbered cards count as their face values.

3. Each player chooses three cards to form a three-digit number that represents a percent and the remaining two cards form a two-digit number.

4. Calculate the percent of the number.

5. Players compare their results. The one with the greatest value wins.

Renée's Turn

The digits I can use are 0, 3, 6, 1, and 4.
I will take 630% of 41.
6.30 × 41 = 258.3
My result is 258.3.

4.9

Percent Change

YOU WILL NEED
• a calculator

GOAL

Solve problems involving changes described as percents.

LEARN ABOUT the Math

In 2005, the number of movie tickets sold in Canada increased 0.5% to 120.3 million.
Suppose it increased another 0.5% in 2006.

❓ How many tickets would have been sold in 2006?

A. Why can you describe the ticket sales in 2005 as 100.5% of the sales in 2004?

B. How many tickets were sold in 2004?

C. How many tickets would have been sold in 2006?

Reflecting

D. Why are the ticket sales in 2006 not 101% of the sales in 2004?

E. How could you have calculated the number of tickets for 2004 if you knew the percent increases from 2004 to 2005 and from 2005 to 2006, and the number of tickets sold in 2006?

F. If a percent increase is 10%, is the old value 90% of the new one? Explain.

WORK WITH the Math

Example 1 | Calculating a percent increase

This year, Jasleen's song library increased by 40%. She has 420 tunes in it now. How many songs did she have before?

Holly's Solution

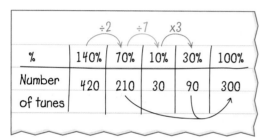

She used to have 300 tunes.

If the song library increased 40%, now it is 140% of what it was before.

I used a ratio table. I tried to get an equivalent ratio where the percent was 100% instead of 140%. First, I got to 70% and then I tried to find a way to get 30% so I could add the two columns to get the 100%.

Lam's Solution

140% = 1.40

I know that 420 tunes is 140% of the old number of tunes.
I wrote 140% as a decimal.

$1.4 \times \blacksquare = 420$

Then I wrote an equation to relate the old number of tunes to 420.

$10 \times 1.4 \times \blacksquare = 10 \times 420$
$\quad\quad 14 \times \blacksquare = 4200$

I decided to multiply both sides of the equation by 10 to get rid of the decimal.

$\blacksquare = 4200 \div 14$
$\quad = 300$

She used to have 300 tunes.

I divided both sides by 14.

Example 2 | Calculating a percent decrease

Ellen had $800 in her bank account. She withdrew $80 to buy a gift for her friend.

a) By what percent did the balance decrease?
b) What percent of the old balance is the new balance?

Taira's Solution

a) $\dfrac{80}{800} = \dfrac{1}{10}$

$\dfrac{1}{10} = 10\%$

The percent decrease is 10%.

To calculate the percent, I had to compare the amount withdrawn to the original balance, not the new balance, using a ratio or fraction. Then I wrote it as a percent.

b) $100\% - 10\% = 90\%$.

The new balance is 90% of the old one.
I checked by comparing 720 to 800.

$\dfrac{720}{800} = \dfrac{9}{10}$

$= 0.9$

$= 90\%$

I had to subtract from 100% to find the amount that remained.

A Checking

1. Calculate.
  a) a 30% increase from 50   **c)** a 20% decrease from 50
  b) a 150% increase from 50   **d)** a 0.5% decrease from 50

2. The population of a town with 8500 people increased 8% last year.
  a) How do you know that the increase was less than 850 people?
  b) What percent of 8500 is the new population?
  c) What is the new population?
  d) What percent of the new population is the old population?

B Practising

3. Calculate the percent increase or decrease.
  a) from 200 to 100   **c)** from 50 to 200
  b) from 80 to 90   **d)** from 500 to 450

4. Exports of wood to China from Canada increased by 150% from 2000 to 2005. What percent describes the amount of wood exported in 2005 compared to the year 2000?

5. A car dealer reported a 4.5% drop in car sales to 520 cars. What percent of the original car sales was the new total?

6. Sam increased the savings in his bank account by 200% when he added a birthday gift from his grandmother. Now he has $330. How much was the gift?

7. In 2001, the population of Nunavut was 26 745. In 2006, it was 30 782.
   a) What was the percent increase in population? Explain your thinking.
   b) If the increase continues at the same rate, what population would you expect in 2011?

8. The graph shows the number of Internet users in Canada in January 2006 and January 2007.

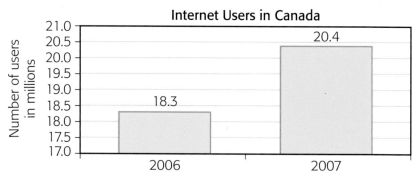

   a) What was the percent increase?
   b) What is the January 2007 value as a percent of the January 2006 value?

9. a) In April 2007, home sales in Calgary dropped 11.01% from the sales in March 2007. There were 3505 homes sold in April. How many homes were sold in March?

   b) The 3505 homes represent a 3.88% increase in home sales from April 2006. How many homes were sold in April 2006?

10. Kendra said that her amount of homework increased 400% when it went from one half-hour of work to 2 h of work. Do you agree? Explain.

11. The number of students attending francophone schools in Alberta increased from 1600 in 1994 to 3800 in 2004. What was the percent increase?

12. A child's mass increased from 30.0 kg to 40.0 kg in two years. Skin makes up about 16% of the mass of a body. About how many kilograms of skin did the child gain during the two years?

13. The growth in visitors to a community website from 2006 to 2007 was 117%. The number of visitors was 8.9 million in 2006. How many visitors were there in 2007?

14. Canadian digital download sales increased 122% from 2005 to 2006. The growth rate was much higher than in the United States or Europe. There were 14.9 million downloads in 2006. How many downloads were there in 2005?

15. a) Gasoline prices increased from 114.9¢/L to 118.9¢/L in one month. What was the percent increase, to the nearest tenth of a percent?

    b) If the price for a container of gourmet chocolate-covered potato chips increased at the same rate as in part a), what would be the new price of a $7.50 container?

16. The price of a computer decreased by 25%.
    Which of these procedures would give the new price? Explain.
    A. multiply current price by 1.25
    B. multiply current price by 0.25 and subtract from the present price
    C. multiply current price by 0.75
    D. take $\frac{3}{4}$ of the current price

Reading Strategy

Monitoring Comprehension

Identify the signal words in these questions. How can understanding these words help you solve math problems?

Double Your Money

You might think it would take 10 years for an amount to double if it increases by 10% each year.

You would be wrong! You can calculate how long it takes.

1. Imagine you have $1. Calculate its value after a year if it increases by 10% in that year.

2. Use the new value to calculate the value after a 10% increase on that new value.

Year	Value at start of year	Value at end of year
1		
2		

3. Repeat until you get to $2. How long did it take?

4. Repeat steps 1 to 3 for an increase of 15% each year. How long did it take?

5. Determine the percent that would allow you to double your money in two years.

1. Use a grid to model and calculate each.
   a) 110% of 70   **b)** 37.5% of 180

2. Andrea calculated 0.035×50 to determine a certain percent of 50. What percent was it?

3. An addition to a house increases the floor area from 275 m² to 300 m². By what percent was the original floor area increased?

4. The Mackenzie River is the longest river in Canada. It is 4241 km long, but the Nile River is about 158% as long. About how long is the Nile River?

5. The number of students who bought lunch in a school cafeteria increased 0.8% from January to February. If 125 students bought lunch in February, how many bought lunch in January?

6. A pair of jeans purchased in Manitoba cost $44.99 before taxes. They are on sale for 15% off.
   a) If PST is 7% and GST is 5%, how much would the jeans cost after taxes?
   b) What percent of the original regular price is the price with taxes?

7. The number of new homes on a street increased by 300% from January to March and by 100% from March to July. By what percent had the number of houses increased from January to July?

What Do You Think Now?

Revisit What Do You Think? on page 143. How have your answers and explanations changed?

Chapter **Review**

Frequently Asked Questions

Q: How can you solve percent problems using fractions?

A: You can relate the percent to an equivalent fraction and multiply or divide by that fraction.

For example, to calculate 125% of 48, you can write 125% as $\frac{125}{100} = \frac{5}{4}$ and multiply 48 by $\frac{5}{4}$.

$$\frac{5}{4} \times 48 = 5 \times 48 \div 4$$
$$= 5 \times 12$$
$$= 60$$

Q: How and when can you combine percents?

A: When you are adding, subtracting, multiplying, or dividing two percents of the same number, you can perform the calculation with the percent values and then apply them to the number.

For example, to calculate the GST and PST on an item, you can add the two percents and then multiply by the price.

When you are considering percents of two different numbers, you must calculate each value separately and then compute.

For example, 20% of 50 + 10% of 40 is not 30% of either 50 or 40; 20% of 50 + 10% of 40 = 10 + 4 = 14; 14 is 28% of 50 and it is 35% of 40.

Q: How do you calculate percent change?

A: When an amount increases or decreases, you can describe the percent change by relating the increase or decrease to that amount.

For example, if you increase 100 to 105, the increase of 5 is 5% of the original amount of 100. The final amount, 105, is 5% + 100% = 105% of the original amount.

If you decrease 100 to 95, the decrease of 5 is 5% of the original amount of 100. The final amount is 95% of the original amount.

Practice

Lesson 4.1

1. Use grids to model and calculate each amount. One full grid represents 100%.
   a) 205% **b)** 140% **c)** 330% **d)** 118%

2. Describe a situation where you might use 200%.

3. **a)** Write 12:5 as a percent.
   b) Why would you not write the rate 12 L in 4 min as a percent?

Lesson 4.2

4. Use a thousandths grid to represent each percent.
   a) 0.2% **b)** 4.1% **c)** 10.9%

5. Rick's class is 5.2% of the number of students in the school. If there are 32 students in his class, how many students are in the school?

Lesson 4.3

6. Use a fraction, a decimal, and a percent to describe each shaded area. One full grid represents 100%.
   a) 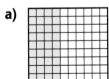 **b)**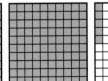

7. Describe each as a percent.
   a) $\frac{5}{2}$ **b)** 0.004 **c)** 1.58

**Eye Colour Among
Canadian School Children**

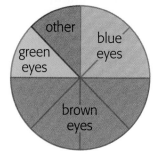

8. A Canadian census showed that the eye colour among Canadian school children could be described by the circle graph. What percent of the students had green eyes?

Lesson 4.4

9. Solve.

   a) 15% of ▦ = 6

   b) 32% of 65 = ▦

   c) $\frac{45}{18}$ = ▦%

   d) 0.8% of 2 500 000 = ▦

10. A sugar–and–water mixture of 250 g contains 8 g of sugar. What percent of the mixture is sugar?

Lesson 4.5

11. Calculate.

   a) 14% of 80   b) 118% of 20   c) 1.5% of 3000

12. In Alain's class, 15 students play in the local soccer league. They make up 6% of the league. How many students are in the league?

Lesson 4.6

13. Write each amount as a percent of the regular price of the jeans.

   a) the sale price with 35% off

   b) the cost with 5% GST only

Lesson 4.8

14. Luke bought a hockey sweater with a regular price of $68.95. The sweater was on sale for 35% off, and the taxes were 12%. Determine each amount.

   a) the discount   c) the taxes

   b) the sale price   d) the purchase price

Lesson 4.9

15. Calculate the percent increase or decrease.

   a) from 50 to 200   c) from 300 to 3000

   b) from 80 to 60   d) from 1000 to 100

16. A population increased by 15% from 1996 to 2001 and by 22% from 2001 to 2006. What percent is the increase from 1996 to 2006?

Chapter **Task**

YOU WILL NEED

- a calculator
- a measuring tape or ruler

Task | Checklist

✔ Did you use the different types of percents required?

✔ Did you write a fraction as a percent and include percent increases or decreases?

✔ Are your calculations clear and easy to follow?

✔ Are your descriptions clear and easy to understand?

137%, 6% + 7%, 0.21%

All About You

You can describe your life using many different numbers and measurements.

❓ How could you describe yourself using percents?

- You must use at least 10 percent values.
- Some percents have to be greater than 100% and some have to be less than 1%.
- Some percents have to describe an increase or decrease.
- Some percents have to involve combining percents.
- Some descriptions have to involve starting with a fraction and then rewriting it as a percent.

A. Think about your height.
- What could you compare it to so the percent describing it is greater than 100%?
- What could you compare it to so the percent describing it is less than 1%?

B. Think about the number of people in your family.
- How could you describe yourself in relation to your family with a percent greater than 100?
- Why would you probably not use a percent less than 1%?

C. Think about the length of your foot compared to the lengths of your fingers. What percents could you use to compare them?

D. Imagine that your adult height is 107% of your current height. If your arms were also 107% as long, how long would they be?

E. Complete the description of yourself following the rules above. Show your calculations.

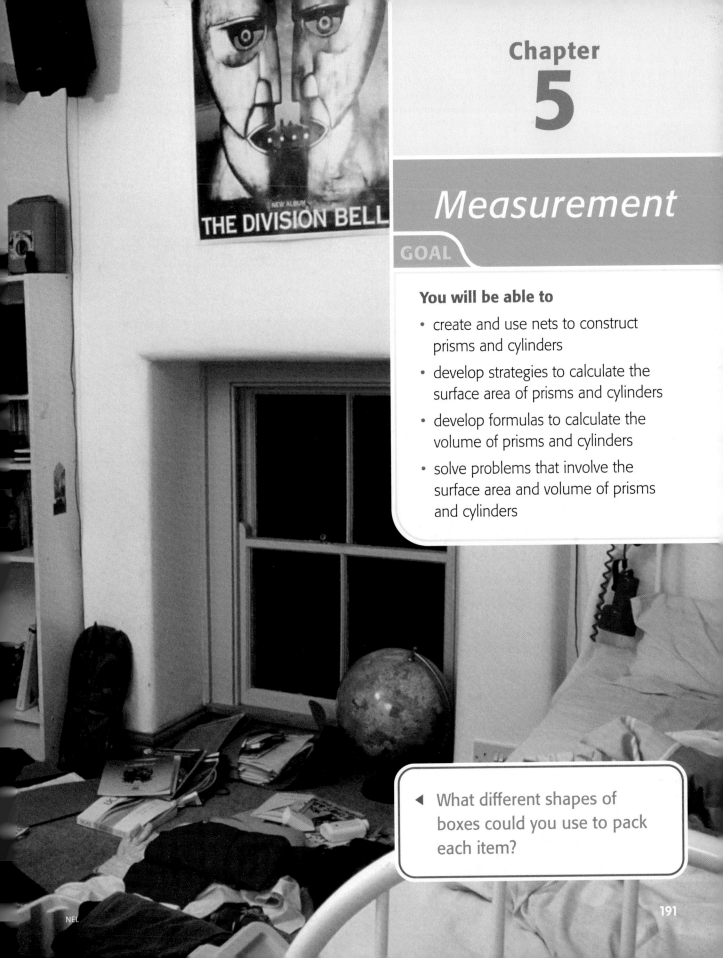

Chapter 5

Measurement

GOAL

You will be able to

- create and use nets to construct prisms and cylinders
- develop strategies to calculate the surface area of prisms and cylinders
- develop formulas to calculate the volume of prisms and cylinders
- solve problems that involve the surface area and volume of prisms and cylinders

◀ What different shapes of boxes could you use to pack each item?

Getting **Started**

Planning a Park

Allison has designed this park for her neighbourhood. The residents have asked that 80% of the park be grass.

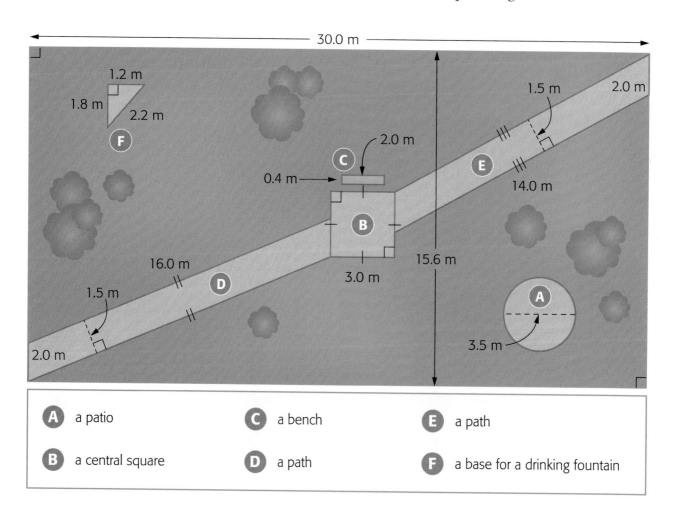

A a patio	**C** a bench	**E** a path
B a central square	**D** a path	**F** a base for a drinking fountain

❓ Will Allison's design have enough grassy area?

A. What is the total area of the park?

B. What area does each feature occupy?

C. What percent of the park will be grass?

What Do You Think?

Decide whether you agree or disagree with each statement.
Be ready to explain your decision.

1. There is enough paper to cover all six faces of this box.

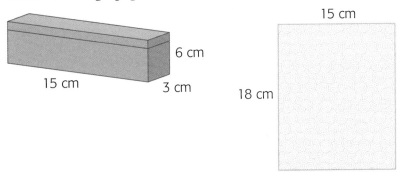

2. You can build the box in question 1 from this design.

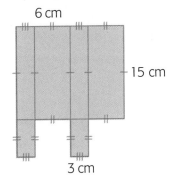

3. If you double the length of each side of a cube, you double the total area of its faces.

4. If you double the length of each side of a cube, you double its volume.

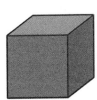

5.1

Exploring Nets

YOU WILL NEED

- Nets of Buildings I–VI
- 1 cm Grid Paper
- a ruler
- scissors
- tape

GOAL

Build 3-D objects from nets.

EXPLORE *the Math*

net

a 2-D pattern you can fold to create a 3-D object; for example, this is a net for a cube:

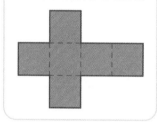

Brian wants to add a train station, a grain elevator, a water tower, and a small hut to his model railroad. He has the **nets** of five buildings, but they are not labelled.

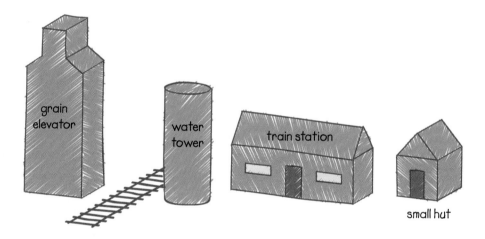

❓ Which nets can Brian use to construct the buildings?

5.2

Drawing the Nets of Prisms and Cylinders

YOU WILL NEED

- 1 cm Grid Paper
- scissors
- transparent tape
- a compass

Draw nets of prisms and cylinders.

service building

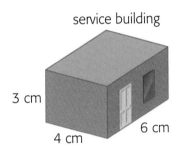

3 cm
4 cm
6 cm

tent

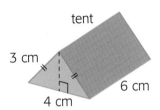

3 cm
4 cm
6 cm

2 cm
4 cm

water tank

LEARN ABOUT *the Math*

Nikita is building a model campground. She plans to make the service building using a rectangular prism, tents using triangular prisms, and the water tank from a cylinder. She asked Misa to help her make nets for the models.

❓ How can Nikita and Misa draw nets of the models?

A. Draw the floor of the service building.

B. Draw the four walls around the floor and then the roof of the building. Draw them so the net folds to make a rectangular prism. Label the net with its dimensions.

C. Draw the floor of the tent. Draw the other four faces around it to make a net of the tent.

D. Draw the top of the water tank. Below it, draw the side of the water tank as if it were laid out flat. Draw the bottom of the water tank below that.

E. Cut out, fold, and tape your nets to make the models.

Reflecting

F. When you drew each net, how did you decide where to place each face in relation to the others?

WORK WITH *the Math*

Example 1 | Creating a net for a rectangular prism

Nikita wants to create a net of a model of a general store
in her model campground. It is 9 cm long, 5 cm wide, and 4 cm high.

Nikita's Solution

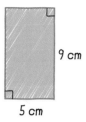

9 cm

5 cm

I started with the floor. I drew a rectangle 5 cm wide by 9 cm long.

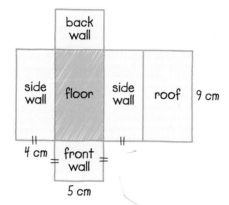

back wall

side wall | floor | side wall | roof | 9 cm

4 cm | front wall

5 cm

I drew the walls so they touched the floor and I drew the roof to touch one of the walls.

I know my net was correct, because when I folded it, the store was 9 cm long, 5 cm wide, and 4 cm high.

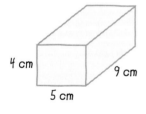

4 cm

9 cm

5 cm

Example 2 | Creating a net for a triangular prism

Preston wants to create a net of a model of a large tent for
the campground. It is 9 cm long, 6 cm wide, and 4 cm high.

Preston's Solution

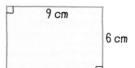

9 cm

6 cm

I started with the floor. I drew a rectangle 6 cm wide by 9 cm long.

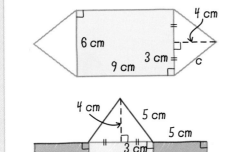

$c^2 = a^2 + b^2$
$= (3\text{ cm})^2 + (4\text{ cm})^2$
$= 25\text{ cm}^2$
$c = 5\text{ cm}$

I needed two triangular walls. I knew each wall had a base of 6 cm and a height of 4 cm. I split one of the triangular walls into two right triangles. To figure out the side lengths of the walls, I used the Pythagorean theorem with one of the right triangles.

I drew the other walls. Each one was 5 cm wide by 9 cm long.

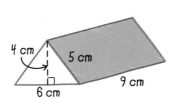

I know my net was correct, because when I folded it, the tent was 9 cm long, 6 cm wide, and 4 cm high.

Example 3 | Creating a net for a cylinder

Allison is building a model fuel storage tank in the shape of a cylinder for the campground. It must be 12 mm in diameter and 22 mm high.

Allison's Solution

I drew the top of the cylinder. I could have started with the side, too.

$C = \pi d$
$\doteq 3.14 \times 12$
$\doteq 38\text{ mm}$

I drew the curved side laid out flat, as a rectangle. I knew it was 22 mm high. To determine its width, I calculated the circumference of the circle. I drew another circle for the base on the bottom.

I know my net was correct, because when I folded it, the storage tank was 22 mm high and 12 mm in diameter.

Communication | Tip

The symbol "$\doteq$" means approximately equal to.

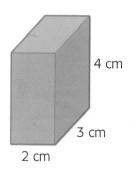

4 cm

3 cm

2 cm

A Checking

1. Draw a net of the prism on the left.

2. Which net(s) will fold to make this prism?

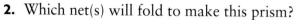

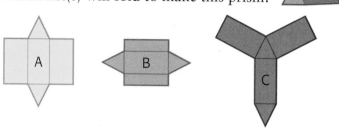

A

B

C

B Practising

3. Draw a net of the prism on the left.

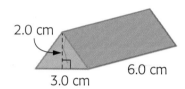

2.0 cm

6.0 cm

3.0 cm

4. Draw a net for each container.

   a)
   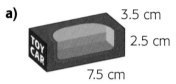
   3.5 cm

   2.5 cm

   TOY CAR

   7.5 cm

   b)

   3 cm   RAISINS

   18 cm

   c)

   Cookies

   6.5 cm

   12.0 cm

5. a) I have a rectangle in the middle, with a triangle attached to each of the two short sides and a rectangle attached to each of the two long sides. What net am I?

   b) I am made up of six congruent squares attached by their sides to form a T. What net am I?

6. a) What two prisms could you use to make this model of a house?

   b) Create a net of each prism. Check that they work by cutting them out and folding to create a model of a house.

7. Draw a net for a box that would just hold the tiles, stacked in one pile. Each box has to be the same shape as the tiles it holds.

a) 30 triangular floor tiles 2 mm thick

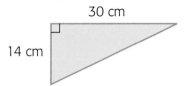

Reading Strategy

Visualizing

Picture each net in your mind. Sketch what you think the nets will look like before using the measurements to create your drawings.

b) 30 rectangular floor tiles 3 mm thick

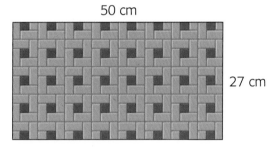

c) 30 circles 2 cm thick

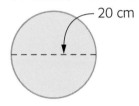

8. Jenna has 8 rolls of tape. Each roll is 40 cm in circumference and 7 cm high. Draw a net of a rectangular box that will fit all of the rolls in one layer.

9. a) Explain what strategies you can use to recognize whether a net is for a rectangular prism, a triangular prism, or a cylinder.

b) Explain what strategies you can use to draw a net for a rectangular prism, a triangular prism, and a cylinder. Draw an example of one of them.

Determining the Surface Area of Prisms

YOU WILL NEED

- 1 cm Grid Paper
- a calculator
- a ruler

GOAL

Develop strategies to calculate the surface area of prisms.

LEARN ABOUT the Math

The managers of a mint factory are choosing a box to hold breath mints. They will choose the box that uses the least amount of cardboard, including 10% more for overlap and folding.

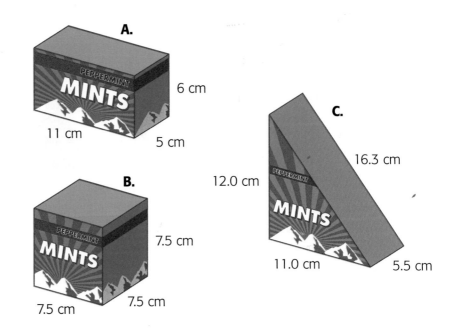

A.

6 cm

11 cm

5 cm

B.

7.5 cm

7.5 cm

7.5 cm

C.

16.3 cm

12.0 cm

11.0 cm

5.5 cm

? Which box should be chosen?

Example 1 | Determining a rectangular prism's surface area

I determined the surface area (SA) of box A using a net.

Aaron's Solution

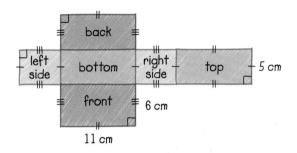

I imagined laying the box flat. I drew the net of the box and labelled the faces. Each face is a rectangle.

Area of front = 11 cm x 6 cm
= 66 cm²
Area of back = 11 cm x 6 cm
= 66 cm²
Area of right side = 5 cm x 6 cm
= 30 cm²
Area of left side= 5 cm x 6 cm
= 30 cm²
Area of top = 11 x 5 cm
= 55 cm²
Area of bottom = 11 cm x 5 cm
= 55 cm²

I calculated the area of each face.

SA = front + back + right side + left side + top + bottom
= 66 cm² + 66 cm² + 30 cm² + 30 cm² + 55 cm² + 55 cm²
= 2(66 cm²) + 2(30 cm²) + 2(55 cm²)
= 302 cm²

To determine the surface area, I added all the areas. I noticed that the front and back had the same area. So did the sides, and so did the top and the bottom.

302 cm² x 0.10 = 30 cm²
Total area of cardboard
= 302 cm² + 30 cm²
= 332 cm²
Box A uses 332 cm² of cardboard.

They want 10% more for overlap, so I calculated 10% and added it to the surface area.

Example 2 | Determining a cube's surface area

I determined the surface area of box B by recognizing that all of the faces are congruent.

Nikita's Solution

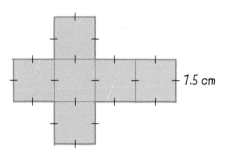

7.5 cm

I drew the net. I noticed each face was 7.5 cm by 7.5 cm. The faces were congruent.

SA = 6 x area of one face
   = 6 x 7.5 cm x 7.5 cm
   = 337.5 cm²

I multiplied the area of one face by the number of faces.

Total area of cardboard
= 337.5 cm² + 33.8 cm²
= 371.3 cm²
Box B uses 371.3 cm² of cardboard.

I added 10% to the surface area.

Example 3 | Determining a triangular prism's surface area

I determined the surface area of box C using the formula for the area of a triangle.

Brian's Solution

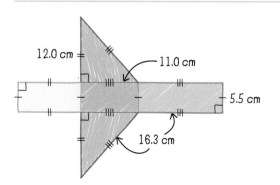

12.0 cm

11.0 cm

5.5 cm

16.3 cm

I drew the net.

Area of one triangle
= (b x h) ÷ 2
= (11.0 cm x 12.0 cm) ÷ 2
= 66.0 cm^2
Area of two triangles = 2 x 66.0 cm^2
= 132.0 cm^2

I calculated the area of the two triangles.

Area of rectangles
= 12.0 cm x 5.5 cm + 11.0 cm x 5.5 cm + 16.3 cm x 5.5 cm
= 66.0 cm^2 + 60.5 cm^2 + 89.7 cm^2
= 216.2 cm^2

I calculated the area of the rectangles.

SA = 132.0 cm^2 + 216.2 cm^2
= 348.2 cm^2

The surface area is the sum of the areas of the triangles and rectangles.

Total area of cardboard
= 348.2 cm^2 + 34.8 cm^2
= 383.0 cm^2
Box C uses 383.0 cm^2 of cardboard.

I added 10% to the surface area.

Box A uses 332 cm^2, box B uses 371.3 cm^2, and box C uses 383.0 cm^2 of cardboard. Box A uses the least cardboard.

Reflecting

A. How does drawing the net of a prism help you calculate its surface area?

B. Why did Nikita's calculation require fewer steps than Brian's or Aaron's?

WORK WITH the Math

Example 4	Calculating a triangular prism's surface area

Calculate the surface area of this prism.

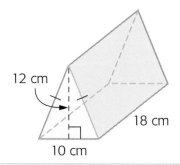

Solution

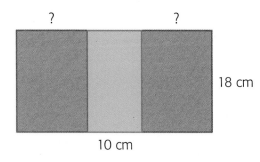

First sketch the part of the net that shows the rectangular faces. The widths of two rectangles are unknown.

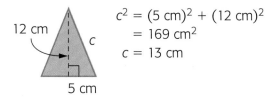

$$c^2 = (5\text{ cm})^2 + (12\text{ cm})^2$$
$$= 169\text{ cm}^2$$
$$c = 13\text{ cm}$$

The widths were sides of the triangular base. Use the Pythagorean theorem to figure out what they are.

Draw the full net.

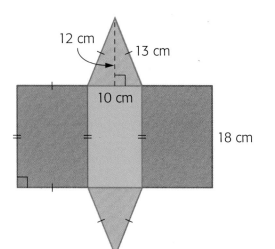

Area of two triangles
= 2 × (12 cm × 10 cm) ÷ 2
= 120 cm²

Area of two side rectangles
= 2 × (18 cm × 13 cm)
= 468 cm²

Area of base rectangle
= 18 cm × 10 cm
= 180 cm²

SA = 120 cm² + 468 cm² + 180 cm²
   = 768 cm²

The surface area is 768 cm².

Calculate the area of the faces. Multiply the areas of congruent faces.

The surface area is the sum of all areas.

A Checking

1. Draw a net for each prism.

   A. 4.5 cm, 8.0 cm, 3.2 cm

   B. 4.8 cm, 5.1 cm, 3.6 cm, 9.2 cm

   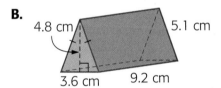

2. Calculate the surface area of each prism in question 1.

B Practising

3. **a)** Sketch a rectangular prism 3 cm by 5 cm by 6 cm.
   b) What is the surface area of the prism?

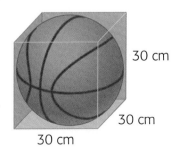

30 cm
30 cm
30 cm

4. A sports company packages its basketballs in boxes. The boxes are shipped in wooden crates. Each crate holds 24 boxes.
   a) Model three possible crates. Use centimetre cubes.
   b) Draw nets for the three crates you modelled.
   c) Calculate the surface area of each crate you modelled.
   d) Which crate uses the least amount of wood?

5. Marilynn has 1 m² of paper to wrap a box 28 cm long, 24 cm wide, and 12 cm high for a present. Does she have enough paper?

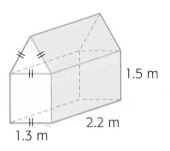

1.5 m

2.2 m

1.3 m

6. Alan is painting the walls and ceiling of his room, which is 4.2 m long, 3.7 m wide, and 2.6 m high. The window is 60 cm long by 40 cm high. The door is 2 m high by 85 cm wide.
   a) Determine the surface area of the walls in the room.
   b) He will use two coats of paint. A 4 L can of paint can cover 36 m². How many cans of paint does he need to buy?

7. Jordan is building this doghouse. (He will cut the door in the doghouse later.) How much wood will he need?

8. Which object has the greater surface area? Explain how you know.

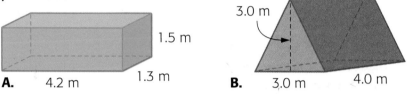

1.5 m

1.3 m

3.0 m

A. 4.2 m

B. 3.0 m   4.0 m

9. Adrian cuts a cube into smaller cubes. Is the total surface area of the smaller cubes less than, greater than, or equal to the surface area of the original cube? Explain your thinking with words, diagrams, and calculations.

10. a) Draw a rectangular prism with a surface area of 24 cm².
    b) Draw a new rectangular prism where the sides are twice as long as the original. How does its surface area compare with that of the original?
    c) Draw a new rectangular prism where the sides are half as long as the original. How does its surface area compare with that of the original?

11. a) Calculate the surface area of a rectangular prism 10 m long, 8 m wide, and 6 m high.
    b) What might be the dimensions of a triangular prism with the same height and surface area as the prism in part a)?

12. Why might you need to calculate the surface area of a prism?

13. a) How many areas would you add to calculate the surface area of a triangular prism? Explain.
    b) How many areas would you add to calculate the surface area of a rectangular prism? Explain.

More than One Way to Net a Cube

Some students were asked to draw a net of a cube. This is what they drew.

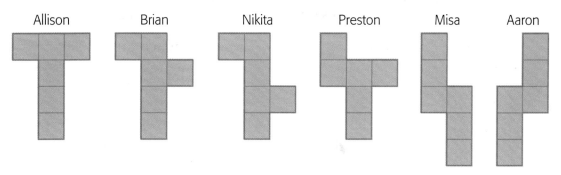

Allison   Brian   Nikita   Preston   Misa   Aaron

Allison said, "We all drew different nets."

Brian said, "Misa's net and Aaron's net are really the same, though. They are just reversed."

Preston said, "All of our nets are correct. I wonder if there are other nets we could draw."

1. There are other nets of cubes. How many can you discover?

2. How many nets can you draw for a box in the shape of a cube that has no lid?

5.4 Determining the Surface Area of Cylinders

GOAL

Develop strategies to calculate the surface area of a cylinder.

LEARN ABOUT the Math

Preston and Misa are making cardboard packages for cookies for a school fundraiser. Each package will hold 12 cookies. They decide to add 5% additional cardboard for overlap.

? How much cardboard do they need for each package?

A. Draw a net of the package.

B. Label the height of the package.

C. What is the area of the top of the package?
What is the area of the bottom of the package?

D. What is the area of the curved part of the package?

E. What is the surface area of the whole package?

F. What area of cardboard is needed for the package?

Reflecting

G. Which surface of a cylinder is affected by the cylinder's height?

H. Write a formula for the surface area of a cylinder.

WORK WITH the Math

| Example 1 | Estimating the surface area of a cylinder |

Can A is 6 cm in diameter and 9 cm high.
Can B is 5 cm in radius and 4 cm high.
Which can has the greater surface area?

Aaron's Solution

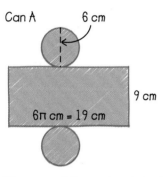

Can A

6 cm

9 cm

6π cm = 19 cm

I drew the nets. The curved side became a
rectangle. The width of the rectangle is the
circumference of the circular base. For can A,
the diameter is 6 cm, so the rectangle is about
3.14 × 6 cm = 19 cm wide.

The area of the rectangle is about
10 cm x 20 cm = 200 cm².
The area of each circle is about
3 x 3 cm x 3 cm = 27 cm². (SA = πr²)

I estimated using easier numbers.

SA ≐ 27 cm² + 27 cm² + 200 cm²
≐ 254 cm²
Can A has a surface area of about 254 cm².

I added all the areas.

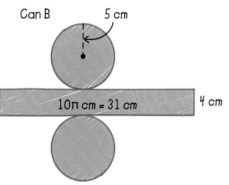

Can B

5 cm

10π cm = 31 cm

4 cm

For can B, the diameter was 10 cm, so the
rectangle was about 3 × 10 = 30 cm wide.

The area of the rectangle is about
4 cm × 30 cm = 120 cm².
The area of each circle is about
3 × 5 cm × 5 cm = 75 cm².

SA ≐ 75 cm² + 75 cm² + 120 cm²
≐ 270 cm²
Can B has a surface area of about 270 cm².
Can B has the greater surface area.

I added all the areas.

Example 2 | Calculating the surface area of a cylinder

Allison is wrapping a cylindrical candle 7.5 cm high and 3.5 cm in diameter as a present for her mother. Allowing 5% for overlap, what area of wrapping paper does she need?

Allison's Solution

The radius is 3.5 cm ÷ 2 = 1.8 cm.

Area of top and base

$= 2 \times \pi \times r \times r$

$\doteq 2 \times 3.14 \times 1.8$ cm $\times 1.8$ cm

$\doteq 20.3$ cm^2

| The top and the base have the same area. I determined the area of one face and doubled it. I decided not to estimate using 3 instead of 3.14 because my estimate might come out too low. |

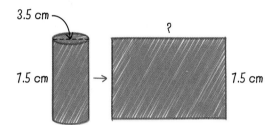

$\pi d = \pi \times 3.5$ cm

$\doteq 10.99$ cm

$\doteq 11.0$ cm

Area of curved surface $= C \times h$

$= \pi d \times h$

$\pi d \times h \doteq 11.0$ cm $\times 7.5$ cm

$\doteq 82.5$ cm^2

When you unroll the curved side of the candle, it forms a rectangle. The sides of the rectangle are the circumference of the base and the height of the cylinder. The circumference of the base is πd.

$SA \doteq 20.3$ cm$^2 + 82.5$ cm^2

$\doteq 102.8$ cm^2

The surface area is the sum of all the areas.

Total area of paper

$\doteq 102.8$ cm$^2 + 5.1$ cm^2

$\doteq 107.9$ cm^2

I need about 108 cm^2 of paper.

I added 5% to determine the total area.

A Checking

1. Determine the surface area of each cylinder, using the net.

a)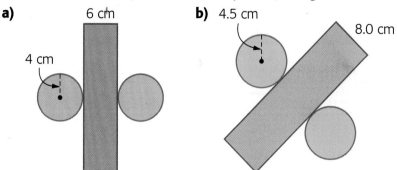
6 cm

4 cm

b) 4.5 cm

8.0 cm

B Practising

2. Calculate the surface area of each cylinder.

a)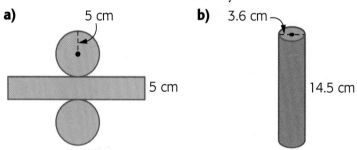
5 cm

5 cm

b) 3.6 cm

14.5 cm

3. Determine the surface area of each cylinder.

	Diameter (cm)	Height (cm)
a)	10.0	8.0
b)	10.0	6.5
c)	10.0	9.4

4. A farmer is buying wrap to protect her hay bales. Each bale is 2 m in diameter and is 3 m high. The top and the bottom of the bales are not enclosed. How much wrap does each bale require?

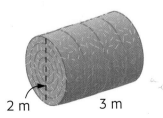

2 m   3 m

5. A can of frozen juice that is 6.7 cm in diameter and 11.8 cm high is made of a cardboard tube, and a metal top and metal bottom. Suppose 24 cans are recycled.
   a) Determine how much cardboard is recycled.
   b) Determine how much metal is recycled.

6. a) This railway car is 3.2 m in diameter and 17.2 m long. Calculate its surface area.
   b) A can of paint covers 40 m² and costs $35. Estimate the cost to paint the railway car.

7. Explain how two cylinders can have the same height but different surface areas.

8. This acrobatic stunt is from the Cirque de Soleil. Each wheel is about 30 cm wide and 2.5 m in diameter. What is the surface area of each wheel?

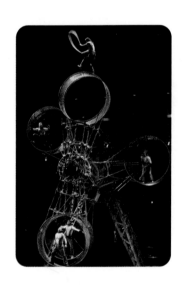

9. Brian is buying burlap to protect his three apple trees against winter weather. He will wrap the burlap around the bottom 150 cm of each tree trunk. The trees are 25.1 cm, 29.8 cm, and 31.4 cm in circumference. About how much burlap will he need?

10. Calculate the surface area of each cylinder.

   a) 2.1 m   b) 2300 cm   c) 2.5 cm

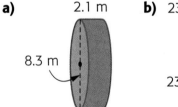  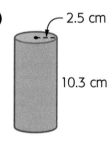

   8.3 m   23.0 m   10.3 cm

11. A cylindrical CD case has a surface area of 372.0 cm². Each CD is 0.1 cm thick and 11.0 cm in diameter. How many CDs can the case hold? Explain, with the help of formulas, what you did.

12. How are calculating the surface area of a cylinder and calculating the surface area of a prism alike? How are they different?

Frequently Asked Questions

Q: How do you calculate the surface area of a prism?

A: The surface area is the sum of the areas of the faces. For a rectangular prism, three pairs of faces are congruent: the front and back, the left and right sides, and the top and bottom. So calculate the area of one face in each pair and double that. Add to determine the total area.

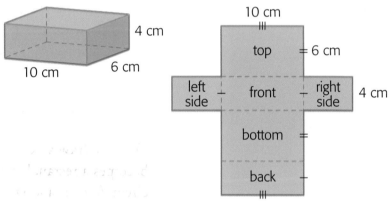

Surface area = 2 × area of top + 2 × area of front
$$+ \; 2 \times \text{area of left side}$$
$$= 2(6 \text{ cm} \times 10 \text{ cm}) + 2(4 \text{ cm} \times 10 \text{ cm})$$
$$+ \; 2(4 \text{ cm} \times 6 \text{ cm})$$
$$= 120 \text{ cm}^2 + 80 \text{ cm}^2 + 48 \text{ cm}^2$$
$$= 248 \text{ cm}^2$$

For a triangular prism, two of its five faces, the triangular bases, are congruent. The other three faces may or may not be congruent. To calculate the area of the bases, you may need to determine their height.

By the Pythagorean theorem, each base of the following prism has a height of 4.0 cm.

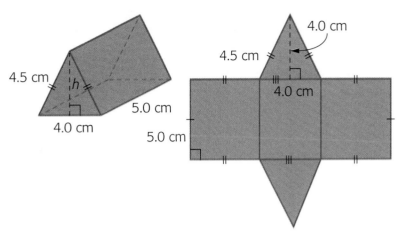

Surface area = 2 × area of bases + 2 × area of sides
+ area of bottom
= 2(4.0 cm × 4.0 cm ÷ 2) + 2(4.5 cm × 5.0 cm)
+ (4.0 cm × 5.0 cm)
= 16.0 cm² + 45.0 cm² + 20.0 cm²
= 81.0 cm²

Q: **How do you calculate the surface area of a cylinder?**

A: You can draw a net, if you wish. The curved surface
becomes a rectangle where length is the cylinder's
circumference and width is the cylinder's height. The base
and the top are congruent, so they have the same area.

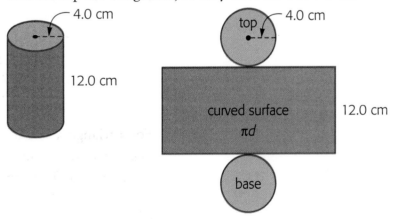

Surface area = 2(area of base) + area of curved surface
= 2(π × r × r) + (πd × h)
≐ 2(3.14 × 4.0 cm × 4.0 cm)
+ (3.14 × 8.0 cm × 12.0 cm)
≐ 401.9 cm²

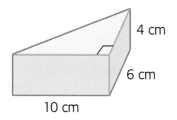

4 cm

6 cm

10 cm

Practice

1. Draw the net of this prism.

2. State whether each net will fold to make a soup can. If it will not, explain why.

a) 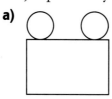 **b)** 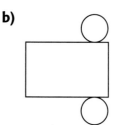 **c)**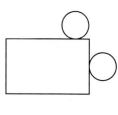

3. Megan is painting a rectangular box 18 cm by 5 cm by 2 cm. What surface area does she need to paint?

120 cm

4. Emma's dad is building a triangular hay trough for his horses, as shown. How much wood will he need?

150 cm   3.0 m

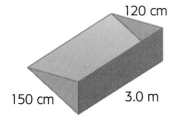

5. Sketch a net for each cylinder, and label its dimensions. Then calculate the surface area.

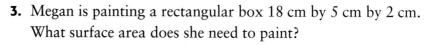

	Item	Radius (cm)	Height (cm)
a)	potato-chip container	4	8
b)	coffee can	7.5	15.0
c)	CD case	8.5	20.5
d)	oil barrel	25.0	80.0

6. Karim is painting a barrel 1.2 m high and 0.3 m in radius. Including the top and bottom, what area will the paint have to cover?

5.5 Determining the Volume of Prisms

Develop and apply formulas for the volume of prisms.

LEARN ABOUT the Math

Misa wants to buy a piece of cheese.

❓ Which piece of cheese is the better buy?

| Example 1 | Calculating the volume of a rectangular prism |

I used a model to calculate the volume of piece A.

Misa's Solution

This prism has 60 cubes, so its volume is 60 cm³.

I modelled one layer with centimetre cubes. The area of the base was 60 cm² and the height was 1 cm.

This prism has 120 cubes, so its volume is 120 cm³.

For two layers, the area of the base was 60 cm² and the height was 2 cm.

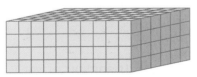

This prism has 240 cubes, so piece A has a volume of 240 cm³.

For four layers, the area of the base would be 60 cm² and the height 4 cm. I thought the volume would be 240 cm³. I was right.

Example 2 | Calculating the volume of a triangular prism

I imagined a model to calculate the volume of piece B.

Brian's Solution

This prism has 70 cubes, so its volume is 70 cm³.

I modelled a rectangular prism 1 cm high with the same length and width as piece B.

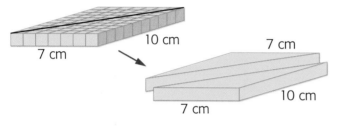

I imagined cutting it along the diagonal to form two congruent triangular prisms. Each piece would have half the volume of the original prism.

Volume of one layer = 70 cm³ ÷ 2, or 35 cm³

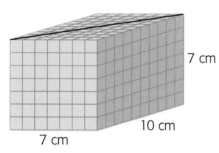

This prism has 490 cubes, so its volume is 490 cm³.

I modelled a rectangular prism with the same width, length, and height as piece B.

Piece B has half the volume of this prism.

Volume of B = 490 cm³ ÷ 2, or 245 cm³

Piece B is the better buy.

Reflecting

A. Write a formula for the volume of a rectangular prism.

B. Is every triangle half of a rectangle?

C. Write a formula for the volume of a triangular prism.

WORK WITH the Math

Example 3 | Calculating the volume of a rectangular prism

Calculate the volume of this prism.

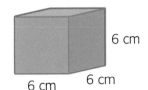

6 cm
6 cm   6 cm

Solution

Area of base = length × width   Calculate the area of the base.
$B = l \times w$
$= 6 \text{ cm} \times 6 \text{ cm}$
$= 36 \text{ cm}^2$

Volume $= B \times h$ Multiply the area of the base by the height.
$= 36 \text{ cm}^2 \times 6 \text{ cm}$
$= 216 \text{ cm}^3$

This prism has a volume of 216 cm³.

Example 4 | Calculating the volume of a triangular prism

Calculate the volume of this prism.

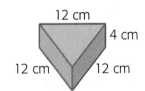

12 cm
4 cm
12 cm   12 cm

Solution

h 12 cm

6 cm

$h^2 = (12 \text{ cm})^2 - (6 \text{ cm})^2$ Calculate the height of the base.
$= 144 \text{ cm}^2 - 36 \text{ cm}^2$ Use the Pythagorean theorem.
$= 108 \text{ cm}^2$
$h \doteq 10 \text{ cm}$

$A = B \times h \div 2$ Determine the area of the base.
$= 12 \text{ cm} \times 10 \text{ cm} \div 2$
$= 60 \text{ cm}^2$

$V = B \times h$ Multiply the area of the base by the height
$= 60 \text{ cm}^2 \times 4 \text{ cm}$ of the prism.
$= 240 \text{ cm}^3$

This prism has a volume of about 240 cm³.

Communication | Tip

In a formula, h can refer to the height of a triangle, or to the height of a prism. Take care to use the appropriate value.

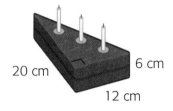

20 cm

6 cm

12 cm

A Checking

1. Calculate the volume of each prism.

a)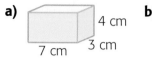
7 cm   3 cm   4 cm

b)
5.0 cm   2.0 cm   4.3 cm

c)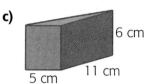
5 cm   11 cm   6 cm

B Practising

2. a) This slice is half the volume of a rectangular cake. What was the volume of the whole cake?
   b) Calculate the volume of this slice of cake.

3. Calculate the volume of each prism.

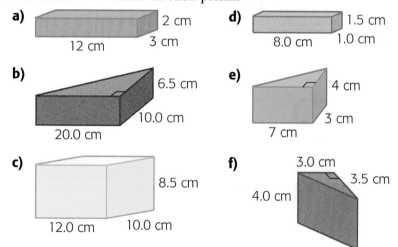

a)
12 cm   3 cm   2 cm

d)
8.0 cm   1.0 cm   1.5 cm

b)
20.0 cm   10.0 cm   6.5 cm

e)
7 cm   3 cm   4 cm

c)
12.0 cm   10.0 cm   8.5 cm

f)
4.0 cm   3.0 cm   3.5 cm

4. a) Determine the volume of prism A.
   b) Do you need to calculate to determine the volume of prism B? Explain.

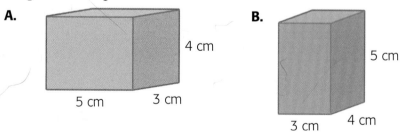

A.
5 cm   3 cm   4 cm

B.
3 cm   4 cm   5 cm

5. a) Determine the volume of prism A.

b) Do you need to calculate to determine the volume of prism B? Explain.

A.

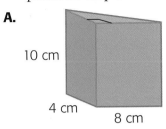

10 cm

4 cm

8 cm

B.

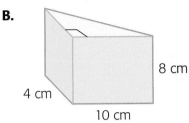

8 cm

4 cm

10 cm

6. Sketch a rectangular prism with each set of dimensions and then calculate its volume.

a) $l = 8$ cm, $w = 8$ cm, $h = 8$ cm

b) $l = 0.5$ cm, $w = 0.5$ cm, $h = 2.0$ cm

c) $l = 3.5$ km, $w = 2.0$ km, $h = 3.0$ km

7. Copy and complete the table for rectangular prisms.

	Length (cm)	Width (cm)	Height (cm)	Volume (cm³)
a)	6	6	8	
b)	4.5	5.0		216.0
c)	3		3	27

8. Copy and complete the table for triangular prisms.

	Length (cm)	Width of Base (cm)	Height of Base (cm)	Volume (cm³)
a)	6	6	8	
b)	3	5		300

9. Anthony needs to buy nails for his carpentry project. The hardware store sells these boxes of nails for the same price. Which one should he buy? Explain your choice with a sketch, calculations, and words.

A.

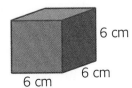

6 cm

6 cm

6 cm

B.

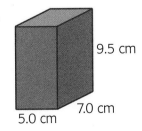

9.5 cm

7.0 cm

5.0 cm

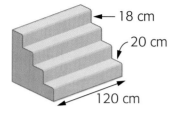

18 cm
20 cm
120 cm

10. Samantha has to pack 30 books in a box. Twenty books are each 28 cm by 21 cm by 2 cm. Ten books are each 20 cm by 18 cm by 3 cm. What is the least volume the box can have?

11. The concrete steps to Brian's front door are shown. What volume of cement was needed to build the steps?

12. a) Draw a rectangular prism with a volume of 24 cm³.

b) Draw a new rectangular prism where the sides are twice as long as the original. How does its volume compare with that of the original?

c) Draw a new rectangular prism where the sides are half as long as the original. How does its volume compare with that of the original?

13. Raisins are sold in two different boxes. Which one do you think is better in terms of getting more raisins for your money?

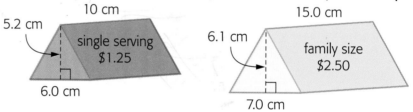

10 cm
5.2 cm
single serving
$1.25
6.0 cm

15.0 cm
6.1 cm
family size
$2.50
7.0 cm

14. Allan's teacher bought solid water colour cakes in a tray, as shown.

a) Determine the volume of each colour.

b) Which colour had the greatest volume?

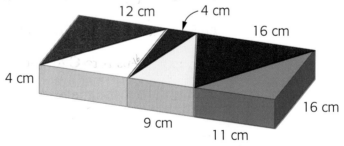

12 cm
4 cm
16 cm
4 cm
16 cm
9 cm
11 cm

15. Estimate the volume of space in your classroom.

16. Will a rectangular prism and a triangular prism have the same volume if they are both the same height? Explain.

5.6 Determining the Volume of Cylinders

YOU WILL NEED
- 1 cm Grid Paper
- a compass
- centimetre cubes
- a calculator

GOAL

Develop a formula for the volume of a cylinder.

LEARN *the Math*

Allison is going to buy some modelling clay. Each cylinder costs $5.

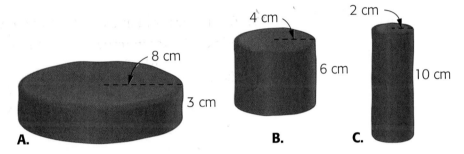

A.   **B.**   **C.**

❓ Which choice is the best buy?

A. Draw a circle with the same radius as the base of cylinder A. Estimate its area.

B. Stack centimetre cubes to model the height of cylinder A.

C. Estimate the volume of cylinder A.

D. Repeat steps A to C for the other two cylinders.

E. Which choice is the best buy? Explain.

Reflecting

F. How can you estimate a cylinder's volume using its radius and height?

G. Use the formula for the volume of a rectangular prism to create a formula for the volume of a cylinder. Explain your thinking.

WORK WITH *the Math*

| **Example 1** | Calculating the volume of a cylinder |

Calculate the volume of this cylinder.

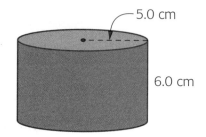

Allison's Solution

Volume of cylinder
= area of base x height
= π x r x r x height
≐ 3.14 x 5.0 cm x 5.0 cm x 6.0 cm
≐ 471.0 cm³
The volume is about 471.0 cm³.

I calculated the volume the way I would calculate the volume of a prism: I multiplied the area of the base by the height.

| **Example 2** | Using volume to solve a problem |

A tube of cookie dough is 942 cm³ in volume and 10 cm in diameter. Each cookie will be 1 cm thick. How many cookies can Nikita make?

Nikita's Solution

Volume of one cookie
= area of base x height
= π x r x r x h
≐ 3.14 x 5.0 cm x 5.0 cm x 1 cm
≐ 78.5 cm³

I calculated the volume of one cookie.

Total volume ÷ volume of one cookie
= 942 cm³ ÷ 78.5 cm³
= 12
I can make 12 cookies.

To determine how many cookies I could make, I divided the total volume of the cookie dough by the volume of one cookie.

A Checking

1. Calculate the volume of each cylinder.

a)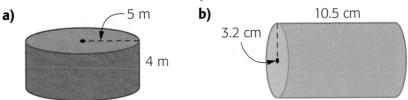

-5 m

4 m

b)

10.5 cm

3.2 cm

B Practising

2. Calculate the volume of each cylinder.

a)

-14.4 cm

12.6 cm

b) 2.5 cm

7.3 cm

3. Determine the volume of the cylinder you could create with each net.

a)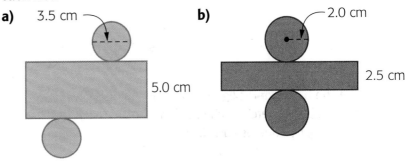

3.5 cm

5.0 cm

b)

2.0 cm

2.5 cm

Reading Strategy

Summarizing

In your own words, how would you summarize the key idea in this lesson?
How does it apply to this problem?

4. There are 12 people in Mandy's exercise class. Each one has a water bottle like this. They fill their bottles from a water cooler that is 20 cm in radius and 90 cm in height. Estimate how many times they can fill up their water bottles before the cooler needs to be refilled.

20.0 cm

10.0 cm

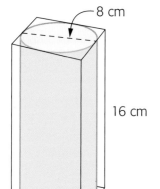

8 cm

16 cm

5. Estimate the number of litres of water in this swimming pool. Recall that 1000 cm³ = 1 L.

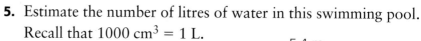

5.4 m

120 cm

6. A cylindrical candle is sold in a gift box that is a square-based prism. Determine the volume of the empty space in the box.

7. Determine the height of a cylinder with a base area of 50.2 cm² and a volume of 502.4 cm³.

8. Loren is putting $2 coins into a plastic tube to take to the bank. The tube has a volume of 26.9 cm³. A $2 coin is 1.75 mm thick and 28.00 mm in diameter. How many $2 coins will the tube hold?

1.75 mm

.175 cm

2.8 cm

9. Which container holds more? Justify your answer.

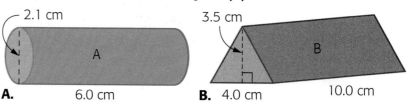

2.1 cm

A

A. 6.0 cm

3.5 cm

B

B. 4.0 cm   10.0 cm

10. Which holds more flour, a cylinder 10.0 cm high and 7.0 cm in diameter or a cylinder 7.0 cm high and 10.0 cm in diameter?

11. These two metal cans both hold the same amount of soup.
    a) Determine the height of the can of chicken soup. Show your solution.
    b) Which can uses more metal? Show your work.

A.

7.5 cm

8.0 cm

Soup

MUSHROOM

B.

10.0 cm

Soup

CHICKEN

12. How are calculating the volume of a prism and calculating the volume of a cylinder alike? How are they different?

5.7

Solve Problems Using Models

GOAL

Use models to solve measurement problems.

LEARN ABOUT *the Math*

Brian's mom has 8 m³ of sand left over from a gardening project. She asked Brian to design a wooden sandbox, with a bottom and a top, for his little sister, Sally. Brian has decided that the sandbox should have these features.

- It should be 50 cm deep, so Sally can climb in and out easily but still have enough to dig in.
- It should use the least amount of wood to save money.
- Its base should be square or triangular.

❓ Which design should Brian choose?

Example 1 | Measuring rectangular and triangular prisms

I decided to use a model to solve the problem.

Brian's Solution

1. Understand the Problem

I assume the sand will fill the sandbox, so I will imagine each of my models is made of sand. Each model will be 0.5 m deep and contain 8 m³ of sand.

2. Make a Plan

I know one dimension and the volume of each sandbox, so I can figure out the other dimensions.

3. Carry Out the Plan

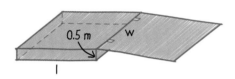

$V = Bh$

$8 \text{ m}^3 = l \times w \times 0.5 \text{ m}$

$16 \text{ m}^2 = l \times w$

The box is a square, so $l = w = 4.0$ m.

I used the lid of a greeting card box to represent the square sandbox. A square sheet of paper can represent the top.

I used the volume to figure out the other dimensions.

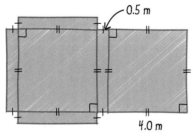

$SA = 2(4.0 \text{ m} \times 4.0 \text{ m}) + 4(4.0 \text{ m} \times 0.5 \text{ m})$

$= 32.0 \text{ m}^2 + 8.0 \text{ m}^2$

$= 40.0 \text{ m}^2$

I opened up the box lid to form the net of the sandbox. I determined the surface area of the lid and of the sheet of paper.

There are two congruent squares and four congruent rectangles.

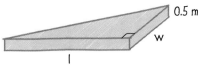

$V = (l \times w \div 2) \times h$

$8\ m^3 = (l \times w \div 2) \times 0.5\ m$

$16\ m^2 = l \times w \div 2$

$32\ m^2 = l \times w$

I chose 8.0 m for l and 4.0 m for w. By the Pythagorean theorem, the third side is 8.9 m.

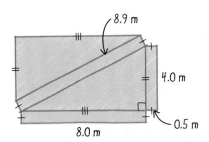

$SA = 2[(8.0\ m \times 4.0\ m) \div 2] + 0.5\ m(4.0\ m + 8.0\ m + 8.9\ m)$

$= 32.0\ m^2 + 10.5\ m^2$

$= 42.5\ m^2$

We should build the square sandbox because it has less surface area and so it will use less wood.

I used a plastic sandwich container to represent the triangular sandbox. I thought that the top of the container could represent the cover.

I used the volume to figure out the other dimensions.

I put the values I knew into the formula.

I divided both sides by 0.5. That is like multiplying by 2.

I multiplied both sides by 2 again.

I decided to choose 8.0 and 4.0 because they are factors of 32, and they are easy numbers to work with.

I cut the box to make the net and then I calculated the surface area.

4. Look Back

I checked my calculations. They look correct.

I thought that the sand would fill the box to the brim, but now I think it would be better not to fill the box to the top, so that the sand will not spill out.

Reflecting

A. How did Brian's models help him figure out how much wood was needed to make the sandbox?

WORK WITH *the Math*

Example 2 | Solving a problem using models

A soup can has a capacity of 350 mL and radius of 3.0 cm. Which box uses less cardboard?

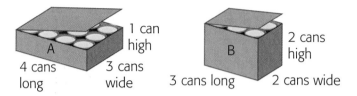

A — 4 cans long, 3 cans wide, 1 can high

B — 3 cans long, 2 cans wide, 2 cans high

Nikita's Solution

---

1. Understand the Problem

Each can is 3.0 cm in radius and holds 350 mL of soup.
I will assume that each can has a volume of 350 cm³.

---

2. Make a Plan

I will use the volume to figure out the height of each can.
Then I will determine the surface areas of the boxes.

---

3. Carry Out the Plan

$V = \pi \times r \times r \times h$

$350.0 \text{ cm}^3 \doteq 3.14 \times 3.0 \text{ cm} \times 3.0 \text{ cm} \times h$

$12.4 \text{ cm} \doteq h$

I calculated the height of a can.

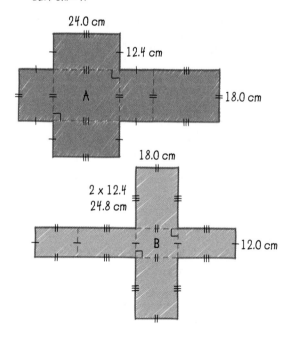

24.0 cm

12.4 cm

A

18.0 cm

18.0 cm

2 x 12.4
24.8 cm

B

12.0 cm

I determined the dimensions of each box.

$SA = 2(18.0 \text{ cm} \times 24.0 \text{ cm}) + 2(12.4 \text{ cm} \times 24.0 \text{ cm})$
$+ 2(12.4 \text{ cm} \times 18.0 \text{ cm})$
$= 1905.6 \text{ cm}^2$

$SA = 2(12.0 \text{ cm} \times 24.8 \text{ cm}) + 2(18.0 \text{ cm} \times 24.8 \text{ cm})$
$+ 2(12.0 \text{ cm} \times 18.0 \text{ cm})$
$= 1920.0 \text{ cm}^2$

Box A has less surface area, so it uses less cardboard.

A Checking

1. A can of vegetable juice has a capacity of 284 mL and is 3.2 cm in radius. Twenty-four cans of juice will be packed in open boxes, and then wrapped in plastic. Which arrangement uses less plastic?

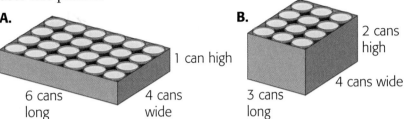

A. 1 can high — 6 cans long — 4 cans wide

B. 2 cans high — 3 cans long — 4 cans wide

B Practising

2. Circular tea bags are packaged in cylinders 8.0 cm high that are also 400 cm³ in total volume. The cylinders are packed in boxes for shipping.
   a) Draw a model for two different boxes that would each hold 24 tea cylinders.
   b) In which box would you ship the tea cylinders? Explain.

3. Fritz is making a stained-glass window. This window is shaped like a rectangle 0.5 m wide by 2.5 m long, with a semicircle above the rectangle.
   a) Draw an outline of the window. Label the dimensions.
   b) How much glass does Fritz need?

4. A package of rice crackers is in the shape of a prism with a base area of 18.0 cm² and a volume of 216 cm³. The base is a right isosceles triangle. The packages are shipped in boxes with a volume of 5184 cm³.
   a) How many packages of crackers are in each box?
   b) Model two different boxes that would hold the packages. Explain which box you would use.

5. A pizza box measuring 34 cm by 34 cm by 5 cm contains a pizza that is 30 cm in diameter. About what percent of the box is occupied by the pizza and what percent is not?

6. Modelling is often a useful way to solve a problem. Is there a time when you would not use a model to solve a problem that involves surface area?

Matching Geometric Solids

YOU WILL NEED
- Geometric Solids Cards I–V
- a calculator

In this game, you will match cards of solids and their nets.

Number of players: 2–4

How to Play

1. Deal five cards to each player. Place the remaining cards in a pile on the table, face down.

2. In turn, put any matching pair of cards in front of you on the table. For example, you can match a net and a surface area, a 3-D object and a net, a 3-D object and a volume, or a 3-D object and a surface area. Then pick up two more cards from the pile.

3. If you cannot match any cards, ask another player for a matching card. If she has one, put the match on the table and take two more cards from the pile. If she does not have one, she says, "Go fish!" Then you pick one card from the pile. If you can make a match now, then do so, and take two more cards. If you cannot, then it is the next player's turn.

4. If you disagree with a player's match, make a challenge. If he is correct, he keeps the cards. If he is wrong, he gives you one of his matches.

5. The game is over when no one has any cards left.

6. The winner is the player who makes the most matches.

Nikita's Turn

I had this card.

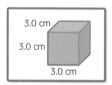

3.0 cm
3.0 cm
3.0 cm

I could not match it with any of my other cards, so I asked Preston if he had one with $V = 27.0 \text{ cm}^3$ on it. He did not, so he said, "Go fish!" I took this card from the pile: so I had a match. I put down those two cards and took two more from the pile.

$SA = 54.0 \text{ cm}^2$

1. Calculate the surface area of each prism.

   a) 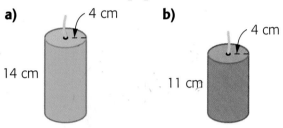 4.3 cm

   22.5 cm   3.0 cm

   b) 15 cm

   15 cm   15 cm

   c) 7.0 cm

   24.0 cm   3.5 cm

2. Draw a net for the paper that is needed to wrap each candle.

   a) 4 cm

   14 cm

   b) 4 cm

   11 cm

3. Which one of the following two statements is true? Explain.
   a) The volume of cylinder B is twice the volume of cylinder A.
   b) The surface area of cylinder B is twice the surface area of cylinder A.

   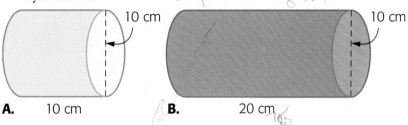

   A. 10 cm   10 cm

   B. 20 cm   10 cm

4. Calculate the surface area of each prism.

   a) 3.0 cm

   6.0 cm   8.0 cm

   b) 6.0 cm

   4.0 cm   15.0 cm

   c) 5.0 cm

   10.0 cm

   7.0 cm

   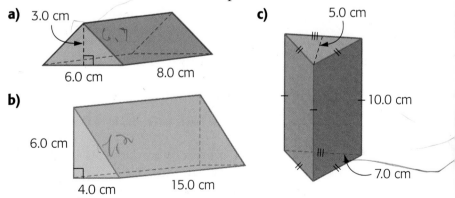

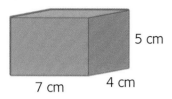

5. a) Determine the volume of this prism.

b) Triple the width, length, and height of the prism. What is the volume now?

5 cm

7 cm   4 cm

6. Which backpack holds the most?

A.

26 cm

20 cm   10 cm

B.

32 cm

16 cm   8 cm

C.

28 cm

14 cm   12 cm

7. Calculate the surface area and volume of each cylinder.

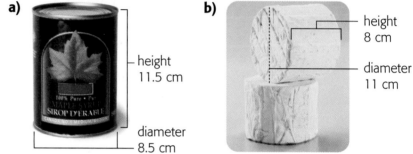

a)

height 11.5 cm

diameter 8.5 cm

b)

height 8 cm

diameter 11 cm

8. Icarus Airlines does not allow passengers to board an airplane with luggage that is more than 22 700 cm³ in volume. Would a passenger be allowed to board an airplane with this suitcase? Explain.

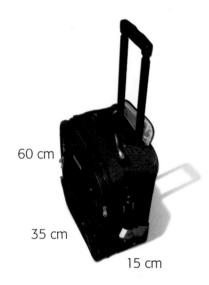

60 cm

35 cm

15 cm

9. A package of microwave popcorn is 8 cm wide, 10 cm long, and 1200 cm³ in volume. The packages are shipped in boxes with a volume of 24 000 cm³.

a) How many packages of popcorn are in each box?

b) Draw two different boxes that would hold the packages. Explain which box you would use.

What Do You Think Now?

Revisit What Do You Think? on page 193. Have your answers and explanations changed?

Chapter **Review**

Frequently Asked Questions

Q: How do you calculate the volume of a rectangular prism?

A1: You can model the prism using centimetre cubes.

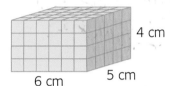

This prism has 120 cubes, so its volume is 120 cm³.

A2: You can multiply the area of the base by the height.

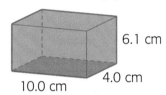

Volume = area of base × height
$$= (10.0 \text{ cm} \times 4.0 \text{ cm}) \times 6.1 \text{ cm}$$
$$= 244.0 \text{ cm}^3$$

Q: How do you calculate the volume of a triangular prism?

A1: You can divide the volume of a rectangular prism with the same width, length, and height by 2.

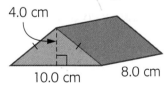

The volume of a rectangular prism 10.0 cm by 4.0 cm by 8.0 cm is 320.0 cm³, so the volume of this triangular prism is 320.0 cm³ ÷ 2 = 160.0 cm³.

A2: You can multiply the area of the base by the height.

Volume = area of base × height
$$= [(10.0 \text{ cm} \times 4.0 \text{ cm}) \div 2] \times 8.0 \text{ cm}$$
$$= 160.0 \text{ cm}^3$$

Q: How do you calculate the volume of a cylinder?

A: You can multiply the area of the base by the height.

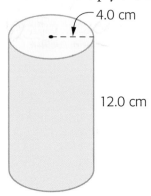

4.0 cm

12.0 cm

Volume = area of base × height
$$= (\pi \times r \times r) \times h$$
$$= \pi \times 4.0 \text{ cm} \times 4.0 \text{ cm} \times 12.0 \text{ cm}$$
$$\doteq 603.2 \text{ cm}^3$$

Practice

Lesson 5.2

1. Draw a net for each object.
   a) a rectangular prism 8 cm by 5 cm by 3 cm
   b) a cube with a side length of 6 cm
   c) a prism 6 cm high with an isosceles triangular base 5 cm wide and 4 cm high
   d) a cylinder 10 cm in diameter and 7 cm high

2. Explain how to determine the surface area of a rectangular box. Draw a net to support your explanation.

3. Match each net with its 3-D object. Explain your choice.

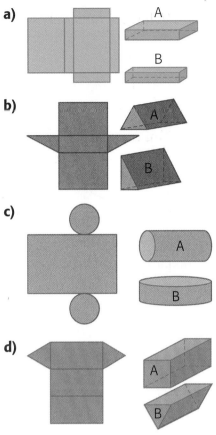

a)

A

B

b)

A

B

c)

A

B

d)

A

B

Lesson 5.3

4. Sketch each object and label its dimensions.
   Then calculate its surface area.

	Item	Length (cm)	Width of base (cm)	Height of base (cm)
a)	tissue box	22	7	10
b)	cereal box	16.3	5.0	27.5
c)	cheese in the shape of triangular prism	25.0	18.0	2.5

5. Ryan is making a cover for his hamster's cage. The cage is
   80 cm long, 50 cm wide, and 40 cm high. How much material
   will he need, if he allows 5% more for the seams of the cover?

6. How much waxed paper will Jake need to cover a cylindrical candle that is 6 cm in radius and 20 cm high?

7. Jeanette is comparing two full boxes of the same kind of buttons at a store. Both boxes cost $2.99. Explain which box is the better buy.

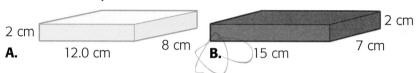

A. 2 cm   8 cm   12.0 cm   **B.** 15 cm   2 cm   7 cm

8. An apartment building has a square entrance hall. There is a triangular planter in each corner of the hall. Each planter is 45 cm deep, and the two sides against the wall are each 90 cm long. What volume of soil is needed to fill all four of these planters?

9. What might be the dimensions of a cylindrical container that contains 750 mL of yogurt?

10. Each week, the Fergusons put out one full round can of grass clippings for collection. The can is 50 cm in diameter and 65 cm high. What volume of grass do they put out each week?

11. A company packages DVD collections in rectangular cases 20.0 cm high, 2 cm thick, and 600 cm^3 in volume. The cases are then packed into boxes for shipping.
   a) Draw and label two boxes of different dimensions that would hold 10 DVD collections that are packed tightly together.
   b) In which box would you ship the collections? Explain.

Chapter **Task**

Moving Day

You are moving and you want to pack all of your own special belongings. Some are very large, others are small.

❓ How much material and how much space would you need?

A. Select 10 items of different sizes and shapes to pack. Include items in the shape of rectangular prisms, triangular prisms, and cylinders.

B. Measure each item.

C. Write a description of each object and its dimensions.

D. Each box will hold one item. Draw a net for each box. Label the dimensions.

E. Calculate the amount of cardboard needed to make each box. Add 10% to allow for overlap.

F. Calculate the volume of each box.

G. Determine what percent of the moving truck your boxes will occupy.

2.5 m

5.0 m

3.0 m

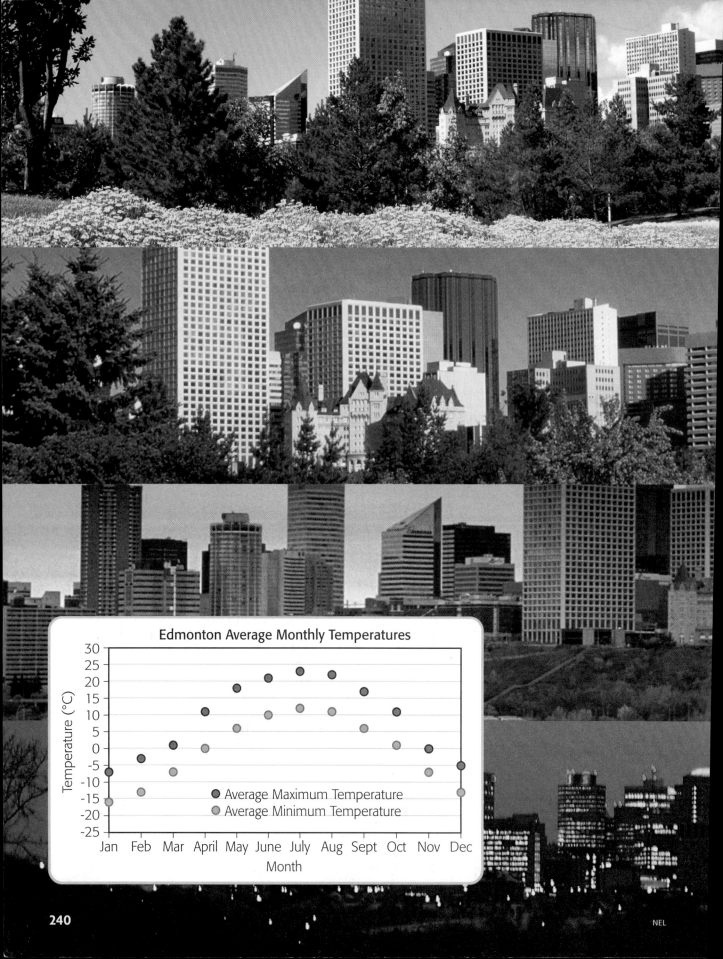

Edmonton Average Monthly Temperatures

Average Maximum Temperature
Average Minimum Temperature

Integers

GOAL

You will be able to

- represent multiplication and division of integers using concrete materials, drawings, and number lines

- record the multiplication and division of integers symbolically

- solve problems that involve addition, subtraction, multiplication, and division of integers

◄ How do you think the average monthly minimum and maximum temperatures were calculated?

Getting **Started**

YOU WILL NEED
- a red spinner and a blue spinner, each divided into eighths
- two paper clips
- red and blue counters
- number lines
- red and blue coloured pencils

Spinning Numbers

Elena has a red spinner that shows positive numbers and a blue spinner that shows negative numbers. Each spinner is divided into eight equal sections. She spins one spinner and records the number. She spins the other spinner and records the number.

❓ What are the greatest and least sums and differences possible?

A. Spin both spinners. Record the sum and the difference in a chart like the one below. Repeat this nine more times.

Positive number (red)	Negative number (blue)	Sum	Difference

B. Does the order in which you add the numbers affect the sum? Explain.

C. Does the order in which you subtract the numbers affect the difference? Explain.

D. Can you get a sum of 0? Can you get a difference of 0? Explain.

E. What is your greatest sum?
What is the greatest sum you could get?

F. What is your least sum? What is the least sum you could get?

G. What is your greatest difference?
What is the greatest difference you could get?

H. What is your least difference?
What is the least difference you could get?

What Do You Think?

Decide whether you agree or disagree with each statement.
Be ready to explain your decision.

1. 5×4 can be thought of as the repeated addition $4 + 4 + 4 + 4 + 4$. You can use this strategy to multiply any two integers.

2. You can divide 20 by 4 by subtracting 4 repeatedly from 20 and counting the number of subtractions needed to get a remainder of 0.

$$
\left.
\begin{array}{l}
20 - 4 = 16 \\
16 - 4 = 12 \\
12 - 4 = 8 \\
8 - 4 = 4 \\
4 - 4 = 0
\end{array}
\right\} \quad 20 \div 4 = 5
$$

You can use this strategy to divide any two integers.

3. The product of two integers is probably always greater than their quotient.

6.1

Integer Multiplication

GOAL

Use patterns to predict the products of integers.

LEARN ABOUT the Math

Guy and Elena thought they could use coloured counters to model integer multiplication.

> ❓ **How can you determine the product of two integers?**

- A positive integer may be written without a + sign in front of it.
- Use brackets to separate the sign of a negative integer from any operation that comes immediately before it in a mathematical expression. For example, write $-3 + (-4)$ to separate the sign of -4 from the addition operation.
- Instead of using a × sign, you can use brackets to separate the factors in a product. For example, 3×5 and $3(5)$ represent the same product.

Example 1 | Modelling positives × negatives

Use integer counters to model products of the form $(+) \times (-)$.

Guy's Solution

$3 \times (-2)$

$3 \times (-2) = -6$

$5 \times (-3)$

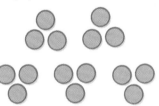

$5 \times (-3) = -15$

$2 \times (-5)$

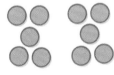

$2 \times (-5) = -10$

The examples I used show that $(+) \times (-) = (-)$.

I tried a few examples of $(+) \times (-)$.

I knew that a product tells the number of identical groups of counters to combine. I used the first factor to tell the number of groups and the second factor to tell the number of negative counters in a group.

I can use this strategy to model any product of $(+) \times (-)$ as groups of negative counters.

Example 2 | Modelling negatives × positives

Calculate −2 × 3.

Vanessa's Solution: Using a property of multiplication

-2 x 3 = 3 x (-2) = -6
I think -2 x 3 = -6.

I remembered that, when you multiply whole numbers, the order does not matter. I assumed that would be true for integers.

Kaitlyn's Solution: Using a pattern

3 x 3 = 9 ⎤ -3
2 x 3 = 6 ⎬ -3
1 x 3 = 3 ⎬ -3
0 x 3 = 0 ⎬ -3
-1 x 3 = -3 ⎬ -3
-2 x 3 = -6 ⎦

I used a multiplication pattern. My pattern shows that, when you decrease the first factor by 1, the product decreases by 3.

I continued this pattern until the first factor was −2.

Joseph's Solution: Using a property of integers

-2 x 3 = 0 - 2 x 3
      = 0 - 6
      = -6
-2 x 3 = -6

I knew that −2 means 0 − 2, so I assumed that −2 × 3 is the same as 0 − 2 × 3.

Example 3 | Using reasoning to multiply two negatives

Calculate −2(−3).

Elena's Solution: Using a multiplication pattern

3(-3) = -9 ⎤ +3
2(-3) = -6 ⎬ +3
1(-3) = -3 ⎬ +3
0(-3) = 0 ⎬ +3
-1(-3) = 3 ⎬ +3
-2(-3) = 6 ⎦

Guy told me that, when you multiply (+) × (−), the product is negative. I used a multiplication pattern that shows that, each time the first factor is decreased by 1, the product increases by 3.

Mark's Solution: Using counters and a property of integers

-2 x (-3) = 0 - 2 x (-3)

-2(-3) = 6

−2 means 0 − 2, so you can say that −2 × (−3) is the same as 0 − 2 × (−3).

I represented 0 with 2 groups, each containing 3 0-pairs. Then I subtracted 2 groups of 3 blue counters.

Reflecting

A. Why does it make sense that the products in each pair are opposites?

2×3 and -2×3
-2×3 and $-2 \times (-3)$

B. How can you predict the sign and value of the product of two integers? Summarize your answer using the chart.

×		Second integer	
		+	−
First integer	+		
	−		

WORK WITH the Math

Example 4	Modelling negatives × positives

Use counters to show why $-3(5) = -15$.

Solution

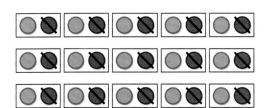

Think of −3(5) as 0 − 3(5).
This means you have to remove 3 groups of 5 positive red counters from 0.

So make 3 groups of 5 0-pairs and remove the red counters.

Example 5 | Determining factors of an integer

Represent 6 as a product of two integers in as many ways as possible.

Solution

6 can be factored as

1×6 and 6×1
$-1 \times (-6)$ and $-6 \times (-1)$
2×3 and 3×2
$-2 \times (-3)$ and $-3 \times (-2)$

If the product is positive, either both factors are positive or both are negative.

Example 6 | Creating a context requiring multiplication

Describe a situation that requires multiplying two integers to answer a question.

Solution

The water level in a tube is dropping at a rate of 3 mm/s.

a) How far will it drop in 10 s?

b) If the height of the water is now 150 mm, what was the height 10 s ago?

You can think of the rate at which the water level dropped as a negative integer (-3 mm/s).

$10 \times (-3) = -30$ mm

Then you can think of the time as negative if you think about what happened in the past.

$$150 + (-10) \times (-3) = 150 + 30$$
$$= 180 \text{ mm}$$

A Checking

1. Write an expression that has the same product.
   a) $3(-4)$ **c)** $-2(-7)$
   b) $-3(1)$ **d)** $-5(-4)$

2. Multiply the integers in each expression using counters.
   a) $2 \times (-5)$ **b)** $-4(-3)$ **c)** $-6(2)$

B Practising

3. Calculate.
   a) -3×4 c) $-5(-5)$
   b) $4(-2)$ d) -8×2

4. Represent each using a model.
   a) $5 \times (-2)$ b) -5×2 c) $-5 \times (-2)$

5. Write the integer multiplication represented by each counter model.

   a)

   b)

   c)

   d)

6. Calculate.
   a) -2×10 c) $2 \times (-8)$ e) $5 \times (-6)$
   b) $-10 \times (-2)$ d) $-8 \times (-2)$ f) -5×6

7. Which two integers would make each true?
   a) The sum of the integers is 23 less than the product.
   b) The sum of the integers is 28 more than the product.
   c) The sum of the integers is 73 more than the product.

8. Complete the following.
   a) $6 \times \blacksquare = (-3) \times 4$ c) $\blacksquare \times 4 = (-6) \times \blacksquare$
   b) $\blacksquare \times (-3) = 5 \times \blacksquare$ d) $\blacksquare \times (-2) = (-6) \times \blacksquare$

9. Explain why the product of any two integers is the same as the product of their opposites.

10. A deck of cards has two cards each of the integers from -5 to 5. Suppose you are dealt two cards from the deck and multiply the numbers on those cards.
    a) Which two cards would give you the greatest product?
    b) Which two cards would give you the least product?

Reading Strategy

Questioning

What questions can you ask to help you understand the problem?

11. Replace the ▨ with =, <, or > to make each statement true.

a) $-1 \times (-2)$ ▨ -4 **d)** $3 \times (-1)$ ▨ -2

b) $4 \times (-5)$ ▨ -20 **e)** $-6 \times (-2)$ ▨ 11

c) $-2 \times (-4)$ ▨ 7 **f)** -4×2 ▨ -7

12. a) Write -16 as a product of two integers in as many different ways as possible.

b) Write 16 as a product of two integers in as many different ways as possible.

13. The product of three integers is –24. Name five possibilities for the three integers.

14. Write each as a product.

a) $-9 + (-10) + (-11)$ **c)** $12 - (-7) - 20$

b) $(-17) + (-8) + (-25)$ **d)** $(-12) + (-18) - 10$

15. Jasmine has 50 shares of a company. The value of each share went down by $2 today. Express the total change in value of Jasmine's shares as an integer calculation.

16. a) Explain why each of these equations is true.

     A. $7 \times (-2) = -7 \times 2$ **B.** $(-2) \times (-7) = 2 \times 7$

b) Create a situation in which each expression could be used to solve a problem.

17. How can you predict the sign of each product without actually calculating it?

a) $-3 \times (-2) \times 4$ **b)** $4 \times (-5) \times 6$

18. Each pattern is based on multiplying integers. Complete each pattern and write a rule for the pattern.

a) $1, -3, 9, -27, 81,$ ___, ___, ___

b) $-3, 6, -12,$ ___, ___, ___

19. You multiplied four integers together, and the answer was negative. What do you know about the signs of the integers?

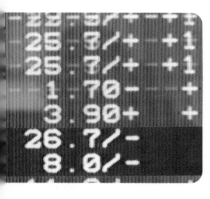

6.2 Using Number Lines to Model Integer Multiplication

YOU WILL NEED
• Number Lines

GOAL

Use a pictorial model to represent integer multiplication.

LEARN ABOUT *the Math*

Sanjev made a movie for his media class. Now he must edit it. He can rewind or fast-forward through the movie at different speeds. The speed is measured in frames per second (fps). He resets the counter to 0 before he advances or rewinds the movie.

? How can Sanjev name the frame he will reach after rewinding or fast-forwarding for a given amount of time?

A. The frame counter is set to 0. You rewind at 10 fps. Complete the following chart showing the frame counter for 1 s, 2 s, 3 s, and 4 s. Use a dotted arrow to show each jump and a solid arrow to show the result.

Rewind time (s)	Number line model	Ending frame	Equation
1	$1(-10) = -10$ 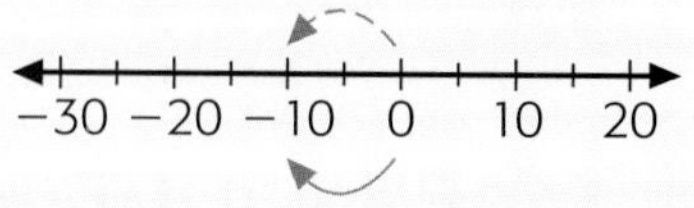	-10	$1(-10) = -10$
2	$2(-10) = -20$ 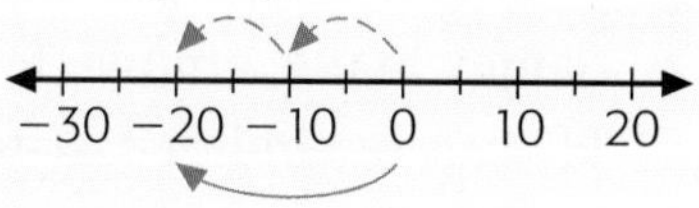	-20	$2(-10) = -20$
3			
4			

B. Predict the ending frames if you rewind for 10 s, 20 s, and 30 s, respectively.

C. You fast-forward at 10 fps and notice that the counter shows 0 when you stop. Complete the following chart showing the starting frame number for each fast-forward time.

Fast-forward time (s)	Number line model	Starting frame	Equation
1	$1(10) = 10$ 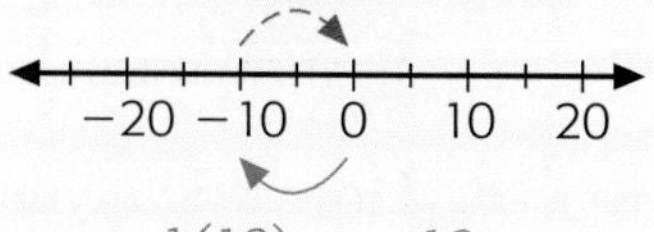 $-1(10) = -10$	-10	$-1(10) = -10$
2	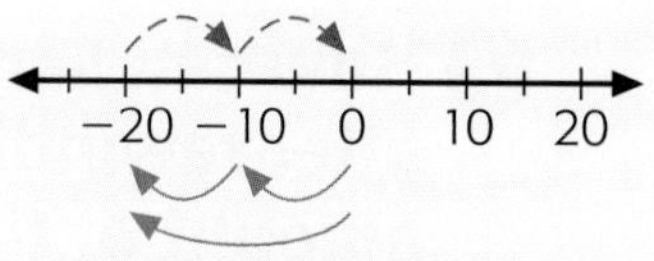 $-2(10) = -20$	-20	$-2(10) = -20$
3			
4			

D. Predict the starting frame if you had fast-forwarded for 10 s, 20 s, and 30 s, respectively, and arrived at frame 0.

E. You rewind at 10 fps and notice that the counter shows 0 when you stop. Complete the following chart showing the starting frame number for rewind time.

Rewind time (s)	Number line model	Starting frame	Equation
1	$-1(-10) = 10$ 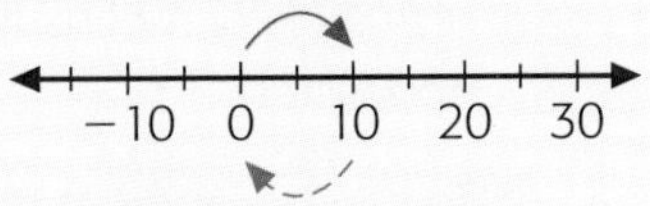 $1(-10) = -10$	10	$-1(-10) = 10$
2	$-2(-10) = 20$ 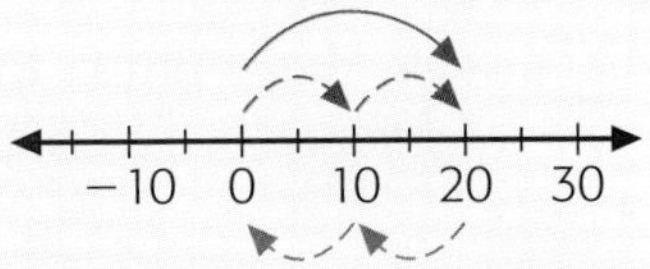	20	
3			
4			

F. Predict the starting frame if you had rewound for 10 s, 20 s, and 30 s, respectively, and arrived at frame 0.

Reflecting

G. In parts C and E, why does it make sense to treat the time as negative when you write the multiplication equation for the starting frame?

H. How would you decide whether to use counters or a number line to represent an integer multiplication?

WORK WITH the Math

Example 1 | Modelling an integer product

Multiply $-3 \times (-2)$ using a number line model.

Mark's Solution

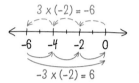

$-3 \times (-2)$ means the same as $0 - 3 \times (-2)$, which is the opposite of $3 \times (-2)$.

To show $3 \times (-2)$, I drew 3 dotted blue arrows going left from 0, with 2 units to each arrow. The arrows stop at -6.

To show its opposite, $-3 \times (-2)$, I drew 3 solid red arrows going right from -6 back to 0. These arrows go to the right 6 units. So the answer must be 6, which is the opposite of -6.

Example 2 | Using integers to solve distance problems

Kenji walks to the west at 80 m/min.
a) Where will he be after 5 min?
b) Suppose that Kenji walked to the west for 18 min. How far must he walk to return to his starting position? In which direction must he walk?

Michel's Solution

I knew that 80 m/min means 80 m every minute.
I imagined a number line where my starting point was 0.
I drew my number line with West negative and East positive.

a) $5 \times (-80) = -400$
Kenji will be 400 m to the west.

I multiplied $5 \times 80 = 400$.
I knew that if he was walking to the west, he would end up west of 0 and that had to be negative.

b) $18 \times (-80) = -1440$
Kenji must walk 1440 m to the east.

I multiplied $18 \times 80 = 1440$.
If he walked to the west to get somewhere, he must have started somewhere to the east of that place.

A Checking

1. Write the multiplication sentence that the blue arrows in each model represents.

a)

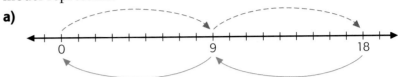

b)

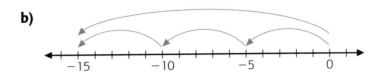

2. Dario is on a cycling trip. He started at 0 km.
   He is now at position 20 h × (−20 km/h).
   When did he reach each of the following positions?
   Draw a number line to show how you got your answer.
   a) 10 h × (−20 km/h)
   b) 8 h × (−20 km/h)
   c) 0 km

B Practising

3. Model $-4 \times (-3)$ on a number line. Calculate the product. Explain what you did.

4. Use a number line to show how to determine $(-4)(-7)$.

5. Write each as a multiplication and then calculate the result.

a)

b)
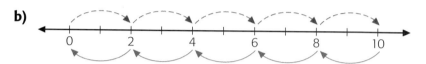

6. a) Write the multiplication equation modelled by each number line diagram.

b) Why do the products represented by each diagram have the same value?

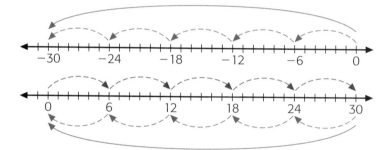

West   East
−   +

0
Start here

7. Write an integer multiplication sentence for each description.

a) Tyler rode a bus to the west for 4 h at 100 km/h.

b) Jenna babysat for 3 h, earning $5/h.

c) The temperature fell 2 °C a day for 6 days.

8. Multiply.

a) $0 \times (-30)$

b) $7(-20)$

c) $-4(-20)$

d) $-15(4)$

e) $-6(-30)$

f) $-20(-50)$

9. a) Determine the greatest product you can form using any pair of numbers from this list. Show how you know.
$-20, -10, 0, 10, 15$
b) Describe a problem situation for which the greatest product might be a solution.

10. The product of two integers is between -20 and -25. Give five possible pairs of integers for which this is true.

11. Explain how you might use a number line to solve $-9 \times \blacksquare = 108$.

12. Each pattern is based on multiplication. Fill in the next three terms and explain the pattern rule.
a) $-20, 100, -500, \_\_, \_\_, \_\_$
b) $5, -55, 605, \_\_, \_\_, \_\_$

13. Multiply.
a) $-5 \times 3 \times (-8)$
b) $-10 \times 2 \times (-5) \times (-6)$

14. The product of five different integers is -80.
a) What is the least possible sum of these integers?
b) What is the greatest possible sum?
c) Is it possible for the product of four different integers to be -80? Explain.

15. Use a number line model to show that these products are equivalent.
a) -12×10 and $12 \times (-10)$
b) $-15 \times (-20)$ and 15×20

16. a) How could you use a number line model to explain why $(-) \times (+) = (+) \times (-)$?
b) How could you use a number line model to explain why the product of two negative numbers is positive?

Mid-Chapter **Review**

Frequently Asked Questions

Q: How can you multiply integers?

A: You can use counters, a number line, or repeated addition. The following models show that

$$(+) \times (+) = + \qquad\qquad (-) \times (+) = -$$
$$(+) \times (-) = - \qquad\qquad (-) \times (-) = +$$

Multiplication question	Counter model	Number line model
$4 \times 3 = 12$	4 groups of 3 positive (red) counters give a total of 12 positive (red) counters.	$4 \times 3 = 12$ The end point tells that $4 \times 3 = 12$.
$4(-3) = -12$	4 groups of 3 negative (blue) counters give a total of 12 negative (blue) counters.	$4(-3) = -12$ The end point tells that $4(-3) = -12$.
$-4 \times 3 = -12$	$-4 \times 3 = 0 - 4 \times 3$ $0 - 4 \times 3$ means subtract 4 groups of 3 red counters from 0. Use the zero principle, and add 4 groups of 3 red counters and 4 groups of 3 blue counters. Then subtract the 4 groups of 3 red counters. You are left with 4 groups of 3 blue counters, or 12 blue counters.	$-4 \times 3 = -12$ The length and direction of the arrow tells that $-4 \times 3 = -12$.

$-4(-3) = 12$

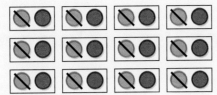

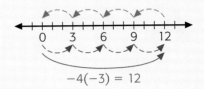

$-4 \times (-3) = 0 - 4(-3)$
$0 - 4(-3)$ means subtract 4 groups of 3 negative (blue) counters from 0. The result is 4 groups of 3 positive (red) counters, or a total of 12 positive (red) counters.

The length and direction of the arrow tells that $-4 \times (-3) = 12$.

Practice

Lesson 6.1

1. Represent each expression using a counter model.
   a) $2 \times (-5)$ **b)** $-3 \times (-4)$ **c)** -2×4

2. Calculate.
   a) -6×2 **d)** $-1 \times (-8)$
   b) $6 \times (-3)$ **e)** $0 \times (-9)$
   c) $-5 \times (-4)$ **f)** $(-7)(-8)$

3. Replace the ▨ with =, <, or > to make each statement true.
   a) $-2 \times (-2)$ ▨ -4 **d)** $-3 \times (-1)$ ▨ 4
   b) $2 \times (-10)$ ▨ -20 **e)** $0 \times (-4)$ ▨ -1
   c) $-2 \times (-5)$ ▨ 7 **f)** $3 \times (-3)$ ▨ -3

Lesson 6.2

4. Represent each expression using a number line model.
   a) $5 \times (-8)$ **b)** $-6 \times (-4)$ **c)** -5×9

5. When playing a game, Matt lost eight points in each of his last three turns.
   Show how to use integers to determine the change in his score after these three turns.

6. Determine the least product you can form using any pair of numbers from this list. Show how you know.
   $-30, -20, 0, 10, 15$

7. Create and solve a problem for $8 \times (-10)$.

6.3

Exploring Uses of Integer Division

GOAL

Investigate situations that can be modelled using integer division.

EXPLORE the Math

Elena and Vanessa keep track of changes in their weekly basketball scores. They record a positive change if a score goes up from the previous week and a negative change if a score goes down.

Elena's Basketball Record					
Week	2	3	4	5	6
Change in score	+5	−2	−2	−3	+7

Vanessa's Basketball Record					
Week	2	3	4	5	6
Change in score	−15	−8	−12	+20	+5

The girls want to compare their average weekly score changes. That means each has to add her scores and divide by the number of weeks, which requires a division involving a negative number.

❓ What other kinds of situations can be represented using a division involving two integers?

6.4

Integer Division

YOU WILL NEED
- red and blue counters
- Number Lines

GOAL

Use integer tiles and number lines to model integer division.

LEARN ABOUT *the Math*

The Science Centre uses a Van de Graaff generator to create large static charges.

Both spheres start with a neutral or 0-charge. A motor turns a belt on a pulley at a constant speed. The movement of the belt over the pulley transfers negative charges to the small sphere at a constant rate.

? **If you know the charge and the time the motor has been running, how can you determine the charge rate?**

Example 1 | Dividing a 2-digit integer by a 1-digit integer

Running the motor for 8 s resulted in a charge of −40 on the small sphere and a charge of +40 on the large sphere. Determine the charge rate.

Guy's Solution: Using integer tiles to model (−) ÷ (+)

The rate at which the small sphere gained its charge is

total charge gained ÷ time = -40 ÷ 8.

I knew that electrons moved to the small sphere from the larger one. That meant the small sphere gained a negative charge.

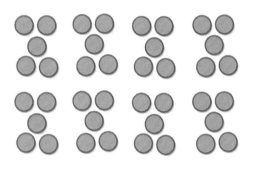

I used 40 negative (blue) tiles to represent the final charge on the small sphere.

I arranged the counters into 8 equal groups, 1 group for the charge transferred each second.

The number of groups shows the number of seconds. The counters in each group represent the charge transferred each second.

The divisor represents the number of groups and the quotient represents the counters in each group.

$$\frac{\text{final charge of -40}}{\text{8 seconds}} = \frac{-40}{8}$$
$$= -5$$

The small sphere gained -5 charges per second.

Kaitlyn's Solution: Using integer tiles to model (−) ÷ (−)

The rate at which the large sphere lost its charge is

total charge lost ÷ time = -40 ÷ (-8).

The electrons that moved to the small sphere started on the large sphere. I imagined going back in time to see how fast they had been transferred. That meant using a negative value for the 8 s.

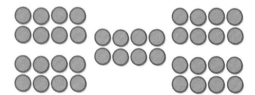

I represented dividing −40 by −8 by regrouping 40 negative (blue) counters into groups of 8. The counters in each group represent the charge transferred each second.

There are 5 groups.
The large sphere lost electrons at a rate of 5 charges/s.

The divisor represents the number of counters in each group, and the quotient represents the number of groups.

Sanjev's Solution: Using a number line to model (−) ÷ (+)

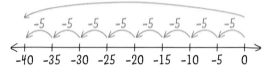

The charge rate is
final charge of -40 ÷ 8 s
= -40 charges ÷ 8 s
= -5 charges/s

I used a number line to show how the small sphere was charged.
Since the charge was −40, I drew an arrow from 0 to −40.

Then I divided the arrow into 8 equal sections, one for each second.

The number of sections is the denominator. The length and direction of each section shows the charge rate.

Mark's Solution: Relating integer division to integer multiplication

To determine the charge rate on the small sphere, I have to solve

▦ = -40 ÷ 8

This is the same as solving ▦ x 8 = -40.
▦ must be negative.

▦ = -5

The small sphere was gaining charges at -5 charges/s.

I knew that every division equation has a related multiplication equation.
I knew that $5 \times 8 = 40$. If the product is negative, one of the factors has to be positive and the other has to be negative.

Reflecting

A. Why were the students correct to use division to determine the rates?

B. How can you use the signs of integers in a division to predict the sign of the quotient?

Example 2 | Solving a problem using division

The table below shows the daily low temperatures for one week in Winnipeg. Calculate the average daily low for the week.

Mon.	Tue.	Wed.	Thur.	Fri.	Sat.	Sun.
−11 °C	−11 °C	−12 °C	−10 °C	−9 °C	−9 °C	−8 °C

Solution

Total of the temperatures = −70.

Average daily temperature for the week

$$= \frac{-70}{7}$$
$$= -10$$

Calculate the average by dividing.

$$\frac{\text{total of the temperatures}}{\text{number of days}}$$

The average low for the week was − 10 °C.

A Checking

1. Calculate.
   a) $-45 \div (-5)$

   b) $\dfrac{0}{-8}$

   c) $81 \div (-9)$

   d) $\dfrac{-56}{7}$

2. Match each division equation with the related multiplication equation. Write the missing integers.
   a) $-16 \div (-8) = \blacksquare$
   b) $16 \div 8 = \blacksquare$
   c) $-16 \div 8 = \blacksquare$
   d) $16 \div (-8) = \blacksquare$

   A. $\blacksquare \times (-8) = 16$
   B. $\blacksquare \times (-8) = -16$
   C. $\blacksquare \times 8 = 16$
   D. $\blacksquare \times 8 = -16$

B Practising

3. Write the division equation represented by each model.
   a)

   b)

4. Write a multiplication equation for each division. Then solve the division.

   a) $-72 \div (-9)$ **c)** $66 \div (-11)$

   b) $84 \div 7$ **d)** $-800 \div 20$

5. Divide.

   a) $40 \div (-5)$ **d)** $-121 \div (-11)$

   b) $-24 \div 6$ **e)** $0 \div (-10)$

   c) $\dfrac{-64}{-8}$ **f)** $\dfrac{54}{9}$

6. Nadia says that $\dfrac{-8}{-2}$ cannot represent a mean change in score. Do you agree? Why or why not?

7. Estimate each quotient.

   a) $844 \div (-4)$ **d)** $-168 \div 8$

   b) $-319 \div (-11)$ **e)** $136 \div (-17)$

   c) $448 \div (-32)$ **f)** $-575 \div (-23)$

8. Determine each quotient. Multiply to check any two.

   a) $\dfrac{48}{-12}$ **d)** $\dfrac{192}{-12}$

   b) $\dfrac{-32}{8}$ **e)** $\dfrac{-256}{32}$

   c) $\dfrac{-27}{-9}$ **f)** $\dfrac{-243}{-9}$

9. a) Copy and complete the following charts.

a	b	$a \times b$	Example
+	+		
+	−		
−	+		
−	−		

a	b	$a \div b$	Example
+	+		
+	−		
−	+		
−	−		

   b) How is determining the sign of a product the same as determining the sign of a quotient?

10. Determine the missing integer in each equation.

a) $40 \times \blacksquare = -800$

b) $\blacksquare \times (-11) = -132$

c) $25 \times \blacksquare = 2500$

d) $\blacksquare \times 24 = -192$

11. The quotient for $-35 \div 5$ is the opposite of the quotient for $-35 \div (-5)$. Why does this make sense?

12. Explain how you know that $4 \div (-2) = -4 \div 2$ and that $(-4) \div (-2) = 4 \div 2$.

13. Emma's scores for the first nine holes of a golf game are given below.

Hole	1	2	3	4	5	6	7	8	9
Score	+1	−1	+3	+3	+2	0	0	−1	+2

Each positive integer represents a score above par. Each negative integer represents a score below par. What is Emma's mean score per hole?

NEL

14. Sanjay has a small investment. Over seven days, the value of his investment changed as shown:

-11 ¢, -24 ¢, $+9$ ¢, $+6$ ¢, $+8$ ¢, -5 ¢, $+3$ ¢

a) What is the mean change in the value of his investments?
b) What is the difference between the mean value and the lowest recorded value?
c) What is the difference between the mean value and the highest recorded value?

15. Calculate.

a) $-3 \times (-8) \div (-4)$

b) $\dfrac{(-6)(6)}{-4}$

c) $-63 \div (-7)(-9)$

d) $\dfrac{-144 \div 12}{-3}$

e) $(7)(-6) \div (3)(-7)$

f) $(-2)(-9) \div (2)(-3)$

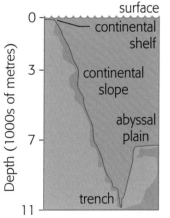

16. The Marianas Trench is the deepest spot in the world's oceans. It is located in the Pacific Ocean, just east of the Philippines. The maximum depth of the Marianas Trench is 10 962 m. The maximum depth of Lake Superior is 406 m.

Create and solve an integer division question using this information.

17. Predict the sign for each quotient without actually computing the final answer. Explain how you know.

a) $\dfrac{-125}{25}$

b) $\dfrac{84}{-7}$

c) $\dfrac{-91}{-7}$

6.5

Order of Operations

GOAL

Apply the rules for the order of operations with integers.

LEARN ABOUT *the Math*

Joseph won a contest, but he has to answer the following skill-testing question before he can claim the prize:

$$\frac{6 \div (-3) + [(4 - (-5)) \times (-7)]}{4 - 5}$$

❓ What is the answer to the skill-testing question?

Example 1	Evaluating an expression in fraction form

Use the order of operations to evaluate the skill-testing question.

Joseph's Solution

$$\frac{6 \div (-3) + [(4 - (-5)) \times (-7)]}{4 - 5}$$

I used the same order of operations for integers as I would have for other numbers.
I started by determining the value of the numerator.
I calculated what is in the innermost brackets.

$$= \frac{6 \div (-3) + [9 \times (-7)]}{4 - 5}$$

I calculated what is in the square brackets.

$$= \frac{6 \div (-3) + [-63]}{4 - 5}$$

I divided.

$$= \frac{-2 + [-63]}{4 - 5}$$

I added to calculate the numerator.

$$= \frac{-65}{4 - 5}$$

I subtracted to calculate the denominator.

$$= \frac{-65}{-1}$$

I divided the numerator by the denominator.

$$= 65$$

The answer is 65.

Reflecting

A. Chiyo says, "If an expression has a numerator and a denominator, like $\dfrac{-6 + (-10)}{(-4)(2)}$, the last calculation is division." Is Chiyo correct? Explain.

B. If you used a different order of operations, would your answer be different? Explain. Use an example.

WORK WITH *the Math*

Example 2 | Calculating using fewer steps

Calculate the answer to this skill-testing question.

$$\frac{[8 \times (-2) - 7] - 10 \div (-5)}{-3 - 4}$$

Vanessa's Solution

Numerator [8 x (-2) - 7] - 10 ÷ (-5)	I calculated the numerator first. I did three steps at the same time, since the calculations do not affect each other. $8 \times (-2) = -16$, $-16 - 7 = -23$, and $10 \div (-5) = -2$.
-23 - (-2) = -21	The numerator is -21.
Denominator -3 - 4 = -7	Then I calculated the denominator. It is like an expression in brackets.
$\frac{-21}{-7} = 3$	I know that a fraction can represent division. I also know that a negative integer divided by a negative integer is positive.

A Checking

1. Calculate.

   a) $-9 - (-6) \div 6$

   b) $4 \times (-8) - (-5)$

   c) $-8 \times (-3) - (-8) \div (-4)$

   d) $\dfrac{-16}{[-2 - (-18)] \times (-1)}$

B Practising

2. In each expression, which calculation(s) should you do first?
   a) $-5 + (-6) \times (-8) \div 2$
   b) $-8 \times 6 \div (-2) - [-9 \times (-3)]$

3. Calculate.
   a) $-2 + (-3) \times (-8 + 4)$
   b) $-9 - (-8) \times 7 + [6 \times (-2)]$
   c) $7 \times [8 - (-2) \times (-6)]$
   d) $[-2 - (-8)] \times (-5)$
   e) $35 + (-4) \times (-8) - 7$
   f) $18 \times (-3 - [8 \times (-5)])$

4. There is an error in this solution.

$$3 \times (-8) \div (-2 - 4) = -24 \div (-2 - 4)$$
$$= 12 - 4$$
$$= 8$$

   a) Find the error.
   b) Explain how to correct the error.

5. Calculate.
   a) $\dfrac{-6 + (-10)}{(-4)(2)}$
   d) $\dfrac{27 + (-18) \div (-2)}{(-2 + 5)(2)}$

   b) $\dfrac{49 \div (-7)}{1 + (-2)(-3)}$
   e) $\dfrac{-9 + (-16) - 10}{(-7)(10) \div (-2)}$

   c) $\dfrac{28 \div (-4 - 3)}{(-2 + 4) \times 2}$
   f) $\dfrac{[6 + (-38)] \div 4(-2)}{(-2 + 4)(5 - 6)}$

6. a) Evaluate with a calculator.
   $$-147 + 156 \div (-4) + 405 \div (-15)$$
   b) Does your calculator follow the order of operations? How do you know?

7. Using brackets, group the terms in this expression to get the least possible result.

$40 \times 6 - 3 \times 4 - 5$

8. The formula for converting temperatures from Fahrenheit (F) to Celsius (C) is $C = (F - 32) \times 5 \div 9$.
Use the formula to calculate $-40\ °F$ in degrees Celsius.

9. This chart shows the predicted high temperatures in Iqaluit for a week in November. Use an integer expression to determine the mean predicted high temperature for the week.

Day	Predicted high temperature (°C)
Monday	−4
Tuesday	−4
Wednesday	0
Thursday	1
Friday	−1
Saturday	−2
Sunday	−4

10. Copy each equation. Identify the missing operation signs.
   a) 36 ▮ (4 ▮ 1) ▮ 2 = 24
   b) −12 ▮ 4 ▮ (−3) = −24
   c) −15 ▮ (−12) ▮ 6 ▮ 16 = −47

11. Adrian bought some shares in four companies. This chart shows how his shares changed in value over one month. Write an integer expression that could be used to determine the change in the total value of his shares. Evaluate your expression.

Company	A	B	C	D
Number of shares	10	100	50	30
Value of each share Aug. 1 ($)	42	5	38	19
Value of each share Sept. 1 ($)	39	4	42	21

12. The price of gold changes daily. One week, the price started at $675 per ounce on Monday and changed −$2 each day for 3 days, and then +$8 each day for the next 2 days.
   a) Complete the chart.

Day	Starting price ($)	Final price ($)	Change in price ($)
Monday	675		
Tuesday			
Wednesday			
Thursday			
Friday			

   b) Calculate the mean final price of gold for the week.
   c) Calculate the mean change in price for the week.

13. Create an integer expression that shows why the rules for the order of operations are needed. Explain how your expression shows this.

14. How is the process for calculating the value of an integer expression the same as the one you use for a whole number expression? How is it different?

6.6 Communicate about Problem Solutions

GOAL

Explain the process of solving an integer problem.

LEARN ABOUT the Math

The cards below were the last three cards that Guy was dealt in a game. Guy followed the instructions correctly, but maybe not in the order shown. Now he is at −12 on the board. Where was he three turns ago?

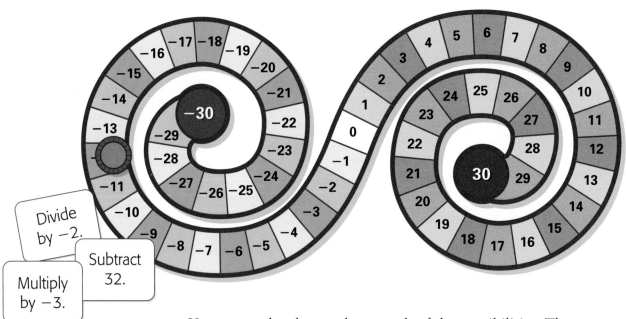

Divide by −2.

Subtract 32.

Multiply by −3.

Vanessa used a chart to keep track of the possibilities. Then she asked Elena to read her solution. Elena asked Vanessa the questions shown.

Vanessa's Solution

If the last card was ...	Guy came from ...	If the card before was ...	Guy came from ...	If the other card was ...	Guy came from ...
Divide by -2.	24	Subtract 32.	56: impossible		
Divide by -2.	24	Multiply by -3.	-8	Subtract 32.	24
Subtract 32.	20	Multiply by -3.	impossible (not an integer)		
Subtract 32.	20	Divide by -2.	-40: impossible		
Multiply by -3.	4	Divide by -2.	-8	Subtract 32.	24
Multiply by -3.	4	Subtract 32.	36: impossible		

Elena's Questions

Why did you use a chart to solve the problem?

How did you choose the column headings?

How did you fill each "Guy came from ..." column?

How did you fill each "If the ... was ..." column?

Did you justify your conclusion that a position was not possible?

Did you state and justify your result for the problem?

❓ How can Vanessa improve her solution?

A. Which of Elena's questions do you think are good questions? Why?

B. How should Vanessa answer Elena's questions?

C. What other questions would be helpful to improve Vanessa's work?

Reflecting

D. Which parts of the Communication Checklist did Elena cover well?

WORK WITH *the Math*

Example 1 | Using a diagram to explain a solution

Carla climbed halfway down a cliff before resting the first time. Then she climbed halfway down the remaining distance and rested for a second time. After climbing halfway down the final distance, Carla was 6 m from the bottom of the cliff. Use an integer to describe Carla's distance, in metres, from the top of the cliff. Explain your thinking.

Joseph's Solution

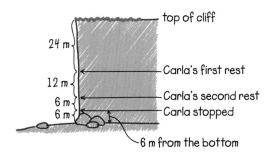

I drew a diagram to show the stages in Carla's climb down the cliff. I imagined that the top of the cliff was 0, and that down was negative and up was positive.

Carla finished 6 m from the bottom of the cliff, halfway between the bottom of the cliff and the location of her second rest. So she climbed down 6 m after her second rest. That is 0 + (−6).

At her second rest, Carla must have been 12 m from the bottom.

Carla's second rest was halfway between the bottom of the cliff and the location of her first rest. At her first rest, Carla must have been 24 m from the bottom. So she climbed down 12 m after her first rest. That is 0 + (−6) + (−12).

Carla's first rest was halfway between the bottom and the top of the cliff. So she climbed down 24 m before her rest. That is −24 m.

That is 0 + (−6) + (−12) + (−24).

0 + (−6) + (−12) + (−24) = −42

The integer −42 describes Carla's distance in metres from the top of the cliff.

A Checking

Use the game board below to answer questions 1 to 3.

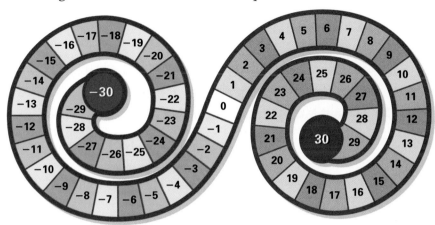

1. **a)** Write the instructions for three cards to go from −10 to 10 on the game board. Then write two other solutions.
   b) Rewrite the instructions in part a) to go from 10 to −10. Explain your thinking.

B Practising

2. These were Guy's last three cards before he landed on −2. Where did he begin? How do you know?

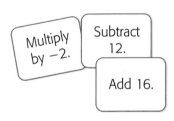

3. These were Guy's last four cards before he landed on −7. Where could he have begun? Explain how you determined your answers.

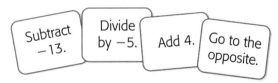

4. Samara walked 3 km to the west. Then she walked twice as far going toward the east. She continued toward the east for another kilometre, stopping 2 km east of Lauren's home. When Samara started walking, how far was she from Lauren's home? Explain how you know.

5. **a)** Change a problem in this lesson to create a different problem, or make up a new integer problem.
   b) Explain how to solve the problem.

Peasant Multiplication

Russian peasants used this method to multiply whole numbers without the use of multiplication tables.

The Peasant Multiplication Algorithm

A. 11×23

11	23

B.

5	46
~~2~~	~~92~~
1	184

Write the two numbers you wish to multiply in two columns.
Divide the number on the left by two. Ignore any fractional portion. Double the number on the right. If the number on the left is even, cross out the entire line.
Repeat the steps until the number on the left is 1. Add the numbers in the right column that have not been crossed out.

C. $23 + 46 + 184 = 253$
$11 \times 23 = 253$

1. Use Peasant Multiplication to calculate each product.
   a) 47×15 **c)** 36×47
   b) 15×47 **d)** 47×36

2. Why is it a good idea to place the lower multiplier in the left column?

3. Use Peasant Multiplication to help you calculate each integer product.
   a) -25×13 **c)** $-16(-21)$
   b) $43(-17)$ **d)** $-23\,958 \times 584$

Target Zero

Number of players: 2 to 4

When using a standard deck of cards, aces count as 1, numbered cards count as their face values, and jokers count as 0. Red cards are positive, and black cards are negative.

YOU WILL NEED
- Integer Cards (two of each card)
  OR
  standard deck of cards (including 2 jokers) with face cards removed

Rules

1. Shuffle the cards. Deal five cards to each player.

2. Place the remaining cards in a pile with one card facing up. This is the target card.

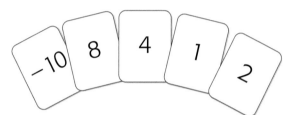

3. Players have 1 min to write an integer expression that uses all of their five cards and has a value as close as possible to the value of the target card. The integers can be combined using operations and brackets.

$$(-10 + 8)(4 - 1 + 2)$$

$$-10 + 8 + 4 - 1 - 2$$

4. Players evaluate their expressions.

   Each player receives a score equal to the positive difference between the value of her or his expression and the value of the target card. An exact match gives a score of 0.

$$(-10 + 8)(4 - 1 + 2) = -10 \rightarrow \text{score is 1}$$

$$-10 + 8 + 4 - 1 - 2 = -1 \rightarrow \text{score is 8}$$

5. Repeat steps 1 to 4 ten times. The winner is the player with the lowest final score.

Chapter **Self-Test**

1. Use counters or a number line to represent each expression.
   - a) $5 \times (-2)$
   - b) $-2 \times (8)$
   - c) $6 \times (-10)$
   - d) $-5 \times (-5)$
   - e) $\dfrac{-25}{5}$
   - f) $-36 \div (-9)$

2. Calculate.
   - a) $6 \times (-1)$
   - b) -9×3
   - c) $-12 \times (-12)$
   - d) $-96 \div (-16)$
   - e) $-98 \div 14$
   - f) $88 \div (-11)$

3. Determine the missing values.
   - a) $-34 \times \blacksquare = 306$
   - b) $28 \times \blacksquare = -336$
   - c) $\blacksquare \div 8 = -7$
   - d) $\blacksquare \div (-18) = 23$

Company	A	B	C	D
Number of shares	50	70	100	25
Change in price per share ($)	−2	+5	−3	−8

4. Marcus recorded this information about his shares. Estimate how much money, in total, he has gained or lost.

5. Which two integers have a product of -120 and a sum of -2?

6. How much greater or less is $5 + (-2)(-8)$ than $-8 + (-2)(5)$?

7. Calculate.
   - a) $-2 \times (-5)$
   - b) $-12 \div 4 \times (-7) - (-2) + 10$
   - c) $18 \times [-3 - (8)(-5)]$
   - d) $\dfrac{-54 + 18 \div (-2)}{(-3 - 4)(-1)}$

8. Use the following integers once each, and any necessary arithmetic operations and brackets, to make an expression equal to -96.
   $-10, -4, 3, 4, 10$

What Do You Think Now?

Revisit What Do You Think? on page 243. How have your answers and explanations changed?

Chapter **Review**

Frequently Asked Questions

Q: **How can you divide integers?**

A: You can use counters, a number line, or a related multiplication equation.

Division question	Counter model	Number line model	Related multiplication
$12 \div 3 = 4$	The number of groups is the quotient.	The number of small arrows is the quotient.	$12 \div 3 = \blacksquare$ is related to $\blacksquare \times 3 = 12$
$-12 \div (-3) = 4$	The number of groups is the quotient.	The number of small arrows is the quotient.	$-12 \div (-3) = \blacksquare$ is related to $\blacksquare \times (-3) = -12$
$-12 \div 3 = -4$	The number of blue counters in each group is the quotient.	The length and direction of each small arrow is the quotient.	$-12 \div 3 = \blacksquare$ is related to $\blacksquare \times 3 = -12$
$12 \div (-3) = -4$	Dividing a positive integer by a negative integer cannot be represented easily using counters or a number line.		$12 \div (-3) = \blacksquare$ is related to $\blacksquare \times (-3) = 12$

Q: **How do you evaluate integer expressions that involve several operations?**

A: Follow the same order of operations that you use with whole numbers and decimals:

Evaluate the contents of brackets first. Divide and multiply from left to right. Add and subtract from left to right.

Practice

Lesson 6.1

1. Calculate.
   - a) -4×4
   - b) $-8 \times (-2)$
   - c) $0 \times (-1)$
   - d) -5×4

2. Predict the sign of each product without calculating it. Explain how you predicted.
   - a) $-1 \times (-2) \times 4$
   - b) $4 \times (-2) \times 5$

Lesson 6.2

3. Calculate.
   - a) $-10(-8)$
   - b) $16(-5)$
   - c) $-6(12)$
   - d) $-21(-11)$

4. The product of five different integers is -24. Write two possible lists of integers for which this is true.

Lesson 6.4

5. Calculate.
   - a) $-32 \div 8$
   - b) $36 \div (-9)$
   - c) $-27 \div (-3)$
   - d) $75 \div (-25)$

6. Determine the mean of each group of integers.
   - a) $10, -8, -16, -6$
   - b) $-21, 9, 15, -30, -3$

Lesson 6.5

7. Replace each ▦ in the equations with $+$, $-$, $\times$, or $\div$.
   - a) -58 ▦ (-36) ▦ $(-15) = -37$
   - b) -4 ▦ (-3) ▦ $28 = 40$

8. Estimate.
   - a) $9 \times (-3) + (-15) \div 3$
   - b) $(-45) \div 5 + 7 - (-12)$

9. Melissa says, "When I combine integers using several operations, I always get the right answer if I do the operations from left to right." Use examples to explain whether she is right or wrong.

Chapter **Task**

Mystery Integers

Select four integers. Do not tell anyone what they are. Make up a set of four clues that will allow someone to guess the integers you chose. All four of the clues must be necessary.

The clues must

- use all four operations somewhere in the four clues
- include comparing integers

For example, suppose that your integers are $-8, 7, 5$, and -3. Here are three possible clues:

- The sum of the four integers is 1.
- If you order the integers from least to greatest, the product of the two middle integers is -15.
- If you subtract the least integer from the greatest integer, and divide the difference by 3, the quotient is 5.

❓ **What four clues can you write to describe your four integers?**

A. The three clues above do not give enough information to figure out the integers. What additional clue would give enough information?

B. Select any four integers of your own and make up four clues. Remember that all of the clues must be necessary. It should not be possible to figure out all the integers with only some of the clues.

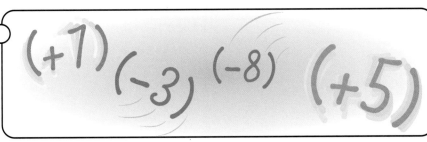

Chapter 7

Tessellations

GOAL

You will be able to

- use angle measurements to identify regular and irregular polygons that might tessellate

- identify and describe translations, reflections, or rotations in a tessellation

- use and describe ways to create a tessellation

◀ This tile pattern uses two different squares. Do you think a tiling pattern could be made using two or more types of triangles?

Getting Started

Completing a Circle

Taira and Holly are determining the different angles that can be used to complete a circle. They are placing wedges at a point until the circle is completed.

❓ What angle should Taira and Holly use to complete the circle?

A. How many angles of 60° can be used to complete the circle?

B. How many angles of 90° can be used to complete the circle?

C. List three other combinations of angles that make a complete circle.

D. What angle should Taira and Holly use to complete their circle?

NEL

What Do You Think?

Decide whether you agree or disagree with each statement.
Be ready to explain your decision.

1. Every hexagon has six angles greater than 90°.

2. The only shape that makes a good floor tile is a rectangle.

3. If you cut a square floor tile into two shapes and rearrange the pieces, the new shape will also make a good tile.

Exploring Tiling

GOAL

Use polygons to tile.

EXPLORE *the Math*

Lam is helping his mother design a tiling pattern for an outdoor table. He wants to use regular polygons in his design.

? **Which shapes can Lam use to tile the tabletop?**

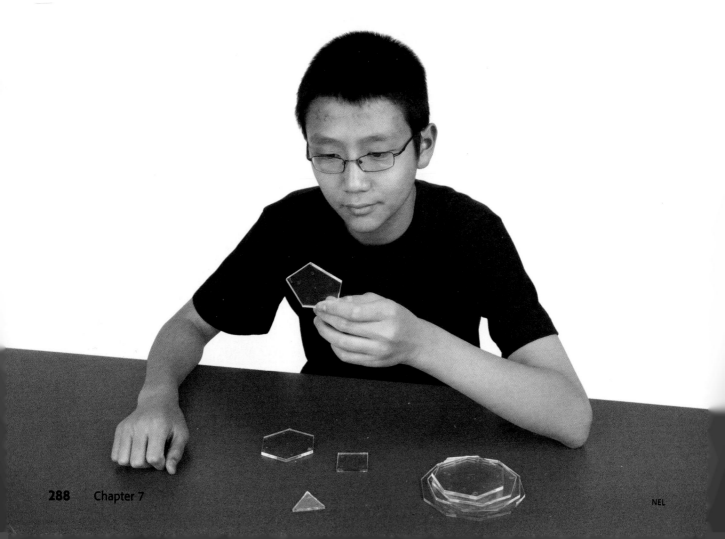

7.2 Tessellating with Regular Polygons

YOU WILL NEED
- Polygon Tiles
- Polygon Tiles Cards I
- Polygon Tiles Cards II
- grid paper
- tracing paper

tessellation
the tiling of a **plane** with one or more congruent shapes without any gaps or overlaps

plane
a flat surface that goes on forever in two different directions

GOAL

Use angle relationships to identify regular polygons that tessellate.

LEARN ABOUT the Math

Angèle is designing a **tessellation** for a scrapbook page.

- She traced around a square to start the tessellation.
- She marked one vertex of the square.
- She lined up the sides and corners of each square she traced.

Angèle wants to design other scrapbook pages with tessellations of equilateral triangles and regular pentagons.

? Which of her regular polygons can Angèle use to tessellate her scrapbook page?

A. How many squares surround the first vertex (X) in Angèle's tessellation?

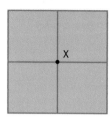

B. How many squares can surround vertex Y?

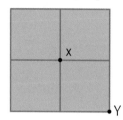

C. How do you know that Angèle's tessellation will cover the plane?

interior angle

the inside angles of a polygon

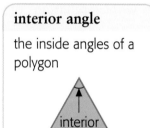

D. What is the measure of each **interior angle** in the square?

E. Determine the angle total at each vertex of your tessellation.

F. Record your data from parts A–D in the second column of a table like this one.

	Equilateral triangle	Square	Regular pentagon
Does the polygon tessellate? (yes or no)		yes	
Number of shapes at each vertex			
Interior angle measure			
Sum of angles at each vertex			

G. Predict the values for the table for equilateral triangles and regular pentagons. Test your prediction by trying to tessellate with those shapes.

Reflecting

H. How could you predict the number of angles that will fit together at the centre vertex from knowing the interior angle measure of each shape?

I. Could exactly three copies of any regular polygon fit around each vertex in a tessellation? Explain.

WORK WITH the Math

| Example 1 | Predicting whether a shape will tessellate |

Show whether a regular heptagon tessellates.

John's Solution

I knew from measuring that the interior angles of a heptagon are about 129° each.

2 x 129 = 258°

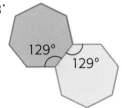

Two heptagons would cover about 258°. For the shape to tessellate, it has to cover 360° with no overlaps.

3 x 129 = 387°

Three heptagons would cover about 387°. That is too much. The third heptagon would overlap the first two.

So regular heptagons do not tessellate.

A **Checking**

1. Try to tessellate with a regular hexagon. Explain why it does or does not work.

B **Practising**

2. Predict whether a regular octagon will tessellate. Explain.

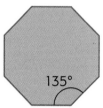

3. A regular dodecagon has interior angles of 150°.
   a) Predict whether it will tessellate. Explain.
   b) Predict whether a smaller, regular dodecagon will tessellate. Explain.

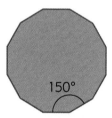

4. Jordan predicts that a regular decagon will tessellate. He says it will work because 360 ÷ 10 is 36 with no remainder. Is Jordan right or wrong? Explain.

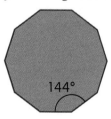

5. What has to be true about the size of the interior angle of a regular polygon for it to tessellate?

7.3

Tessellating with Quadrilaterals

> **GOAL**
>
> **Create and describe tessellations of quadrilaterals.**

LEARN ABOUT *the Math*

Renée is designing a stained glass window. She wants to tile it with only quadrilaterals.

❓ Which of Renée's quadrilaterals tessellate?

A. Create a tessellation by translating or rotating a rectangle. Sketch your tessellation.

B. Repeat part A with a parallelogram.

C. Repeat part A with a rhombus.

D. Which of the quadrilaterals can you use to tessellate?

Reflecting

E. Compare your tessellations with those of a few classmates. Are they all the same?

F. Look at the angles surrounding each vertex in the tessellations you sketched. What is the sum of the angles? How do you know?

WORK WITH *the Math*

Example 1	Using transformation to tessellate

Tessellate with this quadrilateral.

Holly's Solution

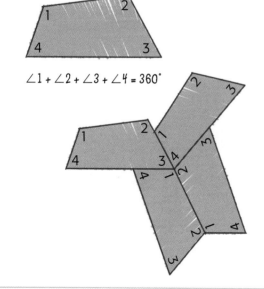

$\angle 1 + \angle 2 + \angle 3 + \angle 4 = 360°$

I knew that the interior angles of a quadrilateral always have a sum of 360°. I also knew that, for a shape to tessellate, the sum of the angles around the vertex has to be 360°.

I matched the quadrilaterals so that each angle, 1, 2, 3, and 4, appeared at each vertex once. The sum of the angles at the vertex was 360°, but I could not extend the pattern to make a tessellation.

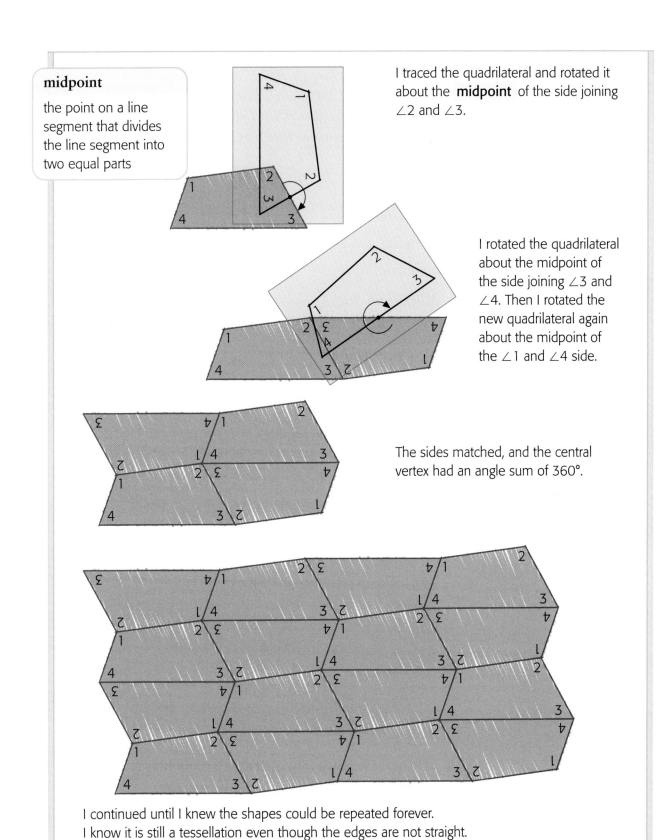

midpoint

the point on a line segment that divides the line segment into two equal parts

I traced the quadrilateral and rotated it about the **midpoint** of the side joining ∠2 and ∠3.

I rotated the quadrilateral about the midpoint of the side joining ∠3 and ∠4. Then I rotated the new quadrilateral again about the midpoint of the ∠1 and ∠4 side.

The sides matched, and the central vertex had an angle sum of 360°.

I continued until I knew the shapes could be repeated forever.
I know it is still a tessellation even though the edges are not straight.

A Checking

1. **a)** Create your own quadrilateral.
   b) Sketch a tessellation with your quadrilateral.
   c) Describe how you tessellated with it.

B Practising

2. **a)** Create a tessellation with rhombuses using only reflection and translation. Sketch your tessellation and describe it.
   b) Repeat part a) using rotation about the midpoints of the sides.

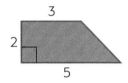

3. Sketch and describe two different tessellations with this right trapezoid.

4. **a)** Create a kite.
   b) Tessellate with the kite.
   c) Sketch and describe the tessellation.

5. **a)** Create a trapezoid.
   b) Try to tessellate with it by rotating around a vertex.
   c) Try to tessellate with it by reflecting and translating.

6. Asuka wants to re-create this tessellation design. What transformation should she start with?

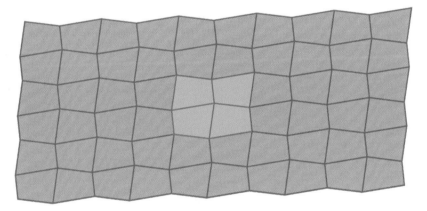

7. **a)** Create a new quadrilateral you think may not tessellate.
   b) Try to tessellate with your quadrilateral.
   c) Did anybody in your class make a quadrilateral that did not tessellate? What do you think this means about quadrilaterals?

7.4

Tessellating with Triangles

GOAL

Create and describe tessellations of triangles.

LEARN ABOUT *the Math*

Ivan notices that some tiles in his home are right isosceles triangles.

He wonders if other types of triangles tessellate.

❓ Which types of triangles tessellate?

A. Divide a rectangle along its diagonal to create two right triangles. From what you know about rectangles, predict whether these triangles will tessellate. Explain your prediction.

B. Try to tessellate with an acute isosceles triangle, using reflection and translation. Does it tessellate? Explain.

C. Divide a parallelogram into two congruent triangles. How does thinking of each triangle as half a parallelogram show that this type of triangle will tessellate?

D. Which types of triangles tessellate?

Reflecting

E. Why do you think that any acute, right, or obtuse triangle can be drawn as half a parallelogram?

F. When you create a tessellation with triangles, why are there always two copies of each angle at each vertex?

WORK WITH *the Math*

Example 1	Using transformations to tessellate a triangle

Create a tessellation with a right triangle.

Taira's Solution: Reflecting and translating

I used geometry software to translate the triangle 0 cm up and the distance of the base to the right a few times to make a row.

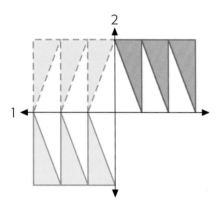

I drew a horizontal reflection line and reflected the row across it.
Then I drew a vertical reflection line and reflected the top row across that.

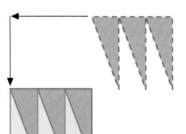

Then I translated the reflected row enough units to the left and down to fit it in the gaps of the original row.

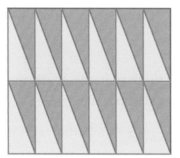

I translated the six right triangles until they tiled the plane.

John's Solution: Rotating about a vertex and translating

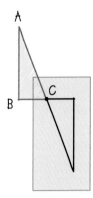

I rotated the triangle 180° clockwise (cw) about point C.

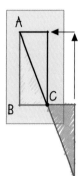

Then I slid the rotated triangle up the same distance as the height and to the left the length of the base so that the two hypotenuses matched up. The two right triangles formed a rectangle.

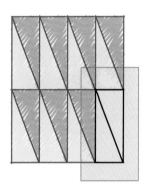

I translated the rectangle until I knew that the tessellation could be extended forever.

Angèle's Solution: Rotating about a midpoint and translating

I constructed the midpoint of the hypotenuse. I rotated the triangle 180° cw about that midpoint. The two triangles formed a rectangle.

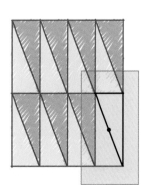

I translated the rectangle until I knew the tessellation could be extended forever.

Example 2 | Using rotation to tessellate

Create a tessellation with a scalene triangle.

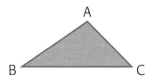

Ivan's Solution

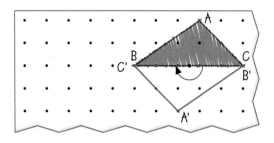

I started by rotating the triangle 180° cw about the midpoint of *BC*.

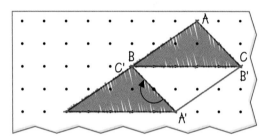

Then I rotated the new triangle 180° cw about the midpoint of *A'C'*.

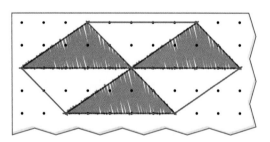

I continued to rotate about the midpoint of each side until the triangles formed a hexagon.

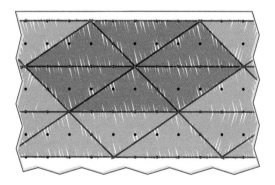

I tessellated with the hexagon until I knew it could be repeated forever.

Lam's Solution

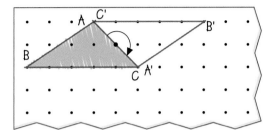

I started by rotating the triangle 180° cw about the midpoint of *AC*.

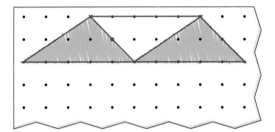

I made a row of triangles that formed a trapezoid. I knew that a trapezoid is a quadrilateral, which always tessellates.

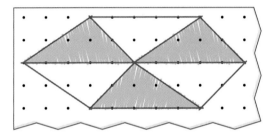

I reflected my row of triangles across a horizontal line below it.

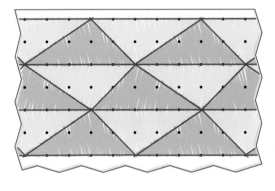

I tessellated with the trapezoid until I knew it could be extended forever.

A **Checking**

1. Create a new shape by rotating a right isosceles triangle 180°
   about the midpoint of one of the sides.

   a) What shape did you make?

   b) Will the new shape tessellate? Explain.

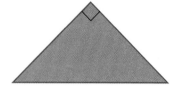

2. Create a new shape by rotating a right isosceles triangle 90°
   either clockwise or counterclockwise about the right angle.

   a) What shape did you make?

   b) Will the new shape tessellate? Explain.

B **Practising**

3. **a)** Draw a scalene triangle that is different from the one below.

   b) Tessellate with your scalene triangle by rotating.

   c) Tessellate with your scalene triangle by reflecting.

   d) Compare the two tiling patterns that you created.

4. Create two different tessellations with an isosceles triangle.
   Describe how you created each.

5. Can you always create at least two different tessellations from
   any triangle? Explain.

Tessera

Number of players: 2 to 4

Rules

1. Player 1 selects one card from the pile of Polygon Tile Cards.

2. Player 1 has 1 min to make a tessellation with the selected polygon. If the rest of the players agree that the design is a true tessellation, Player 1 gets one point. If the rest of the players do not agree that the design is a true tessellation, the player who correctly explains why it is not a tessellation gets one point.

3. Take turns to play until all of the polygons have been used.

4. The player with the highest score wins.

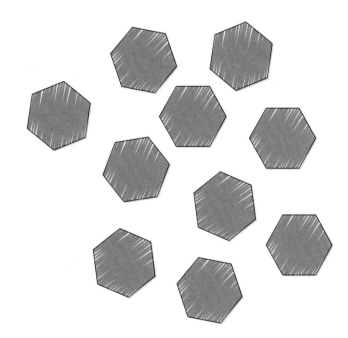

Frequently Asked Questions

Q: How can you tell that a shape tessellates?

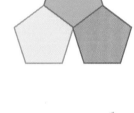

A: If it is not possible to arrange copies of the shape so that the angles at any vertex add up to 360°, then the shape will not tessellate.

If copies of the shape can be arranged so that the angles at each vertex add up to 360°, then you should try to tessellate it to see if it works.

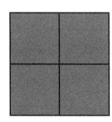

Q: Which polygons tessellate?

A: All triangles and all quadrilaterals tessellate.

Of the regular polygons, equilateral triangles, squares, and hexagons tessellate.

Q: How can you create a tessellation?

A: You can create a tessellation by translating, rotating, or reflecting the shape so that there are no gaps or overlaps.

You can then repeat the process with other copies of the combined shape.

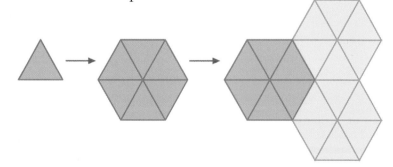

Practice

Lesson 7.2

1. A loonie is a regular 11-sided polygon. Does it tessellate?
Explain.

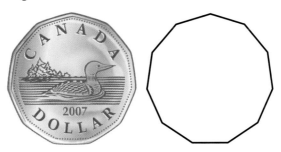

Lesson 7.3

2. Create two different tessellations from a rhombus.
Describe how you got each tessellation.

3. Karim wants to re-create this tessellation. He highlighted a
section of it. What transformations of a single quadrilateral
can he use to create the highlighted section?

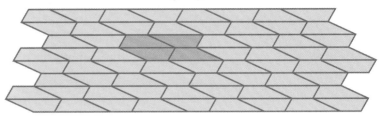

Lesson 7.4

4. Marc started to tessellate with this right isosceles triangle by
rotating it 180° about the midpoint of *AC*.
Erynn started by reflecting it across *BC*.
Will their tessellations be the same or different? Explain.

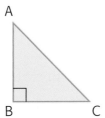

7.5

Tessellating by Combining Shapes

YOU WILL NEED
- Polygon Tiles
- Polygon Tiles Cards I
- Polygon Tiles Cards II
- grid paper

GOAL

Combine two or more regular polygons to form a tessellation.

LEARN ABOUT the Math

Taira is designing a tile pattern for the centre of the garden. She would like to use two regular polygons in her tessellation design.

❓ How can Taira choose two regular polygons that will create a tessellation if they are used together?

A. Choose an equilateral triangle and a square. What is the size of the interior angle in each shape?

B. Predict which combinations of equilateral triangles and squares will tessellate. Explain your reasoning.

C. Use the angle measurements in part A to predict how equilateral triangles and squares will surround each vertex in a tessellation. Explain your reasoning.

D. Check your predictions in parts B and C by creating a tessellation of equilateral triangles and squares. Sketch your tessellation.

E. Choose a different combination of two or more regular polygons. Predict whether this combination will tessellate. Explain your reasoning.

F. Create a tessellation to check your prediction in part E.

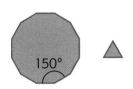

Reflecting

G. Each interior angle in a regular dodecagon (12 sides) is 150°. Why is it reasonable that a combination of regular dodecagons and equilateral triangles could tessellate?

H. Why is it helpful when the two regular polygons you are using to tessellate with have equal side lengths?

WORK WITH *the Math*

Example 1	Predict tessellations based on angles

How can you tell whether combinations of regular octagons and squares will tessellate?

Ivan's Solution

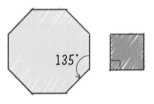

I knew from measuring that the interior angle of a regular octagon is 135°. Each interior angle of a square is 90°. I can try to tessellate the two shapes together if I can find combinations of the interior angles that add up to 360°.

$135° + 135° + 90° = 360°$

I can try to tessellate by placing two octagons and one square at a vertex.

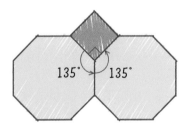

The interior angles added up to 360°.
My prediction worked for the centre vertex.

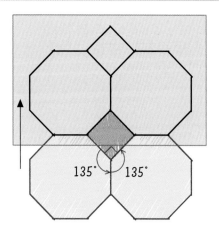

I tested my prediction. I traced the whole combination and translated it up the height of the octagon.

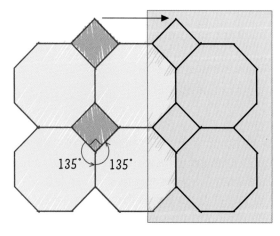

Next, I translated the square and two octagons to the right by the width of the octagon.

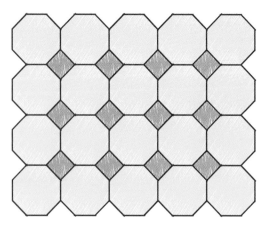

I continued the pattern until I knew it could be extended forever.

A Checking

1. Predict whether a combination of regular hexagons and squares will tessellate. Explain.

B Practising

2. Predict whether a combination of regular pentagons and equilateral triangles will tessellate. Explain.

3. **a)** Choose two regular polygons that have not been discussed, which you think will tessellate if they are used together. Explain your choice.
   b) Sketch your tessellation.
   c) Describe how you got your tessellation.

4. Regular dodecagons do not tessellate. What shape could you combine with a regular dodecagon to create a tessellation? Explain.

5. Erica combined a hexagon, a square, and a triangle to start a tessellation. She is sure that it will tessellate. Do you agree? Explain.

Reading Strategy

Evaluating

Choose an answer to the question. Write statements to defend your answer. Then evaluate your answer.

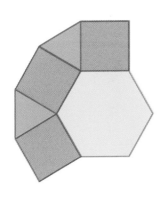

Regular polygon (number of sides)	Approximate size of interior angles
Equilateral triangle (3)	60°
Square (4)	90°
Pentagon (5)	108°
Hexagon (6)	120°
Heptagon (7)	129°
Octagon (8)	135°
Nonagon (9)	140°
Decagon (10)	144°
Hendecagon (11)	147°
Dodecagon (12)	150°

7.6

Tessellating Designs

GOAL

Create and tessellate with an irregular polygon.

LEARN ABOUT *the Math*

John saw a copy of this M.C. Escher drawing on a poster. He wondered how the artist managed to get all of the birds to fit together so well.

He thought that Escher used a square as the basic shape for this artwork.

The black section from the top of the square can be cut out and translated to the bottom of the square.

The black section from the right of the square can also be cut out and translated to the left.

❓ How can you make an irregular tessellating tile?

Example 1 | Creating an irregular tile by translating

Create an irregular tessellating tile from a square.

Lam's Solution

I changed the left side with a curve.

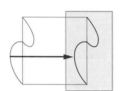

I translated the curve to the right side.

I changed the bottom of the square with another curve.

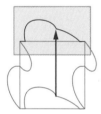

Then I translated the curve up to the top side of the square.

I thought the new tile looked like a knight on a horse. I drew in the picture and cut out the tile.

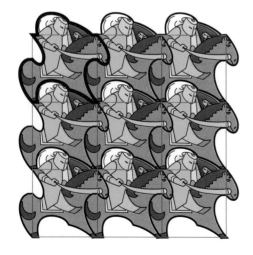

Then I translated the tile over and over to create a tessellation.

Example 2 | Creating an irregular tile by rotating

Create a tessellating shape from a regular hexagon.

Taira's Solution

I traced a design over half of one side.

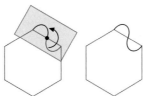

I rotated the design 180° about the midpoint of the side that I changed.

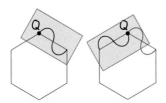

I rotated 120° cw about Q to move the design to the next side.

I continued to rotate and trace the design until all of the sides were changed. I thought my irregular tile would tessellate because it was created from a regular hexagon, which I know tessellates.

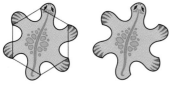

I thought that the new shape looked like a lizard, so I drew some lizard details on it. I cut out the lizard.

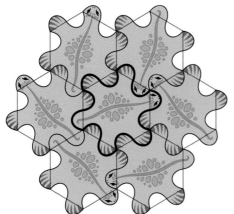

I tried to tessellate with the new tile. I was right. The tiles fit together. I continued to translate the lizard tile until I knew the tessellation could be extended forever.

Reflecting

A. Do you think that using the strategies in Examples 1 and 2 would make a regular pentagon tile tessellate? Explain.

B. In Example 1, the part that was cut out of one side was added to the opposite side. Why was this important to make the tessellation work?

C. In Example 2, the rotation was done using half of each side. Why was this important to make the tessellation work?

WORK WITH the Math

Example 3	Creating an irregular tessellating tile

Create an irregular tessellating tile from a parallelogram.

Solution

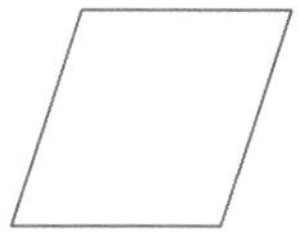

Parallelograms always tessellate.

Change one of the sides.

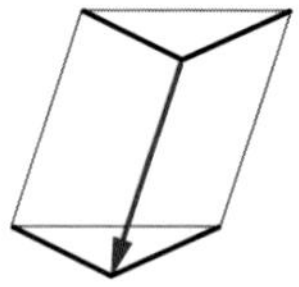

Translate the changed side to the opposite side of the shape.

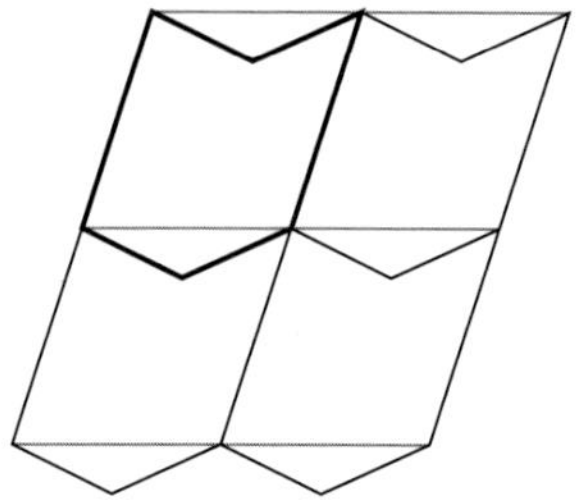

Tessellate the new shape by transforming it over and over.

A Checking

1. **a)** Create a new tile from a square by doing the following:
   - Change the left side and translate it to the right side.
   - Use a different change for the top and translate it to the bottom side.
   - Cut out the tile.

   b) Will the new tile tessellate? Explain.

B Practising

2. **a)** Create an irregular tessellating tile from a rectangle. Sketch it.

   b) Describe how you created it.

   c) How do you know it will tessellate?

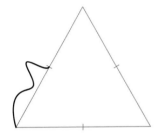

3. Chris started to change a triangle tile by adding a bump to half of one side.

   a) Show how you could finish changing the tile so that it will tessellate.

   b) How you do know your new tile will tessellate?

   c) Decorate the shape to make a design.

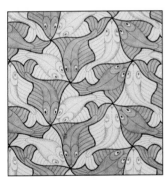

4. This fish tessellation pattern was created by M.C. Escher.

   a) What basic shape do you think Escher started with?

   b) What transformations do you think Escher did with his basic shape? Explain.

   c) Look at the side of the basic shape that has the fish with the double tail fin. How did Escher change this side of the basic shape?

5. Draw a square. Change each side by drawing a curve from one vertex to the adjacent vertex. Is it likely that this shape will tessellate? Explain.

Exploring Tessellations in the Environment

Investigate tessellations in the environment.

EXPLORE *the Math*

Ivan and Holly saw these patterns around their school and decided they are tessellations.

What other tessellations do you see around your school?

? How did people create the tessellations that you have seen?

7.8

Communicate about Tessellations

Describe the transformations in a tessellation.

LEARN ABOUT the Math

John created this tessellation design.

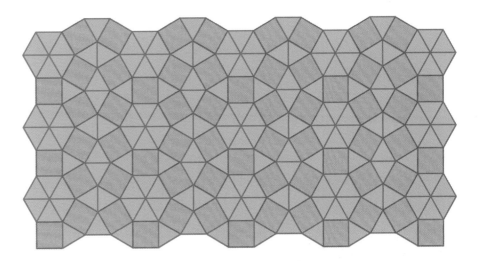

Renée wants to make the same design on a computer. John tries to describe the tessellation to Renée.

❓ How can John improve his description?

John's Description

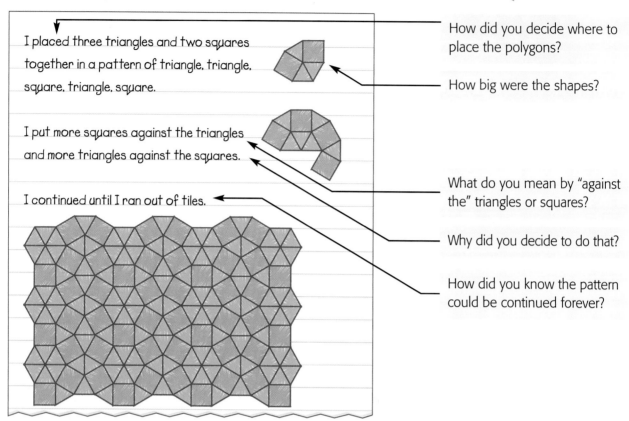

I placed three triangles and two squares together in a pattern of triangle, triangle, square, triangle, square.

I put more squares against the triangles and more triangles against the squares.

I continued until I ran out of tiles.

Renée's Questions

How did you decide where to place the polygons?

How big were the shapes?

What do you mean by "against the" triangles or squares?

Why did you decide to do that?

How did you know the pattern could be continued forever?

Communication Checklist

✔ Did you clearly explain all the steps in your reasoning?

✔ Did you use pictures or diagrams to show your steps?

✔ Did you use words and pictures that were mathematically clear and correct?

✔ Did you justify your conclusions?

A. Use Renée's questions and the Communication Checklist to improve John's description.

B. Which parts of the Communication Checklist did Renée deal with in her questions?

Reflecting

C. Which parts of John's tessellation is hardest to describe using only words? Why?

D. How do the sketches make John's description easier to understand?

WORK WITH *the Math*

| Example 1 | Describing the steps for a tessellation |

Explain how you would create this tessellation.

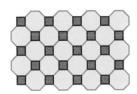

Solution

 Start with just octagons. The vertex angles do not add up to 360°.

 The gap between the octagons is exactly 90°. Add a square to the vertex.

 Translate the two octagons and the square up and to the right so the bottom left sides of the new position of the octagons sit against the top right sides of the old ones.

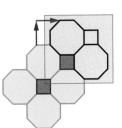 Translate the octagons up to the right again. Each gap is filled by a square with each side length being one unit.

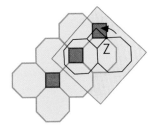 Rotate the last two octagons and square 90° cw around vertex Z.

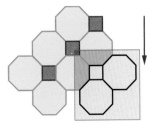 Then translate the rotated shapes down.

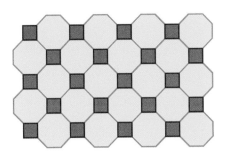 Continue until you think the shapes can be repeated forever. There are no gaps, and the angle measurements at each vertex add up to 360°.

A Checking

1. Describe how to tessellate with a regular hexagon.

B Practising

2. Use the Communication Checklist to help you explain why regular pentagons do not tessellate.

3. Find a picture of a tessellation. Describe how the artist might have created the tessellation.

4. **a)** Determine two ways to tessellate with a kite.
   b) Compare the two tessellations. Use the Communication Checklist to improve your comparison.

Alphabet Tessellations

YOU WILL NEED
• Alphabet Letters

abcdefghi
jklmnopqr
stuvwxyz

Shapes that tessellate can be created to look like letters of the alphabet.

For example, here is a tessellation for the letter "a."

1. Choose two other letters to show that they tile.

2. Make your own version of a stylized letter that tessellates.

1. Determine whether each tile can tessellate.
   Explain your answers.

   a)

   b)

2. **a)** Create a tessellation with a regular dodecagon and two other regular polygons.

   b) Describe your tessellation using transformations.

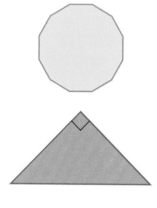

3. Bill started to tessellate with a right isosceles triangle by reflecting across the hypotenuse. Derek started by rotating about the midpoint of the hypotenuse.
   Compare the two patterns.

4. **a)** Combine squares and equilateral triangles to meet at a single vertex.

   b) Try to tessellate that combination of shapes using transformations.

   c) Does it tessellate? Explain.

5. **a)** Use rotations or translations to modify this trapezoid.

   b) Use the new shape to create a tessellation.

What Do You Think Now?

Revisit What Do You Think? on page 287. How have your answers and explanations changed?

Frequently Asked Questions

Q: How can you choose regular polygons to combine to make a new shape that tessellates?

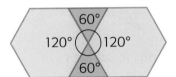

A: Examine the interior angles of the regular polygons. Choose combinations of angles that add up to 360°. Make sure the side lengths of all of the polygons are the same. Try to tessellate the combination.

For example, the interior angles of two hexagons and two triangles add up to 360°.

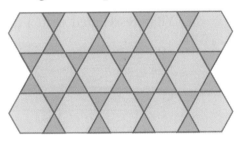

Q: How can you change a tile so that it will tessellate?

A: Start with a shape that you know will tessellate. Change the opposite sides the same way, using appropriate transformations.

Translation

   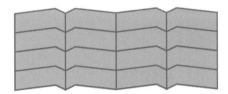

Rotation

    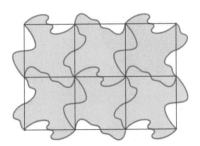

Practice

Lesson 7.2

1. The hardware store does not sell nonagon-shaped (9-sided) tiles. Use angle measurements to explain why.

Lesson 7.3

2. **a)** Create a tessellation with this quadrilateral.

   b) Can the tessellation be done another way? Explain.

3. Sabrina says that this quadrilateral does not tessellate even though the angle sum at the centre vertex is 360°. Do you agree? Explain your thinking.

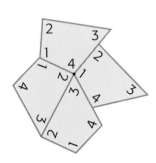

Lesson 7.4

4. Yifan tessellated with a triangle this way.

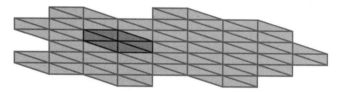

   Patrick tessellated with the same triangle this way.

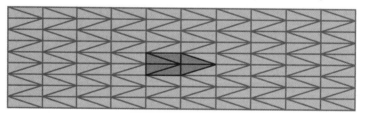

   How did Yifan and Patrick transform the triangle differently to create their tessellations?

Lesson 7.5

5. A regular dodecagon has interior angles of 150°. Which two polygons could you combine it with to create a tessellation? Explain your reasoning.

60°   90°   108°   120°

Lesson 7.6

6. Change a kite tile to make a tessellating design. Explain what you did to change the tile.

Chapter **Task**

Wall Design

You have been asked to create a tessellation design for the wall of your school's main entrance. The school wants to use a modified tile that is decorated with a symbol of the school.

? **How can you tessellate with a modified tile for the school wall?**

A. Choose a polygon to start with.

B. Modify the polygon any way you wish.

C. Decorate your modified polygon with a symbol of your school.

D. Tessellate with your modified polygon.

E. Write a detailed description that someone else could follow to recreate your tessellation design.

Cumulative **Review**

1. Which block would you have to attach to a yellow hexagon pattern block to make the total area 150% of the original area?

   A.    **C.**

   B.    **D.**

2. The number of elk at a park increased by 5% in 2006 and by 10% in 2007. What is the two-year percent increase in the elk population?

   A. 15.5%   **B.** 15%   **C.** 115%   **D.** 115.5%

3. Daria earns a commission of 5.3% of the value of her sales. What would her commission be on sales worth $150 000.00?

   A. $79 500.00   **C.** $795.00
   B. $7 950.00   **D.** $79.50

4. Which of the following does NOT represent the same percent as the others?

   A. 0.0625   **B.** 6.25%   **C.** $\dfrac{1}{16}$ **D.** $\dfrac{25}{4}$

5. Which net(s) will fold to make the object to the left?

   A. 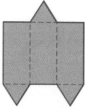   **C.**

   B.   **D.** all of them

6. Which list correctly orders the following shapes from least surface area to greatest surface area?

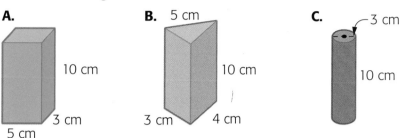

A.   **B.** 5 cm   **C.** ⌐3 cm

10 cm   10 cm   10 cm

3 cm   3 cm   4 cm

5 cm

A. A, B, C   **B.** A, C, B   **C.** C, B, A   **D.** B, A, C

7. A metal prism has a cylindrical hole drilled through it as shown at the left. What percent of the original volume of the prism remains?

A. less than 60%   **C.** between 70% and 80%
B. between 60% and 70%   **D.** between 80% and 90%

⌐2 cm

10 cm

5 cm

5 cm

8. Which expression is most correctly represented by the following picture?

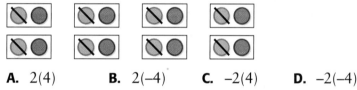

A. 2(4)   **B.** 2(–4)   **C.** –2(4)   **D.** –2(–4)

9. Inigo calculated the value of $\dfrac{-36 + [1 - (-5)]}{2(-3)}$ to be 7. Which operation did Inigo most likely do incorrectly?

A. addition   **C.** multiplication
B. subtraction   **D.** division

10. Which of the following regular polygon tiles will NOT tessellate?

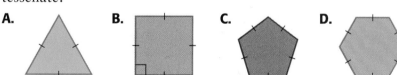

A.   **B.**   **C.**   **D.**

11. What percent of the regular polygons with 10 or fewer sides can be made to tessellate?

A. 37.5 %   **B.** 33.3 %   **C.** 30 %   **D.** 20 %

Women's Speedskating Record Times

Time

0:07:12
0:05:46
0:04:19
0:02:53
0:01:26
0:00:00

500 m   1000 m   1500 m   3000 m   5000 m   team pursuit

Event

☐ Olympic Record   ☐ World Record

You will be able to

- compare the strengths and limitations of different types of graphs
- communicate about the choice and format of a graph
- interpret graphs and identify inappropriate conclusions
- identify ways that graphs can misrepresent data

◀ In 2007, Canadian speed skater Cindy Klassen held the world records for 1000 m, 1500 m, and 3000 m. What conclusions about world and Olympic record times can you draw from the graph?

Getting **Started**

YOU WILL NEED
• grid paper

Different Graphs

Elena and Mark read about an online vote to determine the New Seven Wonders of the World. They decided to conduct their own survey.

The New Seven Wonders of the World

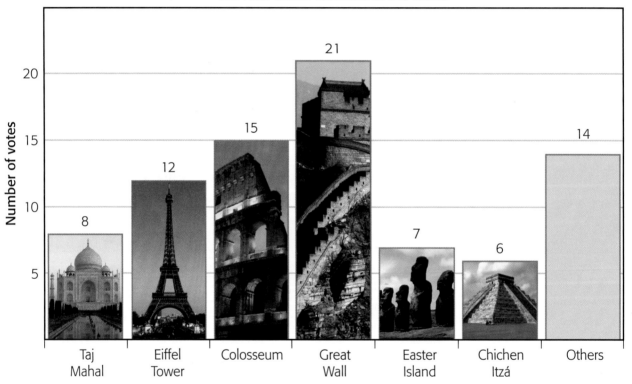

❓ What information can a graph give you?

A. Can the graph be used to decide what the New Seven Wonders of the World should be? Why or why not?

B. Can you use a pictograph to display the data? Explain.

C. Can you use a line graph to display the data? Explain.

D. If you used a circle graph to display the data, what would the whole represent? How would you decide how big to make each part?

E. Construct a line graph, circle graph, or pictograph to display the data. Why did you choose that type of graph?

What Do You Think?

Decide whether you agree or disagree with each statement.
Be ready to explain your decision.

1. These graphs probably show the same data.

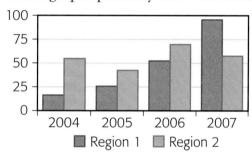 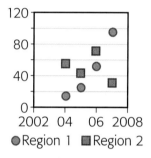

2. The graph shows that Ian's monthly math scores are increasing quickly.

Ian's Math Scores (%)

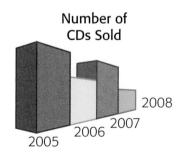

Number of
CDs Sold

3. The graph shows that sales of CDs were greatest in 2007.

4. You can use the circle graph to determine how many times heads was tossed.

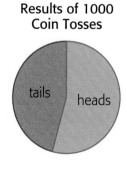

Results of 1000 Coin Tosses

8.1

Choosing a Graph to Display Data

YOU WILL NEED
- grid paper

GOAL

Justify the choice of a graph to display data.

EXPLORE the Math

Joseph read that MP3 players are the most popular form of technology used by people under 20. He wondered if the results were the same for his class, so he conducted a survey. He decided to use a bar graph to display his results.

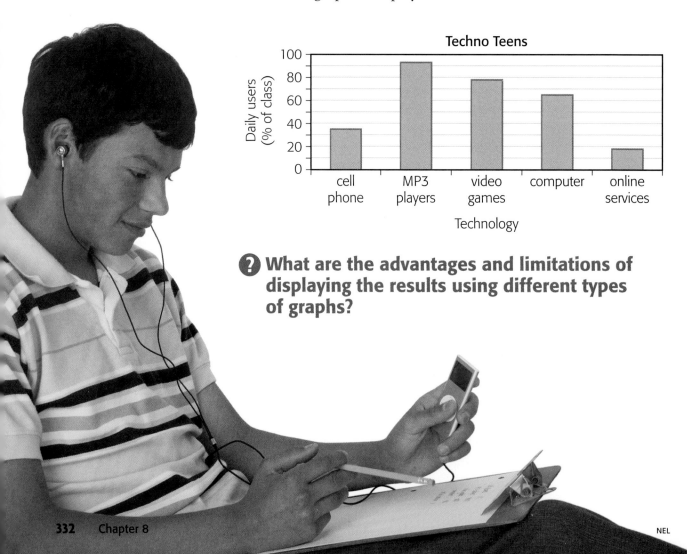

? **What are the advantages and limitations of displaying the results using different types of graphs?**

8.2

Changing the Format of a Graph

YOU WILL NEED
- grid paper
- a ruler
- pencil crayons

GOAL

Compare how different types of graphs present information.

LEARN ABOUT *the Math*

Kaitlyn wants to know how fit her class is. She recorded resting heart rates for all 30 students. She wants to display the data in a graph.

? **How will the format of the graph affect interpretation of the data?**

Resting Heart Rates (beats per minute)

70	60	62	53	76	84	67	62	80	74
70	84	60	76	68	70	72	78	56	64
68	72	70	60	78	80	67	76	66	54

Example 1 | Creating a bar graph

I displayed the data in a bar graph.

Kaitlyn's Solution

53 54 56 60 60 60 62 62 64 66 67 67 68 68 70
70 70 70 72 72 74 76 76 76 78 78 80 80 84 84

First, I ordered the data from the smallest number to largest.

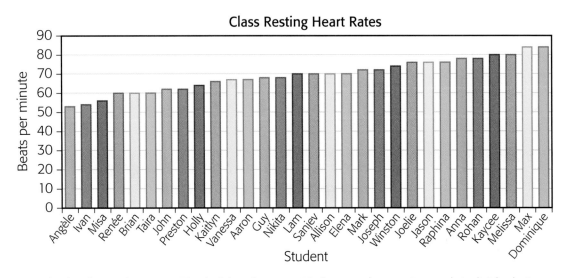

I used a bar for each person. The height of the bar tells you the heart rate of that person.

My bar graph contains each individual piece of data. I can compare the heart rates of individuals. To talk about the whole class is difficult because I have to look at many bars at the same time.

Example 2 | Creating a different bar graph

I grouped the data, then I constructed a bar graph.

Sanjev's Solution

50 – 59: 53, 56, 54
60 – 69: 60, 62, 67, 62, 60, 68, 64, 68, 60, 67, 66
70 – 79: 70, 76, 74, 70, 76, 70, 72, 78, 72, 70, 78, 76
80 – 89: 84, 80, 84, 80

There were many data values, so I organized the data into groups based on the 10s digits.

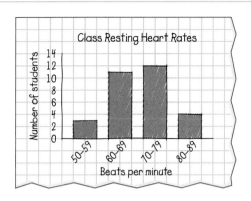

Class Resting Heart Rates

Each bar represents the number of people with heart rates in that group.

I have fewer bars to look at, so it is easier to say things about the whole class. I can see that 23 of 30 heart rates fall in the two middle groups. I do not see which students are in each group though.

Example 3 | Choosing a different graph

I used a circle graph to display the data.

Joseph's Solution

52–59: 53, 54, 56
60–67: 60, 62, 67, 62, 60, 64, 60, 67, 66
68–75: 68, 68, 70, 74, 70, 70, 72, 72, 70
76–84: 76, 76, 78, 78, 76, 84, 80, 84, 80

The range of data is $84 - 53 = 31$. That is about 32, so I used 4 groups of 8 possible data values.

Group size	3	11	12	4
Percent	10	36.7	40	13.3

I calculated each group size as a percent of 30 (the total number of students).

Class Resting Heart Rates
(beats per minute)

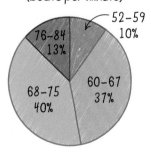

Each wedge represents the percent of the class that is in that group.

I can see that 77% of the class have heart rates between 60 and 75 beats per minute, but I cannot see how many people are in each group.

Reflecting

A. How are the three graphs alike and how are they different?

B. Create questions you could answer best using each of the graphs.

WORK WITH *the Math*

Example 4 | Interpreting graphs

Vanessa and Elena graphed the heights of the students before the class trip to the amusement park.

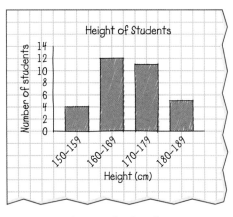

Vanessa's Graph   Elena's Graph

a) How are the graphs different?

b) What conclusions can you make about the heights of the students?

c) Which graph would you use to determine the number of students who could go on a roller coaster ride if you must be at least 162 cm tall? Explain.

Solution

a) The groups for the two graphs are different. In Vanessa's graph there are four groups for data values, each with 10 possible heights. In Elena's graph there are seven groups for data values, each with 5 possible heights.

b) Vanessa's graph shows that 12 out of 32 students are from 160 to 169 cm tall. Elena's graph shows that 7 of those 12 students are from 165 to 169 cm tall. Elena's graph gives more precise information. Her graph also shows that no one is shorter than 155 cm or taller than 184 cm. You cannot tell that from Vanessa's graph.

c) You can only estimate from the graphs. Elena's graph shows that at least 23 students can go on the roller coaster. Vanessa's graph shows that at least 16 students can go on the roller coaster. Elena's graph gives a better estimate.

A Checking

1. Jason surveyed the Grade 8 classes about their pets. He drew three different graphs to display the data.

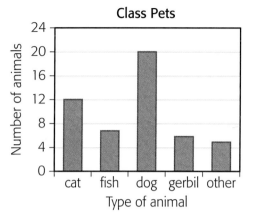

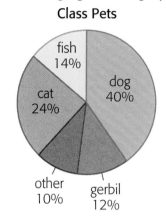

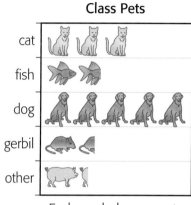

Each symbol represents 4 animals

a) How are all three graphs the same? How are they different?
b) How are the impressions the graphs give different?
c) Is one graph better at presenting the data than another? Explain.

B Practising

2.

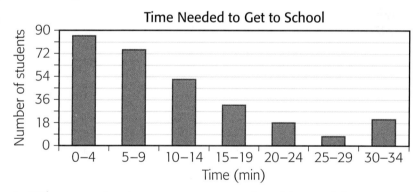

a) What question is easy to answer using this graph?
b) What question about the time to get to school is not as easy to answer using this graph?

3. Gail recorded the daily high temperature for her town for two years. She created two graphs to display the data.

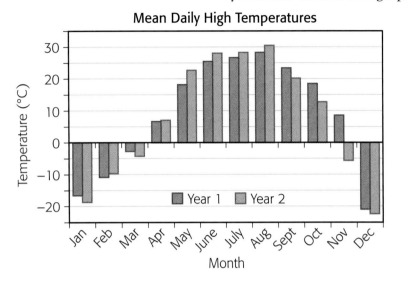

Mean Daily High Temperatures

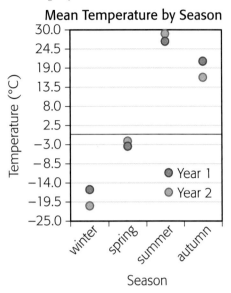

Mean Temperature by Season

Reading Strategy

Inferring

Look at the graphs before reading question 3. What inferences can you make about the data?

a) Which graph could you use to decide the year that was generally warmer? Do both graphs give you the same conclusion?

b) What information is missing in the scatterplot?

4. Manon and Juan recorded the running times for 100 movies. Manon displayed the data in a bar graph that listed each movie individually. Juan grouped the data and created a circle graph.

a) Could Juan have used Manon's bar graph to create his circle graph? How?

b) Why could Manon not use Juan's circle graph to create his bar graph?

5. The following times, in seconds, were recorded for a 100 m race.

13.9 14.3 14.4 13.7 15.2 15.4 14.8 13.9 13.9
14.5 14.7 14.4 13.8 14.2 13.1 13.8 12.4 13.8
12.7 13.4 14.4 13.9 14.0 14.4 14.3 14.5 11.8
14.8 12.9 12.3 12.8 13.7 13.1 15.0

a) Sort the data into groups in two different ways.

b) Create two graphs using your answers from part a).

c) Write a statement about the data that each graph supports.

6. What happens to the bars in a bar graph when you change the size of the groups?

8.3 Communicate about Choosing a Graph

Explain how to choose an appropriate graph for a set of data.

LEARN ABOUT the Math

Sanjev used census data to compare the number of Aboriginal people in Canada in different age groups in 1996 and in 2001. His report included a table and graph.

? How can Sanjev improve his report?

Sanjev's Report

Vanessa's Questions

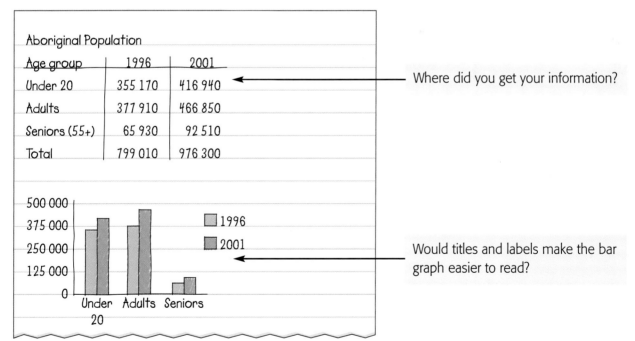

Aboriginal Population

Age group	1996	2001
Under 20	355 170	416 940
Adults	377 910	466 850
Seniors (55+)	65 930	92 510
Total	799 010	976 300

Where did you get your information?

Would titles and labels make the bar graph easier to read?

I chose a double bar graph to show the number of Aboriginal people in each age group for each year. With this graph, I can compare both the number in each age group and the changes in number from 1996 to 2001.

Each blue bar is higher than the green bar, so the graph shows that each age category grew from 1996 to 2001.

Why did you not use other types of graphs?

Which category changed the most? What else does the graph show?

A. Use Vanessa's questions and the Communication Checklist to rewrite Sanjev's report.

Reflecting

B. What parts of the Communication Checklist did Sanjev cover well?

C. How did Vanessa's questions help you improve Sanjev's communication about the populations?

WORK WITH the Math

Example 1 | Using graphs to make decisions

Kaitlyn surveyed 100 households and displayed the results in a bar graph.

How can Kaitlyn use the bar graph to convince her parents she needs her own phone line?

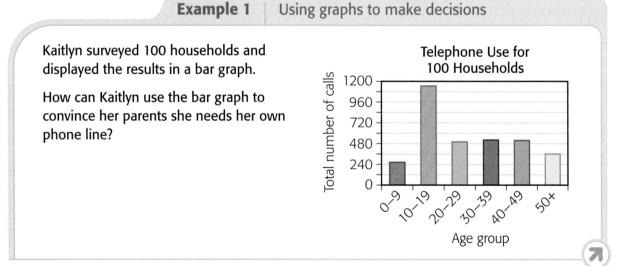

Solution

The graph shows that the 10–19 age group receives many more calls than other age groups. This means that other members of the family probably answer a lot of calls that are not for them. Having a second phone line would make it easier for the whole family.

- How do you budget your money?
- How tall are your classmates?
- How do you spend your day?
- Which four banks give the highest rates of interest?
- How do three magazines compare for number of copies sold in one year?

A Checking

1. Explain why you would use a circle graph to display information about some of the topics on the left, but not others. Use the Communication Checklist to improve your explanations.

2. How might a track and field team use graphs to display their records? What would be the advantage in using each type of graph? Use the Communication Checklist to help write your answer.

B Practising

3. The circle graph shows the breakdown of 55 endangered species in Canada.

Endangered Species in Canada

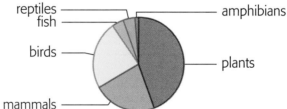

a) Use the graph and the Communication Checklist to write a report about endangered species.

b) Could another type of graph be used to display this data? Explain.

4. Exchange reports from question 3 with a classmate. Make suggestions to help them improve their report.

5. How do the data you collect and the purpose of the graph help you decide which kind of graph to use? Use examples to help you explain.

Mid-Chapter **Review**

Frequently Asked Questions

Q: How do you decide which type of graph you should use to represent data?

A: The type of graph depends on what you want the graph to show.

Type of graph	What the graph shows
line graph	trends
circle graph	how a whole is divided
scatterplot	if there is a relationship between two sets of data
bar graph/pictograph	compare numbers of things in different categories

Q: How does the choice of groups affect the appearance of a graph?

A: Choosing different groups can change the group that a data value belongs to. For example, these bar graphs display the same data but are very different in appearance:

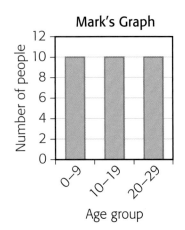

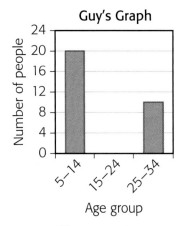

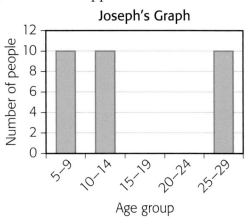

You can often get more information from graphs with smaller groups. For example, Joseph's graph shows there are no people in the 15 to 19 or 20 to 24 age groups. You cannot tell that from Mark's graph.

Practice

1.

Distance (km) Cycled by Bike-a-thon Participants							
17	20	53	27	29	33	36	19
61	13	28	27	16	54	19	42
56	45	8	15	36	25	47	44
32	12	10	65	31	52	35	30

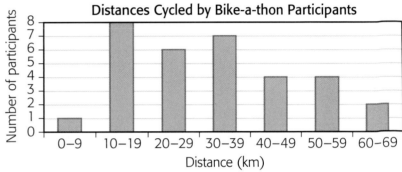

a) Which group of distances was most popular? Use the graph to help you answer.

b) Create another bar graph with different groupings of the data. Use your new graph to decide the most popular group of distances.

c) Compare your answers to parts a) and b). Did using different groups change the interpretation of the graph? Explain.

Top Earning Movies of 2006 (in millions)

1. *Pirates of the Caribbean: Dead Man's Chest* ($423.3)

2. *Cars* ($244.1)

3. *X-Men: The Last Stand* ($234.4)

4. *The Da Vinci Code* ($217.5)

5. *Ice Age: The Meltdown* ($200.1)

Lesson 8.3

2. a) Display this movie data in a graph. Why did you choose that type of graph?

b) Compare your graph with a classmate's. Discuss each of the following:
- Did you choose the same type of graph?
- What impressions do you get from each graph?
- Which graph appears to be the most effective in conveying the information?

c) Write a report for a movie rental company about how they should stock their shelves. Does your graph support your recommendations? Would your classmate's graph support the same recommendations?

Changing the Scale of a Graph

YOU WILL NEED
- pencil crayons
- a ruler
- grid paper or graphing software

GOAL

Explain how changing the scale of a graph can affect its appearance.

LEARN ABOUT *the Math*

Joseph made two graphs to show the results of a survey about favourite types of cheese for sale at a food fair.

Favourite Cheese

Cheese	Number of people
Gouda	951
Cheddar	987
Brie	955

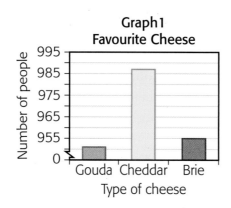

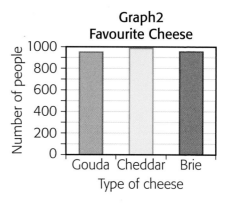

? How does changing the scale of a graph affect its appearance?

A. What is the meaning of the symbol ⌇ on the vertical axis of the graph? Explain how you know this.

B. Do the graphs use the same data? Explain how you know.

C. How do the scales of the two graphs differ?

D. How does changing the scale of the graph affect the conclusions you might draw?

Reflecting

E. Why might Joseph choose one graph over the other?

WORK WITH *the Math*

Example 1 | Changing the scale of a graph

Flena is doing a project on energy conservation. She surveyed 350 households to see how many energy-saving compact fluorescent lamp (CFL) bulbs they were using. What conclusions can she make from the data?

Number of CFL bulbs in use	Number of households
0	73
1-15	153
16-30	124

Elena's Solution

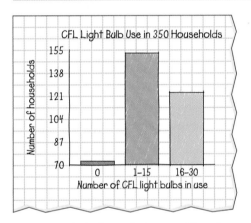

Almost all of the households use CFL bulbs.

I chose a bar graph so that it was easy to compare the number of households in each group.

Since the least value is 73 and the greatest is 153, I let the vertical axis go from 70 to 155.

Kaitlyn's Solution

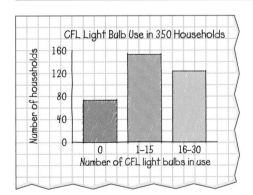

Most households are using energy-saving light bulbs, but about $\frac{1}{5}$ of them are not.

I also chose a bar graph, but my vertical scale started at 0. I think this gives a more accurate impression because I can see better how the whole is divided.

The 0 bar is about half the size of each of the other bars, so it is about $\frac{1}{5}$ of the total.

Example 2 | Changing the scale of a line graph

When Jules Verne wrote the science fiction classic *20 000 Leagues Under the Sea*, one league was about 4 km. How can readers compare leagues to kilometres as they read?

Sanjev's Solution

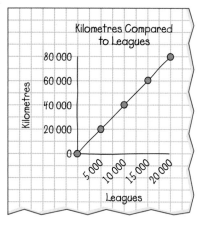

Leagues	Kilometres
0	0
5 000	20 000
10 000	40 000
15 000	60 000
20 000	80 000

I made a table showing leagues and kilometres.

I used the table to create a line graph. Two squares represent 5000 leagues on the horizontal axis and 20 000 kilometres on the vertical axis.

My graph shows that there is a steady rise in the number of kilometres as the number of leagues increases.

Vanessa's Solution

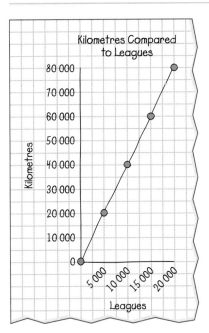

I used Sanjev's table of leagues and kilometres, but I let two squares on the vertical axis represent 10 000 kilometres.

My graph shows a sharp rise in the number of kilometres as the number of leagues increases.

A Checking

1. A vendor at a stadium collected data about favourite hot dog toppings. She used the data to create a bar graph.

Favourite Hot Dog Toppings	
ketchup	300
mustard	275
relish	155
hot peppers	42

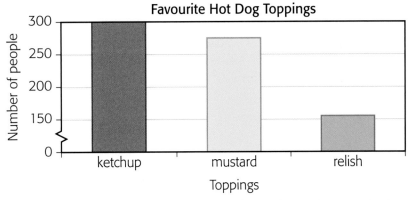

a) What does the graph appear to show about the popularity of the toppings?

b) Make a bar graph with a different scale to show less of a difference between the bars.

2. These two graphs show the number of students participating in provincial science fairs over several years.

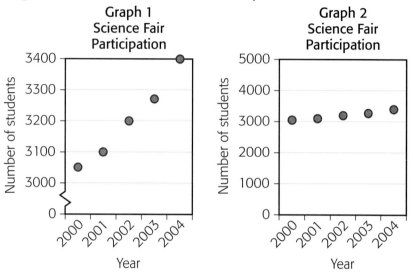

a) Which graph seems to show a greater increase in attendance?

b) Do the graphs appear to show the same data? Explain your reasoning.

c) Which graph might the organizers of the science fair prefer to show parents? Explain your choice.

3. Sagitha used data about the amount of pop the average Canadian drinks in a year to make a bar graph.

Annual Amount of Pop for Each Person	
Year	Amount(L)
1971	54
1981	68
1991	101
2001	113

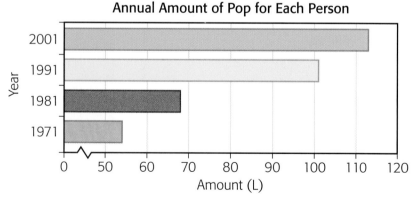

a) Draw another graph that appears to show smaller increases from decade to decade.

b) Describe how your scale differs from Sagitha's scale.

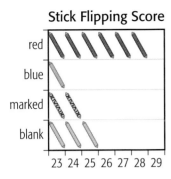

Stick Flipping Score

red
blue
marked
blank

23 24 25 26 27 28 29

4. Your score in a stick-flipping game depends on which side lands face up. Trevor and his friends made a graph showing the number of times each side landed face up during one game.
   a) Can you conclude that the red side lands face up much more frequently than the blue? Explain.
   b) How would you change the graph to better show the results?

5. Students were asked how far they travelled during their summer vacations. The results are shown in this graph.

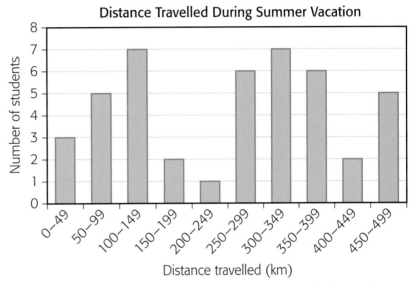

Distance Travelled During Summer Vacation

Number of students

Distance travelled (km)

Create a new graph to show that the majority of the students travelled less than 300 km.

6. How can you change the scale on a graph to make the differences between categories appear less or greater than they really are? Use this graph to help you explain.

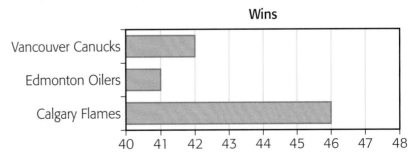

Wins

Vancouver Canucks
Edmonton Oilers
Calgary Flames

40 41 42 43 44 45 46 47 48

8.5

Recognizing Misleading Graphs

YOU WILL NEED
- grid paper

GOAL

Describe how to analyze graphs to be sure the data are represented fairly.

LEARN ABOUT the Math

Vanessa and Guy were contestants in a trivia game show. The graphs show their results.

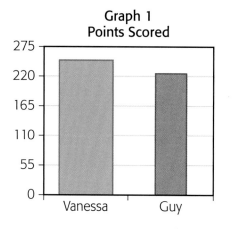

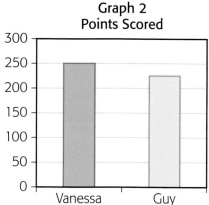

❓ How does one of the graphs create a false impression?

A. Does each graph display the same data? How do you know?

B. What is it that makes the two graphs appear different?

C. Which graph shows that both students scored a similar number of points?

D. What impression does the other graph give?

E. Do you think one of the graphs is misleading? Why or why not?

Reflecting

F. Which graph should be used to compare the results fairly?

G. When might someone want to use the other graph?

WORK WITH *the Math*

| **Example 1** | Analyzing graphs for inconsistencies |

Mark drew a graph to show how the number of music downloads from an online vendor changed over time.

a) What impression does the graph give about the change in the number of downloads?

b) How is this graph misleading?

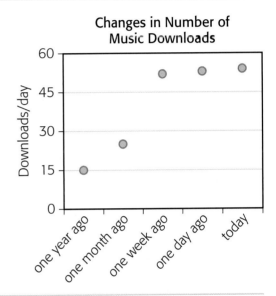

Changes in Number of Music Downloads

Elena's Solution

a) Looking at the points, I can conclude that downloads increased very sharply at first, then tapered off. They still increased, but not at such a great rate as before.

The rate of increase is shown by the change in the heights of the dots.

b) The horizontal scale is evenly spaced, even though the dates it represents are not. The data value for one year ago is probably a mean for the whole year. The data for one day ago and today are not means, they are for only one day. Maybe those two days are outliers. When the mean for this month is calculated, the data could show a big increase, a big decrease, or no change from a year ago or a month ago.

The graph is misleading because it appears that you can use it to predict downloads will increase slowly in the future, but you cannot predict at all using this graph.

When you read the labels, it is possible to figure out what the graph is showing, but Mark could have created a less misleading graph using the means for each month.

| **Example 2** | Identifying inconsistent conclusions |

A company put this graph in a newspaper ad to show how quickly employee pay is rising. Would you want to work for this company?

Kaitlyn's Solution

The graph makes it look like the rates go up a lot, but they do not. I would not want to work for this company.

At first I thought the large shaded area represented the increase in the rate of pay. I looked closely at the graph and realized that the increase in pay is the change in the height, which is tiny.

A Checking

1. These two graphs show the same data.

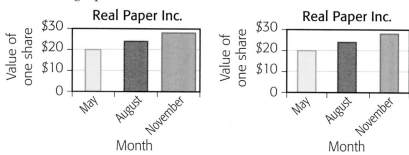

a) Which graph creates a false impression?
b) What false impression is created? Explain.

B Practising

2. A company asked two artists to draw a graph of the company's profits for a six-month period.

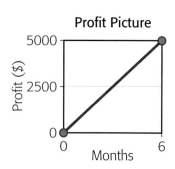

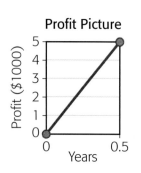

a) How are the graphs alike? How are they different?
b) If you were the president of the company, which graph would you choose to report profits? Explain.
c) Predict the company's profit for the seventh month. What assumption did you make to choose your answer?

3.

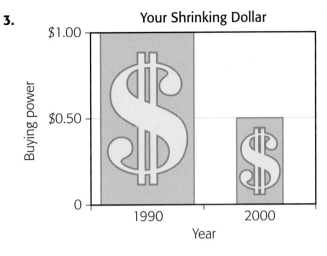

a) Measure and compare the areas of the bars. How do the areas of the symbols compare?

b) Explain how the graph misrepresents the change in the buying power of a dollar.

c) Draw a less misleading graph.

4. A news report said that cancer is the leading cause of death in Canada. Marissa looked up data online and made a circle graph to show that it is not. Should she write to the news station to tell them about their mistake?

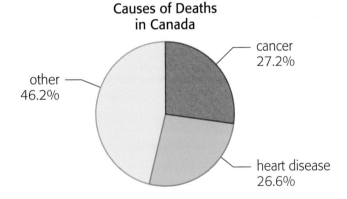

5. When you look at a visual representation of data, what can you look for to be sure the data are represented fairly?

Tricking the Eye

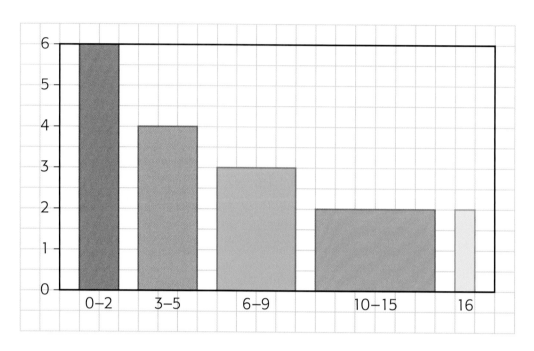

When the bars in a graph have different widths, your eye tends to compare areas instead of heights. Just as in a circle graph, the area of each bar can represent the percentage of all the data that falls in that category.

1. Suppose the height of each bar tells you how many data values are in that group.
   a) How many data values altogether are represented by this graph?
   b) How many bars represent the same number of data values?

2. Suppose the area of each bar tells you how many data values are in that group.
   a) How many data values are represented in this graph altogether?
   b) How many bars represent the same number of data values?

3. Which interpretation, height or area, do you think is a more accurate way to represent the data? Why?

Data Matching

YOU WILL NEED
• game cards

The goal of this game is to match graphs that could be displaying the same data.

Number of players: 2 to 4

How to Play

1. Lay the cards out face down.

2. On your turn, flip any two cards over. If the graphs are displaying the same data, keep the cards and score a point. If the graphs are not displaying the same data, turn them face down again. Your turn is over.

3. When all the matches have been made, the player with the highest score wins.

1. Anne recorded the colours of 100 cars in the parking lot of a supermarket. These are her results.

Colour of car	Number of cars of each colour
white	20
silver	32
black	18
red	12
blue	18

What type of graph would you use to display Anne's data? Explain.

2. A biologist who is studying gulls measured and recorded these wingspans (rounded to the nearest centimetre).

132	145	162	135	142	122	138	124
135	140	128	122	145	138	139	122
146	150	167	128	134	147	151	122

a) Construct two bar graphs, using different groupings for the data.
b) Could you get different impressions of the wingspans from the different graphs you created? Explain.

3. Canadian Western Natural Gas Company reported that prices have dropped since 2001.

Cost of Natural Gas per Gigajoule					
2001	2002	2003	2004	2005	2006
$14.00	$4.00	$5.50	$6.50	$7.50	$13.00

a) What type of graph might you choose to display this data? Explain.
b) What information will your graph show?
c) What other type of graph would be suitable to display this data?

4.

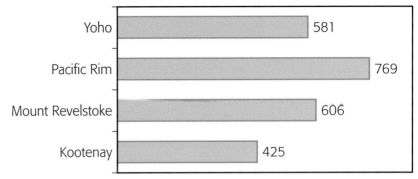

B.C. National Park Attendance

Yoho	581
Pacific Rim	769
Mount Revelstoke	606
Kootenay	425

Thousands of visitors

How could you change the scale of the graph to make the number of Pacific Rim Park visitors look greater? Construct the new version.

5.

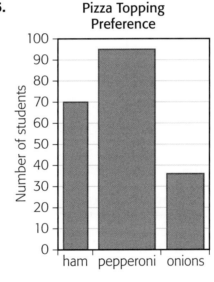

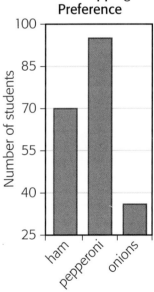

a) How are the graphs the same?
b) How are the graphs different?
c) What impression does each graph give about the students' preferences?
d) Which graph do you feel is presented in a misleading way?

What Do You Think Now?

Look back at What Do You Think? on page 331. How have your answers and explanations changed?

Chapter **Review**

Frequently Asked Questions

Q: How can you change the appearance of a graph?

A: You can change the scale of the graph. This can cause people to have a different impression of the data. For example, these graphs show the same data, but the scale in the one on the right greatly exaggerates the increase in housing prices.

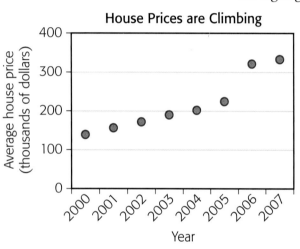

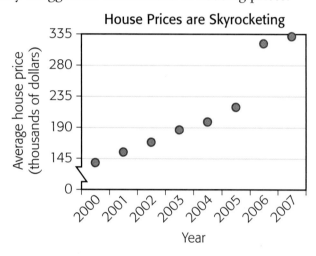

Q: How can a graph misrepresent data?

A: A graph can display data in such a way that a person looking at the graph gets the wrong impression.

For example, enlarging the sector for Growtec in the circle graph makes it appear that they have a larger market share than they really do.

Market Share of Fertilizer Companies

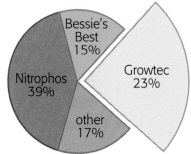

Practice

Country	Life expectancy (years)
Bangladesh	57
Brazil	66
Canada	78
China	70
Ethiopia	50
Iceland	79
India	59
Japan	80
Mexico	73
Norway	78

Lesson 8.2

1. The data show the life expectancy for various countries.
   a) Organize the data shown into groups. Construct a bar graph.
   b) Repeat part a) using different groups. How did your bar graph change?

Lesson 8.3

2. a) Explain why a bar graph is a good choice for the data in question 1.
   b) What other graphs would be appropriate? Explain.

3. Rohan conducted a survey and presented his findings in a graph. He concluded that music is very important to 13-year-olds.

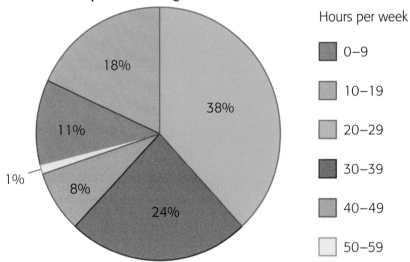

Time 13-Year-Olds Spend Listening to Music

Hours per week
- 0–9
- 10–19
- 20–29
- 30–39
- 40–49
- 50–59

   a) Why is a circle graph a good choice for this purpose?
   b) What details might be a good idea to include?
   c) How does Rohan's graph support his conclusion?

Lesson 8.4

4. Kaycee and Melissa used the same software to create a graph showing the same data.

Lifespans of Various Animals by Kaycee

Lifespans of Various Animals by Melissa

a) How are the graphs different?

b) What does each graph imply about the lifespan of the polar bear compared to the wolf?

c) Describe what would happen if the scale on Melissa's graph started at 15.

Lesson 8.5

5.

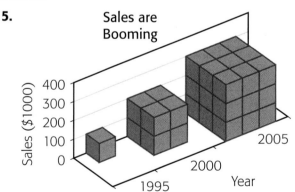

a) How many cubes represent the sales for each year?

b) Does the graph accurately represent the change in sales? Explain.

c) How could the graph be drawn to show the data more fairly?

6. How can you make graphs that display data well, and do not misrepresent the data?

Chapter **Task**

Convincing Statistics

The town is deciding what facilities to build in the new recreational area. You and your friends have been asked to make recommendations. Studies done so far have produced these graphs:

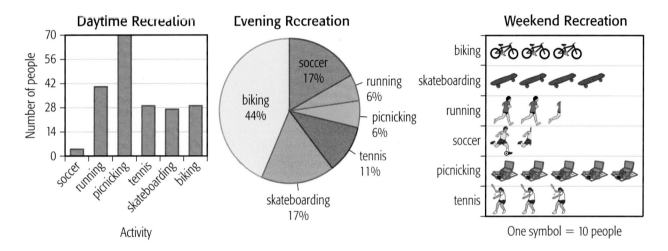

❓ How can you use the graphs to make recommendations?

A. Are the graphs misleading in any way?

B. Which graphs support the argument that picnic areas should be built? Explain.

C. How could you create a new graph to make the case for picnic areas more convincing?

D. How can you use the graphs to make the argument for biking trails convincing?

E. Based on the graphs, what three recommendations would you make? Explain your thinking.

Linear Relations and Linear Equations

GOAL

You will be able to

- represent a linear relation using a table of values and a graph

- describe the relationship between two variables in a table or on a graph

- write an equation you can use to solve a problem

- solve equations that involve integers, and verify the solutions

◄ How is the number of arch-shaped windows along the wings of the Saskatchewan Legislature related to the number of rectangular windows?

YOU WILL NEED
- grid paper
- a ruler
- cubes and counters

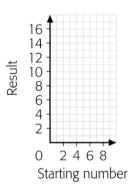

Number Tricks

Ivan created this number trick.
- Choose a number.
- Add 5.
- Multiply by 4.
- Subtract the number you chose.
- Subtract 2.
- Divide by 3.
- Tell me your result, and I can tell you what number you chose!

❓ How can you create your own number trick?

A. The table shows the results of Ivan's trick with two different starting numbers. Copy and extend the chart and test the trick by starting with 3, 4, 5 and 6.

Starting number (n)	Add 5	Multiply by 4	Subtract the original number	Subtract 2	Divide by 3 (result)
1	6	24	23	21	7
2	7	28	26	24	8

B. What rule do you think Ivan uses to predict the starting number?

C. Draw a graph to show how the starting number relates to the result.

D. If someone started with 84, what would the result be?

E. If the result is 243, what was the starting number?

Number Tricks

Result

0 2 4 6 8

Starting number

F. Ivan began making this chart to show how the trick works. Copy and complete the chart to describe the rest of the steps.

Steps in the trick	How it works	Expression
Choose a number.	▢	n
Add 5.	▢○○○○○	$n + 5$
Multiply by 4.	▢○○○○○ ▢○○○○○ ▢○○○○○ ▢○○○○○	$4n + 20$

G. How does the model in step F help you understand the number trick?

H. Make up your own number trick. Use models, graphs, or **algebraic expressions** to show your classmates how your trick works.

What Do You Think?

Decide whether you agree or disagree with each statement. Be ready to explain your decisions.

1. Whenever you use a table of values to describe how two variables are related, you can describe the relationship with a pattern rule.

2. The point $(1, 4)$ is on this graph, so the pattern rule that was used to make the graph must be $y = 4x$.

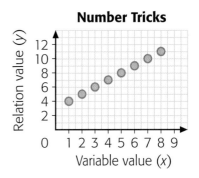

Number Tricks

3. Another way to write the algebraic expression $5(n + 4)$ is $5n + 4$.

4. If two different **equations** use the same letter for the variable, the variable does not have to represent the same amount.

9.1

Making a Table of Values

Create a table of values for a given linear relation.

LEARN ABOUT *the Math*

Taira painted different-sized square tiles to sell at the Winnipeg Folk Festival. She will also sell wooden moulding so that people who buy her tiles can make frames. The moulding is 2 cm wide.

Taira wants to make a table of values that will help her customers decide what length of moulding they need to buy for any size tile.

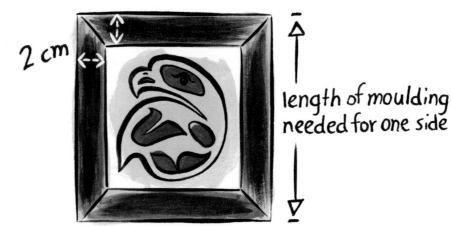

? **How can Taira figure out the length of moulding that someone would need to buy to frame each of her tiles?**

relation

a rule that allows you to use one number to get information about another number

A. Use words to describe the **relation** between the length of one side of the tile and the length of one side of the frame.

B. Write an algebraic expression to describe the relation from part A. Use a variable to represent the length of one side of the square tile.

Length of one side of tile (cm)	Total length of moulding needed (cm)
11	
15	
20	
30	
33	
40	
43	
45	

C. What equation can Taira use to determine the total length of moulding required for all four sides of a frame for a square tile of any size?

D. Use your equation to determine the total length of moulding needed to frame a square tile with sides that are 11 cm long.

E. Copy and complete the table of values to show what length of moulding customers will need to buy to frame each of the other tile sizes.

Reflecting

F. Why is making a table of values a good strategy when there are many different-sized squares?

WORK WITH *the Math*

Example 1	Creating a table of values

Renée runs a dog-walking service. She charges a fee of $3 per walk, plus $1 for every 10 min of the walk. Renée wants to send out flyers for her business. How can she determine sample rates for her flyers?

Renée's Solution

I used t to represent the time I spend walking a dog and I used c to represent the total cost of the walk.

$$\frac{t}{10} + 3 = c$$

Time spent walking, t (min)	Cost of walk, c ($)
15	4.50
30	6.00
45	7.50
60	9.00

I wrote an equation I can use to figure out the cost of a walk if I know how long it lasts.

It costs $1 for every 10 min of walking, so the cost of the walking time in dollars is $t \div 10$ (or $\frac{t}{10}$, which means the same thing). I added 3 for the extra $3 charge.

I used my equation to make a table of values for every 15 min. I substituted the times for t to figure out the costs. I decided to stop at 60 min because most walks would be shorter than that.

A Checking

1. Create a table of values for each equation by substituting values from 1 to 6 for *n*.

    a) $c = 4(n + 3)$ **b)** $t = \dfrac{n}{2} + 7$

2. **a)** Create an equation for each statement.

Statement	Equation
k is equal to half of *n* added to four times *n*	$k = \frac{n}{2} + 4n$
t is equal to five times the sum of four and *n*	$t = 5(4 + n)$

    b) Create a table of values for *n* = 4, *n* = 6, and *n* = 8 for each equation you wrote in part a).

B Practising

3. Write an equation you can use to make a table of values for each situation.

    a) Figure out the cost, *c*, of *n* tickets to a rock concert at $35 per ticket.

    b) Figure out the cost, *c*, of *n* cookies if the price is 2 cookies for $1.

    c) Figure out the cost, *c*, to rent a car for *t* days at $27 per day, if you have a coupon for $15 off the total cost.

4. Choose one situation from question 3. Create a table of values using any five values you choose for one of the variables.

5. Sierra is planning a party. The food will cost $8 per guest and the cake will cost $24.

    a) Write an equation someone can use to figure out the cost of the party for any number of guests.

    b) Create a table of values to show the cost of the party for 5 to 10 guests.

edging

$\leftarrow s \rightarrow$

Reading Strategy

Summarizing

Summarize the steps you will take to solve the problem.

6. Nick and Thao are trying to determine the total length of wooden edging needed to frame cedar planters. The planters are octagonal, but come in different sizes. Each piece of edging is 5 cm longer than one side, s. Nick thinks they should use $L = 16s + 80$. Thao thinks they should use $L = 16(s + 5)$.

    a) Create a table of values for either Thao's equation or Nick's equation. Include rows for these side lengths: 15 cm, 20 cm, and 25 cm.

    b) Compare your table with one that a classmate wrote for the other equation. What do you notice? Why did this happen?

7. Four friends run a lawn care business. They agree to split the profits equally every day, and each friend also agrees to donate $10 of their earnings to a local charity.

    a) Write an equation they can use to determine how much money each friend will receive, after donating to charity, if the business earns t dollars in a day.

    b) Suppose the business earns $320. How much will each friend receive?

8. A rectangle is 2 cm longer than it is wide.

    a) Write an equation you can use to determine the width when you know the length.

    b) Write an equation you can use to determine the perimeter when you know the length.

    c) Create a table of values showing the perimeters of rectangles with these lengths: 10 cm, 12 cm, 14 cm, 16 cm, 18 cm, and 20 cm.

    d) Determine the perimeter of a rectangle with a length of 36 cm. Explain what you did.

9. a) What information can you get from a table of values that you cannot get from the related equation? Give an example.

    b) What information can you get from an equation that you cannot get from the related table of values? Give an example.

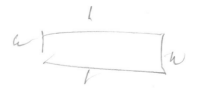

9.2

Graphing Linear Relations

GOAL

Construct a graph from the equation of a given linear relation.

LEARN ABOUT the Math

Angèle plays on a team that is going to an Ultimate Flying Disc tournament.

Six players will travel together and share the cost. Each player will pay an entry fee of $40.

The total travel cost for all six, not counting the entry fees, will be between $300 and $800.

? **How can Angèle figure out how much she might have to pay for the trip?**

Total travel cost (t)	Angèle's cost (a)
300	90
360	
420	

A. Write an equation Angèle can use to calculate her share of the travel cost plus the entry fee. Check your equation using the first pair of values from the table at the left.

B. Continue the table of values to show how Angèle's share of the cost will change as the total travel cost increases from $300 to $800.

Communication | *Tip*

In a table of values, changes to one variable depend on what happens to the other variable. For example, you cannot determine Angèle's cost until you know the total cost of the trip. In a table of values, the amount you need to know first usually goes in the left column. In an ordered pair, it is the first coordinate. On a graph, it is plotted along the horizontal axis.

C. Angèle plans to make a graph to estimate her share of the cost for any total amount from $300 to $800. Which of these points will be on her graph: (300, 90) or (90, 300)? Explain how you know.

D. Draw the axes for Angèle's graph. Choose a scale for each axis that will help you graph all the data from the table, and that will also help you use your graph to determine other possible costs. Give your graph a title.

E. Plot the points from your table of values on the graph. Then place a ruler along the points you plotted. Look for another set of coordinates that could describe an amount Angèle might have to pay.

F. Estimate the amount Angèle would pay if the total cost were $750.

G. Check your answer to part F by substituting the coordinates of the $750 point into your equation from part A.

Reflecting

H. How did you decide what scale to use on each axis?

I. Look at your graph. How does it show that the relation between the total cost and the cost for Angèle is a **linear relation**?

linear relation

a relation whose plotted points lie on a straight line

WORK WITH *the Math*

Example 1 | Graphing and analyzing data

Complete the table for the equation $y = x - 3$.
Graph the points from your table.
Determine the value of x when $y = -7$ using your graph.

x	y
−6	−9
−2	
3	
5	

Holly's Solution

x	y
-6	-9
-2	-5
3	0
5	2

The equation was $y = x - 3$, so I subtracted 3 from each value for x to get the matching value for y.

Some numbers in my table were negative, so I drew a grid with positive and negative numbers. I called the horizontal axis x and the vertical axis y. To mark the number, I found each x-coordinate on the x-axis and then counted up or down to the y-coordinate.

I wanted to know which point that was in line with the rest would have a y-coordinate of −7, so I drew a horizontal line at $y = -7$.

Then I put my ruler along the points and drew a new point where the line met my ruler. Then I drew a line up from the new point to the x-axis. The line met the

When $y = -7$, $x = -4$.

Example 2 | Solving a problem by graphing

Elinor makes custom tables. Each table has two supports, made from metal tubing, as shown. The height of each support is 60 cm, and the width matches the table width.

Elinor has 380 cm of metal tubing. What is the widest table she can make? Use a graph.

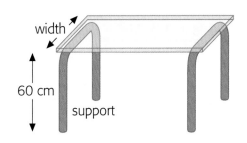

John's Solution

My equation is t = 2(120 + w), where t is the total length of tubing and w is the table width.

The length of tubing in one support is 60 cm + 60 cm + width. A shorter way to write that is 120 + *w*. Each table has two supports so I multiplied 120 + *w* by 2.

I used a spreadsheet to make a table of values. I decided that a table would probably not be less than 20 cm wide or more than 120 cm wide, so I used these amounts to start and end my spreadsheet.

◇	w	t
	20	280
	40	320
	60	360
	80	400
	100	440
	120	480

Tubing Needed for Different Sized Tables

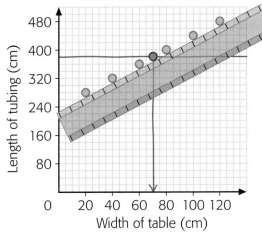

Elinor can make a table 70 cm wide from 380 cm of tubing.

I used my spreadsheet to make a **scatter plot**.

I used 1 square = 5 cm for my horizontal scale so I could show widths from 20 cm up to 120 cm (1.2 m).

I used 1 square = 20 cm for my vertical scale because I figured out I would not need too many squares to show the greatest number, 480 cm.

I printed my graph and drew a line across from 380 cm on the length axis. Then I put my ruler along the points on my graph and drew a new point where the line met my ruler. Then I drew a line down from the new point to the width axis. The line met the width axis at 70, so (70, 380) is a point on the graph.

Example 3 | Describing a relationship between variables

Tuyet manages an amusement park and is checking on the wait times for different rides. She made this graph to show how a customer moves forward in line while waiting for the Free-fall Ride. What does Tuyet's graph show about the relationship between the time spent waiting and the customer's position in the line?

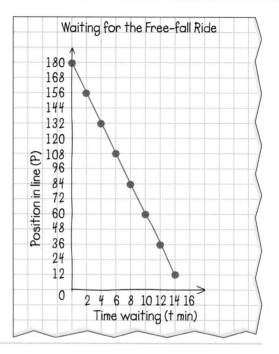

Lam's Solution

Tuyet's graph shows that the person moves up 24 positions in line every 2 min.

The first point on the graph is (0, 180), so a person who just arrived has waited 0 min and is 180th in line. The next point is (2, 156). After 2 min, the person has moved from 180th to 156th. $180 - 156 = 24$, so the person has moved up 24 spaces.

The next point is (4, 132), so after another 2 min, the person has moved up 24 more spaces.

The rest of the points are lined up, so the person keeps moving up 24 spaces every 2 min.

A Checking

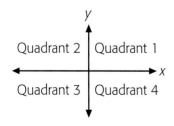

1. **a)** Create a table of values for the equation $y = 8 - 2x$.
   b) Graph the points from your table on a Cartesian coordinate system.
   c) Examine your graph. Do you think it is possible that the graph of this equation will ever contain points in Quadrant 3? Explain your reasoning.

B Practising

2. Treena is going to the fair. Admission to the fairgrounds is $15, and the rides are $5 each.

a) Create a table of values to show how much Treena would pay for admission and for 1, 4, and 10 rides.

b) Graph the data from your table of values. Determine Treena's total cost, including admission, if she goes on 7 rides.

c) If Treena has $75 to spend on rides and admission, how many rides can she go on?

3. a) Create a table of values for the equation $y = \frac{x}{4} + 2$. Choose x-values that are multiples of 4.

b) Graph the points from your table.

c) When $x = 10$, will y be an integer? How do you know?

d) Estimate the value of y when $x = 10$. Use your graph.

4. a) Graph the equation $y = -2(x + 3)$

b) Describe what happens to y each time x increases by 1.

c) When $y = 0$, is x positive or negative?

d) At what point on the graph do the x-values change from negative to positive?

5. At a Pop-a-Balloon game at the fair, you pay $1 and get 3 darts to throw at the balloons. Which graph below could you use to figure out how many darts you could throw for different prices in dollars? Explain how you know.

Graph 1

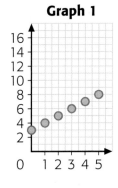

Graph 2

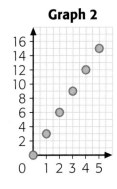

Graph 3

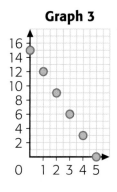

6. Sparkly Clean Window Cleaners charges $4 per window to wash windows in a home. This week, they are offering a $15 discount to all customers with 5 or more windows.
   a) Make a graph to show the window-cleaning cost for homes with 5 to 20 windows. What happens to the cost each time the number of windows increases by 5?
   b) Use your graph to estimate the cost for 17 windows.
   c) Use your graph to estimate the number of windows that could be cleaned for $29.
   d) Why do you think the discount does not apply if a home has fewer than 5 windows?

7. A class at Elmwood School is planning a three-day ski trip. The bus costs $850 and lift tickets cost $75 per person.
   a) Make a graph to show the total cost for 5, 10, 15, and 20 skiers.
   b) What is the total cost for 18 skiers?
   c) What would it cost per student if 14 students went on the trip and shared the cost equally?

8. The large pool at the Pan-Am Pool complex in Winnipeg holds 4700 kL (1 kL = 1000 L). The pool drains at a rate of 40 kL/h.
   a) Graph the relation between the amount of water left in the pool and the number of hours it has been draining.
   b) How much water is left in the pool after 60 h?
   c) Estimate how long the pool will take to drain completely.

9. Match each equation to its graph. Explain your reasoning.
   a) $y = 2x + 5$ b) $y = 5x - 8$ c) $y = -6x + 15$

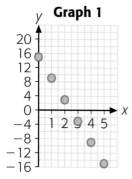
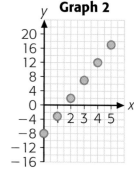
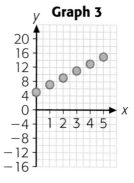

10. What can a graph show you about a situation that you cannot see on a table of values? Give an example from this lesson.

9.3

Exploring Possible Values

YOU WILL NEED
- pattern blocks

GOAL

Explore possible values for variables in a given equation.

EXPLORE the Math

John is competing in the school Think Bowl event.
He will win a point for his team if he can figure out how much each of these special coins is worth. John can use two or more of the clues to help him solve the problem.

Clue 1: If you add the coins and multiply by 3, the sum is $42.

Clue 2: Three green coins and four yellow coins are worth $53.

Clue 3: Four green coins and three yellow coins are worth $45.

Clue 4: Half of the difference between the two coins is $4.

? **What clues can you create about two special coins that are each worth more than John's coins?**

Drawing Diagrams to Represent Equations

Draw a diagram to determine the missing value in an ordered pair.

LEARN ABOUT the Math

Holly's mother sells hand-made chocolates. She charges $1 for every three chocolates, plus $5 for the tin they come in. While Holly is working at the store, a customer arrives with $16 to spend on a tin of chocolates.

Holly knows this equation can help her calculate the cost for any number of chocolates:

$c = \frac{n}{3} + 5$ where c is the cost and n is the number of chocolates.

❓ How many chocolates can the customer buy?

Example 1 | Drawing a diagram

I used a diagram to solve the equation $c = \frac{n}{3} + 5$ when c was 16.

Holly's Solution

$c = \frac{n}{3} + 5$

$16 = \frac{n}{3} + 5$

I had to figure out what n is when c is 16. I rewrote the equation by substituting 16 for c.

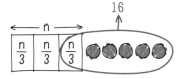

$16 = \frac{n}{3} + 5$ means that if you divide n into 3 equal parts and then you add 5 to one part, you will have 16. I drew a rectangle to show n. Then I divided the rectangle into 3 equal parts and labelled each part $\frac{n}{3}$. I added 5 to one part to make $\frac{n}{3} + 5$.

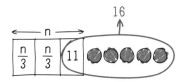

$\frac{n}{3} = 11$ because 11 is what is left if you take 5 away from 16.

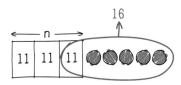

Each $\frac{n}{3}$ part must be 11 because the parts are equal.

$\frac{n}{3} = 11$

$n = 11 \times 3$

$n = 33$

The customer can buy 33 chocolates for $16.

If $\frac{n}{3} = 11$, then n must be 33.

Reflecting

A. How can Holly use her diagram to verify her solution?

B. What are some advantages and disadvantages of Holly's solution?

WORK WITH *the Math*

Example 2 | Solving a more complex equation

Solve the equation $4(d + 5) = m$ when $m = 32$.

Solution A: Dividing both sides by the same amount

$4(d + 5) = m$
$4(d + 5) = 32$

$= 32$

4 groups of $(d + 5)$ equals 32,
so $(d + 5)$ must equal $32 \div 4 = 8$.

Since $d + 5 = 8$, then d must equal 3.

Check:
Left side	Right side
$4(d + 5)$	32
$4(3 + 5)$	
$4(8)$	
32	

Rewrite the equation with 32 instead of m.

Draw a picture to show that $4(d + 5)$ means "4 groups of $(d + 5)$." You can use a box to represent the variable because you do not know what amount it represents. You can draw red counters to represent the constant amount (+ 5).

Figure out the value of each group of $d + 5$.

Then figure out the value of d.

Verify by substituting 3 for d in the original equation.

Solution B: Writing the multiplication differently

$4(d + 5) = m$
$4(d + 5) = 32$
$4d + 20 = 32$

$4d = 12$
$d = 3$

Rewrite the equation with 32 instead of m.
Multiply each part of the $d + 5$ by 4.

$4d + 20 = 32$ means that if you have 4 groups of d and you add 20, the result is 32. Draw a rectangle to represent 32 and divide it into parts that show $d + d + d + d + 20$.

The yellow part of the rectangle is worth 20, so the green part must be worth $32 - 20$ or 12. Each d must be worth 3 because $4(3) = 12$.

Example 3 | Solving an equation involving subtraction

Solve the equation $\frac{x}{4} - 7 = y$ when $y = -19$.

Solution

$\frac{x}{4} - 7 = y$

$\frac{x}{4} - 7 = -19$

Rewrite the equation with −19 instead of y. This equation means, "If you divide x into 4 equal parts and then subtract 7 from one of the parts, the answer is −19."

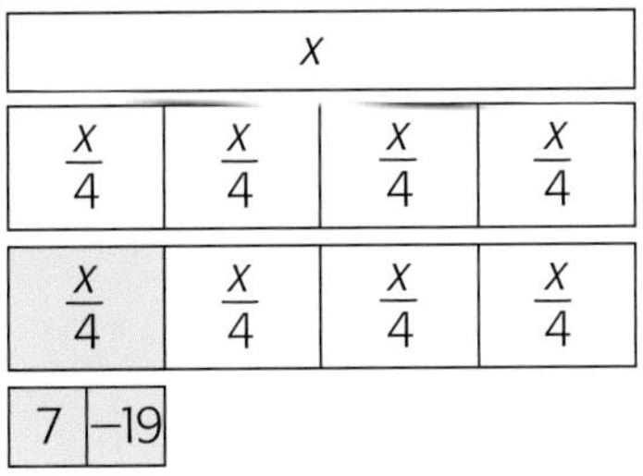

	x		

$\frac{x}{4}$	$\frac{x}{4}$	$\frac{x}{4}$	$\frac{x}{4}$

$\frac{x}{4}$	$\frac{x}{4}$	$\frac{x}{4}$	$\frac{x}{4}$

7	−19

Draw a rectangle to represent x, the starting amount.

Divide x into 4 equal parts to show $\frac{x}{4}$.

The equation says that, if you subtract 7 from $\frac{x}{4}$, there will be −19 left. The yellow part of the picture shows this. It also shows that $\frac{x}{4} = 7 + (-19)$, so $\frac{x}{4} = -12$.

$7 + (-19) = -12,$

$\text{so } \frac{x}{4} = -12$

$4(\frac{x}{4}) = 4(-12)$

$x = -48$

There are 4 groups of $\frac{x}{4}$ in x, so if $\frac{x}{4} = -12$, then $x = -48$.

Check: Left side   Right side

$\frac{x}{4} - 7$ -19

$\frac{-48}{4} - 7$

$(-12) - 7$

-19

Verify the solution by substituting −48 for the variable x in the original equation.

A Checking

1. Solve each equation using a diagram.
   a) $t = 5(n + 1)$, when $t = 30$ b) $p = \frac{x}{3} - 2$, when $p = -5$

B Practising

2. Solve each equation.
   a) $\frac{x}{3} + 23 = y$, when $y = 41$ b) $3x + 9 = y$, when $y = 36$

3. Each diagram is the beginning of a solution to an equation. Write the equation.

a) 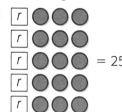 = 25

b)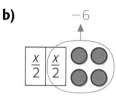

4. Continue each solution in question 3.

5. Solve each equation.

a) $6x + 5 = y$, when $y = 41$

b) $3x - 24 = y$, when $y = 12$

c) $\dfrac{x}{2} + 9 = y$, when $y = -13$

d) $4(x + 7) = y$, when $y = 20$

6. a) Create a table of values for $y = 3x - 4$.

b) Graph the points from your table on a Cartesian coordinate system.

c) Use your graph to determine the values of x when $y = 11$ and $y = -16$.

d) Why is a graph more useful than a diagram when you have to solve an equation for more than one value of the variable?

7. Bowling costs $4 per game plus $2 for shoe rental.

a) Write an equation you can use to determine the cost of bowling for any number of games.

b) During a tournament, Max spent $30. How many games did he bowl?

8. Which of these equations would you solve by drawing a diagram? Explain your choice(s) and show the diagrams you would use.

A. $4x = y$, when $y = 24$

B. $4x + 320 = y$, when $y = 424$

C. $n - 5 = d$, when $d = 0$

D. $\dfrac{x}{3} - 2 = y$, when $y = 3$

Mid-Chapter **Review**

Frequently Asked Questions

Q: How can you graph a linear relation?

n	*c*
40	1200
80	2000
120	2800
160	3600
200	4400
240	5200

A: You can create a table of values using the relation. For example, suppose a sports banquet for up to 240 people costs $20 for each person plus $400. The relation is $20n + \$400 = c$. Decide on reasonable values for one of the variables and create the table.

You need to know the number of people to get the cost, so *n* goes on the horizontal axis.

The *n*-axis will go from 0 to at least 240. You can use a scale of 1 square for 20 people.

The *c*-axis will go from $0 to at least $5200. You can use a scale of 1 square for $400.

Plot points on the scatter plot using the table of values.

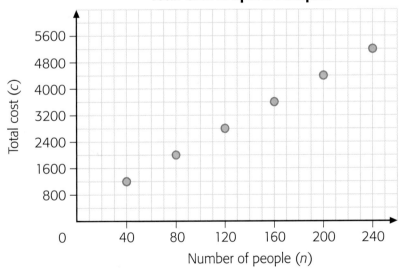

Total Cost of Sports Banquet

Linear Relations and Linear Equations   **383**

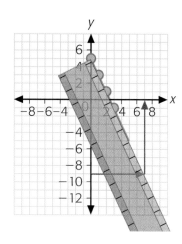

Q: **How can you solve an equation using a graph?**

A: For example, use the graph of $-2x + 5 = y$ to solve $-2x + 5 = -9$.

Step 1:
Place a ruler along the plotted points.
Look for a point on the line formed by the ruler where $y = -9$.

Step 2:
Draw a vertical line from that point to the horizontal axis to find the x-value for that y-value. That point is the value of x that solves the equation.

For $-2x + 5 = -9$, $x = 7$.

Q: **How can you solve an equation by drawing a diagram?**

A: For example, solve $3(d + 2) = t$ when $t = -12$ by drawing a picture to figure out what the equation means.

$$\boxed{d} \,●● $$
$$\boxed{d} \,●● \ = -12$$
$$\boxed{d} \,●●$$

3 groups of $\boxed{d}\,●●$ equal -12.

$3(-4) = -12$, so each group of $\boxed{d}\,●●$ must equal -4.

If $d + 2 = -4$, then d must be -6.

Check.

Left side	Right side
$3((-6) + 2)$	-12
$= 3(-4)$	
$= -12$	

Practice

25n + 50 = c	
n	*c*
3	125
7	225
15	
	550

(handwritten notes alongside table)

Lesson 9.1

1. Complete the table of values for $25n + 50 = c$.

2. A digital television provider charges $30 a month for the basic package, plus $2 for each additional theme group.
   a) Write an equation for the monthly cost of various television packages.
   b) Create a table of values to show the cost of the basic package plus 0, 2, 4, 6, 8, and 10 theme groups.
   c) How much would a basic package plus 7 theme groups cost?
   d) Suppose Jerry's bill is $52. How many theme groups does he get?

Lesson 9.2

3. Graph each relation on the same set of axes.
   a) $y = 4x - 5$ b) $y = -3(x - 4)$ c) $y = \dfrac{x}{2} + 1$

4. Darius is a long-distance truck driver. His average speed is 80 km/h and he takes a 1 h break on each trip. A relation for the number of hours he is on the road, t, is $t = \dfrac{d}{80} + 1$, where d is the distance he drives. Graph this relation.

5. Use your graph from question 4 to determine how many hours Darius takes to drive each distance.
   a) 400 km   b) 640 km   c) 880 km

6. Use your graph from question 4 to determine how far Darius drives in each period of time.
   a) 5 h   b) 8 h   c) 10 h

Lesson 9.4

7. Solve each equation by drawing a diagram.
   a) $4x + 3 = y$, when $y = 23$
   b) $2(x + 5) = y$, when $y = -8$
   c) $\dfrac{x}{5} + 2 = y$, when $y = 6$
   d) $\dfrac{x}{4} - 5 = y$, when $y = 4$

9.5 Solving Equations with Counter Models

YOU WILL NEED

- red and blue cubes
- red and blue counters
- Balance Mat

GOAL

Model and solve linear equations concretely.

LEARN ABOUT *the Math*

The National Hockey League (NHL) is made up of 30 teams in Canada and the United States. Before the NHL expanded in 1967, there were far fewer teams.

If you start with the number of teams before the expansion, add 4, and then multiply by 3, the result is 30, which is the current number of teams in the NHL.

? How many teams were in the National Hockey League before it expanded?

Example 1 | Modelling to solve an equation

I wrote an equation to describe the number of teams and then solved the equation by modelling with cubes and counters on a balance.

Lam's Solution

I used t to represent the number of teams before the 1967 expansion of the NHL.

$3(t + 4) = 30$

$3(t + 4)$

I wrote an equation to show the clues: "Add 4 to t and then multiply by 3."

$3(t + 4)$ means the same as $3 \times (t + 4)$.

I used a red cube to represent t.
I added 4 round counters to show $t + 4$.
To show $3(t + 4)$, I made 3 rows of $t + 4$.

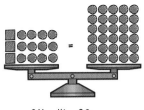

$3(1 + 4) = 30$

$3t + 12 = 30$

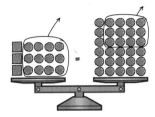

$3t + 12 - 12 = 30 - 12$

$3t = 18$

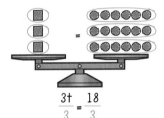

$$\frac{3t}{3} = \frac{18}{3}$$

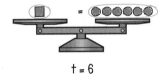

$t = 6$

There were 6 teams in the NHL before the 1967 expansion.

Check: Left side   Right side
$\quad\quad 3(t + 4)$ 30
$\quad\quad = 3(6 + 4)$
$\quad\quad = 3(10)$
$\quad\quad = 30 \checkmark$

I still had to figure out how much t was worth. $3(t + 4) = 30$, so I thought of a pan balance with $3(t + 4)$ on the left side and 30 on the right side. I made a model with cubes and counters.

$3(t + 4)$ was the same as $3t + 12$ because there were 3 t-cubes and 12 counters.

I subtracted 12 counters from each side. The amounts stayed balanced but the 3 t-cubes were alone on one side. That helped me figure out that 3 t-cubes were worth 18.

I noticed that I could make 3 groups of t on the left side and 3 groups of 6 on the right side. This is like dividing both sides by 3.

I took away two of the groups on each side. Since the groups were equal, the amounts that were left stayed balanced. This let me see the value of one red cube, or t.
Then I knew that each t was worth 6.

I verified my solution by substituting 6 for the variable t in my equation. The left side was equal to the right side, so my solution was correct.

isolate

to show the same equation in an equivalent way so the variable is alone on one side

Reflecting

A. Whenever you add, subtract, multiply, or divide on one side of the equation, you need to make the same change on the other side. Why is it important do this?

B. How did **isolating** the three red cubes on one side help Lam solve the problem?

WORK WITH *the Math*

Example 2 | Modelling equations with negative numbers

Solve the equation $3 - 2x = 7$.

Solution A: Solve by balancing

$$3 - 2x = 7$$
$$3 + (-2x) = 7$$

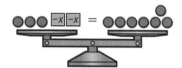

Model the equation with cubes and counters. Use red for positive and blue for negative. You cannot show $3 - 2x$ on the left side, but you can show $3 + (-2x)$, which means the same thing.

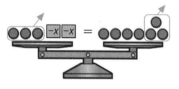

Isolate the cubes on one side by subtracting 3 counters from each side.

$$3 - 3 + (-2x) = 7 - 3$$

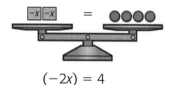

The cubes are alone and the equation still balances.

$$(-2x) = 4$$

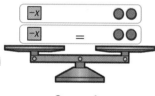

Make two equal groups on each side to determine the value of $-x$.

$$\frac{-2x}{2} = \frac{4}{2}$$
$$-x = 2$$
$$x = -2$$

If $-x = 2$, then x must equal the opposite of 2, or -2.

Check: Left side   Right side
$$\quad 3 - 2x \qquad 7$$
$$= 3 - 2(-2)$$
$$= 3 - (-4)$$
$$= 3 + 4$$
$$= 7 \checkmark$$

Verify the solution by substituting 2 for x in the original equation. The left and right sides are equal, so the solution is correct.

Solution B: Solve using the zero principle

$3 - 2x = 7$

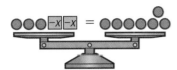

Model the equation with cubes and counters.

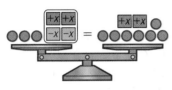

$3 + (-2x) + 2x = 7 + 2x$
$3 + \boxed{(-2x) + 2x} = 7 + 2x$
$3 + 0 = 7 + 2x$

Remove the negative cubes by using the zero principle. Add $2x$ to both sides. The circled cubes are opposites, so their value is 0.

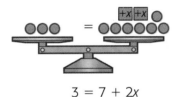

$3 = 7 + 2x$

Now only positive x-cubes are left, so it will be easier to find the value of x.

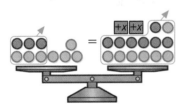

$3 + (-7) = \boxed{7 + (-7)} + 2x$
$-4 = 0 + 2x$
$-4 = 2x$

Isolate the cubes on one side by adding -7 to both sides.

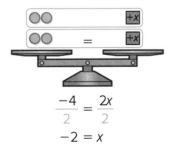

$\dfrac{-4}{2} = \dfrac{2x}{2}$
$-2 = x$

2 x-cubes are worth 4 negative counters. Each x-cube must be worth 2 negative counters, so $x = -2$.

This is the same thing as dividing both sides of the equation by 2.

Example 3 | Modelling equations with fraction solutions

Model and solve the equation $6x - 2 = 1$.

Solution

$6x - 2 = 1$

Model the equation with cubes and counters. Use 2 negative counters to represent -2.

$6x + (-2) + 2 = 1 + 2$

$6x = 3$

Isolate the cubes on the left side using the zero principle. Add 2 red counters to each side to remove the 2 blue counters. The circled counters are opposites, so their value is 0.

There are only 3 red counters on the right side of the equation, so divide each side into 3 equal groups.

$\dfrac{6x}{3} = \dfrac{3}{3}$

2 red cubes have the same value as 1 red counter.

$2x = 1$

To find the value of one red cube, imagine the red counter split in half.

$\dfrac{2x}{2} = \dfrac{1}{2}$

Two cubes are equal to two $\frac{1}{2}$ counters, so one cube is equal to one $\frac{1}{2}$ counter.

$x = \dfrac{1}{2}$

The solution to the equation
$6x - 2 = 1$ is $x = \dfrac{1}{2}$.

Check: Left side   Right side
          $6x - 2$ 1

          $= 6(\frac{1}{2}) - 2$

          $= 3 - 2$

          $= 1$ ✔

Verify the solution by substituting $\frac{1}{2}$ for x in the original equation. The left and right sides are equal, so the solution is correct.

1. Model and solve each equation.
   a) $2(z + 3) = 14$
   c) $-6 = 5x + 4$
   b) $35 = 5(k - 4)$
   d) $-2d + 3 = 9$

B Practising

2. a) Solve $3x + 5 = 26$ using a model. Record your steps.
   b) Explain how your model helped you solve the equation.

3. Write an equation for each model, then solve your equations.

   a) 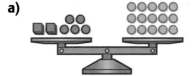   b)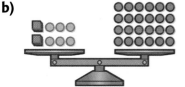

4. a) Solve $4x - 2 = 5$ using models or a diagram.
   b) Why would it be difficult to complete the solution using only cubes and counters?

5. Model and solve each equation.
   a) $4g = -24$
   d) $5a = 13$
   b) $2h - 5 = 11$
   e) $4a + 3 = -3$
   c) $4(m - 2) = 20$
   f) $3(y + 2) = -12$

6. Write each sentence as an equation, then solve the equation.
   a) Seven more than five times a number is 22.
   b) Three less than four times a number is 21.
   c) Four times two more than a number is 32.

7. Solve each equation. Show what you did.
   a) $-3d + 5 = -4$
   b) $-10 = 6x - 4$
   c) $-2(z - 3) = -8$

8. a) Draw a picture to solve the equation $\frac{x}{5} - 4 = 8$.
   b) Why would it be difficult to use cubes and counters to solve an equation where the variable is divided by a number?

9. Jack Nicklaus is one of the greatest golfers of all time. Over his career, he had 20 wins in major tournaments.
   a) If you multiply the number of times he finished third by 2 and then add 2, the result is the number of times he finished first. How many times did he finish third?
   b) If you divide the number of times he finished in the top three by 4 and then subtract 3, you get the number of third-place finishes. How many top-three finishes did Nicklaus have? How many times did he place second?
   c) The Masters Tournament is the most prestigious tournament in golf. Four times one less than Nicklaus's number of Masters wins is equal to his total number of first-place wins. How many times did he win the Masters?

10. Create a balance problem for a classmate to solve. Use small paper bags with heavy counters in them to represent variables. (Make sure to put the same number of counters in each bag.) See if your classmate can write an equation to describe your problem, and then solve it to figure out how many counters you put in each bag.

11. If you are modelling an equation on a real pan balance, what is the reason you cannot use one cube to represent a variable?

12. When you make a model to solve an equation, why does it help to use different materials to represent the variables and the **constants**?

Solving Equations Symbolically

GOAL

Solve a linear equation symbolically.

LEARN ABOUT the Math

The world's largest indoor triple-loop roller coaster is the Mindbender at Galaxyland Amusement Park in the West Edmonton Mall.

Thirty-one people were waiting to get on the Mindbender ride. After they boarded, two trains were full and the third train had five empty seats.

? **How many seats are in each train on the Mindbender?**

Example 1 | Using symbols

Determine the number of seats on each train by writing a symbolic solution.

Renée's Solution

I used n to represent the number of seats in each train.

$$n + n + (n - 5) = 31$$

$$3n - 5 = 31$$

$$3n - 5 = 31$$
$$3n - 5 + 5 = 31 + 5$$
$$3n = 36$$

$$\frac{3n}{3} = \frac{36}{3}$$
$$n = 12$$

There are 12 seats on each train.

Check:

$$12 + 12 + 7 = 31 \ \checkmark$$

Two full trains had *n* people in seats, and one train had *n* − 5 people in seats. There were 31 people altogether.

I replaced *n* + *n* + *n* with 3*n* to simplify my equation.

I wanted to isolate 3*n* on one side so I could see how much it was worth and figure out *n*. To get 3*n* alone, I used the zero principle and added 5 to both sides.

Now I knew 3 full trains had 36 seats. To get *n*, the number of seats on one train, I divided both sides by 3. This kept the equation balanced.

To check, I drew each train and showed the full and empty seats. My picture matched what it said in the problem, so my answer was correct.

Example 2 | Working backwards

Determine the number of seats on each train by working backwards
through the operations.

John's Solution

$3n - 5 = 31$

Forward	Backwards ↑
Start with n.	Result is n.
Multiply by 3.	Divide by 3.
Subtract 5.	Add 5.
Result is 31.	Start with 31.

I wrote the operations that happen to the variable in the equation. Then I worked backwards to figure out what operations I would have to do to change 31 back to n.

Start with 31.

Add 5: $31 + 5 = 36$

Divide by 3: $\dfrac{36}{3} = 12$

Result is n: $n = 12$

I started with 31 and followed my backwards operation steps to figure out n.

Check: Left side   Right side

$3n - 5 31$

$= 3(12) - 5$

$= 36 - 5$

$= 31$ ✔

I verified my solution by substituting 12 for n in the equation. The left side was equal to the right side, so my solution was correct.

Reflecting

A. How is Renée's solution similar to solving equations with cubes and counters?

B. How do you think John knew which operations to use? Could he have done the same operations in a different order?

C. How are John's and Renée's solutions alike?

Example 3	Solving equations involving division

Solve $\dfrac{c}{4} + 1 = 6.$

Solution

$$\dfrac{c}{4} + 1 = 6$$

$$\dfrac{c}{4} + 1 - 1 = 6 - 1$$

$$\dfrac{c}{4} = 5$$

To get c alone on one side of the equation, start by subtracting 1 from both sides.

$$4\left(\dfrac{c}{4}\right) = 4(5)$$

$$c = 20$$

$\dfrac{c}{4}$ means $c \div 4$, so you can figure out what c is by multiplying $\dfrac{c}{4} \times 4$.

Multiply the right side by 4 to keep the equation balanced.

Check:

$$\dfrac{c}{4} + 1 = 6$$

You can verify the solution by using a model. $\dfrac{c}{4} + 1 = 6$ can mean that, if you divide c counters into 4 groups and then add 1 to one of the groups, that group will have 6 in it.

$\dfrac{c}{4} \rightarrow$

Since $c = 20$, start with 20 counters. Divide the 20 counters into 4 groups.

$\dfrac{c}{4} + 1 \rightarrow$

Add 1 counter to one of the groups. Now there are 6 counters in that group, so $\dfrac{c}{4} + 1 = 6$.

$\dfrac{c}{4} + 1$ ✔

The solution is correct.

Example 4 | Solving equations with integers

Solve the equation $12 = -6(y - 4)$.

Solution A

$$12 = -6(y - 4)$$
$$12 = -6y + 24$$
$$12 - 24 = -6y + 24 - 24$$
$$-12 = -6y$$
$$\frac{-12}{-6} = \frac{-6y}{-6}$$
$$2 = y$$

Multiply each term in the brackets by -6.

Subtract 24 from both sides to isolate $-6y$.

Divide both sides by -6 to isolate y.

Check: Left side   Right side

$$12$$

$$-6(y - 4)$$
$$= -6(2 - 4)$$
$$= -6(-2)$$
$$= 12 \checkmark$$

Verify by substituting 2 for y in the equation. The left and right sides are equal, so the solutions are correct.

Solution B

$$12 = -6(y - 4)$$
$$\frac{12}{-6} = \frac{-6}{-6}(y - 4)$$
$$-2 = (y - 4)$$
$$-2 = y - 4$$
$$-2 + 4 = y - 4 + 4$$
$$2 = y$$

Divide both sides by -6 to simplify the equation.

Add 4 to both sides to isolate y.

A Checking

1. Solve each equation and record your steps.

   a) $a + 12 = 60$

   b) $39 = b - 13$

   c) $4s = 72$

   d) $17 = 4a + 5$

   e) $2(n - 4) = 6$

   f) $\dfrac{w}{5} - 3 = 17$

B Practising

2. Solve each equation and record your steps. Show one way to verify each solution.

   a) $q - 17 = -31$

   b) $-117 = -9s$

   c) $\dfrac{z}{6} = -5$

   d) $7d - 11 = 66$

   e) $14(n + 5)42$

   f) $8 = \dfrac{t}{4} - 9$

3. Mei began solving the equation $-7(c - 3) = 49$. Copy and complete her solution.

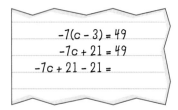

$$-7(c - 3) = 49$$
$$-7c + 21 = 49$$
$$-7c + 21 - 21 =$$

4. Sam began solving the equation $6(r + 2) = 16$. Copy and complete his solution.

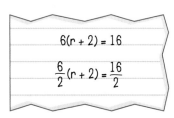

$$6(r + 2) = 16$$
$$\dfrac{6}{2}(r + 2) = \dfrac{16}{2}$$

5. Solve $-3(x - 3) = -18$ in two different ways. Show what you did.

6. Solve each equation and record your steps. Show one way to verify each solution.

   a) $11 = 5x - 4$

   b) $-3m + 7 = 40$

   c) $\dfrac{z}{5} = -7$

   d) $-3(z - 8) = 6$

   e) $9 = 2(x + 3)$

   f) $9 - 7x = -12$

7. Alex says to Callie, "I am thinking of a number. If you divide my number by 8 and then subtract 12, the result is 14." Write and solve an equation to determine Alex's number.

8. a) Carina bought three cafeteria lunches—one for herself and one for each of her two friends. Each lunch had a veggie sub and a dessert. The desserts cost $2 each and Carina paid $18 altogether. Write an equation you can use to determine the cost of each sub.

   b) Solve the equation. How much did each sub cost?

9. Solve each equation and record your steps. Show one way to verify each solution.

   a) $8t - 1 = 5$

   b) $\dfrac{k}{3} - 5 = 7$

   c) $-4(f - 2) = 12$

   d) $\dfrac{m}{6} + 9 = 5$

10. A Grade 8 class held a charity car wash and earned $368. They gave $200 to an animal shelter. They shared the rest of the money equally among four other charities. How much money did each charity receive?

11. Emily and her friends spent the day at the West Edmonton Mall. Each person paid $35 for admission to the Waterpark, and $25 to get into Galaxyland for the evening. The group also paid $40 to rent a cabana at the Waterpark. They spent $700 altogether. How many people were in the group?

12. Six friends took a trip to the Canadian Rockies. They swam in Banff Upper Hot Springs, rode a gondola at Lake Louise, and went on a glacier tour at the Columbia Icefields. Visiting all three attractions cost a total of $426 for the group. The gondola ride was $24 per person, and admission to the hot springs was $8 per person. How much did the glacier tour cost?

13. Aaron said, "When I solve an equation symbolically, it helps if I think about cubes and counters on a pan balance." Do you agree with Aaron? Explain.

9.7 Correcting Errors in Solutions

YOU WILL NEED
- a coin
- grid paper

GOAL

Verify solutions to linear equations and identify and correct any errors.

LEARN ABOUT the Math

Taira played four rounds in a golf tournament. Her final score was 288. She has a 3 handicap. This means that, to calculate her final score for each round, she subtracted her handicap, 3, from the number of strokes she took.

Here are three solutions that try to calculate Taira's mean score for each round before her handicap was applied. The expression $4(s - 3)$ was used to express her total score before the handicap was applied, where s represents the mean score for one round.

? Which one of these solutions is correct?

Solution 1	Solution 2	Solution 3
$4(s - 3) = 288$ 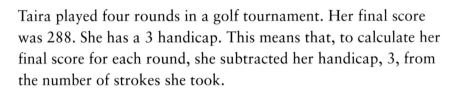 $4(s - 3) = 288$ $4s - 12 = 288$ $4s - 12 - 12 = 288 - 12$ $4s = 276$ $\dfrac{4s}{4} = \dfrac{276}{4}$ $s = 69$	$4(s - 3) = 288$ $\dfrac{4}{4}(s - 3) = \dfrac{288}{4}$ $s - 3 = 72$ $s - 3 + 3 = 72 + 3$ $s = 75$	$4(s - 3) = 288$ $4s - 3 + 3 = 288 + 3$ $4s = 291$ $\dfrac{4s}{4} = \dfrac{291}{4}$ $s = 72\dfrac{3}{4}$

The mean score for each round without the handicap was 69.

The mean score for each round without the handicap was 75.

The mean score for each round without the handicap was $72\dfrac{3}{4}$.

A. Which solution is correct?

B. Describe the error in each incorrect solution.

Reflecting

C. How did you verify each solution and identify any errors?

D. Why is it important to verify the solution to an equation?

WORK WITH *the Math*

Example 1	Identifying and correcting errors

Identify and correct the errors in this solution.

$$-2(x - 1) = -22$$
$$-2x - 2 = -22$$
$$-2x - 2 + 2 = -22 + 2$$
$$-2x = -20$$
$$\frac{-2x}{-2} = \frac{-20}{-2}$$
$$x = 10$$

Taira's Solution

$-2(x - 1) = -22$
$-2x + 2 = -22$
$-2x + 2 - 2 = -22 - 2$
$-2x = -24$
$\dfrac{-2x}{-2} = \dfrac{-24}{-2}$
$x = 12$

Check: Left side   Right side
$-2(x - 1)$ -22
$= -2(12 - 1)$
$= -2(11)$
$= -22$ ✔

I did not have to verify this solution because the problem told me it was incorrect.
I found the errors by checking each step. I noticed a problem in the second line where the person multiplied -2 by -1 and got -2 instead of $+2$. I fixed the problem and then finished the solution.

I verified my solution, and it was right because both sides were equal.

A Checking

1. Verify each solution. Identify and correct any errors.

   a)
   $$4x = 24$$
   $$4x - 4 = 24 - 4$$
   $$x = 20$$

   b)
   $$x + 4 = 3$$
   $$x + 4 - 4 = 3 + 4$$
   $$x = 7$$

   c)
   $$5(x + 2) = 35$$
   $$5(x + 2) \div 5 = 35 \div 5$$
   $$x + 2 = 7$$
   $$x + 2 - 2 = 7 - 2$$
   $$x = 5$$

B Practising

2. Solve each equation and verify your solution.

   a) $5x + 3 = 38$ **b)** $\dfrac{x}{3} + 5 = -4$ **c)** $4(x - 2) = 20$

3. Verify each solution. Identify and correct any errors.

   a)
   $$4(x + 3) = 24$$
   $$4(3x) = 24$$
   $$12x = 24$$
   $$\frac{12x}{12} = \frac{24}{12}$$
   $$x = 2$$

   b)
   $$5(x + 2) = 45$$
   $$5x + 10 = 45$$
   $$15x = 45$$
   $$\frac{15x}{15} = \frac{45}{15}$$
   $$x = 3$$

   c)
   $$5 + 4x = 13$$
   $$5 + 4x - 4x = 13 - 4x$$
   $$5 = 9x$$
   $$\frac{5}{9} = \frac{9x}{9}$$
   $$\frac{5}{9} = x$$

4. Compare the errors you identified in question 3. What do you notice?

5. Solve each equation and verify your solution.
   a) $18 = 3(d - 1)$
   b) $3 - 2k = -9$
   c) $7 = \dfrac{s}{2} + 5$

6. Verify each solution. Identify and correct any errors.

a)
$$56 = 8(x + 3)$$
$$56 = 8x + 24$$
$$56 - 24 = 8x + 24 - 24$$
$$32 = 8x$$
$$\frac{32}{32} = \frac{8x}{32}$$
$$x = \frac{8}{32}$$
$$x = \frac{1}{4}$$

c)
$$\frac{s}{6} + 3 = 11$$
$$6\left(\frac{s}{6}\right) + 3 = 6(11)$$
$$s + 3 = 66$$
$$s + 3 - 3 = 66 - 3$$
$$s = 63$$

b)
$$7x - 2 = -16$$
$$7x - 2 + 2 = -16 + 2$$
$$7x = -14$$
$$x = -2$$

d)
$$2(d + 4) = 10$$

$$d = 3$$

7. Katie's mother is buying school supplies for Katie and her four sisters. In one store she spends $20. She buys a ruler for each child and a package of pens that costs $3. Write and solve an equation to determine the cost of each ruler. Verify your solution.

8. When you solve an equation, why is it important to record your solution steps as well as the answer?

Equation Checkers

Number of players: 2

How to Play

1. Set up the counters on the squares with equations, as in a regular game of checkers.

2. Play as in regular checkers. Before moving, solve the equation of the last square on which you would land.

3. The first player to capture all the counters of the other player wins.

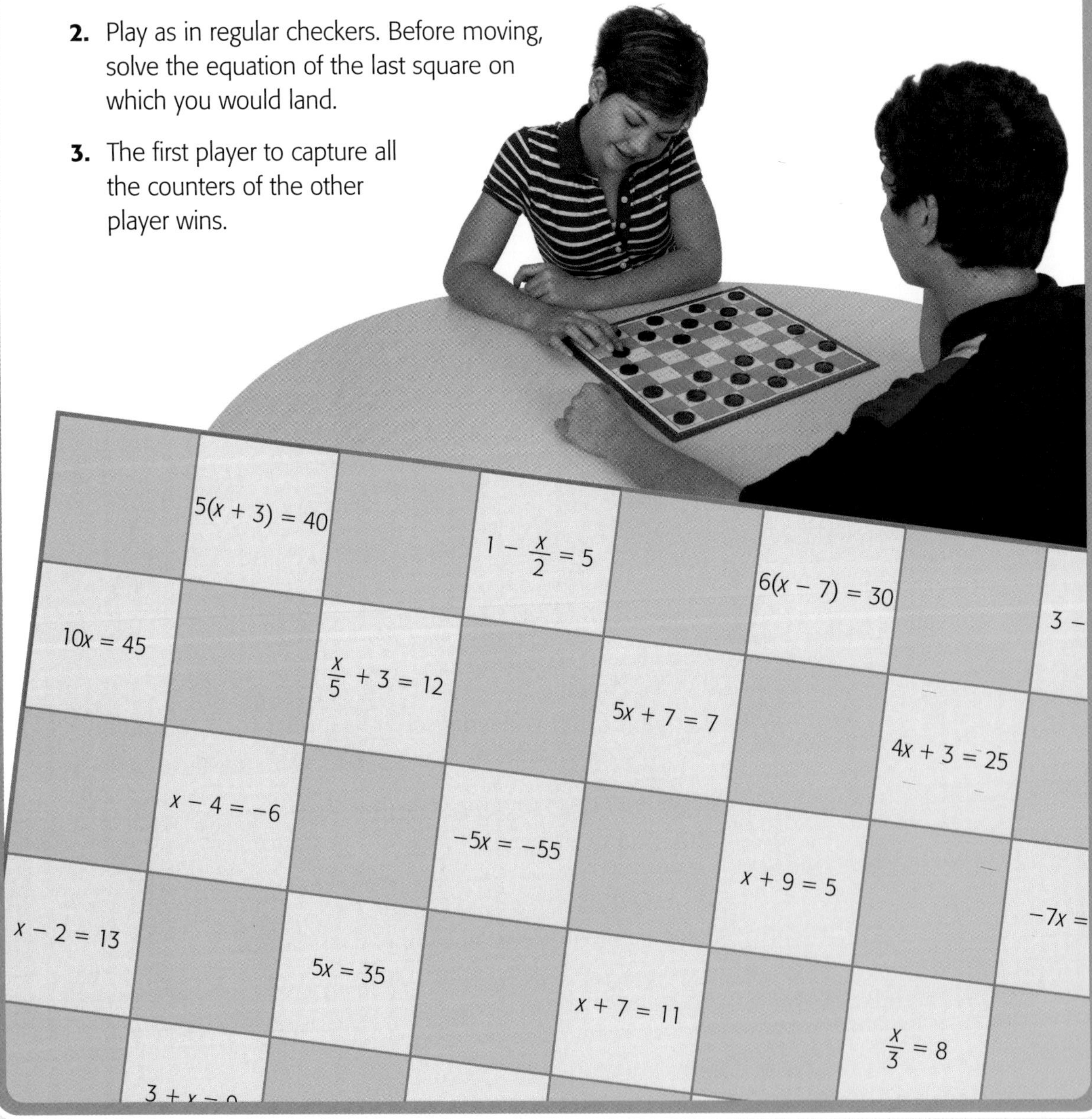

$5(x + 3) = 40$

$1 - \dfrac{x}{2} = 5$

$6(x - 7) = 30$

$3 -$

$10x = 45$

$\dfrac{x}{5} + 3 = 12$

$5x + 7 = 7$

$4x + 3 = 25$

$x - 4 = -6$

$-5x = -55$

$x + 9 = 5$

$x - 2 = 13$

$-7x =$

$5x = 35$

$x + 7 = 11$

$\dfrac{x}{3} = 8$

$3 + x = 9$

Solve Problems Using Logical Reasoning

GOAL

Solve problems that involve equations using logical reasoning.

LEARN ABOUT the Math

What are your target heart rates, Angèle?

My minimum target heart rate is 39 beats per minute more than my resting heart rate. My maximum target heart rate is 36 beats per minute less than twice my minimum target heart rate during exercise. My resting heart rate is 60 beats per minute.

❓ **How can Holly use logical reasoning to determine Angèle's target heart rates?**

Example 1 | Using logical reasoning

Determine Angèle's minimum and maximum target heart rates.

Holly's Solution

1. Understand the Problem

I know Angèle's resting heart rate. I can use that to determine the other rates.

2. Make a Plan

I will relate each pair of heart rates with equations and then solve them.

3. Carry Out the Plan

$r + 39 = m$

I wrote an equation to express Angèle's minimum target heart rate, m, in relation to her resting target heart rate, r.

$60 + 39 = 99$
Angèle's minimum target heart rate is 99 beats per minute.

I substituted her resting heart rate to evaluate her minimum target heart rate.

$2m - 36 = x$

I wrote an equation to relate the maximum rate, x, to the minimum rate.

$2(99) - 36 = x$
$198 - 36 = x$
$162 = x$
Angèle's maximum target heart rate is 162 beats per minute.

I substituted her minimum target heart rate to solve for her maximum heart rate.

4. Look Back

Angèle's minimum heart rate is 39 more than her resting rate.
$60 + 39 = 99$
Angèle's maximum heart rate is 36 beats less than twice her minimum rate.
$2 \times 99 - 36 = 162$

I verified my answers.
My answers matched what it said in the problem.

Reflecting

A. How did Holly use logical reasoning to solve the problem?

WORK WITH *the Math*

Example 2	Using logical reasoning and equations

A senior admission at the Royal Tyrrell Museum is $2 less than an adult admission. A youth admission is $2 more than $\frac{1}{2}$ a senior admission. The youth admission is $6. What are the senior and adult admissions?

Holly's Solution

1. Understand the Problem

I know the youth admission. I can use that to determine the senior admission. Then I can use the senior admission to determine the adult admission.

2. Make a Plan

I will relate each pair of admissions with equations and then solve them.

3. Carry Out the Plan

$$\frac{s}{2} + 2 = y$$

I wrote an equation to express the youth admission, y, in relation to the senior admission, s.

$$\frac{s}{2} + 2 = 6$$

I substituted the youth admission to solve for the senior admission.

$$\frac{s}{2} + 2 - 2 = 6 - 2$$

$$\frac{s}{2} = 4$$

$$s = 8$$

The senior admission is $8.

$$a - 2 = s$$
$$a - 2 = 8$$

I wrote an equation to express the adult admission, a, in relation to the senior admission, s.

$$a - 2 + 2 = 8 + 2$$
$$a = \$10$$

The adult admission is $10.

I substituted the senior admission to solve for the adult admission.

4. Look Back

The senior admission is $8. Half of that is $4.
The youth admission should be $2 more, or $6.
The adult admission is $10. The senior admission is $2 less, or $8. ✔

I verified my answers. My answers matched what it said in the problem.

A Checking

1. Solve this problem using logical reasoning and an equation. Jie has $36 in the bank. She deposits the same amount of money each week. Three weeks later, she has $162. How much money did she deposit each week?

B Practising

2. Vanessa is a Winnipegger who is planning a vacation to Los Angeles. The return fare on Airline A is $65 more than the bus fare. The bus fare is $177 more than one-half of the fare on Airline B. The air fare on Airline A is $464. Determine the Airline B fare and the bus fare.

3. Jasper put together a set of gears in science class. The circumference of the green gear is 24 cm. The circumference of the black gear is 4 cm more than one-third of the green gear. The circumference of the blue gear is half of the black gear. Determine the circumference of the black gear and blue gear.

4. Alexis likes whitewater rafting. A two-day rafting trip on the Elaho and Squamish rivers near Whistler, BC, is $300, while the cost of a one-day trip on the Tatshenshini River in the Yukon is $125.
   a) Write a problem about the cost of the two trips.
   b) Exchange your problem with a classmate. Have your classmate solve your problem to see if it is set up correctly.

5. The students in Mr. Hegel's math class are trying to guess his age. He tells them that his daughter is four years younger than one-third of his age. When asked about his daughter, he tells the class that she is two years older than half of Meg's age. Meg, a student in the class, is 14. How old is Mr. Hegel? Explain your answer.

6. How can using equations make it easier for you to solve problems logically?

Reading Strategy

Inferring

What clues in the text help you better understand the problem?

A Winning Formula for Billiards

YOU WILL NEED
- a ruler
- a protractor

How many rebounds will a billiard ball make on its way to the corner pocket?

Number of rebounds = length of table + width of table – 2

This winning formula only works when:
- The greatest common factor of the length and width is not 1. (Express the ratio of length to width in lowest terms. For example, a table 6 units long and 4 units wide has the same rebound formula as a table 3 units long and 2 units wide. Write 3 + 2 – 2.)
- The table has only corner pockets.
- The length and width of the table are whole numbers.
- The ball is hit from a corner at a 45° angle.
- The rebounds do not include the original hit or the sinking of the ball in the corner pocket.

$$\begin{aligned} \text{Number of rebounds} &= l + w - 2 \\ &= 4 + 3 - 2 \\ &= 7 - 2 \\ &= 5 \end{aligned}$$

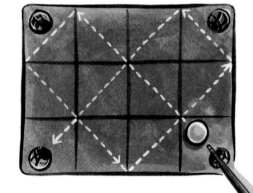

1. Draw models of billiard tables on grid paper with these dimensions: 5 by 3, 6 by 4, 6 by 5, and 12 by 8.

2. For each table, predict (using the formula) the number of rebounds a ball will take to reach a corner pocket.

Size of table	5 by 3	6 by 4	6 by 5	12 by 8
Number of rebounds				

3. Check your predictions by drawing the path of the ball on each table using a ruler and a protractor.

Chapter **Self-Test**

1. **a)** Create a table of values for $y = -3(x - 2)$.
   b) Graph the points. Use your graph to identify four more points to add to your table.

2. Solve. Record your steps and verify your solution.

   a) $3a = 21$ **c)** $2c - 7 = -2$ **e)** $-5 = \dfrac{t}{4} - 3$

   b) $\dfrac{x}{6} = -4$ **d)** $-20 = 4(z - 1)$ **f)** $-2(z - 3) = 12$

3. Allison is flying to Québec in 7 weeks. She has $90 and the return airfare is $405. How much must she save each week? Use an equation.

4. Verify each solution. If the solution is incorrect, identify the error and write the correct solution.

   a)
   $$2(a - 5) = 24$$
   $$2(a - 5 + 5) = 24 + 5$$
   $$2(a) = 29$$
   $$\frac{2a}{2} = \frac{29}{2}$$
   $$a = 14\tfrac{1}{2}$$

   b) $\dfrac{x}{5} + 3 = -5$

   $\dfrac{x}{5}$ and 3 more $= -1$
   $$\frac{x}{5} = -4$$
   $$x = -\frac{4}{5}$$

5. Patrick and John are planning a trip to the Northwest Territories. Trip A lasts for three days. Trip B lasts for six days. Trip C costs $2750 for eight days. Trip C is twice the cost of Trip B, minus $1650. Trip B is twice the cost of Trip A, minus $100. How much is Trip A?

What Do You Think Now?

Revisit What Do You Think? on page 365. How have your answers and explanations changed?

Frequently Asked Questions

Q: How can you solve an equation by balancing?

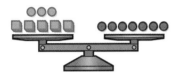
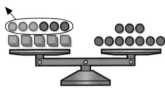
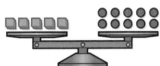

A: An equation is like a level pan balance because the two sides are equal. As you solve an equation, you must add, subtract, multiply, or divide the same way on both sides to keep the balance. For example, solve $-5x - 3 = 7$.

$$-5x - 3 = 7$$
$$-5x - 3 + 3 = 7 + 3 \quad \text{Add 3 to both sides, to balance.}$$
$$-5x = 10$$
$$\frac{-5x}{5} = \frac{10}{5} \quad \text{Divide each side by 5 to}$$
$$-x = 2 \quad \text{determine the value of } -x.$$
$$x = -2 \quad \text{If } -x = 2, \text{ then } x = \text{the}$$

The solution is $x = -2$. $\quad$ opposite, -2.

Q: How do you solve an equation with an expression in brackets?

A1: Sometimes you can isolate the variable by dividing both sides by the multiplier and then adding or subtracting to isolate further. For example,

$$-2(x + 5) = -8 \quad \text{Divide both sides by } -2.$$
$$x + 5 = 4 \quad \text{Add } -5 \text{ to both sides.}$$
$$x + 5 - 5 = 4 - 5$$
$$x = -1$$

A2: Sometimes you multiply through and then solve the equation. For example,

$$-2(x + 5) = -9 \quad \text{Multiply the terms inside}$$
$$-2x + (-10) = -9 \quad \text{the brackets by } -2.$$
$$-2x + (-10) + 10 = -9 + 10 \quad \text{Add 10 to both sides.}$$
$$-2x = +1 \quad \text{Divide both sides by } -2.$$
$$x = -\frac{1}{2}$$

Q: **How can you verify and correct the solution to an equation?**

A: Substitute the solution into the original equation to see whether the left side and right side are equal. If the solution is incorrect, carefully work through each line to find the error.

For example, verify this solution.

$$3 - 4x = 15$$
$$3 - 3 - 4x = 15 - 3$$
$$4x = 12$$
$$\frac{4x}{4} = \frac{12}{4}$$
$$x = 3$$

Check: Left side   Right side
$$3 - 4x \qquad 15$$
$$= 3 - 4(3)$$
$$= 3 - 12$$
$$= -9 \qquad ✗$$

The solution is incorrect. When 3 was subtracted, the left side became $-4x$, not $4x$.

New Solution

$$3 - 4x = 15$$
$$3 - 3 - 4x = 15 - 3$$
$$-4x = 12$$
$$\frac{-4x}{-4} = \frac{12}{-4}$$
$$x = -3$$

Verify the new solution. Check:

Left side   Right side
$$3 - 4x \qquad 15$$
$$= 3 - 4(-3)$$
$$= 3 - (-12)$$
$$= 15 \qquad ✔$$

The new solution is correct.

Practice

Lesson 9.1

1. Janelle is filling a swimming pool at a rate of 120 L/min. When she begins, 4000 L of water are already in the pool.
   a) Write an equation for the amount of water in the pool after t min.
   b) Janelle is tracking water use for a conservation study. Create a table of values for the amount of water in the pool after 15, 30, 45, and 60 min.

Lesson 9.2

2. Janek has $480 in his bank account. Each week, he takes out $24 for karate lessons.
   a) Make a graph to show how the amount in Janek's account changes each week.
   b) How much money is in Janek's account after 7 weeks?
   c) How many karate lessons has Janek taken if he has $264 in his account?

Lesson 9.4

3. Solve each equation by drawing a diagram.
   a) $3(x + 4) = y$, when $y = 27$ b) $\frac{x}{3} - 7 = y$, when $y = 2$

Lesson 9.5

4. Model and solve each equation.
   a) $3t - 4 = 8$ b) $11 = 8z + 5$ c) $5 - 3x = 26$

Lesson 9.6

5. Solve each equation.
   a) $-6(a + 7) = 54$ b) $16 = \frac{t}{8} - 32$ c) $-5x - 9 = -7$

Lesson 9.7

6. Verify the solution. Identify and correct any errors.
$$19 - 7x = -2$$
$$19 - 19 - 7x = -2 - 19$$
$$-7x = -21$$
$$\frac{-7x}{7} = \frac{-21}{7}$$
$$x = -3$$

7. Verify each solution. Identify and correct any errors.

a) $2(d - 2) = -6$

Left side	Right side

$d = -1$

b)
$$-3(p + 6) = -15$$
$$-3(p + 6 - 6) = -15 - 6$$
$$-3p = -21$$
$$\frac{-3p}{-3} = \frac{-21}{-3}$$
$$p = 7$$

Lesson 9.8

8. A whitewater rafting company offers three different tours. The beginners' tour is $19 more than half the cost of the intermediate tour. The advanced tour is $25 less than double the cost of the beginners' tour. The advanced tour is $85. How much do the other two tours cost?

Chapter **Task**

Planning a Dragon Boat Festival

Many Canadian cities host dragon boat festivals, such as this one in Kelowna.

One festival wants to raise money for charity.

- There will be 600 volunteers and between 140 and 180 teams.
- Each team will have 25 members and pay $1600 to enter.
- Each team will compete in three races.
- Each race will have five teams and take 10 min.
- The festival has raised $252 000 from sponsors.
- The racers and volunteers will all celebrate at a dinner that will cost the festival $20 for each person.
- All profits go to charity.

❓ How much money will the festival be able to donate to charity?

Prepare a report for the festival. Support your conclusions with equations, tables of data, and graphs. State any assumptions.

A. Make a graph the schedulers can use to determine the number of races that will be held depending on how many teams there are.

B. Determine the minimum and maximum number of hours the races will take.

C. Determine the minimum and maximum cost of the food for team members and volunteers.

D. You hope to raise $500 000, including the money from sponsors. How many teams need to enter to meet your goal?

E. Additional expenses are $38 000. If you do raise $500 000, how much money will you be able to donate to charity?

TUESDAY	TONIGHT	WEDNESDAY
Cloudy periods High 17 °C POP 20%	Cloudy periods Low 8 °C POP 20%	Isolated showers High 21 °C Low 8 °C POP 30%
THURSDAY	**FRIDAY**	**SATURDAY**
Sunny with cloudy periods High 23 °C Low 11 °C POP 10%	Mainly sunny High 20 °C Low 9 °C POP 10%	Sunny with cloudy periods High 20 °C Low 7 °C POP 10%

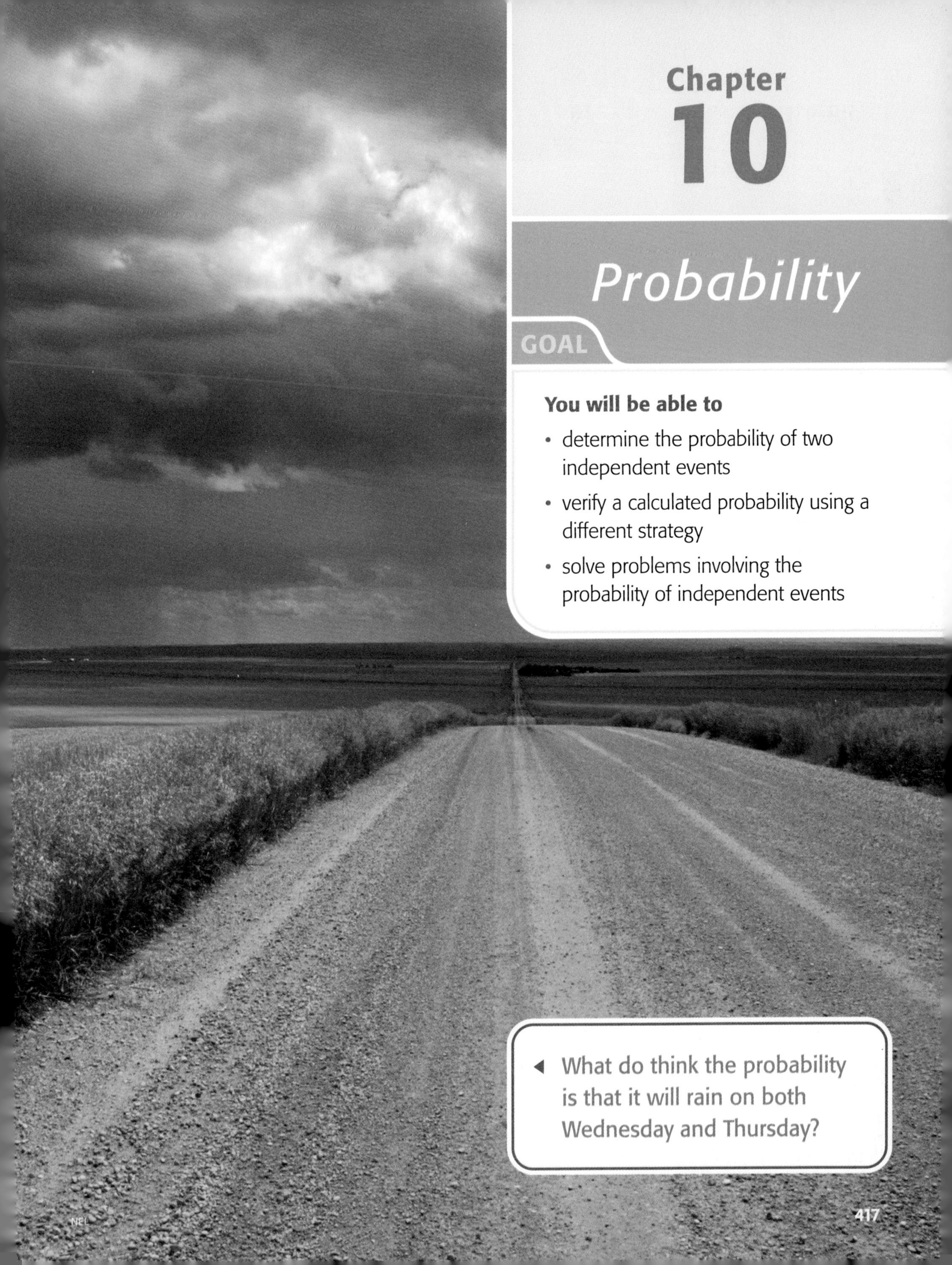

Chapter 10

Probability

GOAL

You will be able to

- determine the probability of two independent events
- verify a calculated probability using a different strategy
- solve problems involving the probability of independent events

◀ What do think the probability is that it will rain on both Wednesday and Thursday?

Getting Started

YOU WILL NEED
• Spinners

Assigning Volunteer Times

Renée volunteered to be an office helper. There are four times when office helpers are needed.

Each month, the four volunteers pick a time period from a hat.

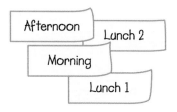

❓ **What is the probability that Renée will get the afternoon time two months in a row?**

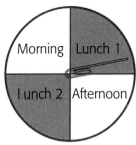

A. Renée made a spinner to model pulling slips of paper from a hat. She spun it twice and got "Afternoon" twice. Does this mean she will always be the afternoon office helper? Explain.

B. Complete this **tree diagram** to represent the possible outcomes of spinning for two different months.

1st month   2nd month

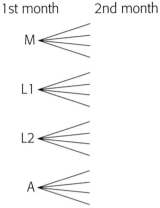

M

L1

L2

A

tree diagram

a way to record and count all combinations of events, using lines to connect the two parts of the outcome

C. Determine the total number of possible outcomes for two spins.

D. Calculate the probability of Renée getting "Afternoon" two months in row. Use the tree diagram. Express the probability as a fraction and a percent.

What Do You Think?

Decide whether you agree or disagree with each statement. Be ready to explain your decision.

1. Adelle spins the spinner and gets a vowel. She is more likely to spin a consonant on her second spin.

2. You cannot calculate the probability that two **independent events** will occur without using a tree diagram.

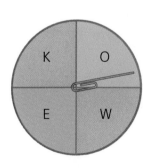

independent events

Two events are independent if the probability of one is not affected by the probability of the other.

3. If there are four possible outcomes for an event, then the probability of each outcome is a fraction with a denominator of 4.

10.1

Exploring Independent Events

YOU WILL NEED
- coloured marbles or counters
- two paper bags or boxes

GOAL

Investigate probabilities of independent events.

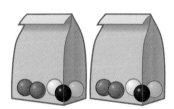

EXPLORE the Math

John and Taira place identical groups of coloured marbles into two bags. John chooses a marble from one bag and Taira chooses a marble from the other bag.

They do this for several different groups of marbles. Sometimes they use more marbles than other times.

? **How can you determine the probability that John and Taira will choose marbles that are the same colour?**

Probability of Precipitation

There are many ideas about what meteorologists mean when they publish the probability that it will rain on a given day.

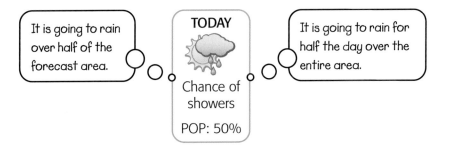

Officially, a probability of precipitation (POP) of 50% means that when similar weather conditions have been reported in the past, 50% of the time there has been rain within 12 hours of the forecast somewhere in the area.

For example, suppose a meteorologist collects data about the current weather around Edmonton. If she finds 50 similar situations, 10 of which resulted in rain somewhere in the area, then the POP is 20% for the next 12 hours.

1. Does rain falling in your forecast area mean that it will rain on your school?

2. **a)** Make a tree diagram to show the outcomes of two consecutive days with a 50% POP for your area.
   b) How likely is it to rain at least once?
   c) How likely is it to rain both days?
   d) How does the probability of rain both days in the forecast area compare to the probability of rain both days at your school?

3. **a)** The POP is 100%. Will it rain today?
   b) The POP is 0%. Will it rain today?
   c) Suppose the POP published at 8:00 a.m. is 20% and you have a picnic at 11:00 a.m. Should you be surprised if it rains on your picnic? Explain.

10.2

Probability of Independent Events

YOU WILL NEED

• Spinners

GOAL

Use pictures or charts to determine the probability of two independent events.

LEARN ABOUT the Math

Holly and Ivan are playing a game. Both spin their spinners. Holly wins if the product is a multiple of 3 but not of 4. Ivan wins if the product is a multiple of 4 but not of 3. Otherwise, it is a tie.

❓ Who is more likely to win?

outcome table

a chart that lists all possible outcomes of a probability experiment

sample space

all possible outcomes in a probability experiment

complementary event

the set of outcomes in the sample space in which the event does not happen; e.g., when rolling a die, the event (rolling 2) has the complementary event (rolling 1, 3, 4, 5, or 6).

Communication | Tip

You can write *P*(Holly wins) as a shortcut for the words the probability of the event "Holly wins."

A. Why are the results of spinning the two spinners independent events?

B. Complete the following **outcome table** for the **sample space** of this situation. The first few entries are filled in for you.

		Ivan's spin		
		3	4	5
	2	2, 3	2, 4	
	4			
Holly's spin	6			
	8			
	10			

C. Draw a tree diagram to verify the outcome table.

D. How many favourable outcomes are there for the event "Holly wins?" How many are there for the **complementary event** "Holly does not win?"

E. How many favourable outcomes are there for the event "Ivan wins?" How many are there for the complementary event "Ivan does not win?"

F. Which is greater, *P*(Holly wins) or *P*(Ivan wins)? Explain how you know.

Reflecting

G. How do you use the number of sections in each spinner to determine the number of rows and columns in the outcome table and the number of branches in the tree diagram?

H. How do you determine the total number of outcomes in the sample space using the outcome table or the tree diagram?

I. Why did it not matter whether you used an outcome table or a tree diagram to determine the probability of one of the students winning?

WORK WITH *the Math*

Example 1 | Using an outcome table

John has all the red face cards from a standard deck and, Taira has all the black face cards from the deck. Each draws one card from their hand without looking.

a) How many different outcomes are possible?
b) Determine P(2 Jacks).

John's Solution

a)

	Taira's Cards					
	J♠	Q♠	K♠	J♣	Q♣	K♣
J♥						
Q♥						
John's K♥						
Cards J♦						
Q♦						
K♦						

I made an outcome table.

There will be 36 outcomes in the table.

I could see there would be 6 rows and 6 columns, so there had to be 6×6 outcomes.

b) The outcome table shows that there are 4 possible ways to choose a pair of Jacks.

	Taira's Cards					
	J♠	Q♠	K♠	J♣	Q♣	K♣
J♥	✓			✓		
Q♥						
John's K♥						
Cards J♦	✓			✓		
Q♦						
K♦						

I used my outcome table and marked the 4 outcomes that had 2 Jacks.

I decided not to use a tree diagram because there would be too many branches.

$$P(2 \text{ Jacks}) = \frac{4}{36} = \frac{1}{9}$$

Example 2 | Using a tree diagram

Suppose you toss a coin and then roll a six-sided die.

a) What is the probability of getting heads and an even number?
b) What is the probability of not getting heads and an even number?
c) Verify your answers.

Lam's Solution

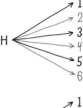

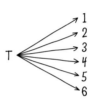

I listed all the possibilities in a tree diagram.
The 12 branches represent 12 equally likely outcomes.

a) Three of the branches start with heads and end in an even number, so three outcomes are favourable.

$P(H \text{ and even}) = \frac{3}{12}$, or $\frac{1}{4}$

b) Not getting heads and an even number and the event in part a) are **complementary events**.

$P(\text{not "}H \text{ and even"}) + P(H \text{ and even}) = 1$

$P(\text{not "}H \text{ and even"}) + \frac{1}{4} = 1$

$P(\text{not "}H \text{ and even"}) = \frac{3}{4}$

c) I made an outcome table to verify my answers. There are three favourable outcomes for $P(H \text{ and even})$ and there are nine favourable outcomes for $P(\text{not "}H \text{ and even"})$.

$P(H \text{ and even}) = \frac{3}{12}$, or $\frac{1}{4}$

$P(\text{not "}H \text{ and even"}) = \frac{9}{12}$, or $\frac{3}{4}$

Example 3 | Identifying events that are not independent

A bag contains 1 white marble, 1 blue marble, 1 green marble, and 1 red marble. Renée removes one marble and then another. Are these independent events?

Renée's Solution

Since I did not put the first marble back in the bag, it was not possible for the first and second marbles to be the same colour. The result of the first draw has an effect on the second draw. The two draws are not independent events.

A Checking

1. Amit has two orange counters, two green counters, and two purple counters in a bag. She draws one counter from the bag and puts it back. She then draws another counter.
   a) Make an outcome table that shows all possible outcomes in the sample space for this experiment.
   b) Determine $P(2 \text{ orange})$.

B Practising

2. Ellie uses the same counters that Amit used. She draws one counter from the bag and then another, without putting the first one back. Are these events independent or not? Explain.

3. Suppose you roll the die and then spin the spinner.

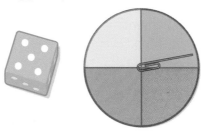

   a) Use an outcome table, organized list, or tree diagram to show the sample space for this experiment.
   b) Determine $P(3 \text{ and yellow})$.
   c) Determine $P(\text{odd number and green})$.

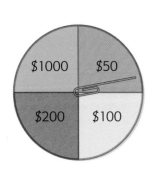

4. Kaycee has won a contest. Her prize will be the sum of two spins of the prize spinner.
   a) Use an outcome table to show Kaycee's possible winnings.
   b) Determine $P(\text{Kaycee wins more than } \$100)$.
   c) Determine $P(\text{Kaycee wins less than } \$500)$.

5. Jenna rolls a four-sided die, numbered 1 to 4. Vi rolls a six-sided die. Determine the following probabilities.
   a) $P(\text{both show 2})$
   b) $P(\text{both show an even number})$
   c) $P(\text{both show a prime number})$
   d) $P(\text{neither shows 3})$
   e) Use a different strategy to determine the sample space and verify your calculations for parts a) to d).

6. Rick spins the spinner and Donna draws the name of a month from a hat.

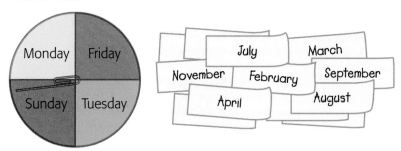

a) Determine P(Friday and April)
b) Determine P(Monday and a month with 31 days)
c) Determine P(Tuesday and a month starting with J)
d) Determine P(Monday and not April)
e) Use a different strategy to determine the sample space and verify your calculations for parts a) to d).

7. Boris has a bag containing five mah-jong tiles: three from the circle suit 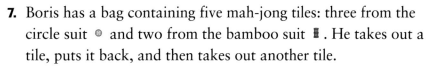 and two from the bamboo suit 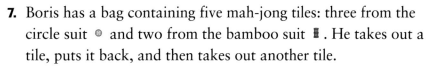. He takes out a tile, puts it back, and then takes out another tile.

a) Explain why selecting the first tile and selecting the second tile are independent events.
b) Determine P(both circle tiles).
c) Determine P(both bamboo tiles).
d) Determine P(1st tile bamboo, 2nd tile circle).
e) Use a different strategy to determine the sample space and verify your calculations for parts a) to d).

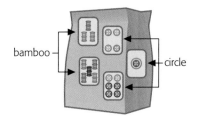

8. a) How can you use a tree diagram or an outcome table to determine the denominator of the probability of two independent events in fraction form?

b) Why is using a tree diagram or an outcome table a good strategy to calculate probabilities involving two independent events?

Reading Strategy

Activating Prior Knowledge

Use what you already know about tree diagrams and outcome tables to help you solve this problem.

10.3

Using a Formula to Calculate Probability

GOAL

Develop and apply a rule to determine the probability of independent events.

LEARN ABOUT the Math

Mrs. Wong gave her class a two-question quiz. There was one True/False question and one five-part multiple-choice question. The correct answers were False and D.

QUIZ Circle the correct answers.

1. The probability of an event may be represented by a fraction between 0 and 10.

   TRUE   **FALSE**

2. Amit draws a card from a standard 52-card deck of playing cards. How many of these possible values for P(drawing an Ace) are correct?

   • $\dfrac{1}{52}$ • $\dfrac{4}{52}$ • $\dfrac{1}{13}$ • about 0.077   • about 0.019

   A. 0   **B.** 1   **C.** 2   **D.** 3   **E.** 4

? **What is the probability that a student can correctly answer both questions by guessing?**

Example 1 | Using an outcome table

Create an outcome table to analyze the sample space.
Then determine P(both correct).

Renée's Solution

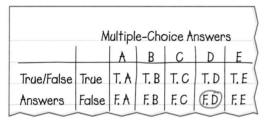

Multiple-Choice Answers					
		A	B	C	D	E
True/False	True	T. A	T. B	T. C	T. D	T. E
Answers	False	F. A	F. B	F. C	(F. D)	F. E

$P(\text{both correct}) = \dfrac{1}{10}$

$P(\text{both correct})$

$= P(\text{correctly guessing T/F}) \times P(\text{correctly guessing M-C})$

$= \dfrac{1}{2} \times \dfrac{1}{5} = \dfrac{1}{10}$

	$\frac{1}{5}$	$\frac{1}{5}$	$\frac{1}{5}$	$\frac{1}{5}$	$\frac{1}{5}$
$\frac{1}{2}$					
$\frac{1}{2}$				$\left(\frac{1}{10}\right)$	

I made an outcome table in which the rows represented the answers to the True/False (T/F) question and the columns represented the answers to the multiple-choice (M-C) question.

There were 10 outcomes and only one represented getting both questions correct.

I noticed that this is like calculating the fraction of the area of the chart that shows the favourable outcome. You calculate the area by multiplying the length by the width. The length of that section was $\frac{1}{2}$ and the width was $\frac{1}{5}$.

Example 2 | Using a tree diagram

Develop and apply a rule for calculating the probability of guessing the correct answer to the True/False question and the correct answer to the multiple-choice question.

Ivan's Solution

True/False   Multiple-Choice

→ 1 way

→ 4 ways

→ 1 way

→ 4 ways

2 x 5 = 10 branches

I drew a tree diagram that showed the number of ways to correctly (blue arrows) and incorrectly (red arrows) answer the questions.

I noticed that the number of ways of getting to an outcome on the right side of the tree was the product of the number of ways of getting to the end of the first branch and the number of ways of getting from there to the second branch.

True/False   Multiple-Choice   Probability

$\frac{1}{5}$ → Correct $\frac{1}{10}$

$\frac{1}{2}$ → Correct

→ Incorrect $\frac{4}{10}$

→ Correct $\frac{1}{10}$

→ Incorrect

→ Incorrect $\frac{4}{10}$

I divided the number of ways of getting to an answer by the number of outcomes for that answer. That told the probability of each choice.

I saw that the probability of guessing both correct answers was the product of the probabilities of correctly guessing each one.

P(both correct)

= P(correctly guessing T/F) x P(correctly guessing M-C)

$= \frac{1}{2} \times \frac{1}{5} = \frac{1}{10}$

Reflecting

A. How could you use Ivan's tree diagram to support Renée's reasoning?

B. Why does it make sense that P(getting both questions wrong) $= P$(getting first one wrong) $\times P$(getting second one wrong)?

WORK WITH *the Math*

Example 3 | Calculating a combined probability

John draws a card from five cards, numbered 1 to 5. He puts the card back and then Renée draws a card. Calculate P(both even).

Solution A: Using an outcome table

		Renée's card				
		1	2	3	4	5
John's card	1					
	2		✔		✔	
	3					
	4		✔		✔	
	5					

Make an outcome table and place a checkmark in the outcomes where both cards were even numbers.

$$P(\text{both even}) = \frac{4}{25}$$

Solution B: Using a rule

$P(\text{both even}) = P(\text{1st card even}) \times P(\text{2nd card even})$
$$= \frac{2}{5} \times \frac{2}{5} = \frac{4}{25}$$

Since John put the card back, the probability of drawing an even card would not be affected by his first draw.

Example 4 | Identifying events that are not independent

Angèle draws a card from five cards numbered 1 to 5 and does not put the card back. Then Taira draws a card. Show that you cannot multiply probabilities to determine P(both even).

Solution

P(both even) will have a denominator of 20. P(even) $\times$ P(even) has a denominator of 25. Since the denominators are different, the product of the probabilities is not the same as the probability of both cards being even.

It is not possible to have any outcomes where the same number is drawn twice, so there would be 20 outcomes in the table. P(even) is a fraction with a denominator of 5.

A Checking

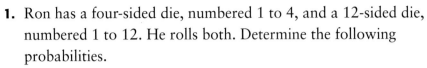

1. Ron has a four-sided die, numbered 1 to 4, and a 12-sided die, numbered 1 to 12. He rolls both. Determine the following probabilities.
   a) P(each shows a 4)
   b) P(each shows an even number)
   c) P(each shows a multiple of 4)

B Practising

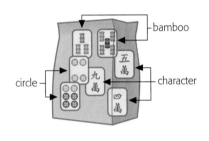

bamboo
circle
character

2. Bo has seven mah-jong tiles in a bag: two from the circle suit, two from the bamboo suit, and three from the character suit. He draws a tile, puts it back, and draws another tile.
   a) Explain why the two draws are independent events.
   b) Determine P(both bamboo tiles).
   c) Determine P(both character tiles).
   d) Determine P(six-of-circles tile and the three-of-bamboo tile).

3. Ram spins the spinner and then draws a card from those shown.

   a) Explain why the spin and the draw are independent events.
   b) Determine P(1, Jack).
   c) Determine P(even number, King).
   d) Determine P(multiple of 5, black card).

A

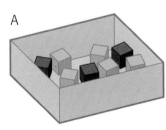

4. One block is taken from box A. Then one block is taken from box B. Determine the following probabilities.
   a) P(both blocks are green)
   b) P(both blocks are black)
   c) P(1st block is green and 2nd is black)
   d) P(1st block is black and 2nd is green)

B

5. a) Determine P(both blocks are the same colour) for the two boxes in question 4.
   b) Explain why you cannot multiply probabilities to answer part a).

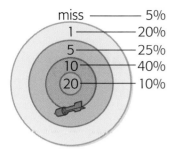

miss ——— 5%
1 ——— 20%
5 ——— 25%
10 ——— 40%
20 ——— 10%

6. Annie is a good dart thrower. The dart board shows the probability that she will hit each ring of the target. She throws two darts.

a) Determine *P*(both darts miss the target).

b) Determine *P*(10 points with each dart).

c) Determine *P*(10 points with first dart and 20 points with the second).

d) Discuss whether or not the results of the two throws are independent events.

7. Rishi has a combination lock for his locker. The lock uses two numbers between 0 and 39. The same number may be used twice. His combination is 35 – 24. Show how to determine the probability that someone could correctly guess the combination.

8. A school soccer team has the following history.
• They win 50% of the games played on rainy days.
• They win 60% of the games played on fair days.
The weather forecast says there is an 80% chance of rain for the next game day.

a) Determine *P*(it rains and they win).

b) Determine *P*(it does not rain and they win).

c) Explain why the probabilities in parts a) and b) do not add to 100%.

9. Situation 1: David has 1 red and 3 green jellybeans in a bag, and Darlene has 1 red and 2 green jellybeans in a bag. David and Darlene each take one jellybean.

Situation 2: Bill has 2 red and 5 green jellybeans in his pocket. Bill takes 2 jellybeans from his pocket.

a) Why can you use the multiplication rule for probabilities to determine *P*(David and Darlene choose red)?

b) Why can you not use the multiplication rule to determine *P*(Bill chooses 2 red jellybeans)?

Communicate about Probability

GOAL

Communicate strategies for determining and verifying probabilities.

LEARN ABOUT the Math

Lam's baseball coach told him that his season batting average was 0.250. Lam was worried because he was out two at-bats in a row.

Taira wrote him a note explaining why he should not be too worried. She asked Holly to look it over before she gave it to Lam.

? **How can Taira make her note more convincing?**

Taira's Note

Lam, your batting average is 0.250. That means the probability that you will be put out in an at-bat is 0.750.

The probability you will be put out two times in a row is:

P(out in the 1st at-bat) x P(out in the 2nd at-bat)

= 0.750 x 0.750 = 0.5625

This is more than 50%. So I think you should not be surprised that you were out in those two at-bats.

I found a spinner simulation on the Internet and used it to model 100 pairs of at-bats. I made two 4-section spinners and spun them 100 times. Orange meant a hit, and any other colour meant an out.

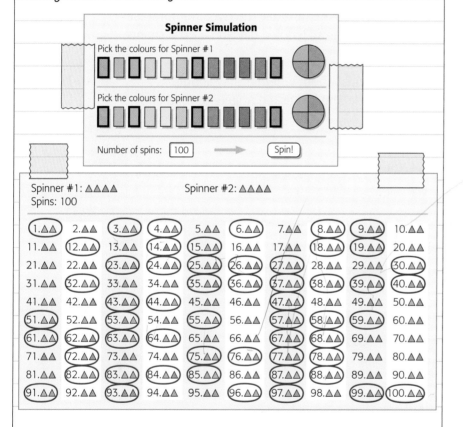

In 100 spins, I got 56 pairs with no orange . That is close to what I calculated the probability of two outs in a row to be, so I think I am right. Do not worry about the two outs. That is not unusual.

Holly's Comments

How do you know this is true?

Arc the two at-bats independent events?

Is this simulation a good model for Lam's at-bats?

Is one set of 100 spins enough to verify your calculations?

Why is your conclusion reasonable?

Communication
Checklist

✔ Did you clearly state all
your assumptions?

✔ Did you justify your
assumptions and
calculations?

✔ Did you justify your
conclusions?

Reflecting

A. Which of Holly's comments do you think is most important for making Taira's note more convincing?

B. What additional suggestions would you provide to help Taira make her note more persuasive?

WORK WITH the Math

Example 1	Justifying a probability calculation

Angèle and Holly are planning a school picnic. If it is raining on the Thursday they have chosen, the event will move to the next day. The weather forecast says there is an 80% chance of rain on the scheduled day and a 40% chance of rain the next day.

Holly has written a letter to the principal about whether they should reschedule the event to another week. She has asked Angèle to read and edit it before she sends it.

Angèle's Editing

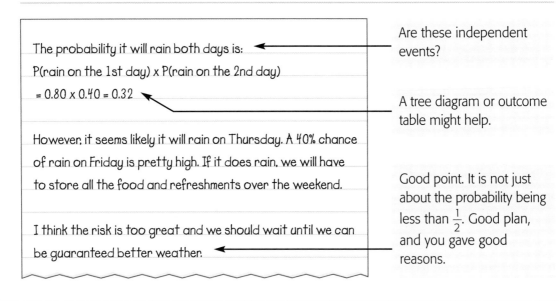

The probability it will rain both days is:

P(rain on the 1st day) x P(rain on the 2nd day)

= 0.80 x 0.40 = 0.32

However, it seems likely it will rain on Thursday. A 40% chance of rain on Friday is pretty high. If it does rain, we will have to store all the food and refreshments over the weekend.

I think the risk is too great and we should wait until we can be guaranteed better weather.

Are these independent events?

A tree diagram or outcome table might help.

Good point. It is not just about the probability being less than $\frac{1}{2}$. Good plan, and you gave good reasons.

1. Lam's batting average is 0.250. Lam says that means, if he gets a hit in his first at-bat, he is sure to be out in his second at-bat. What do you think about Lam's interpretation of his batting average?

B Practising

2. Calvin wrote a letter about whether the band should reschedule their spring picnic to another weekend. What questions would you ask Calvin to improve his letter?

> The probability of rain on Saturday is 20%, and the probability of rain on Sunday is 60%. Since the chances of rain on each day are independent events, the probability it will rain both days is:
>
> P(rain on Saturday) x P(rain on Sunday) = $\frac{2}{10}$ x $\frac{6}{10}$
>
> = $\frac{12}{100}$, or 12%
>
> I think it is safe to have the picnic this weekend.

3. Two yellow cubes, one blue cube, and one green cube are placed in a bag. They are mixed up, and one cube is removed. It is returned to the bag, and the cubes are mixed again. A second cube is removed.

a) Explain how to calculate *P*(drawing 2 yellow cubes).

b) Show how to verify the probability you calculated in part a) using a different strategy.

4. Suppose you toss a coin and then roll a 12-sided die numbered 1 to 12.
   a) Explain how to determine P(heads, even number).
   b) Explain how to verify the probability you calculated in part a) using a different strategy.

5. A dresser drawer contains two socks of each colour: grey, black, and white. Without looking, you reach in, take one sock, and then take another. Explain why P(both socks are grey) is not $\frac{2}{6} \times \frac{2}{6}$.

6. Suppose you have a 30% chance of catching a trout for every day you fish on Rainbow Lake.

   a) Calculate P(2 trout in 2 days).
   b) Show how to use a different strategy to verify your calculation in part a).
   c) Do you think that the result of your first day fishing and the result of your second day fishing are independent events? Explain.

7. A and B are two independent events. If $P(A) = \frac{3}{4}$ and $P(A \text{ and } B) = \frac{9}{20}$, explain how to determine $P(B)$.

8. Suppose you calculate the probability that one event and then another will occur.
   a) Why is showing that events are or are not independent an important part of your explanation of the calculation?
   b) Why is doing the calculation a different way sometimes a good idea?

The Game of Pig

The goal of this game is to be the first player to score 100 points without rolling double sixes.

Number of players: 2 or more

How to Play

1. Players take turns rolling two dice as often as they wish or until they roll a 6.

2. If a player rolls a single 6, the turn ends and the score for the turn is 0.
If a player rolls a double 6, the turn ends and all the player's points are lost.
If a player stops before rolling a 6, the points for the score for the turn are the total of all rolls on that turn. Add this to the total from previous turns.

3. The first player to reach 100 points wins.

Renée's Turn

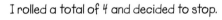

I rolled a total of 6 and decided to roll again.

I rolled a total of 4 and decided to stop.

My score for the turn is 6 + 4 = 10.
I add that to my total. I am now in second place!

Lam	Renée	Angèle
~~9~~	0	~~5~~
~~9~~	~~8~~	~~0~~
~~9~~	~~8~~	14
23	18	

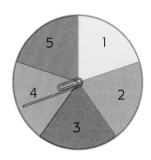

1. You spin the spinner twice.
   a) Make an outcome table to describe the sample space.
   b) Determine P(even, even) and P(odd, odd).
   c) Why are the probabilities different?

2. A multiple-choice quiz has five choices for each question. The correct answers to the first two questions are A and C.
   a) Why is it reasonable to assume that guessing an answer to the second question is independent of guessing an answer to the first?
   b) Calculate P(guessing both correct answers).
   c) Use an outcome table or tree diagram to verify the probability.

3. A lacrosse team wins 70% of its games played on sunny days and 40% of its games played on rainy days. The weather forecast indicates an 80% chance of rain today. Determine the probabilities of these combinations of events.
   a) It will rain and the team will win.
   b) It will be sunny and the team will lose.
   c) Describe a strategy you could use to verify your calculations.

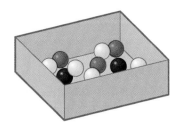

4. Without looking, Yunjin removes a marble from the box, returns it, and then removes another. Determine each probability.
   a) P(both marbles are white)
   b) P(1st marble is white, and 2nd is not red)
   c) P(neither marble is black)

What Do You Think Now?

Revisit What Do You Think? on page 419. How have your answers and explanations changed?

Chapter **Review**

Frequently Asked Questions

Q: How can you calculate the probability of two independent events?

A1: You could examine a tree diagram, organized list, or outcome table for the events. The numerator of the probability will be the number of favourable outcomes, and the denominator will be the number of equally likely outcomes in the sample space.

For example, suppose you spin this spinner twice and wanted to know the probability of both spins having the same number. You could make an outcome table to show the sample space.

		Second spin		
		1	2	3
	1	1, 1	1, 2	1, 3
First spin	2	2, 1	2, 2	2, 3
	3	3, 1	3, 2	3, 3

The favourable outcomes are (1, 1), (2, 2), and (3, 3).

P(both spins are the same number)

$= \dfrac{\text{number of favourable outcomes}}{\text{number of possible outcomes}}$

A2: You can multiply the probabilities of independent events to determine the probability that they will both occur.

For example, suppose you spin the above spinner twice.

P(1st spin is 2, and 2nd spin is odd)
$= P(\text{1st spin is 2}) \times P(\text{2nd spin is odd})$
$= \dfrac{1}{3} \times \dfrac{2}{3} = \dfrac{2}{9}$

Practice

Lesson 10.2

1. You toss a four-sided die, numbered 1 to 4, and spin the spinner.
   a) Use an outcome table to show all possible combinations of die tosses and spins.
   b) Determine $P(1, 20)$.
   c) Determine $P(\text{toss} > 1, \text{spin} < 30)$.
   d) Draw a tree diagram and use it to verify your answers.

2. A paper bag contains three blue marbles and three red marbles. You remove a marble from the bag and then put it back. Then you remove another marble from the bag.
   a) List all the outcomes.
   b) Calculate $P(\text{marbles are different colours})$.
   c) Would the events still be independent if the first marble were not returned to the bag before the second is removed? Explain.

Lesson 10.3

3. A combination lock has two wheels with the letters A to F. The lock combination comes preset from the factory.
   a) Calculate the probability of guessing the correct combination on the first try.
   b) Use a different strategy to verify the probability calculation.

4. A provincial park claims that the probability of spotting moose in the park on any day is 0.15 and the probability of spotting loons is 0.70.
   a) Determine $P(\text{moose and loon on the same day})$.
   b) Determine $P(\text{moose on two consecutive days})$.
   c) Determine $P(\text{no moose for two days})$.
   d) What assumptions did you make?

Lesson 10.4

5. Melik dropped a coin out of each of his pockets. He had one nickel, one dime, and six quarters in the left pocket and eight nickels and four quarters in the right pocket.
   Explain how to determine the probability that Melik dropped the greatest of amount of money possible.

Free Throw

Angèle can sink 60% of her shots from 5 m and 40% from 10 m. She will be required to shoot from each distance as part of the tryout for the school basketball team.

❓ How can you predict the probability that she will sink both shots?

A. Show how to calculate the probability that she will make both shots. Justify the use of your strategy.

B. Conduct an experiment to model Angèle shooting one shot from each of the two distances. Repeat the experiment several times. Do your experimental results verify your calculation in part A? Explain.

C. How else can you verify your calculation in part A? Explain.

D. Holly has the same combined probability of making her two shots as Angèle, but her probabilities for each distance are not the same as Angèle's. Determine two possible combinations that could describe Holly's probability of making a shot from each distance. Justify your strategy.

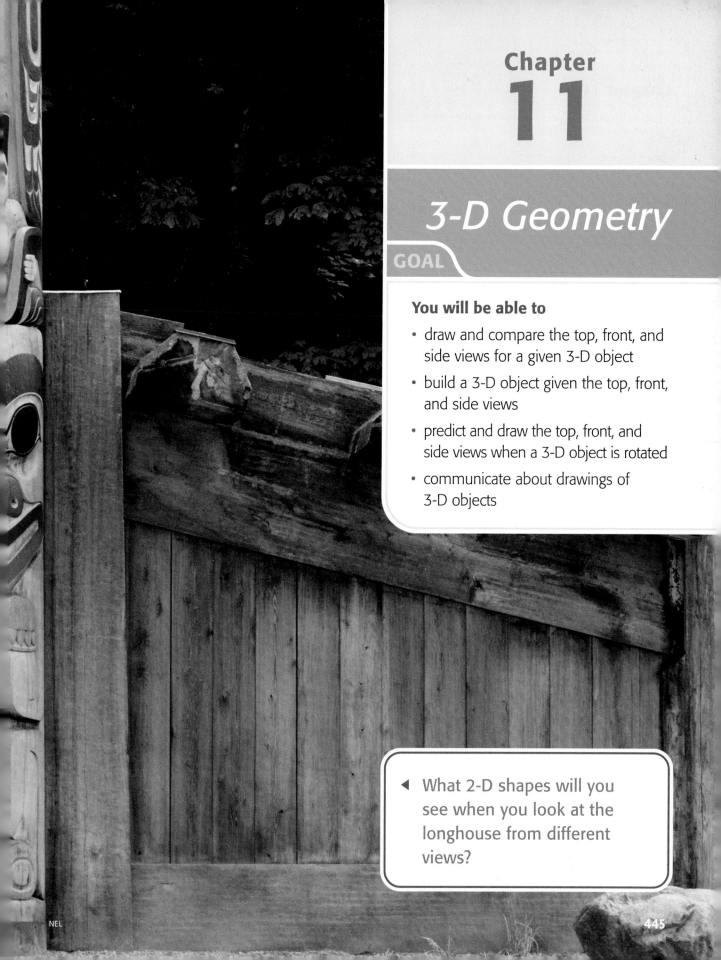

3-D Geometry

GOAL

You will be able to

- draw and compare the top, front, and side views for a given 3-D object
- build a 3-D object given the top, front, and side views
- predict and draw the top, front, and side views when a 3-D object is rotated
- communicate about drawings of 3-D objects

◄ What 2-D shapes will you see when you look at the longhouse from different views?

Getting Started

Identifying Cube Structures

Vanessa built a structure of linking cubes. These photos show the front and side views of her structure.

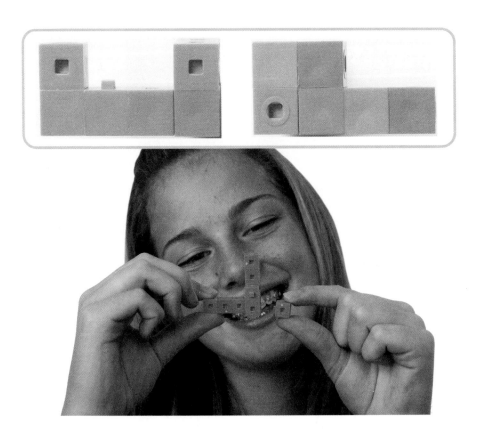

? **How many cubes might Vanessa have used to build her structure?**

A. How do you know that Vanessa's structure is not a rectangular prism?

B. What extra information do you need to tell how many cubes she used?

C. What is the least number of cubes in her structure? Build the structure to show your answer.

D. Can you build a different structure with the same views and the same number of cubes as in C?

E. What is the greatest number of cubes in her structure? Build the structure to show your answer.

F. What other number of cubes might be in her structure? Explain.

What Do You Think?

Decide whether you agree or disagree with each statement. Be ready to explain your decision.

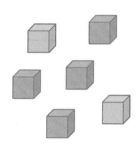

1. If you have a cube structure with two orange cubes and four blue ones, then you will see orange when you look at the front and side.

2. If you link four cubes together, you can see 18 faces when you look at all sides of the structure.

3. A 3-D structure will look the same whether you look at it from the right or the left.

4. You can tell how many cubes are in a structure by looking at a photo of it.

11.1

Drawing Views of Cube Structures

YOU WILL NEED

- linking cubes
- grid paper

GOAL

Use grid paper to draw top, front, and side views of a cube structure.

LEARN ABOUT the Math

Elena and Sanjev each used linking cubes to represent a building in their community. They want to draw different views of their models.

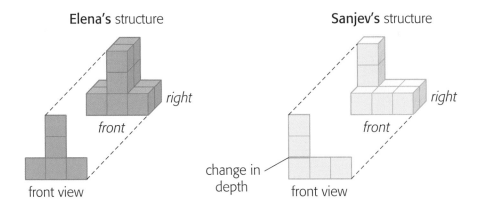

Elena's structure   Sanjev's structure

❓ How can you make top, front, and side views of a cube structure?

A. How do you know that the drawing of each front view is correct?

B. Draw what you would see if you looked at the top view of each structure. Explain how you did it.

C. Draw what you would see if you looked at the right view of each structure. Explain how you did it.

Reflecting

D. Why do the different views of a cube structure not always show the same number of cubes?

E. Can two cube structures have the same front view but different side views? Build models to help you explain.

WORK WITH *the Math*

Example 1	Drawing views of a cube structure

Nolan made a model of a chair using linking cubes. How can he represent the top, front, and right views of his structure?

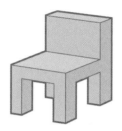

Nolan's Solution

 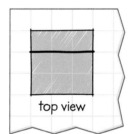

To draw the top view, I looked down at the structure from directly above. To represent what I saw, I drew a 3-by-3 square. The top is not really a square, though. I drew a darker line to show where the surface changes in depth.

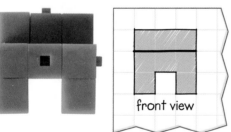

I repeated this for the front view. I represented what I saw when I looked straight at the front of the structure. Then I drew a darker line to show the change in depth.

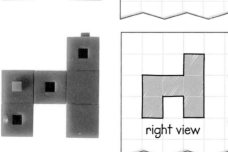

For the right view, I turned the chair so that I was looking straight at the right side. This view had no change in depth.

3-D Geometry **449**

A Checking

1. This structure is built with 7 linking cubes. Visualize what it will look like from the top, front, and right side. Identify each view below as top, front, or right side.

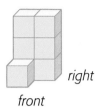

right

front

a)

b)

c)

B Practising

2. a) Build this structure with linking cubes.
b) Rotate your structure so you can see the top, front, and right views.
c) Draw each view, using a thick line to indicate a change in depth.

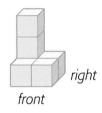

right

front

3. Make a rectangular prism out of linking cubes. Draw the top, front, and side views.

4. What would the top, front, and side views of this prism look like? Explain how you know.

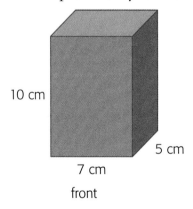

10 cm

5 cm

7 cm

front

5. a) Use up to 20 linking cubes to make an airplane that looks different from the top, front, and sides.
b) Draw the top, front, and right views of the airplane.

6. Draw and label three different views of the table.

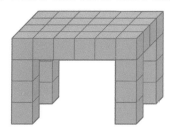

7. a) Build this structure with linking cubes.

b) Rotate your structure so you can see the top, front, and right views.

c) Draw each view, using a thick line to indicate a change in depth.

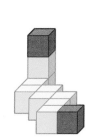

8. a) Build this structure with linking cubes.

b) Draw the top, front, right, and left views of the structure.

c) If you take away the red cubes, which views would look different? How would they be different?

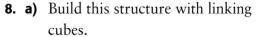

9. Look at the structure in question 8.

a) How could you add a cube so only the top view does not change?

b) How could you add a cube so the number of depth lines is the same in both the left and right views?

10. How are the top, front, and side views of a rectangular prism alike?

11. Can you always tell how many cubes are used in a structure if you know the top, front, and right views? Explain.

Building Cube Structures from Views

YOU WILL NEED
- linking cubes
- grid paper

GOAL

Make cube structures, given their top, front, and side views.

EXPLORE the Math

Habitat 67 is a unique housing development made of stacked modules in the shape of rectangular prisms. It was built for the 1967 Montreal World Exposition and was featured in the movie *Blades of Glory*.

Last week Vanessa used cubes to make a model like Habitat 67. She drew these views of her structure but forgot to include the change of depth lines. She wants to build the model again.

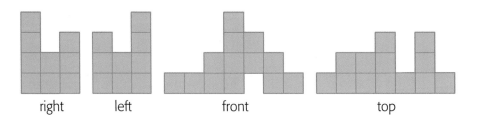

right   left   front   top

? **How many different models with these top, front, and side views can Vanessa build?**

11.3 Creating Isometric Drawings

YOU WILL NEED
- Isometric Dot Paper
- a ruler
- linking cubes

> **GOAL**
>
> Create isometric drawings of cube structures.

LEARN ABOUT *the Math*

Sanjev used cubes to make a model of a platform for the choir. He wants to fax an **isometric drawing** of it to the choir director.

isometric drawing

a 3-D view of an object in which
- vertical edges are drawn vertically
- width and depth are drawn diagonally
- equal lengths on the object are equal on the drawing

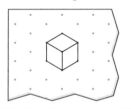

❓ How can Sanjev make an isometric drawing of the model?

Example 1 | Making an isometric drawing

I used isometric dot paper to draw a model of the platform for the choir.

Sanjev's Solution

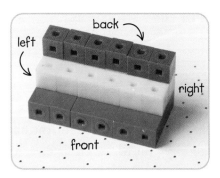

I placed the bottom layer of the structure on paper. I decided which sides of the structure were front, right, left, and back to help me keep track of the views. Then I turned the paper so that the view corresponded to the isometric dot paper.

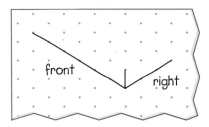

I could see three faces of the front right cube, so I started with that one. I drew the vertical part, then I added the bottoms of the front and right. I used one space for the height, six for the width, and three for the depth. I labelled the front and right faces.

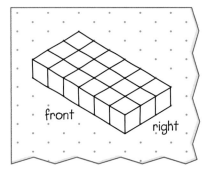

I completed the bottom layer.
I used one space to represent the height, width, and depth of each cube.

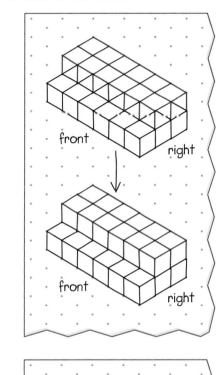

I added the next layer to the structure. I used a different colour to add that layer to my drawing. When the second layer was finished, I erased lines from the first layer that should be hidden.

I repeated this for the top layer.

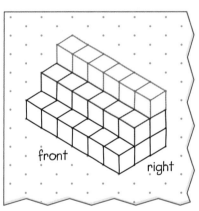

Reflecting

A. Did Sanjev have to draw the whole bottom layer first? Explain.

B. Would you rather use an isometric sketch or views drawn on grid paper to build a cube structure? Explain.

WORK WITH *the Math*

Example 2 | Drawing a cube structure

Make an isometric drawing of this cube structure. Shade your drawing to make it look 3-D.

Solution

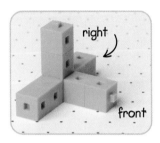

Line up the vertices of the cubes in the structure with the dots of the isometric dot paper. Start by drawing a cube that has three faces visible.

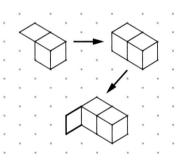

Extend the lines to draw a face that is next to it. Continue extending lines to add other faces.

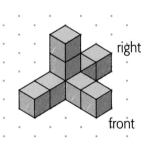

When the drawing matches the cube structure, use three shades of the same colour to fill it in—one for the top faces, one for the front faces, and one for the side faces.

front

Ⓐ Checking

1. Build this cube structure. Make an isometric drawing to represent your cube structure.

2. **a)** Build this cube structure.
   b) Make an isometric drawing of the structure.
   c) Turn the structure to a different view and make another isometric drawing of it.

front

3. **a)** Build this cube structure.
   b) Make two different isometric drawings of the structure.

front

4. Build the following cube structures. Make an isometric drawing of each.

a)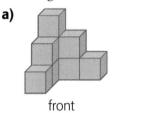

front

b)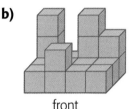

front

5. **a)** Build three different letters of the alphabet with linking cubes.
   b) Draw each letter on isometric dot paper.
   c) Draw the top, front, and right views for each letter.

6. Build this cube structure. Make an isometric drawing of the structure.

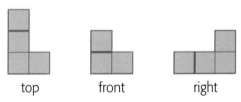

top   front   right

7. **a)** Build two different cube structures that can be represented by the same isometric drawing.
   b) Draw enough face views of each structure to show how they are different.

8. Why might an architect use an isometric drawing instead of face views to show a structure?

Frequently Asked Questions

Q. How do you draw the different views of a cube structure?

A. Draw what you see when you look at the structure straight on. Then look at the structure from a slightly different angle to see changes in depth. Mark the changes in depth with a heavier line. The top, front, left, and right views of a cube structure are shown below.

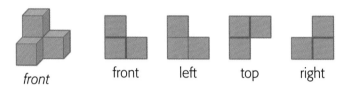

front   front   left   top   right

Q. How do you make an isometric drawing of a cube structure?

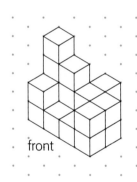

front

A. There are different ways to do this. You can line up the vertices of the cubes with the dots of the triangular dot paper. Then start drawing a cube with three faces. Extend the lines to draw the cubes around it. Continue drawing the cubes until the isometric drawing matches the cube structure.

Another method is to draw the structure layer by layer, erasing hidden lines as you go.

Q: How does an isometric drawing compare with top, front, and side views?

A: An isometric drawing is a single representation of a 3-D object. The drawing is 2-D but it appears to be 3-D. Top, front, and side views are separate drawings of a 3-D object. Each view is 2-D, and it appears to be 2-D.

Practice

Lesson 11.1

1. Draw the top, front, right, and left views of each structure.

   a)

   front

   b)

   front

Lesson 11.2

2. **a)** Make two cube structures that have this top view.

   b) Draw three other views of your two structures.

   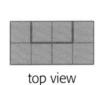

   top view

3. Use these views to build a linking-cube structure.

   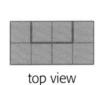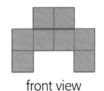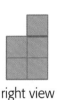

   | top view | front view | left view | right view |

4. The front, left, and right views of a structure all look like this.

   Build the structure and draw the top view.

Lesson 11.3

5. **a)** Build a cube structure using 15 linking cubes.

   b) Make isometric drawings from two different views.

6. **a)** Trade your isometric drawings from question 5 with a partner.

   b) Use your partner's isometric drawing to build a cube structure.

   c) Did your cube structure match your partner's original structure? Why or why not?

11.4 Creating Cube Structures from Isometric Drawings

YOU WILL NEED
- Isometric Dot Paper
- a ruler
- linking cubes

GOAL

Create cube structures based on isometric drawings.

LEARN ABOUT the Math

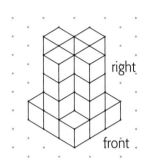

Joseph and Mark are using Elena's isometric drawing to build a cube structure. Joseph thinks the structure has 20 cubes but Mark thinks it has only 19.

❓ How can Elena make sure that they will build the structure correctly?

A. How many cubes are visible?

B. Build a cube structure with 19 cubes that matches Elena's drawing.

C. Build a cube structure with 20 cubes that matches Elena's drawing.

D. Elena says that the structure is made of 22 cubes. Make a cube structure with 22 cubes that matches Elena's drawing.

E. Make a second structure with 22 cubes that matches her drawing.

F. What additional instructions should Elena give to be sure that other people build the structure the way she intended?

Reflecting

G. How can both Joseph's and Mark's models match Elena's sketch when they are made of different numbers of cubes?

H. What clues in the drawing did you use to help build Elena's cube structure?

WORK WITH the Math

Example 1	Building based on an isometric drawing

Build two different cube structures that match this isometric drawing.

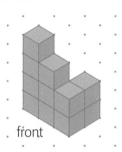

front

Kaitlyn's Solution

I started with the 11 cubes that I can see in the isometric drawing.

To make other structures that match the drawing I would have to add cubes that were hidden, so I turned my structure around.

I could see where to add a cube.

I turned my new structure back to the original position to check that the cube I added was hidden.

Both structures could be represented with the isometric drawing.

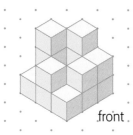

front

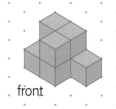

front

A Checking

1. **a)** How many cubes are visible in this isometric drawing?
   b) Build a cube structure that matches the drawing. How many cubes did you use?
   c) Build a different cube structure that also matches the drawing. How are your cube structures different?

B Practising

2. Build a cube structure to match this isometric drawing. Sketch your cube structure so that someone else would build it exactly as you did.

3. Each of these cube structures is made with six cubes. Which structures are the same?

   A.

   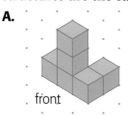

   front

   C.

   front

   B.

   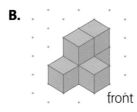

   front

   D.

   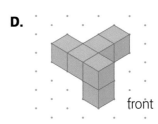

   front

4. Each set of drawings can be used to build the same structure. Which set would you choose to build the structure? Explain.

   A.

   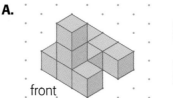

   front

   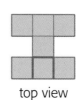

   top view

   B.

   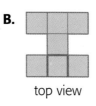

   top view

   front view

Optical Illusions

Isometric drawings can be used to make optical illusions.

Look carefully at this isometric drawing.

Do you see three white walls with a blue cube sitting in the back corner, or do you see a large white cube with a portion taken out?

Follow these steps to make your own optical illusion.

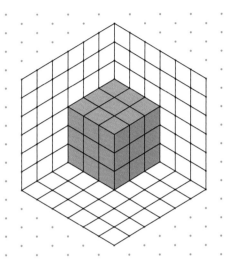

1. Cover a portion of isometric dot paper with hexagons.

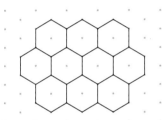

2. Make each hexagon represent a cube by dividing it into three rhombuses, as shown.

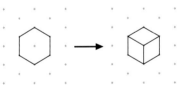

3. Choose a colour scheme for the different types of rhombuses, then use it to colour your drawing.

4. Are you looking down on cubes that come out of the page, or up at them?

Rhombus	Colour
◇	◆
▱	▰
▱	▰

Rotating Cube Structures

YOU WILL NEED
- Isometric Dot Paper
- linking cubes
- grid paper

> **GOAL**
>
> **Make and verify predictions about the views that result from rotating cube structures.**

LEARN ABOUT the Math

Mark's science fair project topic is pulleys and gears. For part of the display, he plans to attach the letters in the word GEARS to five gears in a train. He wondered what the letters would look like as they turned, so he built an E out of linking cubes to see.

? What views will Mark see when the E is rotated?

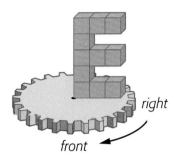

right

front

A. Draw the top, front, and side views of this letter E.

B. Predict and draw the top, front, and side views after the letter is rotated 90° in the direction shown.

C. Predict and draw the top, front, and side views after the letter is rotated 180° from its original position in the direction shown.

D. Predict and draw the top, front, and side views after the letter is rotated 270° from its original position in the direction shown.

E. Check your predictions by building the letter E with linking cubes and rotating it as described in parts B, C, and D.

Reflecting

F. What strategies did you use to predict the views of the rotated letter?

G. What happened to the views as the E was rotated?

Communication | Tip

Horizontally rotating a structure means making it rotate like a merry-go-round.

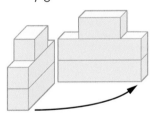

Vertically rotating the structure means making it rotate like a Ferris wheel.

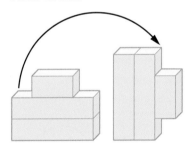

WORK WITH *the Math*

| **Example 1** | Representing views of a rotated structure |

Vanessa made a cube structure and wants to predict the front, top, and right views after vertically rotating the structure 90° clockwise (cw).

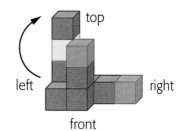

Vanessa's Solution

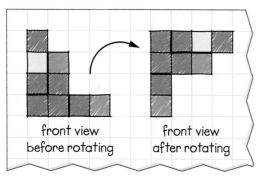

When I vertically rotate the structure 90° cw, the front face remains the front face, the left face becomes the top face, and the top face becomes the right face.

First I drew the front view of my structure. Then I rotated it 90° cw to show what the new front view will be.

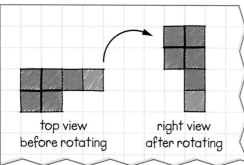

When the structure is rotated, the left and right of the top view will become top and bottom of the right face. The top view will be rotated 90° cw to become the new right view.

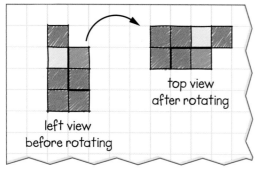

When the structure is rotated, the bottom and top of the left face will become the left and right of the top face. The left view will be rotated 90° cw to become the new top view.

When the structure is vertically rotated 90° cw, the new face views will be old face views that have been rotated 90° cw.

Example 2 | Identifying outlines of a rotated structure

Below are outlines of the front view of this structure in its original position and after it has been horizontally rotated 90° and 180° cw.

A. B. C.

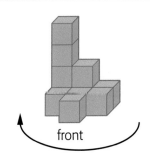

front

Match each outline to the correct rotation.

Guy's Solution

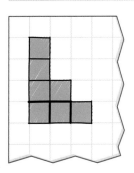

First I built the structure with linking cubes. Outline B matches the front view of the structure in its original position.

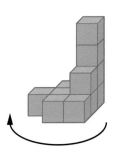 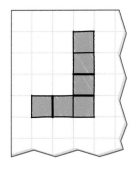

I rotated the structure 90° cw. The new front view matched outline A.

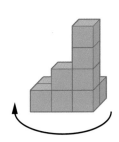 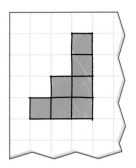

I rotated the structure 90° more so that it was rotated 180° from its original position. The new front view matched outline C.

Example 3 | Rotating a structure to show hidden cubes

Build a structure using at least nine cubes. Make two isometric drawings that together show all of the cubes in your structure.

Kaitlyn's Solution

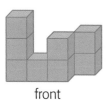

front

First, I built my structure using exactly nine cubes.

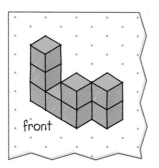

front

I made an isometric drawing from this view. It shows only eight cubes.

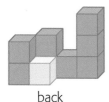

back

I horizontally rotated the structure 180° cw. This view shows a cube that I could not see before the structure was rotated.

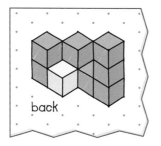

back

I made my second isometric drawing.

Each view shows only eight of the nine cubes, but together they show all of the cubes.

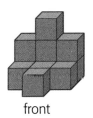

front

A Checking

1. a) Predict and draw the front, top, and right views of this structure.

b) Predict and draw the front, top, and right views of this structure when it is horizontally rotated 180° cw.

c) Build the structure and check your predictions.

2. Rotate this structure horizontally until the outline matches the front view. How was the structure rotated?

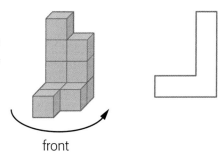

front

B Practising

3. Ruiz and Naghma each built a structure. Naghma thinks the structures are the same. Determine if she is correct and explain your answer.

Naghma's structure   Ruiz's structure

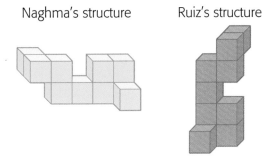

4. Select two red objects that match the blue object on the left.

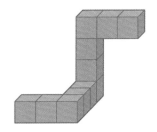

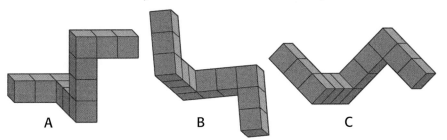

A   B   C

5. a) Draw the front, top, and right views of this model airplane after it has been vertically rotated 90° cw.

b) What would the front, top, and right views be if the model were horizontally rotated 90° cw?

c) Which of these two rotations is a real plane likely to do? Explain.

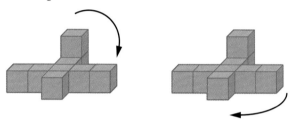

6. Joey constructed letters with linking cubes. These are the front views after the letters have been vertically rotated 180° cw.

a) Which letters did he make?

b) What made it easy to identify the letters?

c) Would it be as easy to identify the letters if they were horizontally rotated 90° cw? Explain.

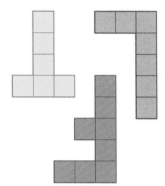

7. Rotate each of these structures until it matches the outline. Describe how each was rotated.

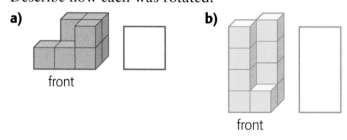

8. Make a structure with 10 linking cubes. Draw the front, top, and right views before and after it has been horizontally rotated 180° cw.

9. What information is provided by looking at different views of a rotated structure?

Real Estate Tycoon

In this game, you own a building once you have collected its top, front, and right views. The goal is to own the greatest number of buildings.

Number of players: 2 to 4

YOU WILL NEED
- building cards
- view cards

How to Play

1. Deal out the building cards. Place your building cards face up in front of you.

2. Spread all the view cards face down in an array so that everyone has access to them.

3. On your turn, flip over a view card. If possible, place it face up beside any of your buildings that it matches. Otherwise, flip it face down again. Your turn is over.

4. An opponent may challenge a match you have made. All players discuss it. If the match is incorrect, the challenger keeps your building card and the view card is turned face down again. If it is a correct match, you get another turn.

5. When you own all of your buildings, you may call the game. The player owning the greatest number of buildings wins. You may also let the play continue in the hope of gaining more buildings through challenges.

6. When all buildings are owned, the player owning the greatest number of buildings wins.

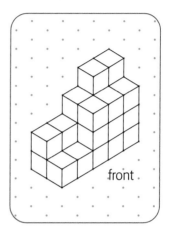

front

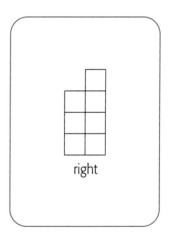

right

Communicate about Views

GOAL

Describe the views necessary to build a 3-D structure.

LEARN ABOUT the Math

Guy wrote to his cousin Robert to tell him about his school project.

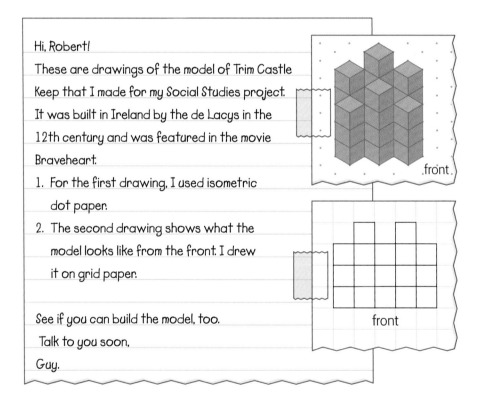

Hi, Robert!

These are drawings of the model of Trim Castle Keep that I made for my Social Studies project. It was built in Ireland by the de Lacys in the 12th century and was featured in the movie Braveheart.

1. For the first drawing, I used isometric dot paper.

2. The second drawing shows what the model looks like from the front. I drew it on grid paper.

See if you can build the model, too.

Talk to you soon,

Guy.

front

front

❓ How can Guy improve his description?

Robert sent back a letter with the following drawings and some questions.

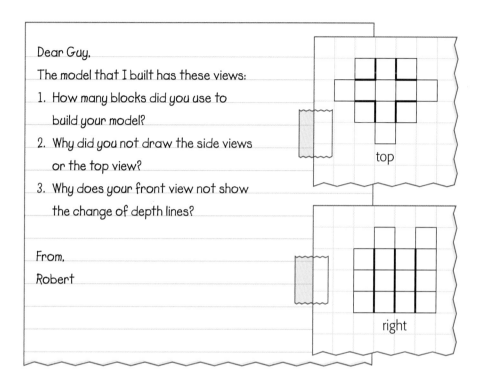

Dear Guy,

The model that I built has these views:

1. How many blocks did you use to build your model?

2. Why did you not draw the side views or the top view?

3. Why does your front view not show the change of depth lines?

From,
Robert

top

right

A. Use the Communication Checklist to explain why Robert's questions could help Guy improve his description.

B. The top view of Trim Castle Keep is symmetric. Improve Robert's drawings of the views to represent the structure accurately.

C. Rewrite Guy's description using Robert's ideas and your own.

Reflecting

D. Explain how the changes improve Guy's description.

Example 1 | Describing a structure

Joseph wrote a description of the structure that he built.
Make suggestions to help Joseph improve his communication.

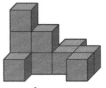

front

Joseph's Description

front

I built my structure with linking cubes.
I drew the structure on isometric dot paper.
I also drew the front and right views to give
more information about the structure.

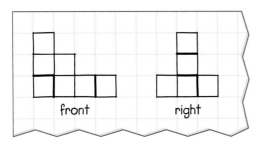

front   right

Elena's Suggestions

I think your drawings are accurate, but they do
not tell me enough to build the structure. I can see
the front and right views in the isometric drawing,
so including those face views did not tell me any
new information.

I can see 9 cubes in your drawing and there are
two places where a cube might be hidden:

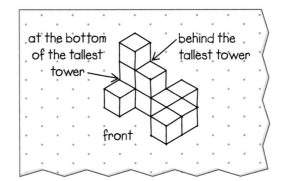

at the bottom
of the tallest
tower

behind the
tallest tower

front

I think there must be a cube at the bottom of the
tallest tower so that all the cubes are linked. The
top view, left view, back view, or an isometric
drawing from another view would show if the
other cube is there or not. You could also say how
many cubes you used.

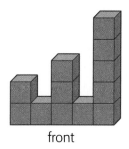

front

A Checking

1. Rosanna is building a 3-D object to display at the math fair. She is creating a plan for building the object. Using the Communication Checklist, write a description of the structure.

B Practising

2. **a)** Describe how to use these top, front, and left views to build a structure.

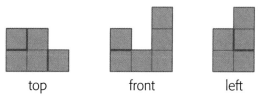

top   front   left

b) Use the Communication Checklist to help you decide what is good about your description and what you can improve.

c) Trade descriptions with a partner. Have your partner use your description to build the structure. If your partner was not able to use your description to build the structure, make changes to make the description clearer.

3. **a)** Build a structure using up to 12 linking cubes.
   b) Make a plan for building the structure.
   - Draw the views of your structure.
   - Make isometric drawings of your structure.
   - Add any other information that needs to be included in your plan to allow someone else to build your structure.

4. **a)** Choose an object in your classroom or at home. Use the Communication Checklist to help you describe the object so that someone could build a model using linking cubes.
   b) Trade descriptions with a partner and follow the steps.

5. If you were building a desk from parts, what should the instructions include to help you build it? Explain.

Reading Strategy

Evaluating

Share your answer with a partner. Does your partner agree or disagree?

Chapter **Self-Test**

1. Which structure matches this set of top, left, right, and back views?

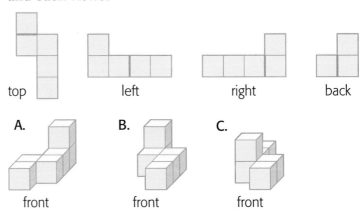

A. front B. front C. front

2. **a)** Use the top, front, and left views to build a cube structure.

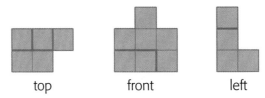

top front left

   b) Draw the right view of the structure in part a).

3. **a)** Build a structure using 10 linking cubes.
   b) Draw the front, top, and side views of your structure.
   c) Rotate your structure vertically 90° cw. Then make an isometric drawing of it that shows the front face.
   d) Ask a classmate to build your structure using your drawings.

4. Both isometric drawings in the margin represent a structure made with eight cubes. Do they represent the same structure? How do you know?

A.

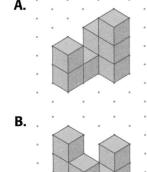

B.

What Do You Think Now?

Revisit What Do You Think? on page 447. Have your answers and explanations changed?

Frequently Asked Questions

Q: How can different structures be represented by the same isometric drawing?

A: An isometric drawing shows only one view of a structure. There could be cubes hidden in that view. For example, both of these structures, shown from the back, correspond to the isometric drawing shown.

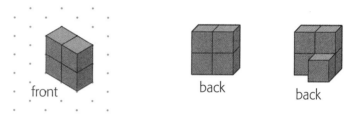

Q: How is it possible to have different isometric drawings of the same cube structure?

A. Different views of the same structure can lead to different isometric drawings. For example, these drawings show the same cube structure, first in its original position and then after being horizontally rotated clockwise.

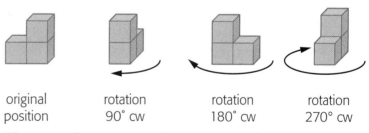

original   rotation   rotation   rotation
position   90° cw   180° cw   270° cw

These are the corresponding isometric drawings:

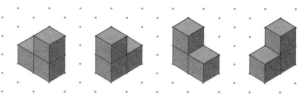

Practice

Lesson 11.1

1. **a)** Build this structure with linking cubes.
   b) Draw the top, front, right, and left views of your structure.
   c) If you take away the red cubes, which views would look different and how would they be different?

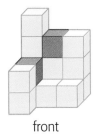

front

Lesson 11.2

2. Allanah built a structure with linking cubes and drew these views. Build Allanah's structure, then draw the back view.

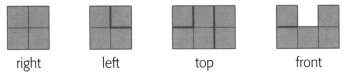

right   left   top   front

Lesson 11.3

3. **a)** Use 20 linking cubes to build a structure.
   b) Make an isometric drawing of your structure.
   c) Make an isometric drawing from a different view.

Lesson 11.4

4. Jared built a model using 11 linking cubes. He made an isometric drawing of his model. Build Jared's model using linking cubes.

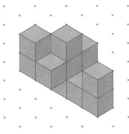

Lesson 11.5

5. Leyla built a model of an inukshuk using linking cubes. She is sending her cousin in Montreal drawings of her model and an explanation of how inukshuks are built.
   a) Build a model of an inukshuk with linking cubes.
   b) Make isometric drawings to show your model horizontally rotated 0°, 90°, 180°, and 270° cw.

Lesson 11.6

6. Write a letter to Leyla's cousin, describing the model in question 5.

3-D Archaeology

Archaeologists must fully describe their dig sites in reports. They use 3-D models and 2-D drawings to record their findings.

❓ How can you provide enough information so that an accurate model can be built of a structure?

A. Use linking blocks to build a model of an ancient building.

B. Provide enough information on paper to make it easy to visualize your model and to build it.

C. Exchange plans with a partner and try to build each other's structures.

D. Check to see if your partner could build your structure. Did you provide enough information for your partner? What other information would help?

1. Students in a gym class were practising the standing long jump. Their best distances are recorded in centimetres:

   185   205   221   186   185   212   222   215   198   200   205
   207   193   186   172   208   225   170   206   215   228   230

   Which type of graph would best show the percentage of the class that jumped a distance of at least 190 m?

   A. a bar graph   **C.** a circle graph
   B. a line graph   **D.** any of the above are equally good.

2. Chad made the first three figures in a pattern using toothpicks.

   The pattern rule he used was $n = 5f + 1$ where n represented the number of toothpicks he needed and f was the figure number. Which graph best represents the relation between the number of toothpicks and the figure number?

   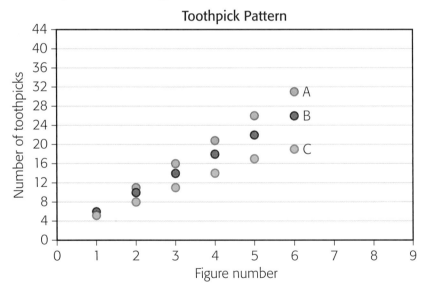

   A. A   **B.** B   **C.** C   **D.** none of these

g	f
0	▲
1	−12
■	0

3. Determine the values for ■ and ▲ in the table of values for the relation $f = 3(g − 5)$.

A. ■ = 5, ▲ = 15   C. ■ = 5, ▲ = 0

B. ■ = 5, ▲ = −15   D. ■ = 0, ▲ = 0

4. A cart has a mass of 40 kg. Bags of flour are placed on the cart. Each bag has a mass of 5 kg. The total mass of the flour and the cart is 240 kg.

Which of the following equations could you solve to determine the number of bags of flour on the cart?

i) $240 = 5b + 40$ **ii)** $5b + 40 = 240$ **iii)** $5b = 240 − 40$

A. only equation i)

B. only equation ii)

C. only equation iii)

D. any of the equations

5. Which solution is correct?

A.
$15 = −5 (a − 6)$
$15 = −5a − 30$
$45 = −5a$
$−9 = a$

C.
$15 = −5 (a − 6)$
$3 = a − 6$
$9 = a$

B.
$15 = −5 (a − 6)$
$15 = −5a + 30$
$−15 = −5a$
$3 = a$

D.
$15 = −5 (a − 6)$
$−3 = −a − 6$
$3 = −a$
$−3 = a$

6. A paper bag contains 5 red balls and 5 green balls. Another bag contains 3 red balls and 7 green balls.

If you draw one ball from each bag, what is the probability that both will be red?

A. 15%   B. 20%   C. 40%   D. 75%

7. Which is the top view of the cube structure?

A.   B.   C.   D.

Glossary

Instructional Words

C

calculate [*calculer*]: Complete one or more mathematical operations; compute

clarify [*clarifier*]: Make a statement easier to understand; provide an example

classify [*classer* ou *classifier*]: Put things into groups according to a rule and label the groups; organize into categories

compare [*comparer*]: Look at two or more objects or numbers and identify how they are the same and how they are different

conclude [*conclure*]: Judge or decide after reflection or after considering data

construct [*construire*]: Make or build a model; draw an accurate geometric shape (e.g., Use a ruler and a protractor to construct an angle.)

create [*inventer* ou *créer*]: Make your own example

D

describe [*décrire*]: Tell, draw, or write about what something is or what something looks like; tell about a process in a step-by-step way

determine [*déterminer*]: Decide with certainty as a result of calculation, experiment, or exploration

draw: 1. [*dessiner*] Show something in picture form (e.g., Draw a diagram.)
2. [*tirer*] Pull or select an object (e.g., Draw a card from the deck. Draw a tile from the bag.)

E

estimate [*estimer*]: Use your knowledge to make a sensible decision about an amount; make a reasonable guess (e.g., Estimate 3210 + 789.)

evaluate [*évaluer*]: 1. Determine if something makes sense; judge
2. Calculate the value as a number

explain [*expliquer*]: Tell what you did; show your mathematical thinking at every stage; show how you know

explore [*explorer*]: Investigate a problem by questioning, brainstorming, and trying new ideas

extend [*prolonger*]: 1. In patterning, continue the pattern 2. In problem solving, create a new problem that takes the idea of the original problem further

J

justify [*justifier*]: Give convincing reasons for a prediction, an estimate, or a solution; tell why you think your answer is correct

M

measure [*mesurer*]: Use a tool to describe an object or determine an amount (e.g., Use a protractor to measure an angle.)

model [*représenter* ou *faire un modèle*]: Show or demonstrate an idea using objects and/or pictures (e.g., Model addition of integers using red and blue counters.)

P

predict [*prédire*]: Use what you know to work out what is going to happen (e.g., Predict the next number in the pattern 1, 2, 4, 7,...)

R

reason [*raisonner* ou *argumenter*]: Develop ideas and relate them to the purpose of the task and to each other; analyze relevant information to show understanding

relate [*établir un lien* ou *associer*]: Describe how two or more objects, drawings, ideas, or numbers are similar

represent [*représenter*]: Show information or an idea in a different way that makes it easier to understand (e.g., Draw a graph. Make a model. Create a rhyme.)

S

show (your work) [*montrer son travail* ou *présenter sa démarche*]: Record all calculations, drawings, numbers, words, or symbols that make up the solution

sketch [*esquisser*]: Make a rough drawing (e.g., Sketch a picture of the field with dimensions.)

solve [*résoudre*]: Develop and carry out a process for finding a solution to a problem

sort [*trier* ou *classer*]: Separate a set of objects, drawings, ideas, or numbers according to an attribute (e.g., Sort 2-D shapes by the number of sides.)

V

validate [*valider*]: Check an idea by showing that it works

verify [*vérifier*]: Work out an answer or solution again, usually in another way; show evidence of

visualize [*imaginer*]: Form a picture in your head of what something is like; imagine

Mathematical Words

A

algebraic expression [*expression* (n.f.) *algébrique*]: The result of applying arithmetic operations to numbers and variables; e.g., $3x$ or $5x + 2$. Sometimes this is just called an expression.

angle bisector [*bissectrice* (n.f.)]: A line that cuts an angle in half to form two equal angles

B

base [*base* (n.f.)]: The side of a shape that is measured for calculating the area or perimeter of a shape. Each base has a corresponding height that creates a 90° angle with the base. Any side of a shape can be the base of the shape.

C

Cartesian coordinate system [*système* (n.m.) *de coordonnées cartésiennes*]: A method (named after mathematician René Descartes) for describing a location by identifying the distance from a horizontal number line (the x-axis) and a vertical number line (the y-axis). The location is represented by an ordered pair of coordinates (x, y). The axes intersect at $(0, 0)$, which is called the origin.

centre of rotation [*centre* (n.m.) *de rotation*]: A fixed point around which other points in a shape rotate in a clockwise (cw) or counterclockwise (ccw) direction; the centre of rotation may be inside or outside the shape

circle graph [*diagramme* (n.m.) *circulaire*]: A graph that shows how the parts make up a whole

circumference [*circonférence* (n.f.)]: The boundary of a circle; the length of this boundary

clockwise (cw) [*dans le sens* (n.m.) *des aiguilles d'une montre*]: Turning in a sense similar to the hands of a clock; e.g., a turn from direction OP to direction OQ is a clockwise turn (Also see **counterclockwise.**)

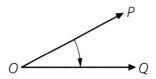

common denominator [*dénominateur* (n.m.) *commun*]: A common multiple of two or more denominators; e.g., for $\frac{2}{3}$ and $\frac{3}{6}$, a common denominator would be any multiple of 6. If you use the least common multiple of the denominators, the common denominator is called the lowest common denominator.

common factor [*diviseur* (n.m.) *commun*]: A whole number that divides into two or more other numbers with no remainder; e.g., 4 is a common factor of 12 and 24

common multiple [*multiple* (n.m.) *commun*]: A number that is a multiple of two or more given numbers; e.g., 12, 24, and 36 are common multiples of 4 and 6

complementary event [*événement* (n.m.) *complémentaire*]: The set of outcomes in the sample space in which the event does not happen; e.g., when rolling a die, the event (rolling 2) has the complementary event (rolling 1, 3, 4, 5, or 6)

constant [*constante* (n.f.)]: A quantity that does not change; e.g., in $2 \times n + 5$, 5 is a constant

convex [*convexe*]: A design where all interior angles measure no greater than 180°

coordinates [*coordonnées* (n.f.pl.) *d'un point ou coordonnées* (n.f.pl.)]: An ordered pair, used to describe a location on a grid labelled with an x-axis and a y-axis; e.g., the coordinates (1, 3) describe a location on a grid that is 1 unit horizontally from the origin and 3 units vertically from the origin

counterclockwise (ccw) [*dans le sens* (n.m.) *contraire des aiguilles d'une montre*]: Turning in a sense opposite to the hands of a clock; e.g., a turn from direction OQ to direction OP is a counterclockwise turn (Also see **clockwise**.)

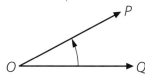

D

diameter [*diamètre* (n.m.)]: A line segment that joins two points on the circumference of a circle and passes through the centre; the length of this line segment

digital root [*racine* (n.f.) *numérique*]: The number obtained by adding the digits of a number, then repeating the digit addition for each new number found, until a single-digit number is reached; e.g., the digital root of 123 is $1 + 2 + 3 = 6$

divisibility rule [*règle* (n.f.) *de divisibilité ou caractères* (n.m.pl.) *de divisibilité*]: A way to determine if one whole number is a factor of another whole number without actually dividing the entire number

dodecagon [*dodécagon* (n.m.)]: A polygon with 12 straight sides and 12 angles

E

equally likely outcomes [*résultats* (n.m.pl.) *également probables*]: Two or more outcomes that have an equal chance of occurring; e.g., the outcome of rolling a 1 and the outcome of rolling a 2 on a 6-sided die are equally likely outcomes because each outcome has a probability of $\frac{1}{6}$

equation [*égalite* (n.f.); *remarque: en français, une équation comporte obligatoirement une inconnue*]: A statement that two quantities or expressions are equivalent; e.g., $4 + 2 = 6$ and $6x + 2 = 14$

equivalent [*équivalent*]: Equal in value; e.g., two equivalent fractions are $\frac{1}{2}$ and $\frac{2}{4}$, two equivalent ratios are $6:4$ and $9:6$, and the fraction $\frac{1}{2}$ is equivalent to the decimal 0.5

equivalent rate [*rapport* (n.m.) *équivalent*]: A rate that describes the same comparison as another rate; e.g., 2 for \$4 is equivalent to 4 for \$8

equivalent ratio [*rapport* (n.m.) *équivalent*]: A ratio that represents the same relationship as another ratio; e.g., $2:4$ is an equivalent ratio to $1:2$ because both ratios describe the relationship of the blue counters to the red counters. There are 2 red counters for each blue counter, but also 4 red counters for every 2 blue counters.

event [*événement* (n.m.)]: A set of one or more outcomes in a probability experiment; e.g., the event of rolling an even number with a six-sided die consists of the outcomes of rolling a 2, a 4, or a 6

experimental probability [*probabilité* (n.f.) *expérimentale*]: In a probability experiment, the ratio of the number of observed favourable outcomes to the number of trials, or repetitions, of the experiment

expression [*expression* (n.f.) *numérique*]: See **algebraic expression** [*expression algébrique* (n.f.)]

F

factor [*facteur* (n.m.)]: One of the numbers you multiply in a multiplication operation

$$2 \quad \times \quad 6 \quad = \quad 12$$
$$\uparrow \qquad\quad \uparrow$$
$$\text{factor} \quad\quad \text{factor}$$

favourable outcome [*résultat* (n.m.) *favorable*]: The desired result in a probability experiment

formula [*formule* (n.f.)]: A rule represented by symbols, numbers, or letters, often in the form of an equation; e.g., area of a rectangle = length $\times$ width, or $A = l \times w$

G

greatest common factor (GCF) [*plus grand diviseur* (n.m.) *commun, ou PGDC*]: The greatest whole number that is a factor of two or more whole numbers; e.g., 4 is the greatest common factor of 8 and 12.

H

height [*hauteur* (n.f.)]: A line segment drawn to form a right angle with the side of a shape

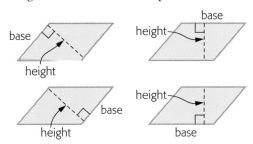

heptagon [*heptagone* (n.m.)]: A polygon with 7 straight sides and 7 angles

hexagon [*hexagone* (n.m.)]: A polygon with 6 straight sides and 6 angles

hypotenuse [*hypoténuse* (n.f.)]: The longest side of a right triangle; the side opposite the right angle

I

improper fraction [*fraction* (n.f.) *impropre*]: A fraction whose numerator is greater than its denominator; e.g., $\frac{5}{4}$ is an improper fraction

independent events [*événements* (n.m.pl.) *indépendants*]: Two events are independent if the probability of one is not affected by the probability of the other

integer [*nombre* (n.m.) *entier ou entier* (n.m.)]: The counting numbers ($+1$, $+2$, $+3$,...), zero (0), and the opposites of the counting numbers (-1, -2, -3,...)

interior angle [*angle* (n.m.) *intérieur*]: The inside angle of a polygon

intersection point [*le point d'intersection* (n.m.)]: The point where two lines or line segments cross each other; e.g., QR intersects ST at intersection point E

isolate [*isoler*]: To show the same equation in an equivalent way so the variable is alone on one side

isometric drawing [*diagramme* (n.m.) *isométrique*]: A 3-D view of an object in which
- vertical edges are drawn vertically
- width and depth are drawn diagonally
- equal lengths on the object are equal on the drawing

K

kite [*cerf-volant* (n.m.)]: A convex quadrilateral with two pairs of equal adjacent sides

L

least common multiple (LCM) [*plus petit multiple* (n.m.) *commun, ou PPMC*]: The least whole number that has two or more given whole numbers as factors; e.g., 12 is the least common multiple of 4 and 6

linear relation [*rapport* (n.m.) *linéaire ou relation* (n.f.) *de variation directe*]: A relation whose plotted points lie on a straight line

line segment [*segment* (n.m.) *de droite ou segment* (n.m.)]: Part of a line with two endpoints; it is named using the labels of the endpoints; e.g., the line segment joining points X and Y is called XY

line segment XY

X ●———————● Y

lowest terms [*sous forme* (n.f.) *irréductible*]: An equivalent form of a fraction with numerator and denominator that have no common factors other than 1; e.g., $\frac{3}{4}$ is the lowest term form of $\frac{12}{16}$, since $\frac{3}{4} = \frac{12}{16}$ and 3 and 4 have no common factors other than 1

M

mean [*moyenne* (n.f.)]: A representative value of a set of data; it is determined by sharing the total amount of the data evenly amongst the number of values in the set; e.g., consider the set of data: 3, 6, 8, 14, 9. There are 5 values, whose sum is 40. The mean is 8, because 40 divided equally among 5 values would give each number the value 8. That is, $40 \div 5 = 8$.

median [*médiane* (n.f.)]: A representative value of a set of data; the middle value of the ordered data. When there is an odd number of values, the median is the middle value; e.g., the median of 2, 3, and 4 is 3. When there is an even number of values, it is the value halfway between the two middle values; e.g., the median of 2, 3, 4, 5, 6 and 6 is 4.5.

midpoint [*milieu* (n.m.)]: The point on a line segment that divides the line segment into two equal parts

mixed number [*nombre* (n.m.) *mixte*]: A number expressed as a whole number and a fraction; e.g., $2\frac{1}{2}$ is a mixed number

mode [*mode* (n.m.)]: A representative value of a set of data; the value or item that occurs most often in a set of data. A set of data might have no mode, 1 mode, or more than 1 mode; e.g., the mode of 1, 5, 6, 6, 6, 7, and 10 is 6.

multiple [*multiple* (n.m.)]: The product of a whole number and any other whole number; e.g., when you multiply 10 by the whole numbers 0 to 4, you get the multiples 0, 10, 20, 30, and 40

N

net [*développement* (n.m.)]: A 2-D pattern you can fold to create a 3-D object; e.g., this is a net for a cube

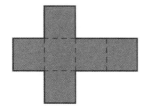

numerical coefficient [*coefficient* (n.m.)]: The multiplier of a variable; e.g., in $2 \times n + 5$, 2 is the numerical coefficient of n

O

octagon [*octogone* (n.m.)]: A polygon with 8 straight sides and 8 angles

opposite integers [*nombres entiers opposés* (n.m.pl.) *ou entiers* (n.m.pl.) *opposés*]: Two integers the same distance away from zero; e.g., +2 and −2 are opposite integers

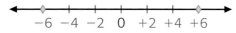

order of operations [*priorité* (n.f.) *des opérations*]: A set of rules people use when calculating, in order to get the same answer. The rules for the order of operations are:
Step 1: Do the operations in brackets first.
Step 2: Divide and multiply from left to right.
Step 3: Add and subtract from left to right.
To remember the rules, think of "BDMAS": Brackets, Divide and Multiply, Add and Subtract.

origin [*origine* (n.f.)]: The point from which measurement is taken; in the Cartesian coordinate system, it is the intersection of the vertical and horizontal axes and is represented by the ordered pair (0, 0)

outcome [*résultat* (n.m.)]: A result of an event or experiment. For example, rolling a 1 is one possible outcome when you roll a die.

outcome table [*tableau* (n.m.) *des résultats*]: A chart that lists all possible outcomes of a probability experiment

outlier [*observation* (n.f.) *aberrante*]: A data value that is far from the other data values

P

parallel [*parallèle*]: Always the same distance apart; e.g., line segments *AB* and *CD* are parallel

part-to-part ratio [*rapport partie/partie*]: A comparison of two parts of the same whole; e.g., 2:4 compares the number of red tiles to the number of blue tiles

part-to-whole ratio [*rapport partie/tout*]: A comparison of part of a whole to the whole (e.g., 2:6 compares the number of red tiles to the total number of tiles) that can be written as a fraction, such as $\frac{2}{6}$

pattern rule [*règle* (n.f.) *de la suite*]: A way to describe a pattern that compares a characteristic of the figure to the figure number; e.g., a pattern rule for the pattern shown below is $b = 4 \times n + 1$, where b is the number of blocks in figure n

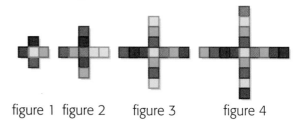

figure 1   figure 2   figure 3   figure 4

percent [*pourcentage* (n.m.)]: A part-to-whole ratio that compares a number or an amount to 100; e.g., $25\% = 25:100 = \dfrac{25}{100}$

perfect square [*carré* (n.m.) *parfait*]: The product of a whole number multiplied by itself; e.g., 49 is a perfect square because $49 = 7 \times 7$

perpendicular bisector [*bissectrice* (n.f.) *perpendiculaire*]: A line that intersects a line segment at 90° and divides it into two equal lengths; any point on the perpendicular bisector to AB is equidistant from endpoints A and B

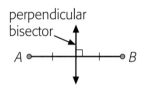

π (pi) [*(pi)* (n.m.) ou **π**]: The ratio of the circumference of a circle to its diameter; its value is about 3.14

plane [*plan* (n.m.)]: A flat surface that goes on forever in two different directions

prime number [*nombre* (n.m.) *premier*]: A number with only two factors, 1 and itself; e.g., 17 is a prime number since its only factors are 1 and 17

probability [*probabilité* (n.f.)]: A number from 0 to 1 that shows how likely it is that an event will happen

proportion [*proportion* (n.f.)]: A number sentence that shows two equivalent ratios or fractions; e.g., $1:2 = 2:4$ or $\dfrac{1}{2} = \dfrac{2}{4}$

Pythagorean theorem [*théorème* (n.m.) *de Pythagore*]: Statement of a relationship in which the sum of the squares of the lengths of the legs of a right triangle is equal to the square of the length of the hypotenuse. This is written algebraically as $a^2 + b^2 = c^2$.

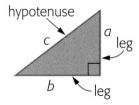

R

radius [*rayon* (n.m.)]: Half the diameter of a circle—the distance from the centre of a circle to a point on the circumference

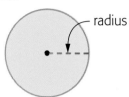

range [*étendue* (n.f.)]: The difference between the greatest and least number in a set of data; e.g., the range of 6, 7, 7, 8, 9 is 3, because $9 - 6 = 3$

rate [*rapport* (n.m.)/*relation* (n.f.)]: A comparison of two amounts measured in different units; e.g., cost per item or distance compared to time. The word "per" means "to" or "for each" and is written using a slash (/); e.g., a typing rate of 250 words/8 min

ratio [*rapport* (n.m.) / *relation* (n.f.)]: A comparison of two numbers (e.g., $5:26$ is the ratio of vowels to letters in the alphabet) or of two measurements with the same units (e.g., $164:175$ is the ratio of two students' heights in centimetres). Each number in the ratio is called a term.

reciprocal [*réciproque* (n.f.)]: The fraction that results from switching the numerator and the denominator; e.g., $\dfrac{4}{5}$ is the reciprocal of $\dfrac{5}{4}$

reflection [*réflexion* (n.f.)]: The result of a flip of a 2-D shape; each point in a 2-D shape flips to the opposite side of the line of reflection, but stays the same distance from the line (Also see **transformation**.)

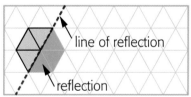

relation [*relation* (n.f.)]: A property that allows you to use one number to get information about another number

repeating decimal [*suite* (n.f.) *décimale périodique*]: A decimal in which a block of one or more digits eventually repeats in a pattern; e.g., $\frac{25}{99} = 0.252\ 525\ ...$, $\frac{31}{36} = 0.861\ 111\ 1\ ...$, $\frac{1}{7} = 0.142\ 857\ 142\ 857...$. These repeating decimals can also be written as $0.\overline{25}$, $0.86\overline{1}$, and $0.\overline{142\ 857}$.

rotation [*rotation* (n.f.)]: A transformation in which each point in a shape moves about a fixed point through the same angle

S

sample space [*espace* (n.m.) *des échantillons*]: All possible outcomes in a probability experiment

scatter plot [*diagramme* (n.m.) *de dispersion*]: A graph that attempts to show a relationship between two variables by means of points plotted on a coordinate grid

solution to an equation [*solution* (n.f.) *d'une équation*]: A value of a variable that makes an equation true; e.g., the solution to $6x + 2 = 14$ is $x = 2$

speed [*vitesse* (n.f.)]: The rate at which a moving object travels a certain distance in a certain time; e.g., a sprinter who runs 100 m in 10 s has a speed of 100 m/10 s = 10 m/s

square root [*racine* (n.f.) *carrée*]: One of two equal factors of a number; e.g., the square root of 81 is 9 because 9×9, or 9^2, $= 81$; sometimes called a root

statistics [*statistique* (n.f.)]: The collection, organization, and interpretation of data

T

terminating decimal [*fraction* (n.f.) *décimal finie*]: A decimal that is complete after a certain number of digits with no repetition; e.g., 0.777

tessellation [*mosaïque* (n.f.)]: The tiling of a plane with one or more congruent shapes without any gaps or overlaps

theoretical probability [*probabilité* (n.f.) *théorique*]: The ratio of the number of favourable outcomes to the number of possible equally likely outcomes; e.g., the theoretical probability of tossing a head on a coin is $\frac{1}{2}$, since there are 2 equally likely outcomes and only 1 is favourable

three-term ratio [*rapport* (n.m.) *à trois termes*]: A ratio that compares three quantities; e.g., the ratio $2:3:5$ (or, 2 to 3 to 5) describes the ratio of red to blue to yellow squares

transformation [*transformation géométrique* (n.f.)]: The result of moving a shape according to a rule; transformations include translations, rotations, and reflections

translation [*translation* (n.f.)]: The result of a slide; the slide must be along straight lines, left or right, up or down (Also see **transformation**.)

tree diagram [*diagramme* (n.m.) *en arbre ou arbre* (n.m.)]: A way to record and count all combinations of events, using lines to connect the two parts of the outcome

```
  1st toss  2nd toss        1st toss  2nd toss
          ┌ H (HH)                  ┌ H (TH)
     H  ─<                     T  ─<
          └ T (HT)                  └ T (TT)
```

trial [*essai* (n.m.) *ou événement* (n.m.)]: A single event or observation in a probability experiment

U

unit rate [*valeur* (n.f.) *unitaire*]: A rate in which the second term is 1; e.g., in swimming, 12 laps/6 min can be written as a unit rate of 2 laps/min

V

variable [*variable* (n.f.)]: A letter or symbol, such as a, b, x, or n, that represents a number; e.g., in the formula for the area of a rectangle, the variables A, l, and w represent the area, length, and width of the rectangle

Z

zero principle [*principe* (n.m.) *de la somme des nombres opposés*]: When two opposite integers are added, the sum is zero; e.g.,

$$(\bigcirc\ \bigcirc) + (\bullet\ \bullet) = 0$$
$$(-2)\ +\ (+2)\ = 0$$

Answers

Chapter 1, p. 1

1.2 Recognizing Perfect Squares, pp. 8–9

1. a), b), d), and f)

2. a) e.g., 1225 equals a whole number, 35, multiplied by itself, so it is a perfect square.
   b) e.g., $484 = 22 \times 22$ or 22^2
   c) e.g., 45 is a whole number, so 45^2 or 2025 must be a perfect square.

3. e.g., The diagram shows that $289 = 17 \times 17$ or 17^2.

4. a) $16 = 4 \times 4$ or 4^2 **c)** $1764 = 42 \times 42$ or 42^2
   b) $144 = 12 \times 12$ or 12^2

5. Yes, e.g., 225 can be written as 15×15 or 15^2.

6. a) 36   **c)** 121   **e)** 625   **g)** 10 000
   b) 81   **d)** 144   **f)** 1600   **h)** 1 000 000

7. e.g., She can group the factors as $(5 \times 9) \times (5 \times 9)$ or 45×45 or 45^2.

8. Yes, e.g., $13 \times 13 = 169$, so 169 is a square, and $31 \times 31 = 961$, so 961 is also a square.

9. e.g., an 8-by-8 and a 2-by-2 square with two congruent 2-by-8 rectangles

10. a) two, 900 and 961
   b) e.g., The greatest perfect square must be 29^2 or 841 because the next square is 30^2 or 900. The least perfect square must be 32^2 because 31^2 is 961.

11. yes

12. e.g., The result will be even if the number squared is even, and odd if the number squared is odd.

13. e.g., Each square number can be written as a number multiplied by itself, so when two square numbers are multiplied, the product can also be grouped to show a number multiplied by itself.

14.

Number	11	12	13	14	15	16	17	18	19	20
Square	121	144	169	196	225	256	289	324	361	400
Ones digit of square	1	4	9	6	5	6	9	4	1	0

15. a) 1   **b)** 4   **c)** 5   **d)** 4

16. No, e.g., if the ones digit of the square is 6 then the ones digit of the number squared can be 4 or 6.

17. e.g., Use the factor 17 to show that $17^2 = 289$.

1.3 Square Roots of Perfect Squares, pp. 13–15

1. a)

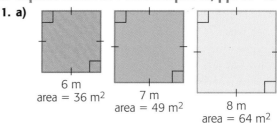

6 m
area = 36 m²

7 m
area = 49 m²

8 m
area = 64 m²

   b) 6 m, 7 m, and 8 m

2. a) 2   **b)** 4   **c)** 9   **d)** 20

3. a) e.g., 7, 21, 21, 63, and $\sqrt{441} = 21$
   b) e.g., 21×21 or $21^2 = 441$

4. 27

5. a) 4-by-16, 8-by-8
   b) e.g., She can choose the square with equal side lengths of 8, which is the square root.
   c) 12
   d) e.g., Sanjev's factor rainbow shows each factor matched to a partner. This matching is like showing the dimensions of rectangles with the same area used in Maddy's method.

6. a) 1   **b)** 0   **c)** 5   **d)** 10   **e)** 20   **f)** 30

7. a) e.g., $\sqrt{31 \times 31}$ is 31 because 31×31 represents the area of a square and 31 is the side length or square root.

b) e.g., $\sqrt{43 \times 43}$ is 43 because 43^2 is a perfect square. The square root of a whole number squared is the whole number.

c) e.g., The factors can be arranged in $\sqrt{2 \times 2 \times 3 \times 3}$ as $\sqrt{(2 \times 3) \times (2 \times 3)}$ $= \sqrt{6 \times 6}$ or 6^2, so the square root must be 6.

8. a) 32   **b)** 121

9. yes

10. 16 m

11. a) e.g., $10^2 = 100$ and $20^2 = 400$, so the square root of 225 must be between 10 and 20.

b) e.g., Only numbers with a ones digit of 5 when squared will also have a ones digit of 5.

c) e.g., The ones digit of the square root must be 5, and the square root must be between 10 and 20, so 15 must be the square root.

12. a) yes   **b)** 26

13. a)

Ones digit of perfect square	Ones digit of square root
0	0
1	1 or 9
2	not possible
3	not possible
4	2 or 8
5	5
6	4 or 6
7	not possible
8	not possible
9	3 or 7

b) No, e.g., the only time you can predict the ones digit of a square root is when the ones digit of the perfect square is 0 or 5.

14. a) 17   **b)** 21   **c)** 47   **d)** 55

15. e.g., Use estimating and predicting the ones digit after squaring, or identify all the factors of 324.

16. a) 10   **b)** 100   **c)** 1000

17. 10 000

18. a) e.g., The only factor that cannot be paired with a different number is 77, which is the square root of 5929.

b) e.g., $77^2 = 5929$

19. e.g., If a whole number has an odd number of factors, then you can pair each factor except for one. This factor must be the square root.

20. e.g., Squaring a number and taking the square root gives the original number.

1.4 Estimating Square Roots, pp. 18–20

1. a) about 3.8   **b)** about 5.5

2. a) 2.8   **b)** 6.5   **c)** 12.8   **d)** 31.3

3. 31.3, e.g., $\sqrt{979}$ should be just greater than $\sqrt{900} = 30$.

4. a) reasonable
b) not reasonable, $\sqrt{15} \doteq 3.9$
c) reasonable
d) not reasonable, $\sqrt{289} = 17$
e) not reasonable, $\sqrt{342} \doteq 18.5$
f) reasonable

5. a) 4.2   **c)** 6.2   **e)** 28.3
b) 8.7   **d)** 12.2   **f)** 62.4

6. a) e.g., Take the square root of the area of the square to determine the side length.
b) e.g., 3000 is between $50^2 = 2500$ and $60^2 = 3600$, so the side length must be between 50 m and 60 m.
c) 54.8 m

7. e.g., **a)** 7   **b)** 20   **c)** 1   **d)** 25

8. a) about 663 m
b) e.g., I calculated $663^2 = 439\ 569$, which is close to 440 000 or 880×500.

9. a) e.g., 29 is between 25 and 36, so $\sqrt{29}$ is between $\sqrt{25} = 5$ and $\sqrt{36} = 6$
b) e.g., 26, 27, and 28

10. a) 4.5 s   **c)** 9.0 s   **e)** 20.1 s
b) 6.4 s   **d)** 13.5 s   **f)** 45.0 s

11. 35

12. a) e.g., choose 20. $20^2 = 400$; $400 + 2 \times 20 = 440$; $440 + 1 = 441$; $\sqrt{441} = 21$; $21 - 20 = 1$
b) All answers are equal to 1.

13. 2025

14. a) 2.236   **c)** 223.607

    b) 22.361   **d)** 2236.068

15. a) When the number increases by a factor of 100, the square root increases by a factor of 10.

    b) 22 360.680

16. e.g., Determine the side length s of the square with area 5 square units to determine the square root. $s^2 = 5$, so s is about 2.2.

Mid-Chapter Review, p. 23

1. a)

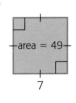

area = 49
7

    c)

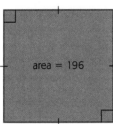

area = 144
12

    b)

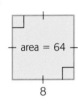

area = 64
8

    d)

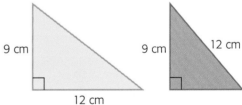

area = 196
14

2. 64, 81

3. C

4. e.g., 11 025 = $(3 \times 5 \times 7) \times (3 \times 5 \times 7)$, which represents 105×105 or 105^2

5. 36, 6

6. e.g., Determine the square root of the area, $\sqrt{900} = 30$, so the side length is 30 m.

7. e.g., The only factor of 81 that is not paired with a partner that is a different number is 9, so $\sqrt{81} = 9$.

8. a) about 3.5   **c)** about 30.4

    b) about 4.1   **d)** about 39.8

9. 100 cm

1.6 The Pythagorean Theorem, pp. 29–31

1. △GHI

2. a) 26 cm   **b)** 8 cm

3. e.g., The sum of the areas of the two smaller squares equals the area of the largest square.

4. a)

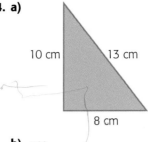

10 cm   13 cm

8 cm

    b) yes

    c) e.g., $10^2 + 8^2 = 164$, but $13^2 = 169$, so the triangle is not a right triangle

5. a) $3^2 + 4^2 = 25$ and $5^2 = 25$

    b) $5^2 + 12^2 = 169$ and $13^2 = 169$

    c) $7^2 + 24^2 = 625$ and $25^2 = 625$

    d) $8^2 + 15^2 = 289$ and $17^2 = 289$

    e) $9^2 + 40^2 = 1681$ and $41^2 = 1681$

    f) $11^2 + 60^2 = 3721$ and $61^2 = 3721$

6. a) yes   **b)** yes

7. about 66 m

8. a) 24 m   **b)** about 23.9 m

9. a) 7.8 cm **b)** 6.3 km **c)** 4.1 cm **d)** 5.8 cm

10. 5 units

11. about 7.1 cm each

12. e.g., If the carpenter measures 5 m from the corner of each wall, then the walls form a right triangle, since $3^2 + 4^2 = 5^2$.

13.

9 cm   9 cm   12 cm

12 cm

14. e.g., If the diagonal of a square has a length of 8 cm, by the Pythagorean theorem the side length of the square can only be $\sqrt{32}$ cm. Many rectangles can have different side lengths with this diagonal.

1.7 Solve Problems Using Diagrams, p. 35

1. 200 cm

2. about 1098 cm

3. 204

4. a) 9   **b)** 11

5. 20 cm

6. about 29.4 km

7. 25

8. e.g., What is the length of x to one decimal place? 11.2 m

Chapter Self-Test, pp. 36–37

1. a) 121   **b)** 196

2. a) e.g., 25 can be written as a whole number multiplied by itself or as 5^2.
   b) $16 + 9 = 4^2 + 3^2$

3. a) 1   **b)** 49   **c)** 225   **d)** 900

4. 4

5. a) 18 cm   **b)** about 6.5 cm

6. e.g., $\sqrt{90}$ is between $\sqrt{81} = 9$ and $\sqrt{100} = 10$, so $\sqrt{90}$ is between 9 and 10, about 9.5.

7. about 807 km

8. $\triangle DEF$

9. about 4.47 units

10. 10 cm and about 7.1 cm

Chapter Review, pp. 39–40

1. a) perfect square   **c)** perfect square
   b) not a perfect square   **d)** not a perfect square

2. e.g., 529 cm^2 is a perfect square, and its square root is the side length of the square.

3. 160 m

4. e.g., A square with an area of 11 cm^2 will have a side length of $\sqrt{11}$ cm. By comparing this square to the other two, $\sqrt{11}$ must be between 3 and 4.

5. a) about 2.6   **c)** about 20.6
   b) about 5.7   **d)** about 30.4

6. about 16.2 m

7. a) e.g., The diagram represents the problem because it shows 9 chairs in front of the square and the remaining 121 chairs in equal rows and columns.
   b) $s^2 + 9 = 130$, where s represents the number of rows and columns
   c) e.g., If $s^2 + 9 = 130$, I can remove 9 chairs from the diagram to get $s^2 = 121$, so s must be 11 because $11^2 = 121$.
   d) 11, 11

8. about 900 km

9. 5 cm, 5.6 cm, and 5.6 cm

10. 30 units

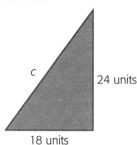

Chapter 2, p. 42

2.1 Multiplying a Whole Number by a Fraction, pp. 49–50

1. $4\frac{2}{3}$

2. a) $\frac{3}{4} + \frac{3}{4} + \frac{3}{4} + \frac{3}{4} + \frac{3}{4}$
   b) $\frac{15}{4}$
   c) $\frac{15}{4}, 3\frac{3}{4}$

3. a) $\frac{2}{3}$ **c)** $\frac{18}{8}, 2\frac{1}{4}$ **e)** $\frac{21}{6}, 3\frac{1}{2}$
   b) $\frac{15}{5}, 3$ **d)** $\frac{8}{5}, 1\frac{3}{5}$ **f)** $\frac{32}{2}, 16$

4. b), c), e), f)

5. $4\frac{1}{6}$ h

6. 4 cups

7. Yes, e.g., a quarter is $\frac{1}{4}$ of a dollar, so multiplying by 17 will tell how many dollars it is worth.

8. a) They are the same—both end up at $\frac{12}{5}$.
   b) e.g., $5 \times \frac{4}{8}$ and $4 \times \frac{5}{8}$

9. a) $\frac{4}{5}$
   b) 40%, 80%
   c) $\frac{4}{5} = 80\%$, so the answers are equal.

10. 11.5

11. e.g., $6 \times \frac{5}{8}$; $3 \times \frac{10}{12}$; $10 \times \frac{3}{5}$

12. e.g., $8 \times \frac{8}{10}$; $35 \times \frac{2}{10}$; $14 \times \frac{4}{8}$

13. e.g., I exercised $\frac{2}{3}$ of an hour, 4 days in a row. How many hours did I exercise?

14. $\frac{4}{5}$

15. $\frac{2}{5}$

16. a) e.g., Each time, you have 5 sets of 2 parts.

   b) e.g., because sometimes the parts are thirds, sometimes fifths, and sometimes sevenths

2.3 Multiplying Fractions, pp. 54–56

1. a) $\frac{4}{9} \times \frac{3}{4}$ **b)** $\frac{3}{7} \times \frac{2}{3}$

2. $\frac{3}{10}$

3. about $\frac{1}{55}$

4. a) $\frac{3}{4} \times \frac{1}{2}$ **b)** $\frac{2}{3} \times \frac{4}{5}$ **c)** $\frac{1}{2} \times \frac{5}{7}$

5. a) $\frac{3}{16}$ **b)** $\frac{4}{15}$ **c)** $\frac{1}{15}$ **d)** $\frac{1}{4}$ **e)** $\frac{1}{5}$ **f)** $\frac{2}{5}$

6. a) $\frac{7}{12}$ **b)** $\frac{1}{6}$ **c)** $\frac{3}{10}$ **d)** $\frac{8}{15}$

7. a) e.g.,    **b)** e.g., $\frac{1}{4} \times \frac{6}{10}$ and $\frac{3}{20} \times \frac{2}{2}$

8. $\frac{1}{5}$

9. a) $\frac{5}{12}$ **b)** 10 h

10. $\frac{4}{15}$

11. a) $\frac{1}{160}$ **b)** $\frac{1}{20}$

12. $\frac{1}{5}$

13. e.g., A gas tank was $\frac{2}{3}$ full. $\frac{3}{5}$ of the gas was used for a trip. What fraction of the tank is still full?

14. a) $2, 1, \frac{1}{2}, \frac{1}{4}, \frac{1}{8}, \frac{1}{16}, \frac{1}{32}$

   b) e.g., To continue the pattern, $\frac{1}{2} \times \frac{1}{2}$ should be half of $1 \times \frac{1}{2}$. Since $1 \times \frac{1}{2} = \frac{1}{2}$, it should be $\frac{1}{4}$.

15. a) $\frac{1}{35}$ **b)** $\frac{1}{12}$ **c)** $\frac{7}{20}$

16. a) 0.12

   b) $\frac{12}{100}$, $\frac{12}{100}$ is the same as 0.12

17. $\frac{1}{100}$

18. The product is less than each fraction because you are taking only a part of either fraction.

19. a) e.g., It is a multiple of 5.

   b) e.g., It might be a multiple of 3, but it does not have to be if you write the fraction in lowest terms. e.g., $\frac{1}{3} \times \frac{3}{5} = \frac{1}{5}$ but $\frac{3}{4} \times \frac{3}{5} = \frac{9}{20}$ and the numerator is a multiple of 3.

2.5 Multiplying Fractions Greater Than 1, pp. 61–63

1. a) e.g., about 4   **b)** e.g., about 49

2. a) $4\frac{4}{5}$ **b)** $2\frac{2}{7}$

3. 1 dozen

4. a) $1\frac{1}{2}$ **b)** $\frac{15}{16}$ **c)** $\frac{8}{15}$ **d)** $2\frac{1}{8}$ **e)** $1\frac{3}{7}$ **f)** $\frac{7}{27}$

5. $11\frac{11}{12}$

6. a) e.g.,   **b)** e.g.,

   c) e.g.,

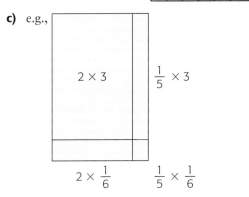

7. a) $7\frac{1}{2}$ **b)** $3\frac{3}{4}$ **c)** $4\frac{4}{5}$ **d)** $7\frac{1}{5}$ **e)** $8\frac{4}{9}$ **f)** $1\frac{11}{24}$

8. a) $3\frac{1}{8}$ cups   **b)** $4\frac{1}{6}$ cups

9. 2 times as much

10. a) e.g., Most likely his estimate would be $3 \times 4 = 12$, so his answer would not be far off his estimate.

   b) e.g., Use a model to show $3\frac{1}{3} \times 4\frac{3}{8} = 14\frac{7}{12}$.

11. $2\frac{2}{9}$

12. Mount Columbia is $26\frac{9}{20}$ times as high.

13. a) $7\frac{41}{50}$

   b) $3\frac{4}{10} = 3.40$, and $2\frac{3}{10} = 2.30$, $3.4 \times 2.3 = 7.82$

   c) e.g., The answers were the same; both times you had to multiply 34 by 23 and adjust the result to make it hundredths instead of ones.

14. e.g., $\frac{8}{5}$, $\frac{5}{4}$, and $\frac{7}{3}$

15. e.g., Mark has $3\frac{1}{2}$ times as many marbles as I have, and Kyle has $2\frac{1}{3}$ times as many as Mark has. how many times as many marbles does Kyle have as I have?

16. Disagree, e.g., $2\frac{2}{3} \times 3\frac{3}{4} = 10$, which is not a mixed number using twelfths.

Mid-Chapter Review, pp. 66–67

1. a) $\frac{1}{5} + \frac{1}{5} + \frac{1}{5} + \frac{1}{5} + \frac{1}{5} + \frac{1}{5}, \frac{6}{5}, 1\frac{1}{5}$

b) $\frac{5}{12} + \frac{5}{12} + \frac{5}{12} + \frac{5}{12}, \frac{20}{12}$ or $\frac{5}{3}, 1\frac{2}{3}$

c) $\frac{3}{5} + \frac{3}{5} + \frac{3}{5} + \frac{3}{5} + \frac{3}{5} + \frac{3}{5} + \frac{3}{5} + \frac{3}{5}, \frac{24}{5}, 4\frac{4}{5}$

d) $\frac{4}{9} + \frac{4}{9} + \frac{4}{9} + \frac{4}{9} + \frac{4}{9}, \frac{20}{9}, 2\frac{2}{9}$

2. a) $\frac{9}{8}$ or $1\frac{1}{8}$ **c)** $\frac{25}{6}$ or $4\frac{1}{6}$

b) $\frac{10}{9}$ or $1\frac{1}{9}$ **d)** $\frac{8}{5}$ or $1\frac{3}{5}$

3. e.g., $8 \times \frac{3}{5}$

4. e.g.,

5. a) $\frac{1}{14}$ **b)** $\frac{3}{4}$ **c)** $\frac{1}{3}$

6. a) $\frac{1}{18}$ **b)** $\frac{12}{35}$

7. a) $\frac{3}{6} \times \frac{2}{5} = \frac{1}{5}$

b) $\frac{2}{4} \times \frac{6}{7} = \frac{3}{7}$

c) $\frac{3}{5} \times \frac{1}{2} = \frac{3}{10}$

8. Yes, e.g., $\frac{2}{8} \times \frac{1}{5} = \frac{2}{40}$, which is equivalent to $\frac{1}{20}$.

9. $\frac{3}{16}$

10. a)

11. a) $1\frac{1}{2}$ **c)** $2\frac{2}{9}$ **e)** $10\frac{5}{16}$

b) $\frac{16}{25}$ **d)** $5\frac{2}{5}$ **f)** $20\frac{2}{5}$

12. $1\frac{2}{5}$

2.6 Dividing Fractions by Whole Numbers, pp. 70–71

1. $\frac{2}{9}$

2. a) $\frac{2}{7}$ **b)** $\frac{5}{21}$

c) You need to use an equivalent fraction in part b) to make equal parts, but not in part a).

3. a) $\frac{1}{4} \times \frac{5}{6}$ **b)** You want $\frac{1}{4}$ of 5 out of 6.

4. a) $\frac{2}{9}$ **c)** $\frac{1}{6}$ **e)** $\frac{2}{15}$

b) $\frac{1}{18}$ **d)** $\frac{1}{10}$ **f)** $\frac{7}{24}$

5. a) e.g., The quotients are $\frac{2}{9}, \frac{7}{16}$, and $\frac{8}{27}$; $\frac{7}{16}$ is almost $\frac{1}{2}$ and $\frac{8}{27} > \frac{8}{32}$, which is $\frac{1}{4}$, but $\frac{2}{9} < \frac{2}{8}$, which is $\frac{1}{4}$.

6. $\frac{5}{24}$ of a can

7. $\frac{5}{24}$

8. a) $\frac{4}{25}$

b) $80\% \div 5 = 16\%$

c) $16\% = \frac{16}{100} = \frac{4}{25}$; that was the answer to a).

9. e.g., **a)** I have $\frac{2}{3}$ of the lawn left to rake. Three of my friends agree to share the job with me. How much do we each have to rake?

b) Each rakes $\frac{1}{6}$ of the lawn.

10. a) You are always dividing 8 pieces into 2 groups, so you get 4 in a group.

b) because the piece sizes are different

11. Yes, e.g., if you divide a fraction by, for example, 5, you divide each piece into 5 and keep one of them. Since the original number of parts was the denominator of the fraction, you would have 5 times as many.

2.7 Estimating Fraction Quotients, pp. 74–75

1. e.g., You can see that about 7 of the $\frac{1}{12}$ make up the $\frac{5}{9}$.

2. a) 2   **b)** 2   **c)** 4

3. e.g., 8 of the tenths are close to $\frac{5}{6}$.

4. e.g., about 2

5. a) about 4   **c)** about 6   **e)** about 8

b) about 6   **d)** about 7   **f)** about 1

6. about 2

7. e.g., $\frac{7}{8}$ is close to 1 and $\frac{2}{7}$ is close to $\frac{1}{4}$. It is easier to figure out how many fourths are in 1.

8. a) e.g., $\frac{1}{4} \div \frac{1}{7}$ **b)** e.g., $\frac{4}{5} \div \frac{1}{4}$

9. a) e.g., $\frac{4}{10} \div \frac{1}{11}$ **b)** e.g., $\frac{1}{3} \div \frac{1}{24}$ **c)** e.g., $\frac{1}{4} \div \frac{1}{80}$

10. about 40

11. e.g., You have $\frac{7}{8}$ of a can of sauce and you need $\frac{1}{3}$ cup for a recipe. How many recipes can you make?

12. e.g., $\frac{5}{6} > \frac{3}{4}$, so not even 1 whole $\frac{5}{6}$ fits into $\frac{3}{4}$.

13. a) e.g., Estimate using $1 \div \frac{2}{10} = 5$ or estimate
  using $\frac{77}{88} \div \frac{14}{88}$, which is about $70 \div 14 = 5$.
b) e.g., I think the first way is easier.

2.8 Dividing Fractions by Measuring, pp. 79–80

1. $\frac{2}{3} \div \frac{2}{9}$

2. $3\frac{1}{2}$

| $\frac{1}{8}$ | $\frac{1}{8}$ | $\frac{1}{8}$ | $\frac{1}{8}$ | $\frac{1}{8}$ | $\frac{1}{8}$ | $\frac{1}{8}$ | |

| $\frac{1}{4}$ | | | |

3. a) $\frac{5}{6}$ **b)** $3\frac{3}{4}$

4. $6\frac{2}{3}$

5. a) $\frac{3}{4} \div \frac{5}{8}$ **b)** $2 \div \frac{2}{5}$

6. a) 15 **b)** $2\frac{1}{10}$ **c)** $6\frac{2}{3}$ **d)** $\frac{18}{25}$

  e.g., Use a common denominator of 30 by
  multiplying the numerator and the denominator of
  $\frac{3}{5}$ by 6 and of $\frac{5}{6}$ by 5. The two fractions are then
  renamed $\frac{18}{30}$ and $\frac{25}{30}$. The $\frac{18}{30}$ fills out $\frac{18}{25}$ of the $\frac{25}{30}$,
  so the quotient is $\frac{18}{25}$.

7. $2\frac{1}{2}$ h

8. e.g., You can pour 10 glasses of juice from a
  pitcher. How many glasses can you pour from $\frac{1}{3}$ of
  a pitcher? Solution: $\frac{1}{3} \div \frac{1}{10} = \frac{10}{3}$, or $3\frac{1}{3}$

9. a) 13 times
b) e.g., Each time Alana checks the turkey there is
  $\frac{1}{3}$ of an hour less time until it is cooked.

10. e.g., Use equivalent fractions with a denominator
  of 10 and divide the numerators. $\frac{6}{10} \div \frac{5}{10} = \frac{6}{5}$

11. a) $\frac{3}{8}$ **b)** $\frac{9}{10}$ **c)** $\frac{16}{27}$ **d)** $1\frac{11}{45}$ **e)** $1\frac{5}{22}$ **f)** $\frac{16}{21}$

12. a) multiplication
b) division or multiplication

13. Yes, order matters; e.g., if one fraction fits into
  another more than once, if you switch the
  fractions, the larger one will not fit in even once.

14. e.g., There are 6 sixths in 1, so if you are trying to
  figure out how many sixths fit into one piece, you
  will get 6. Finding out how many sixths fit inside
  another number is the same as counting how many
  units of 6 pieces can fit inside. One is division by $\frac{1}{6}$
  and the other is multiplication by 6, so they are the
  same thing.

15. a) division
b) e.g., $2\frac{1}{2} \div \frac{1}{3}$ gives a fraction. If each section
  was $\frac{1}{3}$ of an hour long, the quotient would be a
  whole number.

16. e.g., $\frac{5}{a} = \frac{2}{a} + \frac{2}{a} + \frac{1}{a}$; If you divide by $\frac{2}{a}$, you can
  see there are 2 groups of $\frac{2}{a}$ in $\frac{5}{a}$. The $\frac{1}{a}$ is half of $\frac{2}{a}$,
  so there are $2\frac{1}{2}$ groups.

2.9 Dividing Fractions Using a Related Multiplication, pp. 85–86

1. a) $\frac{3}{4}$ **b)** $2\frac{5}{8}$

2. $2\frac{1}{2}$ small cans

3. a) $1\frac{1}{2}$ **b)** $1\frac{1}{2}$ **c)** $\frac{4}{7}$ **d)** $1\frac{1}{5}$ **e)** $\frac{1}{2}$ **f)** $\frac{3}{4}$

4. $3\frac{1}{3}$ snack packs

5. e.g., When dividing, you multiply by the
  reciprocal. You would be multiplying $\frac{7}{8}$ by $\frac{4}{3}$,
  which is greater than 1, and you would get a
  product greater than $\frac{7}{8}$.

6. b) and d)

7. a) $2; \frac{64}{35}$ **b)** $4; \frac{68}{15}$ **c)** $4; \frac{105}{28}$

8. a) 3 **b)** $2\frac{4}{5}$ **c)** $1\frac{5}{6}$ **d)** $3\frac{8}{9}$ **e)** $1\frac{31}{33}$ **f)** $2\frac{29}{35}$

9. a) ii) and iii)
b) e.g., If the first fraction is greater than the
  second, then the answer is greater than 1.

10. a) $2\frac{2}{9}$ **b)** $4\frac{1}{6}$ **c)** not greater than 2 **d)** $2\frac{5}{8}$

11. e.g., $\frac{1}{2}$ and $\frac{4}{3}$

12. a) $13\frac{1}{3}$ pages/min
b) 15 pages/min

13. $3\frac{3}{4}$ pitchers

14. a) $6\frac{2}{3}$ laps   **b)** $4\frac{4}{9}$ laps   **c)** $3\frac{1}{3}$ laps

15. a) 1.5   **b)** $\frac{3}{2}$

   c) e.g., The answers are equivalent.

16. 5 blue blocks

17. a) e.g., A small glass of juice holds $\frac{2}{3}$ as much as a large glass. How many small glasses can you fill by pouring in juice from $1\frac{1}{8}$ large glasses?

   b) e.g., It takes $2\frac{2}{3}$ glasses of juice to fill a pitcher. If you have room to fill $1\frac{2}{5}$ pitchers, what fraction of the $2\frac{2}{3}$ glasses of juice can you use?

2.10 Order of Operations, pp. 90–91

1. a) 9   **b)** $\frac{25}{36}$

2. e.g., $\frac{2}{5} \div \frac{1}{4} + \frac{3}{8} = 1\frac{39}{40}$,

$\frac{2}{5} \div \frac{3}{8} + \frac{1}{4} = 1\frac{19}{60}$,

$\frac{2}{5} + \frac{1}{4} \div \frac{3}{8} = 1\frac{1}{15}$

3. a) $1\frac{1}{12}$ **b)** $1\frac{2}{3}$ **c)** $1\frac{37}{60}$ **d)** $\frac{29}{120}$ **e)** $\frac{37}{10}$ **f)** $\frac{19}{24}$

4. a) e.g., $\frac{1}{2} - \frac{2}{9} \div \frac{4}{5} = \frac{2}{9}$, $\frac{4}{5} - \frac{2}{9} \div \frac{1}{2} = \frac{16}{45}$,

$\frac{4}{5} \div \frac{1}{2} - \frac{2}{9} = 1\frac{17}{45}$

   b) e.g., $\left(\frac{4}{5} - \frac{1}{2}\right) \div \frac{2}{9} = 1\frac{7}{20}$

5. a) and b)

6. a) $\frac{9}{35}$ **b)** $6\frac{7}{12}$ **c)** $12\frac{1}{2}$ **d)** $\frac{22}{28}$ **e)** $5\frac{7}{9}$ **f)** $4\frac{4}{63}$

7. a) i) $\frac{23}{30}$ **ii)** $\frac{101}{120}$ **iii)** $\frac{19}{30}$

   b) e.g., Inserting brackets in the same expression in different places can change the answer.

8. 144

9. $2 + \left(\frac{1}{4} + \frac{1}{3}\right) \times \frac{3}{7} - \frac{2}{5} \times \frac{3}{8} \div \left(\frac{1}{10} + \frac{1}{5}\right)$

10. e.g., $a = \frac{35}{36}$, $b = \frac{1}{36}$, and $c = \frac{5}{6}$

   or $a = \frac{48}{49}$, $b = \frac{1}{49}$, and $c = \frac{6}{7}$

11. a), b), d)

12. e.g., $\frac{4}{5} + \frac{1}{3} \times \frac{3}{5}$

13. e.g., Some students might add before they multiply, and get a different answer.

2.11 Communicate about Multiplication and Division, pp. 94–95

1. a) e.g., 8 out of every 9 students I surveyed had a brother or sister, and $\frac{2}{3}$ of those who had a brother also had a sister. What fraction of the students I surveyed had both a brother and a sister? Solution: $\frac{16}{27}$.

   b) e.g., because you are taking one fraction of another fraction. It is $\frac{2}{3}$ of the $\frac{8}{9}$ that I had information about, not $\frac{2}{3}$ of the whole group.

   c) e.g., $\frac{16}{27}$ is close to $\frac{18}{27}$, which is $\frac{2}{3}$. Since $\frac{8}{9}$ is close to 1, $\frac{2}{3}$ of it should be close to $\frac{2}{3}$.

2. In the first grid, $\frac{2}{3}$ represents the first two rows, and $\frac{3}{5}$ of each row is shaded. This gives 6 shaded boxes out of 15. In the second grid, $\frac{3}{5}$ represents the first 3 rows, and $\frac{2}{3}$ of the row is shaded. This also gives 6 shaded boxes out of 15.

3. a) e.g., Small pizzas are $\frac{3}{5}$ the size of medium ones. There were 3 small pizzas for 4 people to share. What was the size of a medium pizza that each one got?

   b) e.g., Another calculation I could have done would be $\frac{3}{5} \times \frac{1}{4} \times 3$, since dividing by 4 is always the same as multiplying by $\frac{1}{4}$.

4. a) $2 \div \frac{2}{3}$ is the same as $\frac{6}{3} \div \frac{2}{3}$.

   b) e.g., $2 \div \frac{2}{3}$ means that 2 wholes are divided into thirds and the thirds are put in groups of 2.

5. e.g., To calculate $\frac{1}{5}$ of 3.55, I took $\frac{1}{5}$ of each hundredths grid. $\frac{1}{5}$ of the first hundredths grid is 20 hundredths, and $\frac{1}{5}$ of the second and third grids is also 20 hundredths each. $\frac{1}{5}$ of the last grid is $55 \div 5 = 11$ hundredths. This gives a total of $20 + 20 + 20 + 11 = 71$ hundredths, so the total is $3.55 + 0.71 = 4.26$.

6. $\frac{42}{10} \times \frac{2}{10} = \frac{84}{100}$ $\frac{84}{100} = 0.84$

7. a) e.g., $60\% = \frac{60}{100}$ or $\frac{30}{50}$ or $\frac{3}{5}$; $1.5 = 2$ halves $+ 1$ half, or $\frac{3}{2}$.

   b) e.g., No, I think it is easier to calculate 60% of 1 and then 60% of 0.5—60% of 1 is 0.6, and 60% of 0.5 is 0.3, so 60% of 1.5 = 0.9.

8. e.g., Another name for 1 is $\frac{n}{n}$. It does not matter what value you use for n, as long as it is not zero. When you multiply $\frac{a}{b} \times \frac{n}{n}$, you end up multiplying the numerator by n and the denominator by n. Multiplying by 1 does not change anything.

9. Agree; e.g., $1\frac{2}{5} \times \frac{1}{2} = 1.4 \times 0.5 = 0.7$; Disagree; e.g., $1\frac{1}{3} \times \frac{1}{4}$ is about 1.33×0.25; it is easier to multiply as fractions, e.g., $\frac{4}{3} \times \frac{1}{4} = \frac{1}{3}$.

10. e.g., Alike: when you multiply the numerators and multiply the denominators, you are multiplying whole numbers. Different: the answer can be a fraction that cannot be expressed as a whole number.

11. e.g., You know that 6×3 is 18 and $3\frac{1}{2} \times 6$ is 21. Since these numbers are less than or equal to the given numbers, the product of $3\frac{1}{2}$ and $6\frac{1}{3}$ must be greater than 21.

12. e.g., Since $\frac{5}{8}$ is exactly twice the size of $\frac{5}{16}$, it will fit into $\frac{15}{16}$ exactly half as many times.

Chapter Self-Test, p. 96

1. e.g.,

2. a) $\frac{1}{6}$ **b)** $\frac{1}{3}$ **c)** $\frac{24}{35}$

3. e.g., Multiplying by $\frac{5}{6}$ means taking $\frac{5}{6}$ of something; that is only part of it, not all of it, so the answer is less than the number you started with.

4. a) $\frac{3}{8}$ **b)** $\frac{5}{18}$ **c)** $\frac{1}{14}$ **d)** $\frac{15}{56}$

5. e.g., $2\frac{1}{4} + \frac{2}{3} \times \frac{9}{4} = 3\frac{3}{4}$ or $\frac{5}{3} \times \frac{9}{4} = \frac{15}{4}$ or $3\frac{3}{4}$

6. a) $3\frac{3}{10}$ **b)** $4\frac{29}{40}$ **c)** $2\frac{9}{20}$ **d)** $1\frac{5}{27}$

7. a) e.g.,

| $\frac{1}{4}$ | $\frac{1}{4}$ | $\frac{1}{4}$ | $\frac{1}{4}$ |

| $\frac{1}{8}$ | $\frac{1}{8}$ | $\frac{1}{8}$ | $\frac{1}{8}$ | $\frac{1}{8}$ | $\frac{1}{8}$ | $\frac{1}{8}$ | $\frac{1}{8}$ |

b) $\frac{3}{4} \times \frac{8}{5} = 1\frac{1}{5}$

8. a) 2 **b)** $3\frac{1}{8}$ **c)** $\frac{8}{25}$ **d)** $2\frac{4}{5}$

9. a) $\frac{9}{16}$ **b)** $\frac{25}{144}$ **c)** $\frac{1}{4}$

1. e.g.,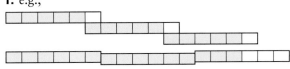

2. a) $6\frac{2}{5}$ **b)** $3\frac{3}{5}$ **c)** $2\frac{4}{7}$ **d)** 8

3. a) $\frac{1}{10}$ **b)** $\frac{1}{3}$ **c)** $\frac{1}{2}$ **d)** $\frac{1}{3}$

4. a) $\frac{3}{5}$ **b)** $\frac{3}{4}$

5.

6. a) $\frac{4}{63}$ **b)** $\frac{6}{35}$ **c)** $\frac{5}{12}$ **d)** $\frac{1}{7}$

7. $\frac{2}{9}$

8. a), c), d)

9. e.g.,

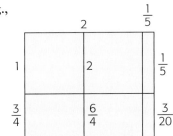

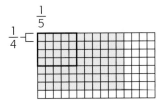

10. a) $\frac{7}{5}$ **b)** $\frac{156}{20}$ or $\frac{39}{5}$

11. 45 employees

12. e.g.,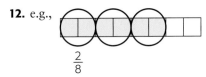

$\frac{2}{8}$

13. a) $\frac{3}{10}$ **b)** $\frac{9}{20}$ **c)** $\frac{2}{15}$

14. e.g., You have halves that you are dividing by 3, or into sixths.

15. a) and c)

16. $\frac{1}{2} \div \frac{1}{4}$

17. e.g.,

18. e.g., Since each set of numbers has a common denominator, you need to compare only the numerators, so $\frac{4}{6} \div \frac{3}{6} = \frac{4}{3}$ and $\frac{4}{5} \div \frac{3}{5} = \frac{4}{3}$.

19. a) 5   **b)** $2\frac{1}{2}$ **c)** $3\frac{1}{3}$ **d)** $1\frac{11}{16}$

20. $\frac{9}{2} \div \frac{1}{4} = 18$

21. $\frac{8}{9}$ of her sugar

22. A; e.g., you can tell which fraction is the largest by comparing the numerators. If the fractions have the same denominator, compare the numerators to determine the greatest value.

23. $3 \times \left(\frac{2}{3} + \frac{1}{3}\right) \div \frac{1}{4} = 12$

24. e.g., 4.5 is $4\frac{1}{2}$, or $\frac{9}{2}$, and 0.5 is $\frac{1}{2}$, so $\frac{9}{2} \times \frac{1}{2} = \frac{9}{4}$, or 2.25.

Chapter 3, p. 102

3.1 Using Two-Term Ratios, pp. 110–112

1. A. $2:5, 2:5 = 4:\blacksquare, 10$
   B. $3:5, 3:5 = \blacksquare:15, 9$
   C. $2:5, 2:5 = 8:\blacksquare, 20$
   D. $3:9, 3:9 = 4:\blacksquare, 12$

2. a) 6   **b)** 15

3. a) e.g.,   **b)** e.g.,

4. a) e.g., 3 to 8, 6 to 16, 12 to 32
   b) e.g., $1:9, 2:18, 3:27$
   c) e.g., $4:3, 8:6, 16:12$
   d) e.g., $\frac{2}{5}, \frac{4}{10}, \frac{6}{15}$
   e) e.g., 1 to 6, 2 to 12, 14 to 84
   f) e.g., $\frac{6}{16}, \frac{9}{24}, \frac{12}{32}$

5. e.g., In figures A and B, 3 out of 5 columns are shaded, representing a ratio of $3:5$. In figure C, 6 out of 10 columns are shaded and both parts of the ratio can be divided by 2, which is the same as $3:5$.

6. a) 3   **b)** 9   **c)** 6   **d)** 20

7. a) e.g., $400:1000$
   b) e.g., 60 to 7
   c) e.g., 200 to 180

8. a) e.g.,
   b) e.g., blue to white $= 3:1$, blue to total $= \frac{3}{4}$
   c) e.g., $6:2$ and $\frac{6}{8}$

9. a) e.g., $30:420 = 1:14$
   b) e.g., $150:2100 = 1:14$
   c) 15 h

10. B

11. 820 bears

12. 172 cm

13. e.g., In the aquatic world races, the U.S. won 35 medals and Australia won 22, so the ratio was $35:22$. It is a ratio, since you are comparing two quantities.

14. a) e.g., The probability is $\frac{8}{30}$, since a 5 was rolled 8 times out of 30. It is a part-to-whole ratio.
   b) $8:4$
   c) yes, rolls of 1 to the rolls of 6
   d) e.g.,

Roll of	1	2	3	4	5	6
How many times	1	2	2	2	2	1

15. a) e.g., the ratio of the number of teachers to the total number of students and teachers on a field trip
   b) e.g., the ratio of the number of times you spin a number on a spinner to the number of times you do not spin that number

16. 12 cm, 16 cm

17. e.g., To get an equivalent ratio, you multiply both terms by the same amount.

3.2 Using Ratio Tables, pp. 116–117

1. a)

Boys	2	20	40	10	30
Girls	3	30	60	15	45

   b)

Bottles of juice	60	6	18	66	54
Bottles of water	90	9	27	99	81

2. a) 54   **b)** 45   **c)** 33   **d)** 96

3. 0.5 L

4. a) 15 **b)** 945 **c)** 14 **d)** 36

5. a) 20.25 kg **b)** 80 kg

6. a) e.g., 3 cm on the map represents 2 000 000 cm or 20 000 m or 20 km.
   b) 10.2 cm

7. 3000 people

8. a) e.g., 4 blue, 9 red, and 16 blue, 36 red
   b) e.g., 8 blue, 9 red; 16 blue, 18 red; 24 blue, 36 red

9. e.g., Using a ratio table is helpful when solving proportions. It is easy to multiply, divide, add, and subtract to determine equivalent ratios.

Mid-Chapter Review, p. 121

1. a) e.g., $8:18$, $16:36$, $32:72$ **b)** yes; yes

2. a) 1 **b)** 35 **c)** 34

3. a) $\frac{3}{8}$ **b)** 1.25 L

4. a) $50:50$ **b)** $16:12$

5. a)

Number of days	7	49	140	28	56
Number of school days	5	35	100	20	40

b)

Number of dimes	1	9	8	6	80
Value of dimes	10¢	90¢	80¢	60¢	800¢

6. 49

7. 20 red, 12 blue, and 4 purple

3.4 Using Rates, pp. 124–125

1. a) e.g., 0.5 goals/game, 20 goals/40 games
   b) e.g., 20 km/2 h, 0.17 km/min
   c) e.g., 2 penalties/5 games, 0.4 penalties/game

2. a) 4 km/h **b)** 8 km

3. a) 108 **b)** 160 **c)** $90 **d)** 4

4. a) 3 CDs
   b) e.g., Since 28 is half of 56, it is easier to divide 4 in half to get 2.

5. a) $1.85/kg **b)** $1.58/L **c)** $12.59/m²

6. a) 1.92 points/game **b)** about 152

7. 9 kg

8. 11 520 times

9. e.g., to decide which of two brands costs less

10. about 11 min

11. e.g., My mom drove 240 km in 3 h. What is her speed in km/h? Answer: Write the distance and time as a ratio, $240:3 = 80:1$. Her speed is 80 km/h.

3.5 Communicate about Ratios and Rates, p. 128

1. yes

2. 1800 flyers. e.g., He gets $1/40 flyers. To get $45, he needs to deliver $45 \times 40 = 1800$ flyers.

3. no

4. a) 55¢
   b) e.g., 550 g of golden raisins
   c) yes

5. 2400 KB, 1200 KB

6. no

7. solution to $8:10 = 20:$ ▪

8. no

3.6 Using Equivalent Ratios to Solve Problems, pp. 132–133

1. 158.4 cm

2. no

3. a) 3.3 min **b)** 13.3 min **c)** 23.3 min

4. about 200 000

5. about 119 min

6. pig: about 367 m, chicken: about 300 m

7. about 79.7 km/h

8. 58.5 cm

9. e.g., for a school of 800 students, 320

10. a) $44.1:30.5$
   b) 21.1 million tonnes

11. a) about 2530 km²
   b) more crowded
   c) 4.9 billion

12. e.g., Set up a proportion, 212 hits/1000 at bats = ▪ hits/400 at bats, and solve for the number of hits.

13. e.g., Two out of every three students who tried out for the musical were girls. If 48 students tried out, how many were boys? Answer: 16

   e.g., Two cans of tuna cost $3. How much will 5 cans cost? Answer: $7.50

Chapter Self-Test, p. 134

1. a) e.g., 15 : 27, 25 : 45   **b)** 50 : 90, 90 : 162

2.

blue	3	24	27	54	51
yellow	4	32	36	72	68
red	8	64	72	144	136

3. a) 10   **b)** 9   **c)** 28   **d)** 21

4. 150 cells

5. $104

6. 45 cats

7. 96 000

8. about 6 min

9. $8.90, e.g., Calculate the unit rate for 1 bar, multiply the unit rate by the number of bars.

Chapter Review, p. 136

1. a) e.g., 18 : 40, 36 : 80   **c)** e.g., 7 to 1, 14 to 2

   b) e.g., $\frac{8}{10}, \frac{16}{20}$ **d)** e.g., 6 : 0.5, 12 : 1

2. a) 72   **b)** 136   **c)** 4

3. a) 1 : 2   **b)** 1 : 4

4.

Boys	15	30	45	5	50
Girls	18	36	54	6	60

5. 82.5

6. $\frac{8}{15}, \frac{4}{15}, \frac{2}{15}, \frac{1}{15}$

7. a) 8 cookies/$1   **b)** 2.5 kg of sugar/$1

8. 3 tosses for 50¢

9. e.g., I would show that 20 : 30 is equivalent to 2 : 3, since 20 ÷ 10 : 30 ÷ 10 = 2 : 3; 2 : 3 is equivalent to 25 : 37.5, not 25 : 35, since 2 × 12.5 : 3 × 12.5 = 25 : 37.5.

10. 400 g of lettuce, 200 g of cabbage, and 150 g of carrots

11. 12 L/100 km

Cumulative Review: Chapters 1–3, pp. 138–139

1. B   **6.** A   **11.** B   **16.** B
2. C   **7.** D   **12.** D   **17.** B
3. C   **8.** C   **13.** B   **18.** D
4. A   **9.** A   **14.** C   **19.** C
5. B   **10.** A   **15.** D

Chapter 4, p. 140

4.1 Percents Greater than 100%, pp.147–149

1. 215%

2.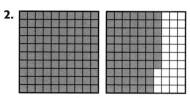

3. 165 cm

4. a)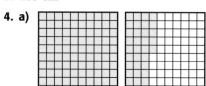

   b)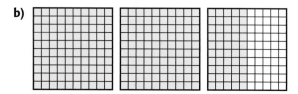

   c)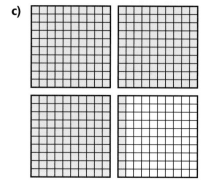

5. e.g., Paul would be correct if the first grid represents 100%, and Rebecca would be correct if the two grids together represent 100%.

6. a) 48   **b)** 260   **c)** 52.8   **d)** 45

7. 350%

8. a) $45   **b)** $155

9. e.g., The comparison would not make sense because litres and hours are different quantities.

10. a) 1110   **b)** 1350

11. a) 320 students   **b)** 40%

12. a) 400%   **b)** 400%   **c)** e.g., about 140%
   d) e.g., What percent of its side length is the perimeter of an equilateral triangle? 300%

13. a) e.g., about 400%   **b)** e.g., about 25%

14. a) e.g., 2 and 10

b) 20%; 2 is $\frac{1}{5}$ of 10 and $\frac{1}{5}$ = 20%

4.2 Fractional Percents, pp. 152–153

1. a)

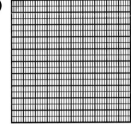

b)

c)

2. 5 g of sugar

3. a) 3.5%   **b)** 4.75%

4. a) 5 g   **b)** 0.5 g   **c)** 12.5 g

5. a) e.g., 2; 1% of 630 is about 600 ÷ 100 = 6, so 0.1% = 0.6; 0.3% is 3 times as much. 3 × 0.6 = 1.8. Since 630 is more than 600, the estimate should be increased to 2.

b)

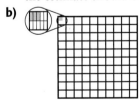

c) 1.89

6. 2.5 g

7. a) 9.3 mL   **b)** 0.3 mL

8. $8000

9. a) 0.1% of a number is the number divided by 1000, and 1 m is equal to 1000 mm. 1000 mm ÷ 1000 = 1 mm.

b) 0.32%

10. a), b), c)

11. when the number is a multiple of 1000

12. No; e.g., 5.1% is 0.1% more than 5%; if the number is very big, then 0.1% could still be a lot. e.g., If the number is 1 000 000, 0.1% is 1000, so the numbers would be 1000 apart.

4.3 Relating Percents to Decimals and Fractions, pp. 157–158

1. a) 75%   **b)** 120%

2. a) 0.011   **b)** $\frac{11}{1000}$

3. a) $\frac{3}{8}$, 0.375, 37.5%   **b)** $\frac{34}{10}$, 3.4, 340%

4. a) $\frac{32}{1000}$, 0.032   **b)** 125%, 1.25   **c)** 6.4%, $\frac{64}{1000}$

5. $\frac{136}{100}$ and 1.36

6. a) 16.67%   **b)** 58.33%   **c)** 25%

7. a) e.g., 40%

b) The bar was 40 mm long and the shaded part was 16 mm, which is 0.4 of 40.

c) e.g., 0.40 and $\frac{2}{5}$

8. a) $\frac{9}{100}$ **b)** 9%   **c)** about 130 min

9. $\frac{41}{10}$ and 4.1

10. 450%

11. a) $\frac{14}{6}$, 233%   **b)** 2 red, 3 blue

12. a) e.g., Set up the proportion $\frac{20}{\blacksquare} = \frac{2.5}{100}$ and solve it by getting a common denominator of 100 × ▪. The numerators of 20 × 100 and 2.5 × ▪ would be equal. To solve 20 × 100 = 2.5 × ▪, divide 20 by 2.5 and then multiply by 100.

b) 0.025 is $\frac{1}{100}$ of 2.5, so there are 100 times as many pieces of size 0.025 as pieces of size 2.5 in a number. So, ▪ ÷ 0.025 = 100 × ▪ ÷ 2.5 and I know from part a) that that is a way to calculate the answer.

13. 100%

14. e.g., To write a decimal as a percent, just multiply by 100 using mental math. If the fraction is an easy one, like $\frac{1}{10}$ or $\frac{1}{100}$, it is easy to write as a percent.

4.4 Solving Problems Using a Proportion, pp. 161–162

1. e.g., The percents go from 0 to 425; 425% is a bit more than 400%, and 400% is 4 groups of 100%. Since 100% is 85 from the second number line, to get 425% of 85 multiply 85 by 4 and add a bit.

2. 32.24 kg

3. a) 108   **b)** 180   **c)** 24   **d)** 11

4. e.g., 32; 20 is a little more than halfway to 100%, so the number is between 30 and 40, or about 32.

5. e.g., **a)**

0%	20%	40%	60%	80%	100%
0	23	46	69	92	115

b)

0%	20%	40%	60%	80%	100%
0	10	20	30	40	50

6. about 2.8 billion downloads

7. a) $\frac{5}{1000}$ **b)** 0.5%   **c)** 20 000%

8. e.g., 3 330 000

9. e.g., 1.26 million

10. e.g., A percent is a ratio where the second term is 100. If you are trying to compare one number to another and write it as a percent, you are trying to get an equivalent ratio where the second term is 100.

4.5 Solving Percent Problems Using Decimals, pp. 165–167

1. a) $0.152 \times 35 = $ ▓, 5.32
   b) $1.24 \times 18 = $ ▓, 22.32
   c) $40 \div 0.055 = $ ▓, 727.27
   d) $30 \div 1.60 = $ ▓, 18.75

2. 560

3. a) 7   **b)** 1.125   **c)** 160   **d)** 3000

4. a) What is 45% of 36?
   b) What is 120% of 45?
   c) What is 0.4% of 180?
   d) 56 is 7% of what number?
   e) 36 is 180% of what number?
   f) 90 is 0.5% of what number?

5. a) $209.99   **b)** $83.99   **c)** $52.49

6. $500

7. about 80

8. about 187

9. The 13.3% of the population that they make up now is a percent of the current population and not the population in 2045.

10. 1 691 648 people

11. $164.62

12. 8

13. a) e.g., Last year, the school population was 400 students. The population grew by 125%. What is the new population?
   b) e.g., A school population is now 400 students, which is 125% of the original population. What was the original population?
   c) e.g., 3.5% of the students in a school of 400 competed in a math contest. How many students competed?

Mid-Chapter Review, p. 169

1. a)

b)

c)

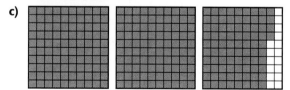

2. a)

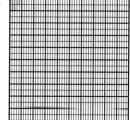

b)

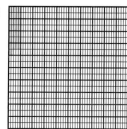

c)

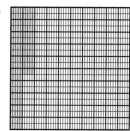

3. action: 20 students, fantasy: 5 students, sports: 15 students

4. a) e.g., 150%, 135 is close to 150, and 95 is close to 100, and $\frac{150}{100}$ is 150%.

b) e.g., 120%, 29 is close to 30, and 26 is close to 25, and $\frac{30}{25}$ is 120%.

c) e.g., 0.5%, 6 is about $\frac{1}{100}$, or 1%, of 640, and 3 is half of that.

5. 27

6. 40

7. a) 15.15 L   **b)** 220 L

4.6 Solve Problems by Changing Your Point of View, p. 173

1. a) 0.8 × price   **b)** 1.05 × price

2. e.g., Double 20% and then add half of the number; or triple 20% and subtract half of the number.

3. $51.44

4. $508.50

5. 64 cm^2

6. e.g., Bella 10 days, Alan 3 days, and Richard 15 days; or Bella 20 days, Alan 6 days, and Richard 30 days

7. $540

8. e.g., When you use a ratio table, you can decide what percents to put together to make the necessary percent, so it is your own point of view.

4.8 Combining Percents, pp. 176–177

1. discount $84.99, final cost $267.71

2. $28 400

3. a) $35.99   **b)** $131.99   **c)** $1.80

4. a) i) $134.96   **ii)** $74.99   **iii)** $24.84
   b) i) $141.71   **ii)** $78.74   **iii)** $26.08

5. Yes; suppose the item was $100, the discount was 10%, and the taxes were 5%. If you do the taxes first and then the discount, you would take 90% of $105 = $94.50. If you take the discount first and then do the taxes, you would take 105% of $90 = $94.50.

6. $87.50

7. the second store

8. a) 14%   **b)** 15.6%

9. The 25% is based on a price of $150, so the added amount is 25% of 150. However, the reduction is based on the new price, which is higher, so the reduction is 25% of a higher number. The reduction is greater than the increase, so the final price is not the original price.

4.9 Percent Change, pp. 181–183

1. a) 65   **b)** 125   **c)** 40   **d)** 49.75

2. a) e.g., 10% of 8500 is 850 and 8% is less than 10%.

b) 108%   **c)** 9180   **d)** 92.59%

3. a) 50% decrease   **c)** 300% increase
   b) 12.5% increase   **d)** 10% decrease

4. 250%

5. 95.5%

6. $220

7. a) 15.09%; 30 782 − 26 745 = 4037. Compare 4037 to the 2001 population since that is the population that increased. $\frac{4037}{26\ 745}$ = 0.1509, so the percent increase is 15.09%.

b) 35 427

8. a) 11.48%   **b)** 111.48%

9. a) 3939 homes   **b)** 3374 homes

10. No, the increase was 1.5 hours, which is 3 times $\frac{1}{2}$ hour. That means the increase was only 300%.

11. 137.5%

12. about 1.6 kg

13. 19.3 million

14. 6.7 million

15. a) 3.5%   **b)** $7.76

16. b), c), d); e.g., A decrease of 25% means the new price is 75% of the old one. The first choice is 125% of the old price, not 75%, but all of the others are 75% of the original price.

Chapter Self-Test, p. 185

1. a) 77   **b)** 67.5

2. 3.5%

3. about 9.1%

4. 6700 km

5. 124 students

6. a) $42.83   **b)** 95%

7. 700%

Chapter Review, pp. 187–188

1. a)
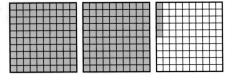

b)
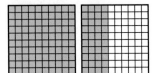

c)
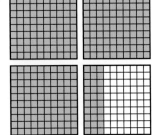

d)
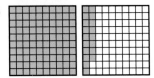

2. e.g., On Tuesday, I did homework for 1 h and on Wednesday I did it for 2 h, so the time spent on homework increased by 200%.

3. a) 240%
b) because the number of litres is not a percent of time

4. a)
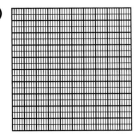

b)
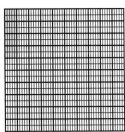

c)
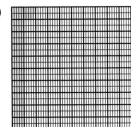

5. 615 students

6. a) $\frac{40}{100}$, 0.4, 40%   **b)** $\frac{205}{100}$, 2.05, 205%

7. a) 250%   **b)** 0.4%   **c)** 158%

8. 12.5%

9. a) 40   **b)** 20.8   **c)** 250%   **d)** 20 000

10. 3.2%

11. a) 11.2   **b)** 23.6   **c)** 45

12. 250 students

13. a) 65%   **b)** 105%

14. a) $24.13   **b)** $44.82   **c)** $5.38   **d)** $50.20

15. a) 300% increase   **c)** 900% increase
b) 25% decrease   **d)** 90% decrease

16. 40.3%

Chapter 5, p. 190

5.2 Drawing the Nets of Prisms and Cylinders, pp. 198–199

1.

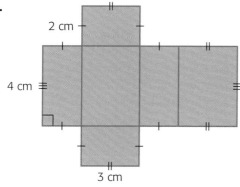

2. A and C

3.

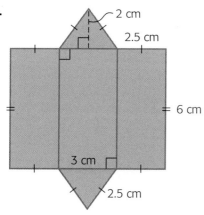

4. a)

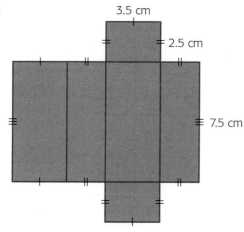

b)

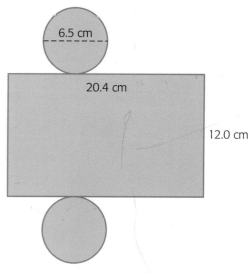

c)

5. a) triangular prism   **b)** cube

6. a) one rectangular prism and one triangular prism with the same width

b)

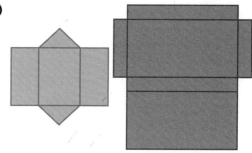

7. a)

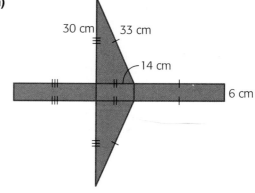

b)

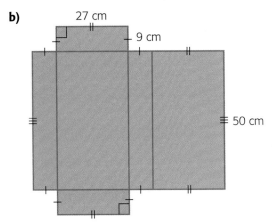

c)

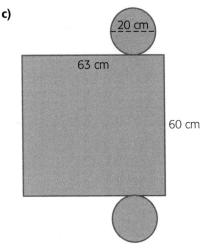

8. e.g., assuming the rolls are in a 1-by-8 array, standing up:

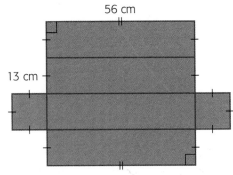

9. a) e.g., If the net has 6 sides, all of them rectangles, then it is likely to be a rectangular prism. If it has 5 sides, 2 of which are congruent triangles and 3 of which are congruent rectangles, it is likely to be a triangular prism. If it has two circles and a rectangle, it is likely to be a cylinder.

b) e.g., For a rectangular prism, draw the base rectangle, and the sides of the base around it. Add the top of the prism to one side. For a triangular prism, draw the base rectangle, and then the triangular bases of the prism at the ends of the rectangle. Draw the two other sides of the prism, connected on each side of the base. For a cylinder, draw two circles with the same radius as the cylinder. In between them, draw a rectangle whose length is the height of the cylinder and whose width is the circumference of the cylinder.

5.3 Determining the Surface Area of Prisms, pp. 205–206

1. a)

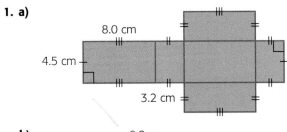

b)

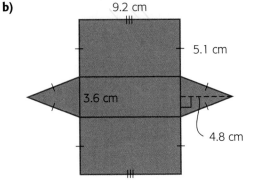

2. rectangular prism 152 cm², triangular prism 144.24 cm²

3. a)

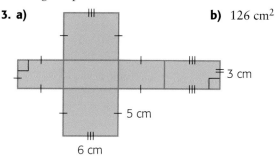

b) 126 cm²

4. a)

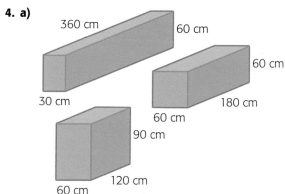

b)

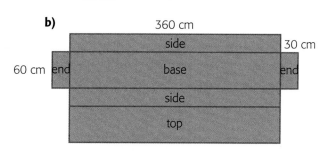

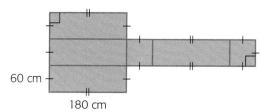

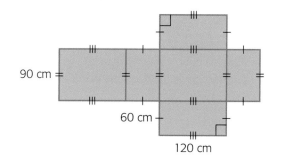

c) 68 400 cm²; 50 400 cm²; 46 800 cm²

d) e.g., The crate with the least surface area is 60 cm by 90 cm by 120 cm.

5. yes

6. a) 39.1 m²   **b)** 3 cans

7. 20.6 m²

8. figure B

9. greater than

10. a) e.g.,

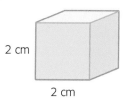

b) e.g., The new surface area is 4 times greater than the original surface area.

c) e.g., The new surface area is $\frac{1}{4}$ of the original surface area.

11. a) 376 m²   **b)** e.g., $h = 6$ m, $b = 6$ m, $l = 17.5$ m

12. e.g., to calculate how much material needs to be used to build or cover the prism

13. a) 5 separate areas but only 2 or 3 different areas

b) 6 separate areas but only 3 different areas

5.4 Determining the Surface Area of Cylinders, pp. 212–213

1. a) about 251 cm²   **b)** about 353.3 cm²

2. a) about 314 cm²   **b)** about 184.3 cm²

3. a) about 408.2 cm²

b) about 361.1 cm²

c) about 452.2 cm²

4. about 19 m²

5. a) about 0.60 m²   **b)** about 0.17 m²

6. a) about 188.9 m²   **b)** $175

7. If both cylinders have the same height but the circular base of each cylinder is different, the cylinders will have different surface areas.

8. about 2.4 m²

9. about 1.3 m²

10 a) about 162.9 m²

b) about 2491.6 m²

c) about 201.0 cm²

11. 53 CDs

12. Alike: you have to calculate the area of each surface and add them together. You can use the formula for the area of a rectangle to calculate at least one face of each. Different: you have to use the formula for the area of a circle to find the surface area of a cylinder.

Mid-Chapter Review, p. 216

1.

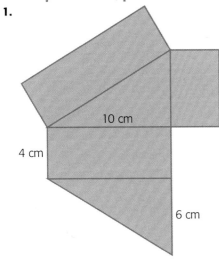

2. a) No, both circular faces are on the same side.
  b) yes
  c) No, circular faces are not on opposite sides.

3. 272 cm^2

4. 8.28 m^2

5. a)

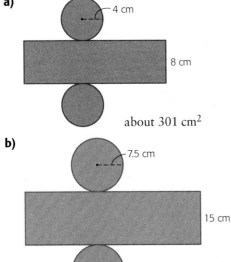

about 301 cm^2

  b)

about 1059.8 cm^2

c)

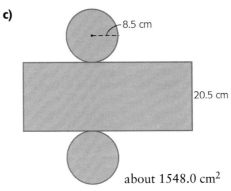

about 1548.0 cm^2

d)

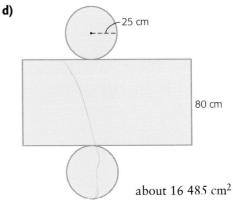

about 16 485 cm^2

6. about 2.8 m^2

5.5 Determining the Volume of Prisms, pp. 220–222

1. a) 84 cm^3 **b)** 43.0 cm^3 **c)** 165 cm^3

2. a) 1440 cm^3 **b)** 720 cm^3

3. a) 72 cm^3 **c)** 1020.0 cm^3 **e)** 42 cm^3
  b) 650.0 cm^3 **d)** 12.0 cm^3 **f)** 21.0 cm^3

4. a) 60 cm^3
  b) No, because B has the same dimensions as A, so they have the same volume.

5. a) 160 cm^3
  b) No, because both A and B are equal to half of a rectangular prism 10 cm × 4 cm × 8 cm.

6. a) 512 cm^3 **b)** 0.5 cm^3 **c)** 21.0 km^3

7. a) 288 cm^3 **b)** 9.6 cm   **c)** 3 cm

8. a) 144 cm^3 **b)** 40 cm

9. B; its volume is greater than A's, so Anthony would get more nails for the same price.

10. e.g., 41 160 cm^3

11. 432 000 cm^3 or 0.432 m^3

12. a)

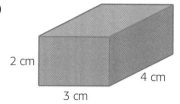

2 cm
4 cm
3 cm

   b) It is 8 times the original.
   c) It is $\frac{1}{8}$ the original.

13. the family size

14. a) red 384 cm³, white 384 cm³, blue 128 cm³, yellow 288 cm³, purple 512 cm³, green 352 cm³
   b) purple

15. e.g., A classroom about 8 m wide, 10 m long, and 3 m high has a volume of 240 m³.

16. no, if the bases are also equal

5.6 Determining the Volume of Cylinders, pp. 225–226

1. a) about 314 m³ **b)** about 337.6 cm³
2. a) about 8204.0 cm³ **b)** about 143.3 cm³
3. a) about 48.1 cm³ **b)** about 31.4 cm³
4. 72 times
5. e.g., about 27 500 L
6. about 220 cm³
7. 10.0 cm
8. 25 coins
9. B
10. the cylinder 10 cm in diameter and 7 cm high
11. a) 4.5 cm **b)** chicken soup can
12. Alike: you use the formula V = area of base × height to calculate the volume. Different: you calculate the area of the base differently, depending on whether it is a rectangle, a triangle, or a circle.

5.7 Solve Problems Using Models, p. 231

1. arrangement B
2. a) e.g., box A: 32 cm by 24 cm by 16 cm (4 cans by 3 cans by 2 cans); box B: 48 cm by 32 cm by 8 cm (6 cans by 4 cans by 1 can).
   b) box A; it uses less material.

3. a)

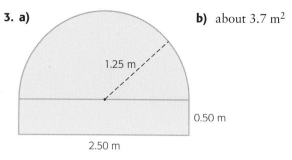

1.25 m
0.50 m
2.50 m

   b) about 3.7 m²

4. a) 24
   b) e.g., box A: 18 cm by 24 cm by 12 cm, surface area of 1872 cm²; box B: 12 cm by 36 cm by 12 cm, surface area of 2016 cm²; use box A as it has less surface area.

5. Assuming the pizza is 3 cm thick, it occupies 37% of the box and does not occupy 63% of the box.

6. yes, when the objects involved are simple

Chapter Self-Test, pp. 233–234

1. a) 354.3 cm² **b)** 1350 cm² **c)** 553.0 cm²
2.

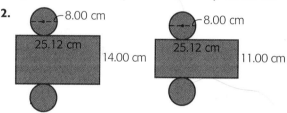

8.00 cm
25.12 cm
14.00 cm
8.00 cm
25.12 cm
11.00 cm

3. statement a)
4. a) 133.8 cm² **b)** 282.0 cm² **c)** 227.0 cm²
5. a) 140 cm³ **b)** 3780 cm³
6. A
7. a) surface area 420.4 cm², volume 652.2 cm³
   b) surface area 466 cm², volume 760 cm³
8. No, the volume is 31 500 cm³.
9. a) 20
   b) e.g.,

20 cm
75 cm
16 cm
40 cm
75 cm
8 cm

   I would use box A, as it uses less material.

Chapter Review, pp. 236–238

1. a)

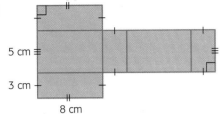

b)

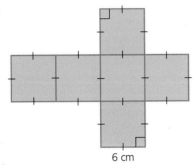

c)

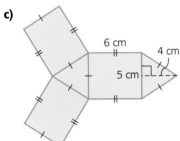

d)

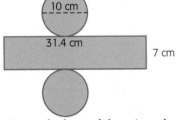

2. e.g., Draw the base of the prism, the two sides, the top part, and the two ends. The top and the base are congruent, the sides are congruent, and the ends are congruent. Calculate the area of each part and then calculate the total of the areas to determine the surface area of the prism.

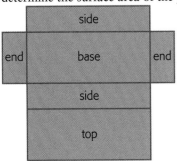

3. a) A: B's base and top are too small.
   b) B: A's base is an equilateral triangle.
   c) A: B's base is too large.
   d) B: A is a rectangular prism.

4. a) 888 cm² **b)** 1334.5 cm² **c)** 1012.5 cm²

5. 15 120 cm², or about 1.5 m²

6. about 980 cm²

7. B, because it has the greater volume.

8. 729 000 cm³

9. e.g., about 15 cm high and a radius of 4 cm

10. 127 562.5 cm³

11. a) e.g.,

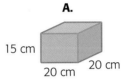
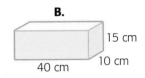

1 case × 1 case × 10 cases   1 case × 2 cases × 5 cases
   b) e.g., box A, because it requires less material.

Chapter 6, p. 240

6.1 Integer Multiplication, pp. 248–250

1. a) e.g., −3(4)   **c)** e.g., 2(7)
   b) e.g., 3(−1)   **d)** e.g., 5(4)

2. a) −10   **b)** 12   **c)** −12

3. a) −12   **b)** −8   **c)** 25   **d)** −16

4. a)

   b)

   c)

5. a) $4 \times (-2) = -8$ **c)** $-4 \times (-2) = 8$
   b) $-2 \times 4 = -8$ **d)** $2 \times 4 = 8$

6. a) −20 **b)** 20 **c)** −16 **d)** 16 **e)** −30 **f)** −30

7. a) e.g., −2, −7 **b)** e.g., −8, 4 **c)** −8, 9

8. a) −2 **b)** e.g., −5, 3 **c)** e.g., −6, 4 **d)** e.g., 9, 3

9. e.g., If you multiply two negative integers, the product is positive, and if you multiply two positive integers the product is positive (e.g., 3 × 6 = 18 and −3 × −6 = 18). If one integer is negative and the other is positive, then the product is negative. It doesn't matter which integer is negative and which one is positive (e.g., −3 × 6 = −18 and 3 × −6 = −18).

10. a) 5 and 5 or −5 and −5, product of 25
b) −5 and 5 or 5 and −5, product of −25

11. a) > **b)** = **c)** > **d)** < **e)** > **f)** <

12. a) −1 × 16, 1 × −16, −2 × 8, 2 × −8, −4 × 4
b) −1 × −16, 1 × 16, −2 × −8, 2 × 8, −4 × −4, 4 × 4

13. e.g., 2, 3, −4; −2, −3, −4; 1, 2, −12; 1, −3, 8; −1, 4, 6

14. a) e.g., 3 × (−10) **c)** e.g., −1 × 1
b) e.g., −25 × 2 **d)** e.g., −4 × 10

15. 50 × (−2) = −100

16. a) In A, each product is −14. In B, each product is 14.
b) e.g., If a golfer scores 2 under par for 7 holes, she is 14 under par. If you spent $7 each day for 2 days, you would have 14 fewer dollars, or −$14. If you had 2 parking tickets for $7 cancelled, you would get your $14 back. If you bought 2 packs of 7 stickers, you would have 14 stickers.

17. a) The product of −3 × (−2) is positive. The product of a positive number and 4 is also positive.
b) 4 × (−5) is negative. The product of a negative number and 6 is also negative.

18. a) −243, 729, −2187. Multiply the previous term by −3.
b) 24, −48, 96. Multiply the previous term by −2.

19. Either there were three positive integers and one negative integer or there were three negative integers and one positive integer.

6.2 Using Number Lines to Model Integer Multiplication, pp. 255–257

1. a) −2 × 9 = −18 **b)** 3 × (−5) = −15

2. a) 10 h ago **b)** 12 h ago **c)** 20 h ago

3.

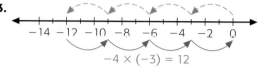

$-4 \times (-3) = 12$

4.

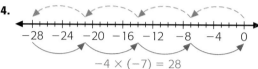

$-4 \times (-7) = 28$

5. a) 5 × 4 = 20 **b)** −2 × 5 = −10

6. a) 5(−6) = −30, −5 × 6 = −30
b) because 5(−6) = −5(6)

7. a) 4 × (−100) = −400
b) 3 × 5 = 15
c) 6 × (−2) = −12

8. a) 0 **c)** 80 **e)** 180
b) −140 **d)** −60 **f)** 1000

9. a) 200 = −20 × (−10)
b) e.g., A negative speed value, in km/h, represents riding a bicycle west, and a positive speed value represents riding east. A positive number tells for how long in hours someone rides, and a negative number tells how long ago they started riding. If Ted started riding 10 hours ago at 20 km/h west, where is he now?

10. e.g., −6 × 4, −4 × 6, −3 × 7, −7 × 3, −11 × 2

11. Draw a blue arrow from 108 to 0. Make 9 equal jumps from 108 to 0 and determine the length of each section. Each section is 12 units long. Since the arrows point left, each represents −12.

12. a) 2500, −12 500, 62 500. Multiply the previous term by −5.
b) −6655, 73 205, −805 255. Multiply the previous term by −11.

13. a) 120 **b)** −600

14. a) −20 **b)** 16 **c)** yes

15. a) -12×10

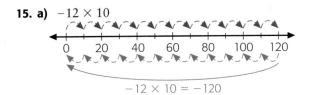

$-12 \times 10 = -120$

$12 \times (-10)$

$12 \times (-10) = -120$

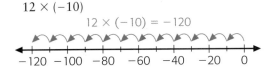

b) $(-15) \times (-20)$

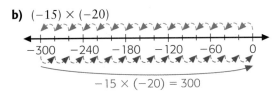

$-15 \times (-20) = 300$

15×20

$15 \times 20 = 300$

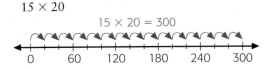

16. a) For $(+) \times (-)$, show a chain of equal left-pointing blue arrows starting at 0. For $(-) \times (+)$, show a chain of red arrows of the same length as the blue one, but ending at 0. Both arrows show the same negative number on the left.

b) For $(-) \times (-)$, show a chain of equal left-pointing blue arrows ending at 0. The starting point of the chain should show the positive product of the negative integers.

Mid-Chapter Review, p. 259

1. a)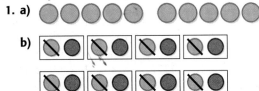

b)

c)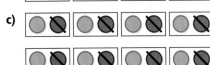

2. a) -12 **b)** -18 **c)** 20 **d)** 8 **e)** 0 **f)** 56

3. a) $>$ **b)** $=$ **c)** $>$ **d)** $<$ **e)** $>$ **f)** $<$

4. a)

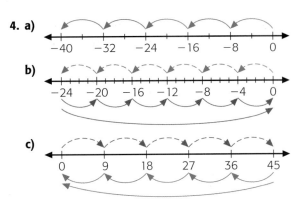

b)

c)

5. $3 \times (-8) = -24$

6. $-30 \times 15 = -450$

7. e.g., Marc took \$10 out of his bank account eight weeks in a row. Express the amount of money that came out of the account as an integer.

6.4 Integer Division, pp. 264–267

1. a) 9 **b)** 0 **c)** -9 **d)** -8

2. a) B, 2 **b)** C, 2 **c)** D, -2 **d)** A, -2

3. a) $15 \div 3 = 5$ **b)** $-10 \div 5 = -2$

4. a) $8 \times (-9) = -72$; $-72 \div (-9) = 8$

b) $12 \times 7 = 84$; $84 \div 7 = 12$

c) $-6 \times (-11) = -66$; $66 \div (-11) = -6$

d) $-40 \times 20 = -800$; $-800 \div 20 = -40$

5. a) -8 **b)** -4 **c)** 8 **d)** 11 **e)** 0 **f)** 6

6. Agree; the mean represents the total score change divided by the number of score changes recorded. The number of score changes recorded must be a positive number.

7. e.g., **a)** -200 **c)** -14 **e)** -7
b) 30 **d)** -20 **f)** 24

8. a) -4 **b)** -4 **c)** 3 **d)** -16 **e)** -8 **f)** 27

9. a)

a	b	$a \times b$	Example
$+$	$+$	$+$	$2 \times 3 = 6$
$+$	$-$	$-$	$2 \times (-3) = -6$
$-$	$+$	$-$	$-2 \times 3 = -6$
$-$	$-$	$+$	$-2 \times (-3) = 6$

a	b	$a \div b$	Example
$+$	$+$	$+$	$6 \div 2 = 3$
$+$	$-$	$-$	$6 \div (-2) = -3$
$-$	$+$	$-$	$-6 \div 2 = -3$
$-$	$-$	$+$	$-6 \div (-2) = 3$

b) e.g., Division can be related to a multiplication operation. You can then use the multiplication rules.

10. a) −20   **b)** 12   **c)** 100   **d)** −8

11. e.g., Modelling these divisions on a number line shows jumps in opposite directions, so the quotients are opposites.

12. $4 ÷ (−2) = (−2)$, since $(−) × (−) = (+)$.
$−4 ÷ 2 = (−2)$, since $(−) × (+) = (−)$.
These expressions are equal. $(−4) ÷ (−2) = 2$, since $(+) × (−) = (−)$. $4 ÷ 2 = 2$.
These expressions are equal.

13. +1

14. a) −2¢   **b)** 22¢   **c)** 11¢

15. a) −6   **b)** 9   **c)** −1   **d)** 4   **e)** 2   **f)** −3

16. e.g., How many times as deep as Lake Superior is the Marianas Trench?
$−10\ 962\ m ÷ −406\ m = 27$ times

17. a) negative, since $(−) ÷ (+) = (−)$
b) negative, since $(+) ÷ (−) = (−)$
c) positive, since $(−) ÷ (−) = (−)$

6.5 Order of Operations, pp. 270–273

1. a) −8   **b)** −27   **c)** 22   **d)** 1

2. a) $(−6) × (−8)$ **b)** $−9 × (−3)$

3. a) 10   **b)** 35   **c)** −28   **d)** −30   **e)** 60   **f)** 666

4. a) $(−2 − 4)$ was not performed first.
b) $3 × (−8) ÷ (−2 − 4) = 3 × (−8) ÷ (−6)$
$$= −24 ÷ (−6)$$
$$= 4$$

5. a) 2   **b)** −1   **c)** −1   **d)** 6   **e)** −1   **f)** −8

6. a) −213
b) Yes; otherwise it would have done the operations from left to right and given the answer −26.85.

7. $(40 × 6 − 3) × (4 − 5) = −237$

8. −40 °C

9. $\dfrac{−4 + (−4) + 0 + 1 + (−1) + (−2) + (−4)}{7}$; −2 °C

10. a) $36 ÷ (4 − 1) × 2 = 24$
b) $−12 + 4 × (−3) = −24$
c) $−15 + (−12) ÷ 6 × 16 = −47$

11. $10 × (39 − 42) + 100 × (4 − 5) + 50 × (42 − 38) + 30 × (21 − 19) = 130$

12. a)

Day	Starting price ($)	Final price ($)	Change in price ($)
Mon.	675	673	−2
Tues.	673	671	−2
Wed.	671	669	−2
Thurs.	669	677	+8
Fri.	677	685	+8

b) $675   **c)** +$2

13. e.g., I have 2 soft drinks and bought 2 more packs, each pack containing 6 soft drinks.
$2 + 2 × 6 = 14$. If calculated from left to right, the result is 24.

14. e.g., Same: the order of operations. Different: with whole numbers you have to consider only the number value, but with integers you have to consider the sign too.

6.6 Communicate about Problem Solutions, p. 277

1. a) e.g., **i)** Multiply by −2. Add 4. Subtract 14.
ii) Subtract 2. Multiply by −3. Subtract 26.
iii) Add 4. Divide by −2. Add 7.
b) Do the opposite operation, in reverse order.
e.g., **i)** Add 14. Subtract 4. Divide by −2.
ii) Add 26. Divide by −3. Add 2.
iii) Subtract 7. Multiply by −2. Subtract 4.

2. 3

3. −28

4. 2 km west

5. a) e.g., These were Guy's last three cards before he landed on −5 on the game board, but maybe not in the order shown: Subtract 2. Add 2. Divide by −3. Where was he three turns ago?
b) e.g., Try the reverse operations in all the different possible orders. He might have been on 7, 15, or 23.

Chapter Self-Test, p. 280

1. a) e.g.,

b) e.g.,

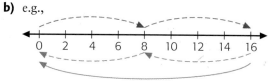

c) e.g.,

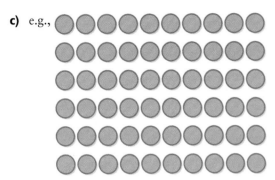

d) e.g.,

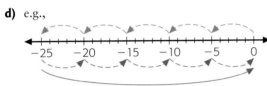

e) e.g.,

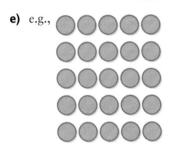

f) e.g.,

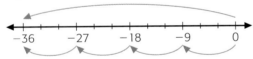

2. a) −6 **b)** −27 **c)** 144 **d)** 6 **e)** −7 **f)** −8

3. a) −9 **b)** −12 **c)** −56 **d)** −414

4. lost $250

5. −12 and 10

6. 39 greater

7. a) 10 **b)** 33 **c)** 666 **d)** −9

8. e.g., $-10 \times 10 - (-4) \times (4 - 3)$

Chapter Review, p. 282

1. a) −16 **b)** 16 **c)** 0 **d)** −20

2. a) positive; $(-) \times (-) = (+)$, then $(+) \times (+) = (+)$
   b) negative; $(+) \times (-) = (-)$, then $(-) \times (+) = (-)$

3. a) 80 **b)** −80 **c)** −72 **d)** 231

4. e.g., $1 \times (-1) \times (-3) \times 4 \times (-2)$ and
   $1 \times (-1) \times (-6) \times 2 \times (-2)$

5. a) −4 **b)** −4 **c)** 9 **d)** −3

6. a) −5 **b)** −6

7. a) $-58 - (-36) + (-15) = -37$
   b) $-4 \times (-3) + 28 = 40$

8. a) e.g., −35 **b)** e.g., 10

9. wrong, e.g., for $2 - 3 \times 4$, using order of operations: $2 - 3 \times 4 = 2 - 12 = -10$, from left to right: $2 - 3 \times 4 = -1 \times 4 = -4$

Chapter 7, p. 284

7.2 Tessellating with Regular Polygons, p. 292

1. A regular hexagon tessellates. e.g., Its interior angles are 120°, and so three regular hexagons fit around a vertex.

2. No, two octagons would cover 270°. Three octagons would cover 405°. The third octagon would overlap.

3. a) No, two dodecagons would cover 300°. A third would overlap.
   b) No, because the interior angles would not change.

4. e.g., No, Jordan is wrong, because he used the wrong division. He divided by the number of sides instead of by the size of the interior angles.

5. e.g., The size of the interior angles must be a factor of 360°.

7.3 Tessellating with Quadrilaterals, p. 296

1. a) b) e.g., I reflected a rhombus along one of its sides. I reflected the second rhombus the same way.

c) e.g., I rotated the quadrilateral about the middle of the slanted side to form a rectangle. I copied and translated the rectangle to form a tessellation.

2. a) e.g., I translated the two rhombuses to the right the width of one rhombus. I continued the translation.

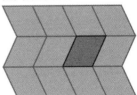

b) e.g., All the figures in this tessellation have the same orientation.

3. e.g., I rotated the trapezoid about the slanted side to form a rectangle. I copied and translated the rectangle to form a tessellation.

I rotated the trapezoid about the midpoint of the slanted side to form a rectangle. I reflected the rectangle along its sides to form a tessellation.

4. e.g., **a) – c)** I rotated the kite about the midpoints of its sides and continued this tessallation.

5. a), b) no tessellation possible
c) e.g.,

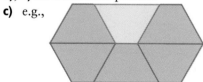

6. rotate a quadrilateral about the midpoint of a side

7. a) b) e.g.,

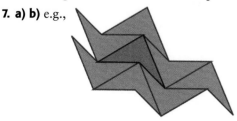

c) No; all quadrilaterals must tessellate.

7.4 Tessellating with Triangles, p. 302

1. a) e.g., a square
b) e.g., Yes, all squares tessellate.

2. a) a right triangle
b) Yes, I can reflect the new triangle along its hypotenuse to make a square, which I know will tessellate.

3. b) e.g., I tessellated by rotating 180° about the midpoint of the longest side to make a parallelogram.

c) e.g., I tessellated by reflecting along the longest side to make a kite on its side.

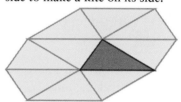

d) e.g., I was tessellating a quadrilateral both times, but the tessellations looked different because one was a kite and the other was a parallelogram.

4. e.g., I reflected over one of the equal sides to create a kite and I rotated 180° around the midpoint of one of the equal sides to create a parallelogram.

5. e.g., Yes, except for equilateral triangles, which always form the same tessellation.

Mid-Chapter Review, p. 305

1. No, because copies of the loonie cannot be arranged so the angles at each vertex add up to 360°.

2. e.g., I translated in the first tessellation and reflected and translated in the second.

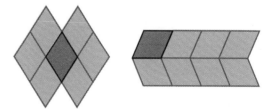

3. e.g., Using the lower right quadrilateral, he can rotate the top side and left side 180° about their midpoints and translate up to the left.

4. the same

7.5 Tessellating by Combining Shapes, p. 309

1. No; no combination of interior angles for hexagons and squares adds up to 360°.

2. No; no combination of interior angles for pentagons and equilateral triangles adds up to 360°.

3. a) e.g., I think hexagons and triangles will tessellate because combinations of their interior angles, 60° and 120°, add up to 360°.

b) e.g.,

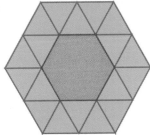

c) e.g., I placed 4 triangles and 1 hexagon at one vertex, and their angle sum was 360°. Once I had my first vertex with my 5 shapes, I continued this combination for the other vertices. This pattern of one hexagon and 18 equilateral triangles can continue forever by translation.

4. A dodecagon and an equilateral triangle; the angle sum at the vertex would be 150° + 60° + 150° = 360°.

5. Yes; the angle sum at the vertex is 360°, and 120° + 90° + 60° + 90° = 360°. The angle of the gap where the hexagon meets the square is 150°. I can fit a square and a triangle into the gap. I can keep repeating that combination at every vertex.

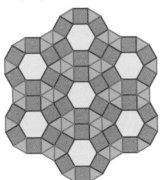

7.6 Tessellating Designs, p. 315

1. a)

 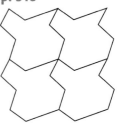

b) Yes, because it is based on a square, and squares tessellate.

2. a) e.g.,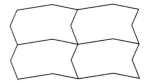

b) e.g., I changed the left side and translated it to the right side. I changed the top and translated it to the bottom.

c) Yes, because it is based on a rectangle, and rectangles tessellate.

3. a) e.g.,

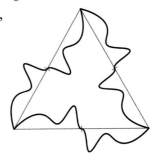

b) It will tessellate because it is based on a triangle, and triangles tessellate.

c) e.g.,

4. a) a rectangle

b) translations, reflections, and rotations

c) e.g., He probably cut out a section from one half of one side and added it to the other half of the same side.

5. e.g., No, because if the same change does not happen on the opposite side, or if half a side is not changed and rotated, then the tiles will not fit together.

7.8 Communicate about Tessellations, p. 320

1. e.g., Translate the hexagon to the left, right, and up and down.

2. e.g., Pentagons do not tessellate because they have no combination in which the interior angles at a vertex add up to 360°.

3. e.g., The artist changed the left and top sides of a rectangle and translated the changes to the right and bottom sides.

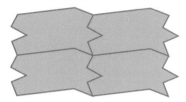

4. a) e.g., 1) Reflect the kite horizontally and translate the image alongside the kite to create a six-sided figure. This figure will tessellate.
2) Rotate the kite 180° cw about its midpoint and translate the image alongside the kite to create a six-sided figure. This figure will tessellate.
b) The result is the same for both methods.

Chapter Self-Test, p. 322

1. a) Yes, it is a triangle, and all triangles tessellate.
b) Yes, it is a quadrilateral, and all quadrilaterals tessellate.

2. a) e.g.,

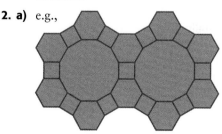

b) e.g., I added a hexagon along the top side of the dodecagon and a square along an adjacent side of the dodecagon. I used translations to add hexagons and rotations to add squares to the dodecagon.

3. The two patterns will be the same.

4. a)

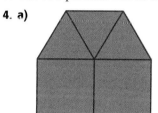

c) No, it is not possible, because no arrangement works.

5. a) b) e.g., Change the left side, then rotate the change 180° about its midpoint and apply it to the right side.

Chapter Review, p. 324

1. The interior angles of a nonagon are 140°, so putting two nonagons together at a vertex gives a centre angle sum of 280°, which will leave a gap of 80°, while putting three nonagons together gives a centre angle sum of 420°, which will cause overlap.

2. a)

b) No, it is not possible to tessellate the quadrilateral in any other way so that all the sides match and the angle sum is 360°.

3. No, all quadrilaterals tessellate, e.g.,

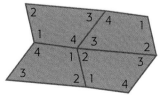

4. Yifan rotated the triangle about the midpoints of its sides until he made a hexagon. Patrick rotated the triangle about the midpoints of its sides until he made a trapezoid. Then he reflected the trapezoid along its base.

5. square and hexagon; e.g., The interior angle of the dodecagon is 150°. That leaves 210° to fill at the vertex. A square has angles of 90° and a regular hexagon has angles of 120°. 150° + 90° + 120° = 360°. There was no way to combine 60° or 108° with 150° and one other shape to total 360°.

6. e.g., I changed the top left (short) side and made the same change to the top right side. I then changed the bottom left (long) side and made the same change to the bottom right side.

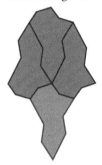

Cumulative Review: Chapters 4–7, pp. 326–327

1. B	**4.** D	**7.** D	**10.** C
2. A	**5.** C	**8.** D	**11.** A
3. B	**6.** C	**9.** B	

Chapter 8, p. 328

8.2 Changing the Format of a Graph, pp. 337–338

1. a) Same: they display the same data. Different: the way the data are displayed.
  b) e.g., In the pictograph, dogs appear to be just a little more popular than cats. The bar graph and circle graph show dogs as much more popular.
  c) e.g., the bar graph, because it is easier to compare the categories.

2. a) e.g., What is the approximate time needed for most students to get to school?
  b) e.g., How many students need less than 2 minutes to get to school?

3. a) e.g., the double-bar graph; yes
  b) e.g., the mean temperature for each month

4. a) e.g., yes, by reading the running times from the bar graph
  b) because Juan's graph would show how many movies are in each group, not the actual running times

5. a) e.g., group by whole seconds and group by half seconds
  b) e.g.,

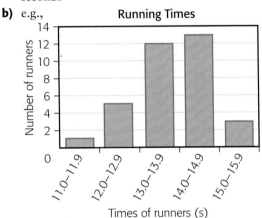

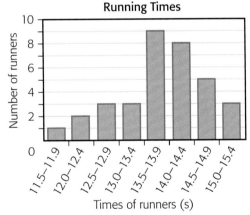

  c) e.g., Graph 1 shows that most runners had a time in the 14.0–14.9 group and Graph 2 shows that most runners had a time in the 13.5–13.9 group.

6. The height of each bar may change.

8.3 Communicate about Choosing a Graph, p. 341

1. e.g., A circle graph would be best for displaying topics in which the data can be grouped into categories that can be compared to the whole, such as budgeting money, time spent on different activities in a day, or comparing the number of copies sold in one year of three different magazines. The values of the categories within these topics may not be as important as the size of the category in relation to the whole.

2. e.g., A track and field team may want to have information about their total number of wins and losses in each event. They could use a bar graph or pictograph to display the frequency of wins and losses for each event and to compare them.

3. a) e.g., Endangered species in Canada include plants and animals. More animals are endangered than plants, but plants make up the largest single group.
   b) e.g., Yes, a bar graph could show numbers instead of percents.

4. e.g., Include the source of the data. Suggest how to lower the number of endangered species. Would another type of graph be better to present the data?

5. e.g., Use a line graph when the data describe a trend, a pictograph or bar graph to describe frequency, and a circle graph to describe parts of a whole.

Mid-Chapter Review, p. 343

1. a) between 10 and 19 km
   b) e.g.,

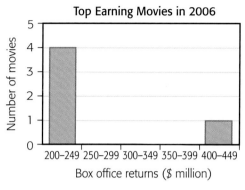

Most rode from 25 to 49 km.

   c) e.g., Yes, the second graph makes it appear that most participants rode a greater distance.

2. a) e.g., I chose a bar graph so that I could compare the data quickly.

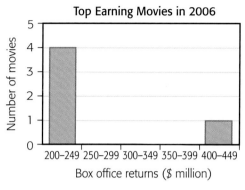

   b) e.g., My classmate used a pictograph. Both graphs showed a big difference between the top earning movie and the others, but I thought the bar graph showed this better.
   c) e.g., *Pirates of the Caribbean: Dead Man's Chest* was the most popular movie, so order more copies of this movie to rent.

8.4 Changing the Scale of a Graph, pp. 347–349

1. a) Ketchup is the most popular, followed by mustard. Relish is much less popular, and hot peppers are not popular at all.
   b) e.g.,

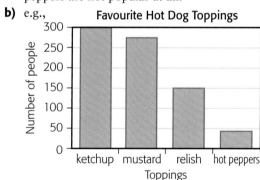

2. a) Graph 1
   b) Yes, the data points are identical.
   c) Graph 1; it shows a greater increase in attendance.

3. a)

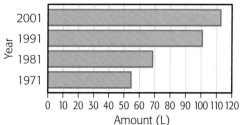

b) e.g., My scale is from 0 to 120 in increments of 10.

4. a) no

b) Draw the number scale from 0 to 29.

5.

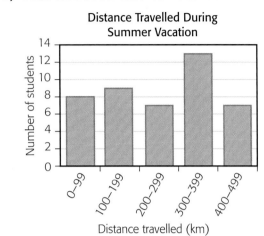

Distance Travelled During Summer Vacation

6. e.g., To make the differences appear less than they are, start the graph at 0. To make them appear greater, start it at 41.

8.5 Recognizing Misleading Graphs, pp. 352–353

1. a) Graph 1

b) The width of the bars makes the differences appear greater than they are.

2. a) e.g., Same: both show increase in profit. Different: Graph 2 is steeper.

b) Graph 2, because the profits appear to increase more quickly

c) about $5800, assuming profits continue to increase at the same rate

3. a) The second one is $\frac{1}{4}$ times the first.

b) The buying power is $\frac{1}{2}$, not $\frac{1}{4}$.

c) Draw the same graph, but with bars the same width.

4. No; it is possible that no single cause in "Other" is greater than 27.2%.

5. e.g., In a bar graph, the scales are evenly spaced and the bars are the same width.

Chapter Self-Test, pp. 356–357

1. e.g., bar graph, to make comparison easier

2. a) e.g.,

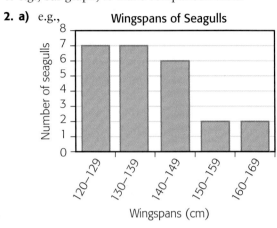

Wingspans of Seagulls

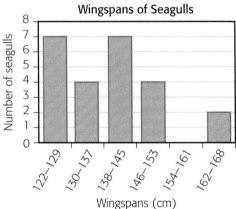

Wingspans of Seagulls

b) e.g., Yes, Graph 1 makes the first groups look similar while Graph 2 makes them look quite different.

3. a) e.g., a line graph to show change over time

b) Even though the 2006 price is less than the 2001 price, there was a large increase from 2002 to 2006.

c) e.g., a bar graph, with the cost for each year as a bar

4. e.g., Start the horizontal scale at 400.

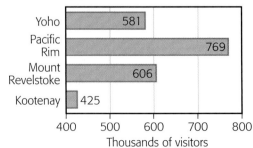

B.C. National Park Attendance

5. a) e.g., They show the same data.
b) The scales are different.
c) e.g., Students like pepperoni the best and onions the least.
d) Each graph is misleading. In the first graph, the bars have different widths, and the scale of the second graph starts at 25, not 0.

Chapter Review. pp. 359–360

1. a) e.g.,

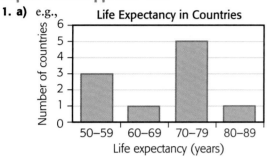

b) e.g.,

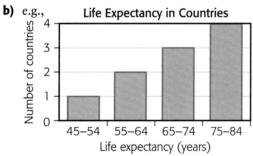

The first bar graph shows a rise and fall in life expectancy, while the second shows a steady rise.

2. a) It is easy to compare the data.
b) e.g., A pictograph can display the same data using the name of the country.

3. a) You can compare the different groups to the whole.
b) e.g., the number of 13-year-olds surveyed; how the survey was conducted; where the survey was conducted
c) The two largest sectors are for 20–29 and 30–39. That means more than 60% of 13-year-olds listen to at least 20 hours of music per week.

4. a) The scales are different.
b) Kaycee's graph shows the polar bear's life is 1.7 times that of the wolf's. Melissa's graph shows the polar bear's life is 3 times that of the wolf's.

c) It would look as if the white-tailed deer, wolf, caribou, and lynx have no lifespan.

5. a) 1995: 1; 2000: 8; 2005: 27.
b) No, the sales in 2000 should be double the sales in 1995, not 8 times greater, and sales in 2005 should be triple the sales in 1995, not 27 times greater.
c) e.g., Draw a bar graph with a scale from 0 to 400, with each square 50.

6. e.g., Use scales that do not exaggerate the data and do not enlarge bars in bar graphs or sectors in circle graphs to create a false impression.

Chapter 9, p. 362

9.1 Making a Table of Values, pp. 368–369

1. a)

n	$c = 4(n + 3)$
1	16
2	20
3	24
4	28
5	32
6	36

b)

n	$t = \frac{n}{2} + 7$
1	7.5
2	8
3	8.5
4	9
5	9.5
6	10

2. e.g., **a)** $k = \frac{n}{2} + 4n$, $t = 5(4 + n)$

b)

n	$k = \frac{n}{2} + 4n$
4	18
6	27
8	36

n	$t = 5(4 + n)$
4	40
6	50
8	60

3. a) $c = 35n$ **b)** $c = \frac{n}{2}$ **c)** $c = 27t - 15$

4. e.g.,

a)

n	$c = 35n$
1	35
2	70
3	105
4	140
5	175

5. a) $8n + 24 = c$

b)

n	c = 8n + 24
5	64
6	72
7	80
8	88
9	96
10	104

6. a) e.g.,

s	L = 16s + 80
15	320
20	400
25	480

b) e.g., The tables are the same because $16s + 80$ and $16(s + 5)$ are equal.

7. a) e.g., $e = \frac{t}{4} - 10$ **b)** $70

8. a) e.g., $w = l - 2$ **b)** e.g., $p = 4l - 4$

c)

Length, l (cm)	Perimeter, p (cm)
10	36
12	44
14	52
16	60
18	68
20	76

d) 140 cm

9. a) e.g., A table shows many solutions at one time and helps me determine a pattern rule.

b) e.g., An equation lets me calculate any value in a relation.

9.2 Graphing Linear Relations, pp. 374–376

1. a) e.g.,

x	y
0	8
1	6
2	4
3	2
4	0

b) e.g.,

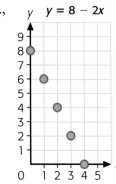

$y = 8 - 2x$

c) no

2. a)

r	c
1	20
4	35
10	65

b) 7 rides cost $50.

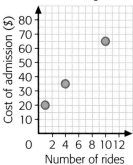

Admission to Fairgrounds

c) 12 rides

3. a) e.g.,

x	y
0	2
4	3
8	4
12	5

b)
$$y = \frac{x}{4} + 2$$

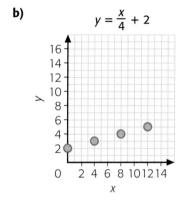

c) no   **d)** e.g., about 4.5

4. a)
$$y = -2(x + 3)$$

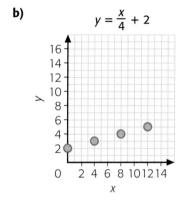

b) y decreases by 2.
c) negative
d) (0, −6)

5. Graph 2

6. a) The cost increases by $20.

Window Cost

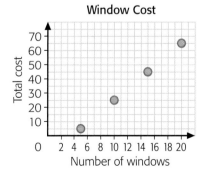

b) e.g., about $55   **c)** e.g., 11 windows
d) e.g., The company would lose money.

7. a)

Total Cost of Ski Trip

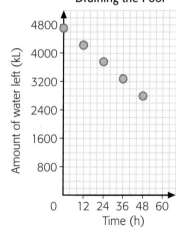

b) $2200   **c)** about $135

8. a)

Draining the Pool

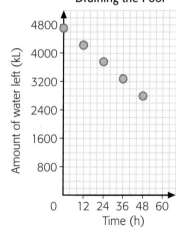

b) 2300 kL   **c)** e.g., about 120 h

9. a) Graph 3   **b)** Graph 2   **c)** Graph 1

10. e.g., how quickly or how slowly the situation is increasing or decreasing

9.4 Drawing Diagrams to Represent Equations, pp. 381–382

1. a) $n = 5$ **b)** $x = -9$

2. a) $x = 54$ **b)** $x = 9$

3. a) e.g., $5(r + 3) = 25$ **b)** e.g., $\frac{x}{2} + 4 = -6$

4. a) e.g., $r = 2$ **b)** e.g., $x = -20$

5. a) $x = 6$ **c)** $x = -44$
b) $x = 12$ **d)** $x = -2$

6. a) e.g.,

x	y
−2	−10
0	−4
2	2
4	8
6	14
8	20

b) e.g., $y = 3x - 4$

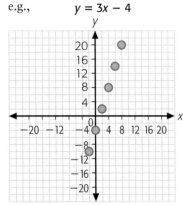

c) $x = 5, x = -4$
d) e.g., A graph displays many solutions.

7. a) e.g., $c = 4g + 2$ **b)** 7

8. e.g., D, because a diagram would make the solution clearer.

Mid-Chapter Review, p. 385

1.

n	c
3	125
7	225
15	425
20	550

2. a) $c = 2t + 30$

b)

Number of theme groups	Total cost ($)
0	$30
2	$34
4	$38
6	$42
8	$46
10	$50

c) $44   **d)** 11

3.

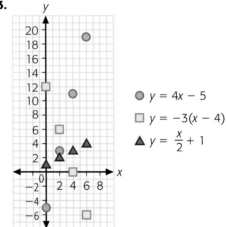

4.

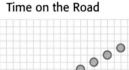
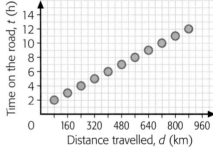

5. a) 6 h   **b)** 9 h   **c)** 12 h
6. a) 320 km   **b)** 560 km   **c)** 720 km
7. a) $x = 5$ **c)** $x = 20$
   b) $x = -9$ **d)** $x = 36$

9.5 Solve Equations with Counter Models, pp. 391–392

1. a) $z = 4$
   b) $k = 11$
   c) $x = -2$
   d) $d = -3$

2. a) $x = 7$
   b) e.g., The model helped me to see what counters to remove on the left side to isolate $3x$.

3. a) $2x + 5 = -15, x = -10$
   b) $2x - 6 = 24, x = 15$

4. a) $x = 1\frac{3}{4}$
   b) The equation simplifies to $4x = 7$, and you cannot divide 7 counters into 4 equal groups.

5. a) $g = -6$
   b) $h = 8$
   c) $m = 7$
   d) $a = 2\frac{3}{5}$
   e) $f = -\frac{3}{2}$
   f) $y = -6$

6. a) $5x + 7 = 22, x = 3$
   b) $4x - 3 = 21, x = 6$
   c) $4(x + 2) = 32, x = 6$

7. a) $d = 3$
   b) $x = -1$
   c) $z = 7$

8. a) $x = 60$
   b) e.g., You cannot divide a cube representing a variable into parts.

9. a) 9
   b) 48, 19
   c) 6

10. e.g., Solve $4x + 3 = 11$. There would be 4 bags and 3 counters on the left side and 11 counters on the right. The value of x is 2.

11. The value of the variable can change but the mass of a cube cannot.

12. e.g., To solve an equation, you need to get a variable alone on one side and a number on the other side. That's how you can tell how much the variable represents. If you can't tell which part is the variable, then you can't get it alone on one side.

9.6 Solve Equations Symbolically, pp. 397–399

1. a) $a = 48$
   b) $b = 52$
   c) $s = 18$
   d) $a = 3$
   e) $n = 7$
   f) $w = 100$

2. a) $q = -14$
   b) $s = 13$
   c) $z = -30$
   d) $d = 11$
   e) $n = -2$
   f) $t = 68$

3. $c = -4$

4. $r = \frac{2}{3}$

5. $x = 9$

6. a) $x = 3$
   b) $m = -11$
   c) $z = -35$
   d) $z = 6$
   e) $x = \frac{3}{2}$
   f) $x = 3$

7. $\frac{x}{8} - 12 = 14$; $x = 208$

8. a) $3(2 + s) = 18$
   b) $s = \$4$

9. a) $t = \frac{3}{4}$
   b) $k = 36$
   c) $f = -1$
   d) $m = -24$

10. $42

11. 11 people

12. $39 per person

13. e.g., Yes, because thinking of the pan balance reminds you to balance the equation.

9.7 Correcting Errors in Solutions, pp. 402–403

1. a) incorrect, $x = 6$
   b) incorrect, $x = -1$
   c) correct

2. a) $x = 7$
   b) $x = -27$
   c) $x = 7$

3. a) incorrect, $x = 3$
   b) incorrect, $x = 7$
   c) incorrect, $x = 2$

4. In each case, variables and constants were added together, which is incorrect.

5. a) $d = 7$
   b) $k = 6$
   c) $s = 4$

6. a) incorrect, $x = 4$
   b) correct
   c) incorrect, $s = 48$
   d) incorrect, $d = 1$

7. $1

8. e.g., so you can check for errors

9.8 Solve Problems Using Logical Reasoning, p. 408

1. $42

2. Airline B $444, bus $399

3. black gear 12 cm, blue gear 6 cm

4. e.g., If you double the cost of the Yukon trip and add $50, the result is the cost of the B.C. trip. The B.C. trip costs $300. How much is the Yukon trip?

5. 39 years old

6. e.g., An equation helps you see what information you have, what information you need, and how to get from what you have to what you need.

Chapter Self-Test, p. 410

1. a) e.g.,

x	y
0	6
1	3
2	0
3	−3

b) e.g.,

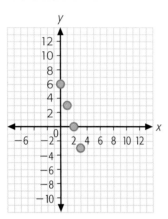

x	y
−2	12
5	−9
−1	9
4	−6

2. a) $a = 7$ **c)** $c = 2.5$ **e)** $t = -8$
   b) $x = -24$ **d)** $z = -4$ **f)** $z = -3$

3. $45

4. a) incorrect, $a = 17$ **b)** incorrect, $x = -40$

5. $1150

Chapter Review, pp. 413–414

1. a) e.g., $w = 120t + 4000$

b) e.g.,

Time, t (min)	Water, w (L)
15	5 800
30	7 600
45	9 400
60	11 200

2. a)

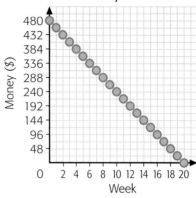

Money in Bank

b) $312   **c)** 9 weeks

3. a) $x = 5$ **b)** $x = 27$

4. a) $t = 4$ **b)** $z = \dfrac{6}{8}$ **c)** $x = -7$

5. a) $a = -16$ **b)** $t = 384$ **c)** $x = \dfrac{-2}{5}$

6. incorrect, $x = 3$

7. a) correct   **b)** incorrect, $p = -1$

8. beginner's tour $55, intermediate tour $72

Chapter 10, p. 416

10.2 Probability of Independent Events, pp. 426–427

1. a)

		Second counter					
		orange	orange	green	green	purple	purple
First counter	orange	OO	OO	OG	OG	OP	OP
	orange	OO	OO	OG	OG	OP	OP
	green	GO	GO	GG	GG	GP	GP
	green	GO	GO	GG	GG	GP	GP
	purple	PO	PO	PG	PG	PP	PP
	purple	PO	PO	PG	PG	PP	PP

b) $\dfrac{1}{9}$

2. not independent

3. e.g.,

		Spin of spinner			
		green	yellow	orange	purple
Roll of die	1	1G	1Y	1O	1P
	2	2G	2Y	2O	2P
	3	3G	3Y	3O	3P
	4	4G	4Y	4O	4P
	5	5G	5Y	5O	5P
	6	6G	6Y	6O	6P

b) $\frac{1}{24}$ **c)** $\frac{1}{8}$

4. a) e.g.,

		Second spin			
		$1000	$200	$100	$50
First spin	$1000	$2000	$1200	$1100	$1050
	$200	$1200	$400	$300	$250
	$100	$1100	$300	$200	$150
	$50	$1050	$250	$150	$100

b) $\frac{15}{16}$ **c)** $\frac{9}{16}$

5. a) $\frac{1}{24}$ **b)** $\frac{1}{4}$ **c)** $\frac{1}{4}$ **d)** $\frac{5}{8}$
e) e.g., An outcome table and a tree diagram give the same results.

6. e.g., with a tree diagram,
a) $\frac{1}{48}$ **b)** $\frac{7}{48}$ **c)** $\frac{1}{16}$ **d)** $\frac{11}{48}$
e) e.g., An outcome table and a tree diagram give the same results.

7. a) Selecting the second tile does not depend on the result of selecting the first tile.
b) $\frac{9}{25}$ **c)** $\frac{4}{25}$ **d)** $\frac{6}{25}$
e) e.g., An outcome table and a tree diagram give the same results.

8. a) The denominator is equal to all possible outcomes in a tree diagram or outcome table.
b) They list all the possible outcomes in the probability experiment.

10.3 Using a Formula to Calculate Probability, pp. 432–433

1. a) $\frac{1}{48}$ **b)** $\frac{1}{4}$ **c)** $\frac{1}{16}$

2. a) The second event does not depend on the first event.
b) $\frac{4}{49}$ **c)** $\frac{9}{49}$ **d)** $\frac{1}{49}$

3. a) The second event does not depend on the first event.
b) $\frac{1}{30}$ **c)** $\frac{1}{6}$ **d)** $\frac{1}{10}$

4. a) $\frac{3}{8}$ **b)** $\frac{3}{20}$ **c)** $\frac{1}{4}$ **d)** $\frac{9}{40}$

5. a) $\frac{21}{40}$
b) The two events are not independent.

6. a) $\frac{1}{400}$ **b)** $\frac{4}{25}$ **c)** $\frac{1}{25}$
d) e.g., The events are independent because one does not depend on the other.

7. $\frac{1}{1600}$

8. a) $\frac{2}{5}$ **b)** $\frac{3}{25}$
c) Probabilities of the team losing are not included.

9. a) The two events are independent.
b) The two events are not independent.

10.4 Communicate about Probability, pp. 437–438

1. e.g., Lam could get a hit in his second at-bat. The probability is 0.250.

2. e.g., How do you know that the events are independent? Should you schedule the picnic for Saturday only, since the chance of rain then is much less likely? Have you shown why your conclusion is reasonable?

3. a) Multiply $P(Y)$ by $P(Y)$: $P(YY) = \frac{1}{4}$
b) e.g., Use an outcome table. There are 4 favourable (YY) outcomes in 16 possible outcomes. $P(YY) = \frac{1}{4}$.

4. a) Multiply $P(\text{heads}) \times P(\text{even})$.
$P(\text{heads, even}) = \frac{1}{4}$
b) e.g., List the possible outcomes: H1, H2, H3, H4, H5, H6, H7, H8, H9, H10, H11, H12, T1, T2, T3, T4, T5, T6, T7, T8, T9, T10, T11, T12. Six of the 24 outcomes are favourable, so $P(\text{H, even}) = \frac{1}{4}$.

5. These events are not independent.

6. a) $\frac{9}{100}$

b) e.g., I made a spinner with 10 equal sections, 3 marked "Catch" and 7 marked "No catch." I did 50 trials of spinning the spinner twice. I got two "catches" in a row 4 times. The experimental probability is $\frac{4}{50}$ or 8%.

c) e.g., Yes, if there are lots of trout in the lake.

7. $P(B) = \frac{3}{5}$

8. a) You need to know because you can only multiply the probabilities of independent events.

b) e.g., It is a good way to check your answer.

Chapter Self-Test, p. 440

1. a)

		Second spin				
		1	2	3	4	5
First spin	1	1, 1	1, 2	1, 3	1, 4	1, 5
	2	2, 1	2, 2	2, 3	2, 4	2, 5
	3	3, 1	3, 2	3, 3	3, 4	3, 5
	4	4, 1	4, 2	4, 3	4, 4	4, 5
	5	5, 1	5, 2	5, 3	5, 4	5, 5

b) $\frac{4}{25}, \frac{9}{25}$

c) There are more outcomes in which both are odd than in which both are even.

2. a) The probability of guessing the second answer correctly is not affected by the first guess.

b) $\frac{1}{25}$

c) e.g.,

		Guess to second question				
		A	B	C	D	E
Guess to first question	A	AA	AB	AC	AD	AE
	B	BA	BB	BC	BD	BE
	C	CA	CB	CC	CD	CE
	D	DA	DB	DC	DD	DE
	E	EA	EB ·	EC	ED	EE

There are 25 outcomes and only AC is favourable so $P(\text{both correct}) = \frac{1}{25}$.

3. a) $\frac{32}{100}$ or 32%   **b)** $\frac{6}{100}$ or 6%

c) e.g., A tree diagram with 8 branches for rain and 2 branches for sun, each one ending with 10 game-outcome branches, gives the same results.

4. a) $\frac{1}{4}$ **b)** $\frac{7}{20}$ **c)** $\frac{16}{25}$

Chapter Review, p. 442

1. a)

		Spinner			
		10	20	30	40
Die	1	1, 10	1, 20	1, 30	1, 40
	2	2, 10	2, 20	2, 30	2, 40
	3	3, 10	3, 20	3, 30	3, 40
	4	4, 10	4, 20	4, 30	4, 40

b) $\frac{1}{16}$ **c)** $\frac{6}{16}$ or $\frac{3}{8}$

d) e.g.,

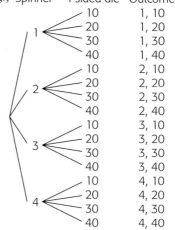

Spinner   4-sided die   Outcome

$P(1, 20) = \frac{1}{16}$ and $P(\text{toss} > 1, \text{spin} < 30)$
$= \frac{6}{16}$ or $\frac{3}{8}$

2. a) e.g.,

		Second marble					
		blue	blue	blue	red	red	red
	blue	BB	BB	BB	BR	BR	BR
First	blue	BB	BB	BB	BR	BR	BR
marble	blue	BB	BB	BB	BR	BR	BR
	red	RB	RB	RB	RR	RR	RR
	red	RB	RB	RB	RR	RR	RR
	red	RB	RB	RB	RR	RR	RR

b) $\frac{1}{2}$ **c)** no

3. a) $\frac{1}{36}$
b) e.g., An outcome table and a tree diagram both give the same result.

4. a) 0.105   **b)** 0.0225   **c)** 0.7225
d) e.g., That seeing moose and seeing loons are independent events.

5. $\frac{1}{4}$

Chapter 11, p. 444

11.1 Drawing Views of Cube Structures, pp. 450–451

1. a) top   **b)** right   **c)** front

2. c)

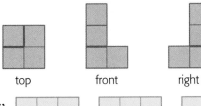

top   front   right

3. e.g.,

top   front   side

4. The top view would be a 7 cm by 5 cm rectangle. The front view would be a 10 cm by 7 cm rectangle. The side views would each be a 10 cm by 5 cm rectangle.

5. e.g., **a)**

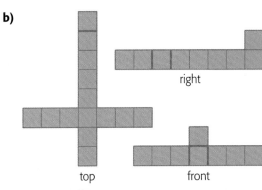

b)

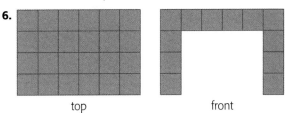

top   front   right

6.

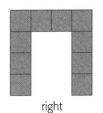

top   front   right

7. c)

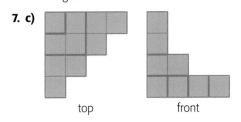

top   front

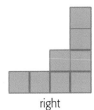

right

8. b)

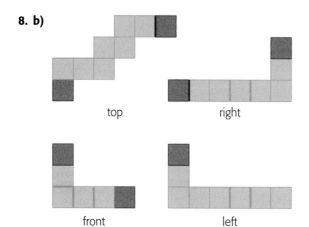

top right

front left

c) All of the views would look different. In the top view, the upper red cube would be yellow and the lower red cube would be missing. In the right view, the upper red cube would be missing and the lower red cube would be yellow with no depth change. In the front view, both red cubes would be missing. In the left view, the red cube would be missing.

9. a) e.g., Add a cube on top of the red cube in the tower.
b) e.g., Add a cube to the left of the front two.

10. They are all rectangles.

11. No, you would need to see the left view in a case where some cubes cannot be seen on the top view or the right view.

11.3 Creating Isometric Drawings, pp. 456–457

1.

front

2. e.g., **b)** **c)**

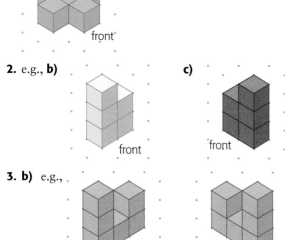

front front

3. b) e.g.,

front front

4. e.g., **a)** **b)**

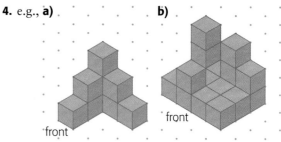

front front

5. a)

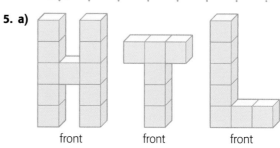

front front front

b) e.g.,

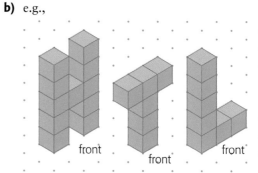

front front front

c) e.g.,

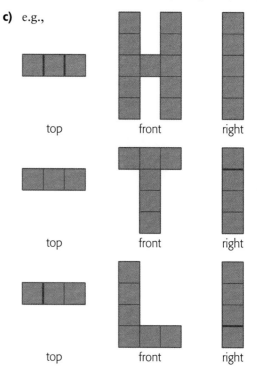

top front right

top front right

top front right

6.

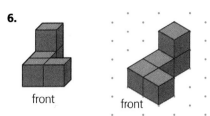

front   front

7. e.g., **a)**   **b)**

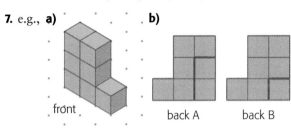

front   back A   back B

8. e.g., to show what the building will look like when it is built. The isometric drawing makes the 2-D picture look 3-D.

Mid-Chapter Review, p. 459

1. a)

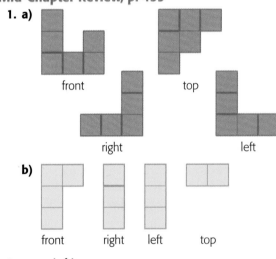

front   top

right   left

b)

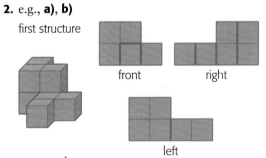

front   right   left   top

2. e.g., **a), b)**

first structure

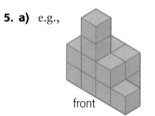

front   right

left

second structure

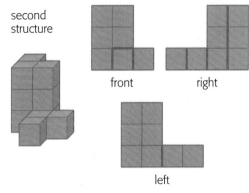

front   right

left

3.

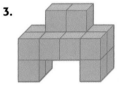

4.

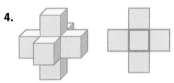

5. a) e.g.,

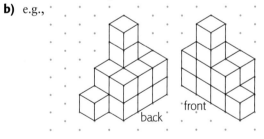

front

b) e.g.,

back   front

6. c) e.g., Yes, my structure did match, because the drawings were clear.

11.4 Creating Cube Structures from Isometric Drawings, p. 462

1. a) 12 cubes

b), c) You can use 13, 14, or 15 cubes, depending on how many cubes are not visible in the isometric drawing of the structure; e.g., in the structure on the left, 2 cubes have been added to the back of the structure; in the structure on the right, 1 cube has been added to the middle of the second tier.

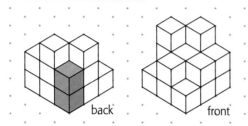

2. e.g.,

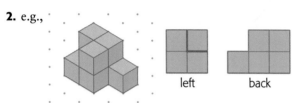

3. A and D are the same

4. e.g., I would choose the drawings in set A. The isometric drawing provides a good representation of the 3-D object.

11.5 Rotating Cube Structures, pp. 469–470

1. a)

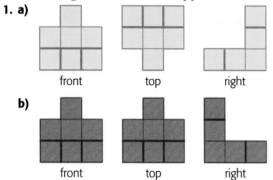

2. The structure was horizontally rotated 270° ccw.

3. Naghma is correct. Ruiz's structure is the same as hers after a vertical rotation of 90° cw.

4. Objects B and C match the blue object.

5. a)

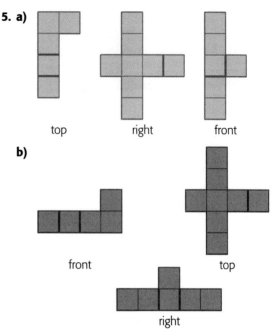

b)

c) e.g., Either rotation could occur in real life, but I think a horizontal rotation is more common. Airplanes bank to the right and the left when making turns. An airplane would only rotate vertically if it were doing aerobatics.

6. a) T, F, and L

b) e.g., They are simple constructions and we use them every day, which makes them easy to recognize.

c) No, because you would only see the side view, which would be a vertical stack of cubes.

7. a) horizontal rotations of 90° cw and 270° ccw

b) Horizontal rotations of 90° cw, 180° cw, and 270° cw all match this view.

8. e.g.,

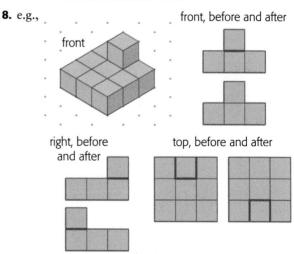

9. e.g., Looking at different views of a structure shows you how you would see the structure as you would if you walked around it. If a structure is not identical on all sides, it gives you information about what features the different sides have.

11.6 Communicate about Views, p. 475

1. e.g., The structure has 12 visible cubes. The top view and side views show cubes behind that are not visible from the front.

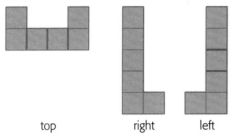

top   right   left

2. a) First, I used 7 cubes to build a structure that matches the front view.

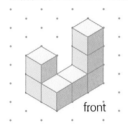

front

Then I turned my structure so the left face is showing. I did not need to add any cubes to match the left view.

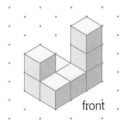

front

Finally, I looked down on my structure and added 1 more cube so the top view of my structure matched the top view shown.

b) My description is good because I sketched isometric drawings to represent what I did at each step. I also told the number of cubes needed each time and used appropriate mathematical language. I could improve my description by including isometric drawings of the back of the structure.

3. a)

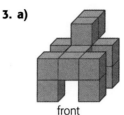

front

b) The structure is made with 12 cubes.

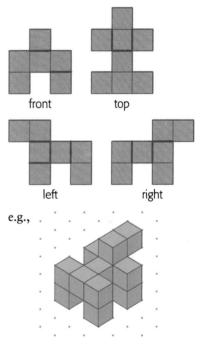

front   top

left   right

e.g.,

The structure is made with 12 cubes. It looks a bit like a dog that is missing its left front leg.

4. a) e.g., I made a model of the computer monitor at home. The model is made with 31 linking cubes. The screen is 5 cubes long by 5 cubes high by 1 cube deep. One cube links the centre of the bottom of the screen with the middle of the base. The base is made up of a row of 5 cubes.

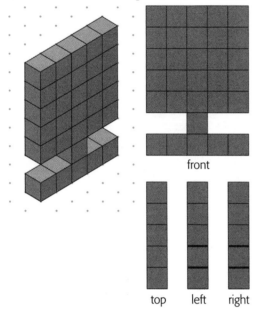

front

top left right

5. Different views give you information about how the pieces are assembled. If you have only one view, you might not know how the parts that are not visible go together.

Chapter Self-Test, p. 476

1. B

2. a)

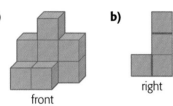

front

b)

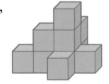

right

3. a) e.g.,

b) e.g.,

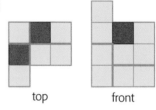

front   top

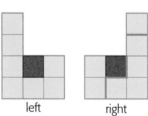

right   left

c) e.g.,

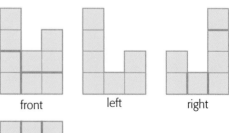

4. They represent the same structure. I made the first structure with linking cubes and rotated it 180° cw.

Chapter Review, p. 478

1. b)

top   front

left   right

c) All views would look different, as shown.

front   left   right

top

2.

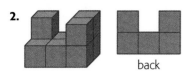

back

3. e.g., **b)**   **c)**

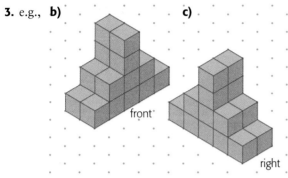

front

right

4.

5. b)

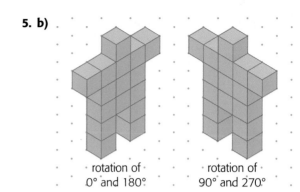

rotation of
0° and 180°

rotation of
90° and 270°

6. e.g., Start with the body. Put nine linking cubes
together to form a rectangle that is 3 cubes wide
and 3 cubes high. Make each leg by connecting
two linking cubes. Stick each leg onto the lower
part of the body. To make the arms, stick one
linking cube to each side of the body, at shoulder
level. Then put one cube on top for the head.

Chapters 8–11

Cumulative Review, pp. 480–481

1. C   **3.** B   **5.** B   **7.** B

2. A   **4.** D   **6.** A

Index

Multiplying/multiplication
  communicating about, 92–95
  dividing fractions using related, 82–86
  fractions greater than 1, 58–63
  fractions less than 1, 52–56
  improper fractions, 58–63
  of integers, 244–250
  mixed numbers, 58–63
  peasant, 278
  whole numbers by fractions, 46–50

N
Nets
  building 3-D objects from, 194
  of cubes, 207
  defined, 194
  of geometric solids, 232
  of prisms and cylinders, 195–199
Number lines
  for modelling integer division, 261–267
  for modelling integer multiplication, 251–257

O
Order of operations
  in calculations involving fractions, 88–91
  and integers, 268–273
Outcome tables, 423

P
Percents
  changes as, 179–183
  combining, 175–177
  using decimals for problem solving, 163–167
  as equivalent decimals/fractions, 154–158
  using equivalent ratios to solve problems, 159–162
  fractional, 150–153
  using fractions to solve problems, 174
  greater than 100%, 144–149
Perfect squares
  identification of, 5–9
  problem creation/solving and, 24
  square roots of, 10–15, 21
Planes, 289
Point of view, solving problems by changing, 170–173
Polygons
  irregular, 310–315
  tessellating with, 289–292
  tiling with, 288

Predicting
  products of integers, 244–250
  views from rotating cube structures, 464–470
Prisms
  drawing nets of, 195–199
  surface area, 200–206
  volume of, 217–222
Probabilities
  communicating about, 434–438
  using formulas to calculate, 428–433
  of independent events, 420, 422–427
  of precipitation, 421
Problem solving
  by changing point of view, 170–173
  using decimals for percent problems, 163–167
  using diagrams, 32–35
  using fractions for percent problems, 174
  integer, 274–277
  using logical reasoning, 405–408
  using models, 227–231
  percentages, 163–167, 174, 175–177, 179–183
  perfect squares, 24
  using proportion, 159–162
  using rates, 122–125
  using ratios, 113–117, 130–133
Proportions
  defined, 107
  problem solving using, 159–162
  solving rate/ratio problems using, 130–133
Pythagorean theorem, 26–31, 41

R
Rates
  birth, 129
  defined, 122
  explaining, 126–128
  problem solving using, 122–125
  using proportions/ratio tables to solve problems, 130–133
Ratios
  explaining, 126–128
  tables, 113–117, 130–133
  three-term, 119
  two-term, 106–112
Reciprocals, 83
Relations, 366
Right triangles, 26–31

Credits

Chapter 1 Opener: A & S Aakjae/Shutterstock; page 2: Steve Yager/Shutterstock; page 10: Alistair Berg/Getty Images; page 13: Photo Bank Yokohama Co., Ltd./Alamy; page 14: Paul Chiasson/CP Photo; page 19: Martin Valent/Shutterstock; page 26: Pythagoras(c.580–500BC) Greek Philosopher and Mathematician, Roman copy of Greek original(marble)/Pinacoteca Capitolina, Palazzo Conservatori, Rome, Italy, Index/The Bridgeman Art Library; page 35: Jeff Vinnick/Getty Images; page 37: ©Nelson Education Ltd.

Chapter 2 Page 50: photos.com; page 52: photos.com; page 63: Alane Kane; page 67: CP PHOTO/Edmonton Sun/Jason Franson; page 75: Design Pics Inc./Alamy; page 86: Stockbyte/Getty Images.

Chapter 3 Opener: jaggat/Shutterstock; page 107: left, blickwinkel/Alamy; middle, Alex Wild Photography; right, Jeff Lepore/Photo Researchers, Inc.; page 108: imagebroker/Alamy; page 112: Richard Fitzer/Shutterstock; page 113: Maxim Petrichuk/Shutterstock; page 122: AFP/Getty Images; page 123: Alfo Foto Agency/Alamy; page 125: Oxford Scientific/Photolibrary/Getty Images; page 137: Front cover from If the World Were a Village, written by David J. Smith and illustrated by Shelagh Armstrong is used by permission of Kids Can Press Ltd., Toronto. Illustrations © 2002 Shelagh Armstrong.

Chapter 4 Opener: Blend Images/Alamy; page 145: Zavodskov Anatoliy Nickolaevich/Shutterstock; page 148: David Lee/Shutterstock; page 154: Ron Niebrugge/Alamy; page 163: istock; page 173: photos.com; page 179: Michael Cogliantry/Getty Images; page 182: top, James P. Blair/Getty Images; bottom, © Galen Rowell/CORBIS; page 184: marianad/Shutterstock; page 185: Galen Rowell/Mountain Light/Alamy.

Chapter 5 Opener: Bubbles Photolibrary/Alamy; page 213: top, Visions of America, LLC/Alamy; bottom, Eric Jamison/Associated Press; page 227: © Patrick Bennett/CORBIS; page 231: Kmitu/Shutterstock; page 234: top right, Dorling Kindersley/Getty Images; bottom, Kristiina Paul; page 239: Jane Norton/istock.

Chapter 6 Opener: top to bottom, Troy and Mary Parlee/Alamy; John Wang/Getty Images; Design Pics Inc./Alamy; © Kevin Burke/CORBIS; page 250: IMAGINA Photography/Alamy; page 255: JUPITER IMAGES/Polka Dot/Alamy; page 266: Radius Images/Alamy; page 272: © Wolfgang Kaehler/CORBIS.

Chapter 7 Opener: © mediacolor's/Alamy; page 287: top, Nancy Brammer/Shutterstock; bottom, Corbis Premium RF/Alamy; page 293: Antonio Iacovelli/Shutterstock; page 297: Marc Hill/Alamy; page 310 & 311: M.C. Escher's Symmetry Drawing E128 © 2007 The M.C. Escher Company-Holland. All rights reserved. www.mcescher.com; page 315: M.C. Escher's Symmetry Drawing E41 © 2007 The M.C. Escher Company-Holland. All rights reserved. www.mcescher.com; page 316: right, Brandon Clark/istock; left, (d) Barry Lewis/CORBIS; page 321: Scott Kim; page 325: Photodisc/Alamy.

Chapter 8 Opener: Doug Pensigner/Getty Images and graph 'Women's Speedskating Record Times' based on data from IOC website http://olympic.org; page 330: left to right, Kharidehal Abhirama Ashwin/Shutterstock; Franck Chazot/Shutterstock; Soundsnaps/Shutterstock; Tan Kian Khoon/Shutterstock; Vladimir Korostyshevskjy/Shutterstock; salamanderman/Shutterstock; page 339: graph 'Aboriginal Population' adapted from Statistics Canada websites www.statcan.ca/Daily/English/980113/d980113.htm and www40.statcan.ca/101/cst01/demo40a.htm; page 341: graph 'Endangered Species in Canada' based on data from http://raysweb.net/specialplaces/pages/canada-es.html and www.sararegistry.gc.ca/species/schedules_e.cfm?id=1; page 343: 'Top Earning Movies of 2006' based on data from celebridiot.com/gossip/index.php/2007/01/02/top-earning-movies-of-2006/; page 349: graph 'Wins' based on data from www.nhl.com/standings/20052006/conference_standings.html: page 353: graph 'Causes of Deaths in Canada' adapted from Statistics Canada website www40.statcan.ca/l01/cst01/health36.htm.

Chapter 9 Opener: Terrance Klassen/Alamy; page 368: Kasia/Shutterstock; page 375: Image Source Shite/Alamy; page 376: Mel Yates/Getty Images; page 382: JUPITER IMAGES/Brand X/Alamy; page 386: Jeff Vinnick/Getty Images; page 392: Harry How/Getty Images: page 393: Danita Delimont/Alamy; page 399: CP PHOTO/Chuck Stoody; page 410: Visual&Written SL/Alamy; page 414: Lisa Moon/Shutterstock; page 415: Jason Kwan/Alamy.

Chapter 10 Opener: Darwin Wiggett/Getty Images; page 433: Marie C. Fields/Shutterstock; page 438: BRUCE COLEMAN INC./Alamy; page 440: JUPITER IMAGES/Comstock Images/Alamy.

Chapter 11 Opener: Ulana Switucha/Alamy; page 452: Megapress/Alamy; page 478: Design Pics Inc./Alamy; page 479: salamanderman/Shutterstock.